Translating England into Russian

Library of Modern Russia

Advisory Board

Jeffrey Brooks, Professor at Johns Hopkins University, USA
Michael David-Fox, Professor at Georgetown University, USA
Lucien Frary, Associate Professor at Rider University, USA
James Harris, Senior Lecturer at the University of Leeds, UK
Robert Hornsby, Lecturer at the University of Leeds, UK
Ekaterina Pravilova, Professor of History at Princeton University, USA
Geoffrey Swain, Emeritus Professor of Central and East European Studies at the University of Glasgow, UK
Vera Tolz-Zilitinkevic, Sir William Mather Professor of Russian Studies at the University of Manchester, UK
Vladislav Zubok, Professor of International History at the London School of Economics, UK

Building on Bloomsbury Academic's established record of publishing Russian studies titles, the *Library of Modern Russia* will showcase the work of emerging and established writers who are setting new agendas in the field.

At a time when potentially dangerous misconceptions and misunderstandings about Russia abound, titles in the series will shed fresh light and nuance on Russian history. Volumes will take the idea of 'Russia' in its broadest cultural sense and cover the entirety of the multi-ethnic lands that made up imperial Russia and the Soviet Union. Ranging in chronological scope from the Romanovs to today, the books will:

- Reconsider Russia's history from a variety of interdisciplinary perspectives.
- Explore Russia in its various international contexts, rather than as exceptional or in isolation.
- Examine the complex, divisive and ever-shifting notions of 'Russia'.
- Contribute to a deeper understanding of Russia's rich social and cultural history.
- Critically reassess the Soviet period and its legacy today.
- Interrogate the traditional periodizations of the post-Stalin Soviet Union.
- Unearth continuities, or otherwise, among the tsarist, Soviet and post-Soviet periods.

- Reappraise Russia's complex relationship with Eastern Europe, both historically and today.
- Analyse the politics of history and memory in post-Soviet Russia.
- Promote new archival revelations and innovative research methodologies.
- Foster a community of scholars and readers devoted to a sharper understanding of the Russian experience, past and present.

Books in the series will join our list in being marketed globally, including at conferences – such as the BASEES and ASEEES conventions. Each will be subjected to a rigorous peer-review process and will be published in hardback and, simultaneously, as an e-book. We also anticipate a second release in paperback for the general reader and student markets. For more information, or to submit a proposal for inclusion in the series, please contact: Rhodri Mogford, Publisher, History (Rhodri.Mogford@bloomsbury.com).

New and forthcoming

Fascism in Manchuria: The Soviet-China Encounter in the 1930s, Susanne Hohler

The Idea of Russia: The Life and Work of Dmitry Likhachev, Vladislav Zubok

The Tsar's Armenians: A Minority in Late Imperial Russia, Onur Onol

Myth Making in the Soviet Union and Modern Russia: Remembering World War II in Brezhnev's Hero City, Vicky Davis

Building Stalinism: The Moscow Canal and the Creation of Soviet Space, Cynthia Ruder

Russia in the Time of Cholera: Disease and the Environment under Romanovs and Soviets, John Davis

Soviet Americana: A Cultural History of Russian and Ukrainian Americanists, Sergei Zhuk

Stalin's Economic Advisors: The Varga Institute and the Making of Soviet Foreign Policy, Ken Roh

Ideology and the Arts in the Soviet Union: The Establishment of Censorship and Control, Steven Richmond

Nomads and Soviet Rule: Central Asia under Lenin and Stalin, Alun Thomas

The Russian State and the People: Power, Corruption and the Individual in Putin's Russia, Geir Hønneland et al. (eds)

The Communist Party in the Russian Civil War: A Political History, Gayle Lonergan
Criminal Subculture in the Gulag: Prisoner Society in the Stalinist Labour Camps, Mark Vincent
Power and Politics in Modern Chechnya: Ramzan Kadyrov and the New Digital Authoritarianism, Karena Avedissian
Russian Pilgrimage to the Holy Land: Piety and Travel from the Middle Ages to the Revolution, Nikolaos Chrissidis
The Fate of the Bolshevik Revolution, Lara Douds, James Harris and Peter Whitehead (eds)
Writing History in Late Imperial Russia, Frances Nethercott
Translating England into Russian, Elena Goodwin

Translating England into Russian

The Politics of Children's Literature in the Soviet Union and Modern Russia

Elena Goodwin

BLOOMSBURY ACADEMIC
LONDON • NEW YORK • OXFORD • NEW DELHI • SYDNEY

BLOOMSBURY ACADEMIC
Bloomsbury Publishing Plc
50 Bedford Square, London, WC1B 3DP, UK
1385 Broadway, New York, NY 10018, USA
29 Earlsfort Terrace, Dublin 2, Ireland

BLOOMSBURY, BLOOMSBURY ACADEMIC and the Diana logo are trademarks of
Bloomsbury Publishing Plc

First published in Great Britain 2020
Paperback edition published 2021

Copyright © Elena Goodwin 2020

Elena Goodwin has asserted her right under the Copyright, Designs and Patents Act,
1988, to be identified as Author of this work.

For legal purposes the Acknowledgements on pp. ix–x constitute
an extension of this copyright page.

Series design by Tjaša Krivec

Cover image: Illustration from Azbuka krasnoarmeitsa ('Alphabet for a Red Army Soldier'),
1921. Written and drawn by Dmitrii Moor.
(© The British Library Board)

All rights reserved. No part of this publication may be reproduced or
transmitted in any form or by any means, electronic or mechanical,
including photocopying, recording, or any information storage or retrieval
system, without prior permission in writing from the publishers.

Bloomsbury Publishing Plc does not have any control over, or responsibility for,
any third-party websites referred to or in this book. All internet addresses given
in this book were correct at the time of going to press. The author and publisher
regret any inconvenience caused if addresses have changed or sites have ceased
to exist, but can accept no responsibility for any such changes.

A catalogue record for this book is available from the British Library.

A catalog record for this book is available from the Library of Congress.

ISBN: HB: 978-1-3501-3399-0
PB: 978-1-3502-4532-7
ePDF: 978-1-3501-3400-3
eBook: 978-1-3501-3401-0

Series: Library of Modern Russia

Typeset by Newgen KnowledgeWorks Pvt. Ltd., Chennai, India

To find out more about our authors and books visit www.bloomsbury.com
and sign up for our newsletters.

Contents

List of Illustrations	viii
Acknowledgements	ix
A Note on the Transliteration and Translations	xi
1 Introduction	1
2 Translated literature in Russia: The 'high art' of realist translation, censorship and key actors within the field	27
3 Translation of British children's literature in Russian context: Responses to political and cultural changes	47
4 J. M. Barrie's *Peter Pan*: Censoring images of the British Empire and Edwardian class society	79
5 Translating Rudyard Kipling's duology about Puck: Empire, historical past and landscape	95
6 A. A. Milne through Soviet eyes: Translating silliness and traditions	113
7 Framing P. L. Travers's *Mary Poppins* in ideological and cultural contexts: Translating features of English national character	127
8 Re-imagining Kenneth Grahame's *The Wind in the Willows*: Images of mythical rural England and the English way of life	151
Conclusion	173
Appendix 1: Englishness in Russian literature	179
Appendix 2: Canon and classics of British children's literature	184
Appendix 3: British children's classics translated into Russian	187
Notes	191
Bibliography	225
Index	247

Illustrations

1	Hook. Illustration by May Miturich-Khlebnikov	86
2	Jolly Roger. Illustration by Ilya Kabakov	87
3	Hook and Peter Pan. Illustration 'This man is mine!' by Francis Donkin Bedford	88
4	The Roman legionaries. Illustration by Sergei Liubaev	105
5	'Hail, Cæsar!' Illustration by Harold Robert Millar	106
6	The adventures of the Table and the Chair. Illustration by Boris Kustodiev	116
7	Three hunters. Illustration by Vladimir Konashevich	117
8	The King's Breakfast. Illustration by Ernest Howard Shepard	122
9	The King and the Lord Chancellor. Illustration by Ernest Howard Shepard	125
10	Mary Poppins. Illustration by Mary Shepard	146
11	Mary Poppins. Illustration by Vadim Chelak	149
12	Mary Poppins. Illustration by Kseniia Shafranovskaia	150
13	Mole and Rat. Illustration by Ernest Howard Shepard	167

Acknowledgements

This book came out of my doctoral thesis at the University of Exeter, and I am grateful for the invaluable support provided throughout the research project. I would like to thank the AHRC for financing my PhD and also for providing the research training support grant which allowed me to travel to Moscow to investigate new material at the Russian State Archive of Literature and Art (RGALI) and the Moscow State Library. Thanks also go to the staff of the British Library, RGALI, the Society for Co-operation in Russian and Soviet Studies and the Lilly Library at Indiana University and special thanks to Aleksei Slobozhan, the late Inna Slobozhan, Alexandra Smith, Alexandra Borisenko, Olga Bukhina and Olga Maeots for finding time, when I was working on my thesis, to discuss and challenge my views on Soviet/Russian translations of English children's literature and censorship.

I am particularly grateful to Tom Stottor who first saw the potential in the work when it was originally commissioned by I. B. Tauris and whose vision and support helped me believe in this book; to Rhodri Mogford, Laura Reeves, the editorial team and the production team at Bloomsbury Academic who provided me with clear-sighted help and guidance during the writing and editing process. Thanks are also due to Olga Sidorova, Olga Ushakova, Jonathan Evans, Sandra Daroczi and Tim Johnson for their interest, ideas and advice as well as for being there to offer a kind word when it was most needed. Special thanks to those who helped to sort out and obtain permissions to use illustrations and extracts from copyright works: Olga Maeots, Hugh Bedford, Vadim Chelak, Catherine Gran, Kristina Kennedy, Sara Toso, Ron Hussey, Danielle Georgiou, Mary Sullivan, Isobel Gahan, Michael O'Brien, Erika Dowell, Natalia Brovchuk, Alexander Marshak, Sergei Liubaev, Kseniia Yakovleva as well as Cotsen Children's Library at Princeton University and RGALI. Not all the illustrations mentioned in the text actually made it into the book because of difficulties in obtaining permissions; in some cases, the copyright holders simply could not be tracked down. However, the images are all clearly referenced and anyone who is interested to see them can find the books which can also be accessed online.

This book has been a lonely project with many long nights and there were times when it felt as if I would never get to the end. I am deeply grateful to my dearest family for standing by me during this challenging intellectual journey: to my husband Phil Goodwin, my son Jacob, my parents Nadia and Valera Shmuratkin and my grandmother Ania for their love and inspiration, unconditional support and emotional comfort. Without them this book would not have appeared. Big thanks go to my friends in England and Russia. Finally, I would like to express my thoughts and gratitude to Nancy Goodwin who is sadly no longer with us but who always believed in my thesis and would have been so happy to see it as a published book.

A Note on the Transliteration and Translations

Transliteration

The Library of Congress system without diacritics is followed for the transliteration from Cyrillic of Russian words and names. When a Russian name has an accepted English spelling, this form was used – for example, Chukovsky instead of Chukovskii.

Translations

Unless otherwise stated, translations are my own and references are made to the original source. All back-translations from Russian to English of citations from primary sources are my own.

1

Introduction

Children's books have always held a special position in Russian literature. For almost a century writing for children was supported and promoted by the state policy aimed at educating and bringing culture to the masses, starting from childhood. In addition, the country was blessed with great talent in this area and a number of great literary figures also wrote for children: Alexander Pushkin, Leo Tolstoy, Vladimir Mayakovsky, Daniil Kharms, Maxim Gorky, Samuil Marshak and Korney Chukovsky, to name but a few. Translated children's literature has occupied a strong place in the system of children's literature since the early days of Soviet Russia. As cultural and cross-cultural socialization starts in childhood and translated literature provides a wealth of material on the peculiarities of foreign cultures, it seems likely that translated children's literature plays a significant role in the process of forming perceptions of other lands and peoples. With regard to translated British children's literature, the way in which the image of England is created helps young readers to form their vision of the country and its culture. This, in turn, contributes to a mutual cultural dialogue and forms the basis for readers' awareness and an understanding of England from childhood.

This book explores how Russian translations of British children's literature construct a literary narrative of England and its culture. The scope of analysis of Russian translations spans about one hundred years, covering Russian translations that appeared during the Soviet period (from 1918 until 1991) and the post-Soviet period (from 1992 until 2015). The starting point of the analysis time frame is based on the idea that not until the October Revolution did the art of literary translation and the emphasis on faithfulness receive focused critical and reflective attention from scholars and translators. From then on, translation was seen as a literary form playing a significant role in Russian literature. Indeed, as Korney Chukovsky states in his 1968 book *Vysokoe iskusstvo: Printsipy khudozhestvennogo perevoda* [*A High Art: Principles of Literary Translation*], it was only after 1917 that accuracy became a universally acknowledged principle in translation.[1]

In general terms, the story of any country takes the form of cultural meanings shared by people and expressed in images, symbols, tales, traditions, events and landscapes.[2] As far as England is concerned, cultural meanings construct and maintain the representation of 'the idea of England as an imagined community', as emphasized in the *Parekh Report*. This idea is shared by large numbers of native people and foreigners who, without interacting with each other, perceive a similar 'mental image of [England's] typical sights and sounds, its customs and habits, the characteristic features of its landscapes and weather, and a sense of what is distinctive about the national character and established institutions'.[3] In the phrase 'translating England', the concept of England is a broad category, encompassing not just the country but its people and culture. Thus, to analyse how it is translated one needs to set certain criteria. That is when the more focused concept of Englishness – characteristics regarded as English – becomes more effective. In a way, England, as a broader concept, and Englishness can be used interchangeably, as characteristics of English culture, society and a way of life. Thus, cultural meanings, which make up the literary story of England, act as a manifestation of Englishness that at the same time relates to the broad concept of England. Therefore, this book will discuss Englishness when analysing translations of England in Russian children's literature.

The notion of Englishness is set apart from the notion of Britishness in this book. The two can sometimes become blurred, especially when approached by foreigners, who have a tendency to equate the two ideas when discussing questions of identity in relation to England and Britain. Nevertheless, there is a clear difference. For example, Iain Chambers divides Britishness into two versions: Britishness as 'Anglo-centric, frequently conservative, backward-looking, and increasingly located in a frozen and largely stereotyped' perception of English culture and 'ex-centric, open-ended and multi-ethnic' Britishness.[4] I have decided to exclude the multi-ethnic component of Britishness, which is more applicable to contemporary British children's literature. Instead, the focus of this book is mainly on Englishness, acknowledging that its stereotyped and conservative nature is Anglo-centric. The Anglo-centric essence of Englishness as 'Merry England' (meaning 'a particular Arcadian attitude to the past, prevalent in Victorian and Edwardian times but with roots stretching back to the turn of the 19th century and with continuing power to the present day'[5]) is expressed to a greater degree in the classics of British children's literature published between the late-Victorian–Edwardian period and the end of the Second World War.[6]

It is this particular Anglo-centrism as 'Merry England' that is represented in the Russian translations of British children's classics discussed in this book. The corpus of English books consists of works published between the late-Victorian–Edwardian periods and the end of the Second World War, as representative examples in which the narrative of England is embedded in the content.[7] The included texts can be regarded as products of the English cultural context, as they contain descriptions of 'Merry England', which explicitly and/or implicitly pertain to a certain time frame: late-Victorian–Edwardian England, as well as England between the First and the Second World Wars. This group of books share common Edwardian cultural features which are easily recognized as manifestations of 'Merry England' by readers around the world, including those who have never seen England and base their perceptions on English literature. Moreover, as Rebecca Knuth emphasizes, English children's books written during the Edwardian period depict an English lifestyle which reflects this epoch and 'most children's books of the late 1920s and 1930s can be seen as carrying forward Edwardian attitudes and tropes'.[8]

The Anglo-centric image of England, which is sometimes projected onto the whole of Britain, seems to be widespread in Russian culture and formed through the agency of stereotypes, which facilitate the mythologization of England in the Russian mind. The two stereotypes, widely held in Russian culture, connoting the mythologized image of mysterious England, are the two Russian expressions – 'dobraia staraia Angliia' [good old England] and 'tumannyi Al'bion' [foggy Albion]. 'Dobraia staraia Angliia' is a Russian version of the English phrase 'Merry England'. According to I. O. Naumova, the Russian phrase is a phraseological calque of the old English expression 'Merrie Olde England' and the widespread expression 'good old times' which is present in various languages around the world and connotes the idealistic perception of the past.[9]

In Russian popular understanding, the phrase 'dobraia staraia Angliia' stands for a conventional image of England of past centuries, symbolizing an island of comfort and calm, traditions and conservatism, law and order, with attributes such as aristocracy and castles, ladies and gentlemen, bowler hats, umbrellas and pipes, afternoon tea and puddings, thatched cottages and roses. The popular symbolic image of the 'dobraia staraia Angliia' can also be found in works by William Shakespeare, Charles Dickens, Oscar Wilde, P. G. Wodehouse, G. K. Chesterton, Arthur Conan Doyle, Agatha Christie, as well as by such writers of children's literature as Lewis Carroll, Kenneth Grahame, A. A. Milne, J. M. Barrie, C. S. Lewis and J. R. R. Tolkien.

The other well-known Russian stereotypical expression of mysterious England – 'tumannyi Al'bion' – was popularized in poetry by Konstantin Batyushkov and Marina Tsvetaeva. The first line of Batiushkov's elegy 'Ten' druga' [The shade of a friend], written in 1814 as he was sailing from England to Sweden, reads, 'I was leaving the foggy shore of Albion'. Tsvetaeva referred to this line of Batiushkov's elegy for her poem 'Ia bereg pokidal tumannyi Al'biona' written in 1918 and dedicated to Byron.[10] This phrase is a well-known toponym in Russian culture associated with England, and as a metaphor it evokes the image of an enigmatic land wrapped in mist, where King Arthur and the Knights of the Round Table once reigned. At the same time, this image is linked in the Russian imagination to an island constantly covered in fog and rarely visited by the sun. Russian nineteenth-century literature offered the image of England as a foggy island shedding not light but melancholy upon the people who lived there.[11] On the whole, both Russian expressions create a positive image of England in Russian culture although a negative perception of England among its people endures, a product of the history between the nations. In the nineteenth century this was connected with commerce and foreign relations, when the image of an unfriendly England with a greedy and self-centred business class developed. Moreover, the Crimean War led to the formation of a new symbolic image of England as 'kovarnyi Al'bion' [perfidious Albion].[12] This negative, mostly stereotypical, image became entrenched in Russian perception and has reappeared in Russian political discourse whenever relations between both countries take a turn for the worse.[13]

The overall perception has been based on opposing views and constructed via different experiences and media: through political discourses prevalent at different periods in Russian history, through the personal experience of people travelling to England, through cinema, theatre, TV and mass media as well as through various fictional and non-fictional sources. In the process of constructing such a perception, literature has played an important role by creating a mythologized image of England in the corpus of Russian national children's literature and by introducing British children's books through translation. During the Soviet period the dominant narrative of this mythologization was political, with state ideology playing a significant role. The post-Soviet period has seen a shift towards the cultural narrative in the mythologization of Englishness. During this period, ideology has still been present, although its nature was modified: the commercial approach to translated literature has superseded the overwhelming influence of state ideology.

Hence, I argue that in Russian translations of British children's classics the construction of Englishness is, on the one hand, affected by censorship and given ideological interpretations and, on the other, partially Russified and reimagined as 'dobraia staraia Angliia'. The degree of modification in representing Englishness varies according to changes in the political situation in Soviet and post-Soviet Russia – political ideology playing a significant role in the Soviet Union and commercial ideology prevailing in post-Soviet Russia.

This book will pursue the following objectives. First, to analyse the literary transfer of images of Englishness from British children's literature to Russian translations during the Soviet and post-Soviet periods in order to discover the extent to which these images were preserved, modified or misrepresented in the translated texts. Secondly, to explain the process of translation in connection to Russian society, namely, how the original texts were found, why they were chosen for translation and who translated them. Thirdly, to explore the reception history of the translated books in Russia by emphasizing on critics and media reviews.

Theory

The book draws on several theoretical ideas proposed by scholars in the fields of translation studies and children's literature (Gideon Toury, André Lefevere, Lawrence Venuti, Zohar Shavit, Emer O'Sullivan and Maria Nikolajeva) that provide a suitable context for analysing the process of translating Englishness and selecting British children's books for translation. With the focus on the assumption that a different culture is assimilated in translation to some degree, reference is made to Gideon Toury's arguments, which state that translated texts are 'facts of target cultures' and that translations should be studied within the context of the receiving cultures.[14] Moreover, the book draws on the hypothesis proposed by André Lefevere who claims that a different culture is 'naturalized' in literary translations.[15] In other words, translations tend to conform more to what the target readers are used to – the literary language and content of the receiving culture. This hypothesis resonates with Lawrence Venuti who emphasizes that foreign texts are 'often rewritten to conform to styles and themes that currently prevail in domestic literatures'.[16]

Theoretical thoughts on translation outlined by Toury, Lefevere and Venuti serve as a justification for the need to look at Russian translation practices, Russian translation norms, translators' personal writings in the form of memoirs, diaries, essays, statements and prefaces for understanding translators' decisions, Russian literature as inspiration for translators in their search for translation solutions, as well as the influence of ideology and censorship (as key factors during the Soviet period) on translation. The purpose of this is to position translated children's books within the context of Soviet and post-Soviet culture.

Through children's literature young readers are educated and entertained. These two purposes are also fulfilled by translated children's books. According to Zohar Shavit, two basic principles govern translation for children: first, the original text should be adjusted in such a way that it is 'appropriate and useful, in accordance with what society regards (at a certain point in time) as educationally good for the child'; secondly, the plot, language and characters should be adjusted in such a way as to fulfil 'society's perceptions of the child's ability to read and comprehend'. The level of adherence to these principles determines the degree to which liberties were taken by translators in making changes to the translated texts.[17] Translators can challenge the prevailing expectations of the receiving culture and to some extent resist adapting the national and cultural context of the original book to the expectations of the receiving culture. For example, translated children's texts, which belong to the group of books celebrated for their aesthetic and literary quality, can enrich the literature of the receiving culture and familiarize children with foreign traditions in literature. However, as happens quite often, young readers are protected from otherness, which foreign literature signifies, on the grounds that children are not able to understand elements of foreign culture and style different from their own. Thus, as Emer O'Sullivan and Maria Nikolajeva assert, translation of children's literature balances between domestication and foreignization.[18]

Hence, these theoretical thoughts prepare the ground for developing the main idea that runs through the book: that the representation of Englishness in children's books translated into Russian would not necessarily be depicted in the same way as shown in the original texts written in English. On the contrary, if it is domesticated, Russian child and adult readers should be able to accept the original text because represented Englishness would not sound too alien. Domesticated culture-bound phenomena from the original text would sound familiar, to some extent reminding Russian readers of Russianness. Such an effect would depend on the readers' response anticipated by translators and the reception of British texts by translators: what translators expect from the translated text, grounding their expectations on existing perceptions and actual information about the culture of the original text.

A few words seem appropriate to clarify the two important concepts that act as the building blocks of the book's methodological approach: politics of children's literature and ideology. The analysis relies on Roderick McGillis's explanation of politics as a broad concept referring to political institutions that overtly and covertly regulate power relations within the field of children's literature and meaning everything that people do in various social situations because children's books can be considered as products of the social system.[19] Logically, the concept of ideology is linked to the politics of children's literature and is employed as an essential tool for contextualizing and analysing the translation process in Russia, in general, and the translation of specific children's books with reference to different Russian representations of Englishness.

The understanding of ideology is based on Ian Mason's definition of the concept and it is applied within the context of Soviet/Russian culture.[20] Ideology is seen as a notion composed of a set of assumptions, principles, views and beliefs, which determine an attitude towards reality for readers and agents of the translation process (who are literary translators, authors of literature, editors, publishers, governing and educational institutions). Ideology is an instrument which enables society to carry out its political and social rhetoric. In translated children's literature, ideology plays a didactic role because stories that are told to children in translated books form images of other cultures from a very early age. Ideology plays a key role in the process of choosing which original text to translate. As a reflection of readers' attitudes towards reality, ideology influences the process of the reception of the translated text. At the same time, as a reflection of the attitudes of producers of translated texts towards reality, ideology influences decisions made by all agents of the translation process. Hence, as a set of assumptions, principles, views and beliefs, ideology is closely connected with the construction of images of Englishness in the original texts, and it is present in the translated children's books produced during the Soviet period and in modern Russia.

Englishness: The concept and categorization

In formulating an approach it is important to set out the contextual background for understanding Englishness as it is perceived in literature and academic discourse. Englishness is seen as a concept constructed in literature, a shared cultural memory of the writers who create it and the readers who interpret it. Its overall portrait is subjective and varies depending on the prevailing ideology that determines each author's concept of English culture. Following this logic, it seems impossible to arrive at a conclusive description or a satisfactory definition. However, various features attributed to Englishness can be derived from literature and scholarship across its various aspects.[21]

For example, the most representative literary work in which most common perceptions of Englishness are summarized is Julian Barnes's satirical and dystopian 1998 novel *England, England*. Although Barnes draws a list of fifty essential features of Englishness, many of the attributes included in his list resonate in children's books: the class system, imperialism, snobbery, the stiff upper lip, hypocrisy, untrustworthiness, thatched cottages, the cup of tea, marmalade, bowler hats, red buses, Robin Hood and His Merrie Men, *Alice in Wonderland*, Queen Victoria and the Magna Carta.[22] Barnes's list is supplemented by Margaret Meek's suggestions on the following attributes of Englishness commonly found in children's literature: the fantasy genre, issues of class, nostalgia, rural landscape and eccentric characters.[23] The historical past and tradition are accentuated by Stuart Hall, according to whom England is ingrained in specific cultural meanings deriving from the concept of heritage: castles, country houses, thatched cottages, cathedrals, churches, gardens, hedgerowed landscapes, rolling countryside and green pastures.[24] The themes of empire and patriotism as attributes specific to the Victorian and Edwardian time frame are highlighted by Rebecca Knuth and Jean Webb.[25] In addition to these features, the following recurring tropes as manifestations of Englishness in literature written in English between 1900 and 1950 are highlighted by Giles and Middleton: England's traditions are represented by historical allusions; English good manners refer to the image of English middle-class gentlemen; the idealized rural landscape symbolizes a pastoral England; domestic England is depicted by the use of images of the English home and family; and finally, urban England is expressed in the form of the English city landscape.[26]

Various features can be attributed to Englishness, and the concept requires a certain level of generalization in order for it to be applied for the purposes of the analysis. Anthony Easthope proposes an idea of Englishness divided into two groups by claiming that the state and culture can be identified as English. On the side of the state, Easthope proposes that Englishness involves certain institutions signifying English national identity (e.g. Parliament, Whitehall, the Old Bailey, the Bank of England, Eton College, the British Broadcasting Corporation, the British Council) and policies associated with them (in other words, how they articulate English national discourse through their actions). On the side of culture, he suggests attributes of Englishness that involve a special environment and way of life: the English language, a canon of English literature, English landscape, English sense of humour and English common sense.[27] By analogy with Easthope's division, in this book the various aspects of Englishness are split into three groups: political and ideological associations of Englishness;

cultural associations of Englishness; and features of English national character. Each group has several features which are specific to English culture and which offer challenges to Russian translators. Thus, they present the chance to assess how translators address these challenges.

The first group, political and ideological associations, refers to the recurring English national themes that include the class system, empire, historical past and traditions. The issue of class plays a considerable role in many children's books written between the Edwardian period and the Second World War. Englishness is represented from the perspective of the class to which an author belongs. Looking at English classics of children's literature, one can observe that many writers are associated with the middle and upper classes, creating their main characters – children and adults – as those who belong predominantly to these class groups. At the same time, when people from the lower classes are portrayed, it is done so that these portraits can provide a contrast. This is quite often achieved through the use of dialect, which as an explicit marker reflects the regional and social nature of the class system.

Politically and ideologically, Englishness is also interrelated with England's imperial past. As Jean Webb suggests, the construction of Englishness in British children's literature of the Victorian and Edwardian period is associated with imperialism: Although England is represented as a manly and heroic centre of the Empire, sometimes the colonial power and heroism of England is questioned and reconsidered.[28] M. Daphne Kutzer puts particular stress on the important role of ideology as a driving force for promoting ideas of, and expanding, the empire. This ideology is all-permeating in classics of British children's literature written in the late nineteenth century and well into the twentieth century. The imperialist enterprise was entirely a male venture and the British believed that good imperial leaders should adhere to such values as hierarchy and resourcefulness, which is reflected in the fiction of the Edwardian period. Such tropes as leadership, honour, courage and morality occur in children's books in relation to empire and English national character and connote the good course of imperialism.[29] Moreover, the themes of empire and patriotism are emphasized in Rebecca Knuth's work, which sees children's literature as a vehicle that shaped English national character. The notion of Englishness in late-Victorian children's books reflects a love of country and summarizes such qualities of the English character as being courageous, manly and patriotic.[30]

The themes of historical past and traditions are also often represented in British children's literature, particularly of the Edwardian period. They are reflected in the widespread tendency to find one's roots in the country's past and the developing interest in local history; in the conviction that Englishness is stored in artefacts and places which was reflected in the founding of the National Trust in 1895 and local museums around the country; in the belief in the greatness of the British Isles and the necessity to maintain and preserve the land.[31] Moreover, these themes are connected through feelings of nostalgia with daily life and the places in which people live.

The second group, cultural associations, relates to landscape and places (city, town, village and home). The third group, features of English national character, refers to the traits commonly associated with English people and includes such tropes as the gentleman, the governess and countryfolk. Features of national character are also linked with the discourses of the fantastic and of silliness. Both discourses are conventional modes of conveying features of national character and hold a considerable place in British children's literature.[32]

The representation of English landscape in Edwardian literature, including children's books, is predominantly focused on the countryside, offering a vision of a green, pastoral land. This representation has a regional character. There is a clear domination of a north–south divide in literary works written during the late-Victorian and Edwardian period. The idealized literary image of the southern English countryside with Tudor-style cottages, gardens and hedges, green fields and rolling hills prevails in most late-Victorian and Edwardian literary evocations of English landscape.[33] In contrast to the image of the south of England, the northern English landscape is depicted as less welcoming, less cultivated, less warm, but still its sharp beauty is clearly expressed by the authors, and the moor, mountains, dales and lakes are the most distinct elements of the image of its scenery.

It is not only landscape that predominates in literary discourses of Englishness. Images of cities, villages and home are also regarded as essential characteristics. London is a typical representation of English cities and is often used as a setting in classics of children's literature. The imagined world of London in these books includes hansom cabs, omnibuses, policemen, housemaids, butlers, gentlemen in bowler hats, department stores, museums, Kensington Gardens and London Zoo, railway stations and trains. English towns and villages are also frequent choices for settings in English classic children's literature. Attributes that pertain to images of the English town and village include country fields, hedgerows, parks, parish churches, village greens and railway stations, thatched cottages, farmhouses and country houses. Moreover, the notion of the English country house is associated with the landed gentry and includes palaces, castles, courts, halls, manors and mansions.

The above types of traditional English houses also symbolize an English home. It is recognized in such rituals as tea drinking and country walks, sitting by the fire and Christmas celebrations which are all centred on the family. The symbolic representation of home as an idealized perception of the nucleus of English life can be viewed as nostalgia for the Golden Age. If one looks at the reality of life in England and depictions of Englishness in children's literature starting from the Edwardian period and up to the Second World War, one would notice an obvious discrepancy between the real and the imagined English worlds. In reality England was to a great extent a class-ridden society and the social gap between the rich and poor was not really reflected in children's literature. The literary idealized English home represented the world of wealthy middle and upper classes. This home was decent and honest and the garden evoked images of an ideal rural past.[34]

The third group, English national character, has a broad spectrum of features among which are politeness, ambiguity, practicality, humour, melancholia, bitterness, hypocrisy, privacy, bravery, personal honour, independence, adventurous spirit and the love of hobbies, as the most representative. Each of these traits can be located within the three tropes symbolically representing the English people: the English gentleman, the governess and countryfolk. The character of the gentleman is so deeply rooted in the English national character that it would probably be almost impossible to imagine English or foreign readers who would not associate England with this image. In general, there are two ways of understanding the concept of a gentleman: a man who holds a high position in society by virtue of noble birth and a man of any social class who abides by moral values and principles. A substantial description of the gentleman, which reflects the upper-class nature of the concept, is given by Christine Berberich: 'top hat, stiff upper lip, public school, emotional frigidity, clubs, ... courteous behaviour, ... good manners, fair play, ..., country houses'. At the same time, Berberich emphasizes the most common moral values that are associated with the gentleman, but without the specifically class-related associations, as 'tradition, honour, loyalty, dignity and duty'. She also connects the image of the Victorian gentleman with imperialism: 'over-moral, stiff-upper-lipped characters, preoccupied with class issues and Empire building, and undisposed to change'.[35]

The image of countryfolk is another manifestation of English national character. This trope is connected with rural England and includes landed gentry and common people. Richard R. Marsh's analysis of literary texts written before the Second World War shows that the structure of the English rural world presented in literature and characterized by class division included the squire, the farmer and the labourer. The squire is depicted as the owner of farms which are leased to tenants, and the farmer, being a tenant or an owner, controls the agricultural labourers.[36] The representation of countryfolk in literature between the early 1900s and the 1940s tends to idealization. For example, the idealized image of the traditional English countryfolk can be seen in Tolkien's character Bilbo Baggins from *The Hobbit*, personifying the essence of rural England as a peasant and a squire, risking his life to protect his home and the traditions of his land. Moreover, although peasants were perceived as the rural poor during the Edwardian period, the idealized perceptions of peasants, who knew the secret of true English life, stood as a true embodiment of the English national character, as Robert Colls notes.[37]

The image of the English governess is most commonly associated with middle- and upper-class families in Edwardian society. Giorgia Grilli describes the governess's uniform in the following way: 'the distinctive cap or a hat . . ., the familiar long grey skirt, the wide belt, the all-important collars, and the boots'.[38] In order to implement her duties efficiently, the governess had to have special character traits such as independence, intelligence, common sense, self-control in any situation, hard work and loyalty to the family who employed her. Ulrike Lentz notes that, on the one hand, the governess was seen as cruel, snobbish and cold-hearted, but on the other she was known for being loving, caring and sympathetic.[39] Famous literary depictions of the governess – Jane Eyre, Agnes Grey, Becky Sharp and Mary Poppins – contain similar character traits to those identified by Grilli and Lentz.

The above-highlighted features of English national character (the third group) are expressed in English literature, including children's literature, through the discourse of the fantastic and the discourse of silliness. The discourse of silliness and its relation to English national character are underpinned by the views of Anthony Easthope. He ascribes common sense and silliness to major traits of English national character and sees them as important characteristics of Englishness. He places silliness in a binary opposition of serious and silly. In this dichotomy silliness is opposed to and at the same time dependent on English common sense and includes humour, nonsense, eccentricity, playful absurdity and exaggeration, and fantasy. In Easthope's view silliness is especially expressed in the works of Lewis Carroll and Edward Lear, in Kipling's *Puck of Pook's Hill*, Barrie's *Peter Pan* and Grahame's *The Wind in the Willows*.[40] Playful absurdity and exaggeration include the state of being not serious and illogical, foolish behaviour, dreamlike states, and inexplicable things and events. Nonsense, as play of the mind, is based on the premise that some aspects of the real world can be distorted, inverted and exaggerated, as explained by Humphrey Carpenter and Mary Prichard. These aspects include the size of people and animals, time and events, outlandish food and other substances. In most cases nonsense involves linguistic attributes, such as invented words, rhymed words, alliteration and literal-minded pedantry.[41] As for eccentricity, which is generally seen as part of the English cult of individual personality, the eccentric behaviour of the English can be seen as the resistance to canons and conventions, as Ernest Barker sees it.[42] Eccentric behaviour is quite often connected in literature with the notion of the English gentleman. For example, well-known literary characters from Charles Dickens's *The Pickwick Papers* – Samuel Pickwick and his travelling companions –are famous eccentrics.

In order to understand how the discourse of the fantastic and Englishness are connected, I draw on Colin Manlove's studies of English fantasy literature.[43] In his view, fantasy literature is a product of English national character. The tendency of the English to bring individuality to whatever they work on is that particular quality that makes England the birthplace and centre of fantasy literature. English freedom of expression, peculiar imagination, nonconformity to limiting rules and stereotypes, eccentricity and the English temperament which is interested in the supernatural – all these aspects of English national character played a significant role in creating the perfect environment for the appearance of the discourse of the fantastic in English literature. Manlove also notes that the fantastic provides the English with the possibility of expressing their love of play with the imagination and the fairy-tale world, and play 'by mixing the supernatural comically with real life, by animating toys, having speaking animals or inventing wholly new worlds with their own rules'. According to Manlove, the following words associated with features of English national character often occur in relation to the discourse of the fantastic: 'conscious, solid, empirical, organized, connected, logical, witty, expansive, accretive, evolutionary, social, creative, various, adventure, quest, circle, happy ending, home, time, desire, nostalgia'. The above-mentioned aspects of English national character become pronounced by means of the discourse of the fantastic and, consequently, can be considered as expressions of English national character in English fantasy literature, including children's fantasy too.[44]

It is important to stress that cultural associations of Englishness and features of English national character create a narrative of the idealized 'Merry England' and pertain explicitly and/or implicitly to the period of time considered in this book – Edwardian England and England between the First and the Second World Wars. Fictional texts, which deal with Englishness, reflect each author's imagined view of England, its culture and people. The essential features of an imagined timeless England cultivated in the literature of the Edwardian period, including children's books, are proposed by Krishan Kumar:

> a country of cathedral cities and small towns and villages set in the 'southern' countryside; ... 'vernacular' domestic architecture ... in the half-timbered 'Tudor' or gabled Queen Anne style; village life centred on the green, the pub and the church, all cosily clustered together.[45]

Kumar states that the Englishness, as described in the works of Edwardian writers, is far from the reality in which modern British society exists. However, such a notion of Englishness is generally supported by many people.[46] According to Knuth, an idealized sense of Englishness was promoted in Edwardian children's books through 'the pseudohistorical concept of medieval and "Merrie Old England" with its atmosphere of cosiness, folk life, and rusticity'. Many Edwardian authors and illustrators of children's books were inspired by the English countryside, which was a place where they could hide from industrialized England. This inspiration resulted in recreated images of an idealized English rural idyll which can be found in the major classics of British children's literature. In this idealized literary England there are lush meadows, gardens, woods, cosy cottages, brave heroes, private boarding schools, as well as village, suburban and city homes as safe places to return to.[47]

The understanding of imagined England in the form of mental images of its distinctive sights and features is shared by many people, writers and readers alike. When the imagined vision of England starts having little or nothing in common with reality, it is likely to become a myth. This myth is connected to the imagined past and present of England. It can be seen as a narrative, in which connotative meanings are attached to English culture-specific events, traditions, social practices, artefacts and the natural environment.[48] Although the English have changed over time, the literary myth of England as a rural idyll, as the land of gentlemen and ladies, as well as the cosy English home, where characters can maintain their privacy, remains very much alive every time readers open English classics of children's literature. This myth is sustained by promoting the image of England as an idyllic place. Such a positive image helps to popularize Englishness as a tourist destination around the world and literary representations of England without doubt still play an effective role in this process.

Russian view of Englishness

This image of an idealized England resonates with a somewhat similar picture formed in Russian scholarly and literary discourse.[49] However, looking back to the nineteenth century, quite often this imagined depiction was influenced by positive and negative stereotypes about the country. The landmark Soviet study of the formation of stereotypes about England was by Nikolay Erofeev, who sheds light on how the image of Englishness became stereotyped in Russian culture during the first half of the nineteenth century. Erofeev concludes that the following stereotypes prevailed, drawn from the Russian nobility and the middle and upper classes who were able to see England themselves: English gentlemen were full of pride and valour; the wet and gloomy climate had affected the development of melancholia as a distinctive trait of national character; also the English, personified in the image of John Bull, were practical, logical, reasonable, hard-working, ethical and honest. At the same time, the widespread Russian view of the English as unemotional and practical-minded was based on the Russian vision of England as a hugely successful industrial and commercial nation. This idea was not drawn from actual facts but rather what Russians thought of the English business class, leading to the creation of a stereotyped portrait of Englishness in the first half of the nineteenth century. This perception did not undergo any particularly radical transformations later on and, as Erofeev concludes, England was idealized in Russian perception to a considerable extent.[50]

As political relations between the two countries changed from warm to cold, Russian fascination with England rose and fell.[51] In the second half of the nineteenth century Russian philosophers and historians – both Westernizers and Slavophiles – were interested in England. On the one hand, England was seen as a dangerous enemy and characterized as Perfidious Albion, an image that was actively disseminated in Russia during 'the Great Game' rivalry between the British and the Russian Empires (famously portrayed by Kipling in his novel *Kim* in 1901). On the other hand, England intrigued the Russian intellectual mind and it was not only the political aspect of Englishness that appealed. Russian philosophers and writers analysed the nature of English national character and the realities of everyday life in England. Korney Chukovsky described the interest in England quite clearly in his 1916 book in which he analysed letters written by English soldiers during the First World War, so the Russian mass reader would feel sympathetic towards the English, saying that

'English literature, poetry, painting, not to mention the great civic consciousness, have fascinated [the Russian intelligentsia] magnetically since our youth'.⁵² So, generally speaking, there was a wealth of widely available information about England in periodicals, fiction, non-fiction and translated literature in pre-revolutionary Russia. For example, periodicals reported on everything that happened in England.⁵³ There was information about English culture, its politics and technological achievements while various aspects of daily life, particularly Edwardian England, regularly appeared in sketches published in Russian newspapers by London-based Russian correspondents, such as Dioneo (Isaak Shklovsky), Korney Chukovsky and Samuil Marshak.⁵⁴

In fact, Chukovsky (1882–1969) and Marshak (1887–1964) played an important role in promoting English culture in Russia. Being renowned Soviet children's poets, translators, literary critics and ardent advocates of children's literature, both of them were also anglophiles, developing a love for English culture in the early stages of their literary careers. Chukovsky worked in London as a reporter for the weekly newspaper *Odesskie Novosti* between 1901 and 1903 then visited England before the October Revolution and again later in life. Marshak studied at the London University from 1912 until 1914 and then visited England several times in his later years. The time they spent in England meant a lot to both of them: not only had they learnt about the culture from personal experience but literature also had a great impact on their choice of books for translation and creative works. Marshak translated English and Scottish poetry (Shakespeare, Burns, Byron, Blake, Keats, Kipling); English and Scottish folk ballads; children's poems by Edward Lear, Lewis Carroll, A. A. Milne; and nursery rhymes. Chukovsky translated the poetry and prose of Wilde, Kipling, Shakespeare, Conan Doyle and Defoe, as well as nursery rhymes. Moreover, their love for British folk poetry, nonsense children's literature and nursery rhymes transformed their writing styles, culminating in original nonsensical poetry full of humour, word play and rhythmic patterns that has been loved by many generations of Soviet and Russian readers.⁵⁵

Post-revolutionary Russia continued to be interested in England, though the level of interest depended on political relations between the two countries. In the 1920s, when the situation between Soviet Russia and Britain worsened, discourse on England included satirical sketches and propaganda slogans, such as 'Nash otvet Chemberlenu' [Our response to Chamberlain] and 'Lordu – v mordu' [Smash the lord in the face], as well as a satirical article *Anglichane, kogda oni liubezny* [The English, when they are polite] written by Alexey Tolstoy, a Russian and Soviet writer, in which he mocks English lords by accentuating their hypocrisy.⁵⁶ Although strongly worded discourse of this kind softened later on, ideological overtones in the representation of England prevailed in Soviet non-fiction. Nevertheless, Soviet writers continued to show a genuine interest and appreciation for the country. The 1984 compilation of publications produced by Soviet writers and journalists called *Sovetskie pisateli ob Anglii* [Soviet writers about England] as an illustrative example.⁵⁷ A collection of sketches and extracts from books and articles included in this volume were written over several decades from the 1920s until the 1980s by famous Soviet writers and journalists who had spent time in England, either working as foreign correspondents or staying as tourists. They provided insightful stories about England, attentively analysing its overall image and depicting the idyllic beauty of the tranquil towns and countryside, thus creating their version of the image of the idealized 'Merry England'.

Of course, all the writings in this volume were infused with Soviet ideology. The authors used a class-based approach to the study of England, which was typical for Soviet times, focusing their attention on the hardships of the English working class, as well as social problems, class differences and stark social contrasts. A similar tendency appears in Soviet non-fiction books about England.⁵⁸ For example, the negativity towards the English, which was widespread in the 1920s and 1930s, was reflected in Il'ia Ehrenburg's view: he called England 'the island of cold-hearted dealers, cunning tradesmen and ruthless colonisers'. He also presented a typical English gentleman to Soviet readers in unflattering tones, closely linking the image with imperialism, colonialism and arrogant attitudes towards the working class, and drawing his portrait from the image of a notable political figure from the 1930s – Neville Chamberlain.⁵⁹ In post-Soviet Russia the portrait of England has been less biased. Clearly, Russian readers nowadays have unrestricted access to a wide range of printed and online publications and are also free to travel abroad. However, compared to the Soviet period, there are considerably fewer non-fictional publications providing a contemporary portrait.⁶⁰

Fiction is another valuable source in which Russian responses to English culture can be found. The theme of England was addressed by many Russian writers, including Alexander Pushkin, Nikolay Leskov, Anton Chekhov, Fyodor Dostoyevsky, Ivan Turgenev, Aleksey Remizov, Evgeny Zamyatin, Vladimir Nabokov and Mark Aldanov. In comparison, Soviet and post-Soviet children's fiction has fewer representations of England. The English historical past was retold by Kir Bulychev in his 1997 book *Angliia: bogi i geroi* [England: gods and heroes], by Mikhail Gershenzon (1940) and Irina Tokmakova (1996) in their versions of the English folk ballads about Robin Hood, by Zinaida Shishova in her 1943 book *Dzhek-solominka* [Jack the straw] and Marina Aromshtam in her 2014 novel *Kot Lantselot i zolotoi gorod, staraia angliiskaia istoriia* [Lancelot, the cat, and a golden city, an old English story]. Vissarion Sisnev (1980) set his novel *Zapiski Vikvikskogo kluba* [Vikvik's Papers] in the real England of the 1970s and Vasily Aksyonov imagined England in his 1972 novel *Moi dedushka – pamiatnik* [My grandfather, the monument]. Dina Rubina imitates the idealized English character and way of life in her 2012 novel *Dzhentl'meny i sobaki* [Gentlemen and Dogs] and Vadim Levin imitates English nonsense poetry in his 1969 book *Glupaia loshad'* [A silly horse]. Also a brief encounter with the English is given in Samuil Marshak's 1927 poem *Pochta* [Mail]. Moreover, episodic depictions of Britain as a colonial empire can be found in Aleksandra Brushtein's 1961 novel *Vesna* [Spring] and Lev Zilov's 1924 poem *Mai i Oktiabrina* [A boy called May and a girl called October]. The negative aspects of English character derived from Britain's imperial past are portrayed in Boris Zhitkov's short stories *Maria i Meri* [Maria and Mary] (1925) and *Urok geografii* [Geography lesson] (1940).[61]

The overall image emerging from Russian depictions in children's literature is twofold and follows the tendency in non-fictional publications aimed at adult readers. Vivid pictures of England created by authors of children's literature often involve representations from opposing ends of the spectrum. Negative depictions mostly prevail in the books created during the Soviet period: when the influence of political ideology is noticeable, as it was during Soviet times, negative nuances in the literary image of England are likely to appear. This negativity has a social aspect, focusing on inequality, the hardships of the working class and the country's imperialist past. For example, Boris Zhitkov's 1925 short story *Maria i Meri* responds to the image of an unjust capitalist country. The author tells his readers about the collision of the Russian schooner, Maria, and the English cargo ship, Mary. The English captain Arthur Parker is portrayed as a heartless man who dislikes the Russians; he gives an order to collide with the schooner and wrecks it purposefully and spitefully. The ideological context is not coincidental, as the 1920s witnessed rather icy relations between Soviet Russia and Britain.[62]

On the other hand, Russian interpretations of Englishness originating from children's literature are idealized and involve prevailing stereotyped perceptions about the way of life, environment, people and culture. In most instances these stereotypes have positive connotations and create an idealized image of England as 'dobraia staraiia Angliia' [good old England] or 'Merry England', with descriptions of country houses, eccentric adventurous gentlemen, polite behaviour, discussions about the weather and a fondness for dogs. The authors consolidate the idealized image of England that is popular among Russian audiences: they offer what readers are expected to like – the myth of good old England. For example, Vasily Aksyonov's 1972 novel *Moi dedushka – pamiatnik* is only partially set in England; but his England is imaginary. His imagined English country house is typical: a white building situated in a park, a spacious courtyard, bright-green grass and pruned bushes.[63] Also Dina Rubina's 2012 novel *Dzhentl'meny i sobaki*, inspired by England and written in the playful style of English nonsensical stories, presents to its readers numerous allusions to idealized Englishness: slices of English-style toasted bread for breakfast, an annual fair in a town called Chesterfield, English-sounding names, a preoccupation with the weather and an affection for dogs.[64]

The twofold image of Englishness emerging from the Russian perspective and the development of the aforementioned arguments is used in this book as a means to demonstrate that the same bipolar tendency to present England positively and negatively is reflected in the representations of Englishness found in Russian translations of children's literature published during the Soviet and post-Soviet periods. Obviously, translated books do not exist in a vacuum. As part of a bigger literary polysystem, translated literature is bound to absorb and respond to literary, cultural and political developments to some degree. If we narrow this idea of interaction between literary systems to the discourse of Englishness in Russia, we see that translated children's literature, along with the national literature, was conducive to the evolution and communication of the story of England on the Russian literary scene. Hence, with the contextual background set out for understanding Englishness in mind, this book brings into focus the story of translating England in Russian children's literature, shedding light on the way that the portrayal of Englishness was manipulated in ideological and cultural contexts.

Structure

Russian fiction and non-fiction published throughout the twentieth and the early twenty-first centuries clearly offer a diverse view and demonstrate a keen interest in England. So what was the fascination among writers and readers? It may well be borne out of a simple desire to learn more about all things foreign, or as Joseph Brodsky suggested, '[i]f you are born in Russia, nostalgia for an alternative genesis is inevitable'.[65] Moreover, curiosity about the culture of the West among the Russians is demonstrated by the popularity of literature translated from major Western languages during the Soviet and post-Soviet periods. For example, according to the latest official print run statistics, almost 13 per cent of all published books in Russia in 2017 were translations of foreign literature, 61 per cent of which were translations from English. Moreover, if in 2008 J. K. Rowling was among the top ten most popular writers of children's literature with the largest print run holding the fifth position, then in 2017 she was pushed out of the list by Holly Webb, who became the second most popular children's author (Korney Chukovsky was the first).[66] This ratio of translated literature continues the dynamic set during the Soviet period, when there was a real willingness to learn about and understand the West. As Sergei Dovlatov once pointed out, Soviet people liked imported goods, and this included translated literature.[67] But who or what generated this clamour? It is possible that it was due to changes in society, literary processes, translation and publishing, not least because of changes in the demands of readers.

Considering Gideon Toury's claim that translations should be studied within the context of receiving cultures, it is important to set the ground for understanding how the world of translated books was formed. With this in mind, Chapter 2 presents the historical background by highlighting the political, social and cultural environment in which Russian translations were created and published. It discusses the ideological conventions of the Soviet literary world by looking at the history of translation theory and praxis and the way translation was regulated in the Soviet Union. As ideology played a key role in the regulation of cultural life in Soviet society, special attention is devoted to the discussion of censorship and translation norms as measures of state control over the translated literature. These ideological constraints shed light on who the key actors within the field of translation were, how Soviet translators anticipated what kinds of texts they might translate and how they went about it. As the Soviet Union imposed restrictions on access to the outside world, an adequate representation of images of foreign cultures was not available. This lack of accessible information led to the misinterpretation of Englishness. The post-Soviet period brought more possibilities for cross-cultural activities between Russia and the outside world, which almost entirely eradicated these flaws in representations of Englishness.

In Chapter 3, a larger contextual picture of British books written for children and translated into Russian will be considered, in order to justify the selection of several translated books chosen for later, closer analysis. The broader context means those British children's books published between the late-Victorian period and the Second World War that were selected for translation into Russian by Soviet and post-Soviet publishers between 1918 and 2017. The larger context also includes the political and cultural dynamic prevalent in Russian society predetermining the development of Russian children's literature which acts as a hosting environment for the translated literature. Analysis of the portrayal of England in translation will narrow in scope to study those English books that portrayed Englishness. Consideration of the views of Soviet/Russian researchers and writers on translated and non-translated British children's literature will form the basis for an understanding of how the translated books fit into the historical and cultural context. This will clarify three questions: which English books children were given to read in the Soviet Union, which English books were not available for Soviet children and what kind of English books that portray Englishness are prevalent in contemporary Russia.

Analysing the bibliographical data about Russian translations will show how translation responded to ideological demands as well as the political and cultural changes which took place during the Soviet and post-Soviet periods. The goal is to identify distinctive trends in the translated texts which appeared in two contrasting periods: Soviet and post-Soviet. This will show that during the former, preference was given to those original books which toed the line of Soviet ideology and reflected the country's social situation, while those that did not comply with the system of values were simply ignored. In such cases censorship was the instrument controlling the selection of titles for translation. In contrast, during the post-Soviet era it was a decision based purely around commercial interests, with themes of national rhetoric having much less sway. This larger contextual picture justifies the choice of books for the case study in the following chapters.

Taking into account the above contextual framework, Chapters 4–8 focus on the detailed case studies, examining the following British children's books and their various translations to gather textual evidence and analyse the translation of various manifestations of Englishness from English into Russian:

- J. M. Barrie, *Peter and Wendy* (1911) translated by Nina Demurova in 1968, an adapted version called *Peter Pan* produced by Irina Tokmakova in 1981, and a translation of the play *Peter Pan* done by Boris Zakhoder in 1967.
- Kenneth Grahame, *The Wind in the Willows* (1908) translated by Irina Tokmakova in 1988, Vladimir Reznik in 1992, Mikhail Iasnov and Aleksandr Kolotov in 1993, Leonid Iakhnin in 2002, Viktor Lunin in 2011.
- Rudyard Kipling, *Puck of Pook's Hill* (1906) and *Rewards and Fairies* (1910) translated by Aleksei Slobozhan (poetry by Galina Usova) in 1984, Gennadii

Kruzhkov and Marina Boroditskaia in 1996, Irina Gurova in 1996, and a 1991 reprint of the 1916 translation by Anna Enkvist which was not available during the Soviet period.

- A. A. Milne, *When We Were Very Young* (one poem only – *The King's Breakfast*) (1924) translated by Samuil Marshak in 1946; *Now We Are Six* (one poem only – *King Hilary and the Beggarman*) (1927) translated by Nonna Slepakova in 1968.
- P. L. Travers, *Mary Poppins* (1934), *Mary Poppins Comes Back* (1935), *Mary Poppins Opens the Door* (1943) translated by Boris Zakhoder in 1968, Igor' Rodin in 1994, Marina Litvinova in 1996.

All the Russian translations were initially published during the Soviet period and afterwards reprinted in post-Soviet Russia. These translations are well represented on the contemporary Russian book market and can be found in bookshops in major Russian cities and the main online bookshops such as ozon.ru, labirint.ru and read.ru. Russian readers (children and their parents) are clearly familiar with these titles. As the results of a Russian survey of 2013 demonstrate, Russian children chose the following translated British children's books for their extracurricular reading (four of these books are included in the detailed case studies): Michael Bond's stories about Paddington Bear, J. M. Barrie's *Peter Pan*, Frances H. Burnett's *The Secret Garden* and *A Little Princess*, Lewis Carroll's *Alice in Wonderland*, Dick King-Smith's *The Sheep-Pig* and *Lady Daisy*, Charles Dickens's *Oliver Twist*, Arthur Conan Doyle's stories about Sherlock Holmes, James Greenwood's *The True History of a Little Ragamuffin*, Kenneth Grahame's *The Wind in the Willows*, C. S. Lewis's *The Chronicles of Narnia*, A. A. Milne's *Winnie-the-Pooh*, J. K. Rowling's books about Harry Potter, R. L. Stevenson's *Treasure Island*, J. R. R. Tolkien's *The Hobbit* and *The Lord of the Rings* and Pamela Travers's books about Mary Poppins.[68]

Each original book chosen for the detailed study contains aspects of Englishness from all three groups previously identified: political and ideological associations, cultural associations and features of national character. However, compared to the originals, these aspects were treated differently in Russian translations, due to ideological influences, and underwent creative transformations. Literary constructions of Englishness through political and ideological associations and expressions of national character were manipulated in an ideological context. The way these features of Englishness were represented depends on the dual role that ideology played in the field of children's literature in the Soviet Union and post-Soviet Russia: in the case of the Soviet Union it was ideological doctrine and censorship; in the case of modern Russia, commercial interests and revived patriotic sentiment. This reflects the shifting nature of the political and cultural climate in Soviet and post-Soviet Russia. With this in mind, the book will analyse how these processes affect Russian representations of the following themes: empire and the historical past in *Puck of Pook's Hill* and *Rewards and Fairies*; empire and the class system in the novel *Peter and Wendy* and the play *Peter Pan*. As for expressions of English national character, the book will look at Russian representations of the discourse of silliness in *The King's Breakfast* and *King Hilary and the Beggarman*, as well as discourses of the fantastic and of silliness in the *Mary Poppins* books.

The larger part of the analysis in Chapters 4–8 focuses on the Soviet period, as the first translations of the analysed books were published before 1991 and the subsequent retranslations, which appeared in the new post-Soviet context, drew on the existing interpretations of Englishness (apart from Milne's poems that were not subsequently retranslated). As Soviet policy imposed restrictions on both the material to be translated and the means by which this should be done, it is interesting to see how both translators as self-censors and editors as censors interfered with the original texts while still managing to build bridges between cultures in this restricted environment. The point of departure for the analysis of Soviet translations is Aleksandra Borisenko's view that the Soviet ideological understanding of childhood affected translated children's literature. Borisenko explains the basic principles for translating books written for children during the Soviet period. It was expected that translators and editors would remove or reduce the effect of everything that was 'sad, morbid, violent, sentimental, ambiguous, complicated, too long, or descriptive'. As a contrasting measure, it was 'advisable to make the text in question' appear cheerful, optimistic, light, straightforward, and dynamic.[69] An understanding of the historical and political context enables a deeper analysis of the representations of Englishness, asking why they were treated ideologically in Russian translations and what subsequent changes in the translations and/or retranslations followed after the fall of the Soviet Union.

Furthermore, the portrayal of Englishness was conveyed in Soviet and post-Soviet translations according to literary norms, requiring translations to be accommodated within the context of the receiving culture and literary tradition. This is another way of looking at the domesticating principle in translation which is supported by André Lefevere's theoretical view about different cultures being 'naturalized' in translations. This tendency refers to cultural associations (landscape and home), features of national character (the gentleman, the governess and countryfolk) and expressions of national character (the discourse of silliness) – they undergo creative transformations in Russian translations, inspired by images of Russianness. These modifications resulted in transforming 'Merry England' of the original classics into the partially Russified 'dobraia staraia Angliia' [good old England], irrespective of whether the translated texts appeared during the Soviet or post-Soviet periods. This is evident in the analysed Russian translations of the following original texts: *The Wind in the Willows*, *Puck of Pook's Hill* and *Rewards and Fairies* and the *Mary Poppins* books.

Chapters 4–8 also include the analysis of pictorial representations of Englishness, focusing on the interaction between illustrations and translated children's literature. Textual and visual elements in a translated children's book complement each other; illustrations can enhance the story. They often reflect the societal conventions and values of both countries in which the original book was written and in which it was recreated in translation. In many cases, they play a significant role in the reception of a translated book; they can add depth to the literary image of England or take away from the meaning by introducing new elements that can be interpreted differently. Hence, I focus on illustrations in *Puck of Pook's Hill* and *Rewards and Fairies*, *Peter Pan*, *The King's Breakfast* and *King Hilary and the Beggarman*, *Mary Poppins* and *The Wind in the Willows*, and discuss how visual images contribute to the distinctive Russian perception of England.

In the original texts, illustrations are subordinated to the written narrative of Englishness. Although the original written texts do not entirely depend on visual images to convey the message (as in picture books, for example), illustrations in each original book are still an important and useful means of adding the visual perception of Englishness to readers' experience of the written texts. Illustrations are only partly essential to extract the meaning of Englishness in the original texts written by Kipling and Barrie; however, they play a more substantial role in the original books by Travers, Grahame and Milne. The way in which original illustrations are coded in their relation to time, place and culture changes in the translated texts. The emphasis of the analysis is on the message of illustrations in the Russian texts – similar to the originals, they depict the idealized England. However, it is a modified version of England and this trend is similar to the way Englishness is represented in textual form. Russian illustrators fill the original meaning with new visual expressions and, by doing this, they offer their own interpretation of England that may or may not correlate with the translators' point of view.

There are two renowned British children's classics – *Alice's Adventures in Wonderland* and *Winnie-the-Pooh* – which have not been included in this corpus of texts chosen for the detailed analysis, although they too reflect the spirit of an idealized 'Merry England' and depict Englishness in the best possible way. Aspects of translation and Englishness in these books have already been widely researched in Russia and in the English-speaking world.[70] Therefore, it seems reasonable to focus on the analysis of Russian translations of the British children's books which have so far not received much scholarly attention.

2

Translated literature in Russia: The 'high art' of realist translation, censorship and key actors within the field

With the October Revolution of 1917 came a new Soviet state and the advent of the idea of retranslating major world classics.[1] The Soviet publishing house Vsemirnaia literatura [World literature] was established under the initiative of Maxim Gorky, a leading Soviet writer and cultural figure, and charged with carrying out this task in September 1918. In 1919 it released a catalogue that included an extensive list of foreign classics and works by lesser-known authors, all written between the late eighteenth century and the early twentieth century, which were to be translated or re-translated. Although this ambitious project ended in December 1924, it increased translation activity, strengthened its position within the Soviet literary system and brought about new developments in theoretical discourse on literary translation as a creative process.[2]

By the mid-1930s, the Soviet school of translation had formulated an initial system of ideas. They were in line with the principles of Socialist Realism[3] that were linked with translation during the First All-Union Conference of Translators held in 1936.[4] During this conference the Soviet literary critic Iogann Al'tman introduced a new term – 'творческий перевод' [creative translation] – which greatly influenced the formation of the Soviet school of literary translation. According to Al'tman, creative translation always stayed true to reality and did not invent individual interpretations; on the contrary, it truthfully re-created the original literary work by accommodating it within the receiving culture. Later, in the 1950s, Al'tman's ideas were developed into the theory of Soviet realist (or adequate) translation by the translation theorist Ivan Kashkin.[5] It was declared that the only acceptable method of translation was based on the principles of Socialist Realism, which would provide ways of achieving adequacy between the translated text and its original. Realist translation was seen as a unified aesthetic system and a single acceptable style. Fidelity to the style and content of the original text was paramount. This could be achieved by depicting everything that was appropriate and progressive according to Soviet ideological dogma.[6]

There were four fundamental principles upon which the Soviet school of realist translation was based, as Lauren G. Leighton explains by referring to the Soviet translation theorist V. M. Rossels: accepting the principle of translatability; acknowledging translation as a literary process; treating translators as writers; and understanding the process of translation not as a copy or an imitation but as an artistic activity in its own right.[7] As it follows from these principles, translation practice was considered equal to literary activity and creativity and was, consequently, treated as high art. Moreover, realist translation was supposed to satisfy readers' demands and the literary tastes of average Soviet readers. It was also considered the best possible method for translating world classics in order to introduce them to the new Soviet audience – the working-class reader. Translation became an independent literary work and it was expected that the translated text would replace the original.

Consequently, translators became co-authors of the original. However, not all of them were capable of producing literary translations which could be considered as works of art in their own right so only the most gifted practitioners were able to succeed. This was perfectly illustrated by Korney Chukovsky who wrote in his diary about Samuil Marshak's demands to be presented as co-author of his own translations, with his name written in capital letters while the original author was demoted to the lowly status of appearing in lower case.[8] Chukovsky's observation was not far from the truth. Although the front covers of Shakespeare's sonnets translated by Marshak did not look exactly as he wished, still, his name was printed in a larger font than the title of the original book, as can be seen in translations published by Sovetskii pisatel' and Gosudarstvennoe izdatel'stvo khudozhestvennoi literatury publishing houses in 1949, 1955 and 1960.

The underlying premise of the Soviet school of realist translation lay in the assumption that everything was translatable, including culture-specific and historic elements (realia), and the peculiarity/uniqueness of the source language (musicality, emotional nuances and structure, especially in poetic translations). The Soviet school focused on the translatability of every element of a foreign text, calling such translation 'adequate'. Hence, ideologically correct Soviet translators who followed the principles of the realist translation could find equivalents to untranslatable elements by using a domesticating strategy. This meant taking into account the role of Russian literature and culture as an accommodating force and treating translated texts as facts of Russian culture (paraphrasing Toury's term).

At the same time, translators could find equivalents by being aware of dominant ideological conventions, which were identified through censorship, and the assumption that 'every translation is more or less an ideological assimilation of the original' as stated in *Literary Encyclopaedia* in 1934.[9]

So, through norms of Socialist Realism, which can be considered as ideological constraints imposed on Soviet literary translation, Soviet authorities could demand how foreign books should be translated. Soviet authorities also controlled what kinds of books could be offered to adult and child readers. According to the literary critic Igor Motiashov, there were four basic criteria for selecting foreign children's books for translation in the Soviet Union: aesthetic, educational, moral and political. The aesthetic criterion meant that the foreign book had to be well written and appeal equally to adult and child audiences. In order to meet the educational criterion, the original book had to be informative and provide authentic and full knowledge about the original culture. A foreign children's book could meet the moral criterion if it promoted diligence, honesty, respect for older people, tolerance, civic responsibility, empathy, and rejection of 'egoism, cruelty, ... falsehood, violence, parasitism, greed', indifference to pain and so on. The political criterion 'expressed the attitude of the publisher and the translator to the existing political situation'. This meant that the book chosen for translation had to be in line with Soviet ideology, according to which all 'racist, militarist, chauvinist, royalist, clericalist, neo-fascist, neo-colonialist, anti-communist, antisocialist, and anti-democratic ideas and views' were rejected.[10] The two last criteria – moral and political – are most closely connected with the idea of censorship and give a more explicit suggestion as to what kind of possible excisions, amendments and substitutions had to be applied in the field of children's literature in order for the translated book to be published.

Censorship as a system of control in the field of foreign literature was a contributing factor to the Soviet Union's cultural isolation from the world. By banning references in translated books to elements of foreign culture that were not in line with Soviet ideology and identifying ideologically correct foreign books suitable for translation, censorship stimulated the creation of imaginary images of foreign cultures contextualized by the Soviet understanding of the outer world. The imaginary images of the capitalist Western world, in particular, were consequences of the necessity to represent the reality depicted in foreign books within the corresponding Soviet context. One can only ponder now whether Soviet translators did this deliberately or whether they were forced to do so by the system of restrictions which laid down the rules that dominated the Soviet literary world. However, it is important to mention that, despite the ideological didacticism and Communist Party control via censorship, children's literature treated 'prescribed historical and ideological themes in a creative way', enabling children's writers to find 'loopholes for originality and retained considerable thematic, stylistic, and generic diversity within it'.[11]

A huge censorship system was built in the Soviet Union between 1917 and 1931, and for up to sixty years its principles did not undergo significant changes, as Herman Ermolaev points out.[12] The hierarchy of the system of Soviet censorship of national and translated literature consisted of five major levels, according to the Russian historian of Soviet censorship Arlen Blium: Communist Party control, the department of political control in the Committee for State Security (KGB), Glavlit, the editor and self-censorship. The main government censorship authority Glavlit, the abbreviation for the Main Administration for Literary and Publishing Affairs at the People's Commissariat for Education of the RSFSR (or Narkompros), played the principal guiding and technical role in the system of control. It implemented instructions issued by the Communist Party and KGB, and policed literature by authorizing books for publishing. It was set up in 1922 and closed down in December 1991.

In respect of censorship in children's literature, the following was written in a circular letter from Glavlit sent to its local authorities in August 1923:

> The [Soviet] Republic pays great attention to the upbringing of young people; hence it is necessary to be especially observant of literature for children and young people. Books containing clearly bourgeois values, praising the old way of life and relations between people, as well as describing religious worship are not allowed. These principles ought to be applied in a delicate way especially in regard to historical literature and classics, full of patriotic ideas and militarism, good-hearted kings and queens, the righteous rich, and so on.[13]

Later, in February 1926, the restrictions imposed on children's literature were even more severe – only children's and young people's literature which promoted communist upbringing was permitted to be published.[14] A circular letter on foreign literature marked 'Classified', which was sent by the Foreign department (Inotdel) of Glavlit to its subordinate authorities in July 1923, listed types of foreign literature banned from importation to the Soviet Union, among which were:

- all works containing ideology that is hostile and alien to the proletariat;
- books of an idealistic nature;
- children's literature containing elements of bourgeois values and praising old [pre-1917] ways and conditions of life;
- works written by authors who were against the October Revolution.[15]

From the late 1950s, additional regulations controlling the circulation of foreign books in the Soviet Union were issued. Notwithstanding the fluctuating nature of censorship regulations, expressed in a slight lessening or tightening of control over foreign literature which depended on the political climate in the country throughout the whole Soviet period, the restrictive principles introduced at the beginning of the Soviet era remained the same.

Censorship also was carried out by editors in publishing houses, journals, magazines, newspapers, TV and radio stations, film studios, theatres and so on. In fact, this was often even more severe than the censorship implemented by Glavlit and even substituted some of its functions. Editors were appointed by the state authorities and under their supervision literary texts underwent severe ideological editing. They had to keep a close eye on all possible nuances (such as obscure citations of forbidden texts and unacceptable allusions) and elements of subtext (in other words Aesopian language) that did not agree with the state ideology.[16] Inna Slobozhan, who was an editor in the Leningrad publishing house Lenizdat from 1956 until 1990s, recalled that an official list of literary themes banned by censorship existed though it was never actually seen by editors. Rather than follow the letter of the code, they had to intuitively guess what a Glavlit censor would cross out from the text. When a censor made remarks on the text forcing an editor to amend the manuscript, the blame was always laid solely on the editor and the consequences were usually severe: disciplinary penalties such as lost bonuses and reprimands. Inna Slobozhan regarded this unpronounced list of forbidden themes as political censorship. The concept of banned themes was interpreted broadly. For example, it was not permitted to write about Sergey Esenin's death, publish the works of Mikhail Bulgakov, or even mention the name of Nikolay Gumilev who was long considered an enemy of the people.[17]

Such themes had to be second-guessed by translators, who were quite often forced to rely on intuition to impose self-censorship, a necessary protective mechanism for any writer or literary translator. This had existed before the October Revolution, but in the Soviet Union, a writer or literary translator tried to foresee what possible ideological, political, aesthetic or other issue the official censor might find in the manuscript and consequently remove it beforehand. Soviet translators had to keep a close watch for bourgeois values in foreign literature and be vigilant in order not to introduce the essence of so-called bourgeois life in the translated works, because a mistake by a translator could turn into a political mistake.[18] For example, as the Russian translator Victor Golyshev recalls, the Soviet Union officially banned only those themes in foreign literature that were connected with pornography, military secrets and anti-Soviet propaganda; however, these subjects could often be widely interpreted.[19] Thus, self-censorship was an everyday tool in the survival kit for all Soviet translators. Also, adherence to the postulates of the Socialist Realist translation can be viewed as another form of self-censorship. As Samantha Sherry argues, the expectation that they would accommodate original texts within the Soviet context meant translators were given the role of authorized interpreters of original texts and encouraged to alter the originals with the purpose of expressing 'what the original should say, rather than what it does say'.[20]

A fragment from the 1979 Soviet film *Autumn Marathon* (directed by Georgii Daneliia; screenplay by Aleksandr Volodin) exemplifies in an allegorical form the role of the Soviet editor as censor. The main character – a literary translator Andrei Pavlovich Buzykin – is notified by his editor that the author whose work he translated would not be permitted for publication. The reason was typical for the Soviet Union: the author has changed his political views, so they are no longer in line with the Soviet position on world politics. Buzykin passively agrees to that and the expression on his face clearly shows that he did not have any choice but to adjust to the new reality. The translator's passivity and conformism points to the existing atmosphere in the Soviet literary translation world: translators did not have absolute freedom in their choices of what and how to translate.

The Soviet Union joined the Universal Copyright Convention in May 1973. Before that foreign authors usually knew nothing about changes in their texts and even books translated into Russian. After May 1973 there was a legal requirement for any translated book, which was in some way modified or adapted, to state that it was printed with abridgments. However, in reality this general statement did not save the situation and, in general, Soviet readers were still unaware of the extent of changes that books underwent during translation, except for those few who could get hold of an original for comparison. It was common practice in the USSR to write prefaces and commentaries to the translated books in which bourgeois values were exposed and criticized. The same was done for the books published in the Soviet Union in the original language by the Progress Publishing House – the foreword and commentaries were written in Russian.

Consequently, the ideological context of the Soviet epoch laid the foundations for creating ideologically correct translations. Hence, the political environment during the Soviet period affected representations of Englishness in Russian translations in such a way that they would inevitably have ideological connotations.

Children's literature was not immune from ideological influences in literary translation, something which is evident from the leading voices in the field. The spokesmen for the realist translation in the context of children's literature were Soviet (Russian) translators of children's literature who were also renowned children's poets: Korney Chukovsky, Samuil Marshak and Boris Zakhoder (1918–2000). They wrote on literary translation in general, as well as on translation in the field of children's literature. Their theoretical views on issues of realist literary translation as a creative and cultural activity created a basis for theoretical ideas on translation in the field of Soviet children's literature.

As mentioned above, Soviet translators did not let untranslatable elements from the original texts penetrate into the Soviet literary system, thus adhering to domesticating principles and focusing on Russian language and culture. Chukovsky stressed that it was necessary for Soviet translators to read Russian literature and to think in Russian; he also emphasized that translation could be called faithful from an artistic point of view only when it recreated the style and content of the original text, accommodating it within the context of Russian culture in such a way that average Soviet readers would easily comprehend. In terms of the translation of culture-specific elements, Chukovsky pointed out to Soviet translators that by using the Russian language, they had to recreate the style of the original and preserve elements specific to the national culture. Regarding the translation of fairy tales, Chukovsky stated that no harm was done if a translation was Russified; in fact, such a transformation turned the original fairy tale into a creative work that belonged to the people of the receiving culture. There was, however, a limit to the degree and Russian folklore was not expected to replace the national peculiarity of the original text.[21]

Like Chukovsky, Marshak treated the translation of children's literature as high art[22] and advocated a domesticating strategy in translation:

> [A translator] must have a profound knowledge of the foreign language and, perhaps, an even more profound knowledge of [one's] own. [A translator] must feel the essence of [his] native language so profoundly so as to avoid giving [himself] up to the foreign, being its slave.[23]

Marshak emphasized that translators were supposed to 'create new – Russian – poems, which retain the thoughts, feelings and melody of the original'.[24] Efim Etkind, a Soviet translator of poetry and a translation theorist, summarized Marshak's translation principles, referring to his translations of Kipling's poems for children: details can be changed; the full content, structure and style of the original is more important.[25]

The fact that Chukovsky and Marshak were anglophiles helps us to see that their knowledge of Russian children's folklore influenced their translations of English nursery rhymes, as well as British folk and nonsense poetry. Being inspired by Russian folklore and Russian children's rhymes, they introduced Russian folk elements quite generously in their translations and emphasized the importance of this approach. They rejected literal translation and promoted the poetic adaptation and accommodation of original poems according to the demands and rules of Russian poetry in terms of rhythm, structure and wordplay. According to them, Soviet translators were expected to know the original culture and focus on creating a portrait of the national character and the poetic peculiarities of foreign nations through the masterful usage of the Russian language.[26]

Although Boris Zakhoder produced less published material about translation practice, compared to Chukovsky and Marshak, he still actively promoted the traditions of Soviet realist translation in the field of children's literature which the pair had developed, believing that translation was high art, and acting as an ideological and moral border guard and cultural mediator. Zakhoder is best known for his adaptations of *Winnie-the-Pooh*, *Mary Poppins*, *Alice's Adventures in Wonderland* and *Peter Pan* (the play). He expressed his views on translation for children as follows: 'Every nation has its own memory. In my translation English memory is replaced by Russian memory, so it would be easier for our children to perceive a foreign fairy-tale. So the fairy-tale becomes fully Russian.'[27] Efim Etkind characterized Zakhoder's method of translation: Zakhoder focused on the re-creation of the essence of the original text, though the form of the original was not so important to him.[28] Indeed, Zakhoder clearly stated in his notes that translation for children meant 're-creating the vividness of the original literary work for readers', which can only be done if a translator possesses intuition, talent and inspiration. He distrusted literalist translation, calling it 'phonetic nationalism', explaining that the nearer translators got to foreign languages in their translations, the more alien these languages and nations would seem to readers of the translated texts. Zakhoder was adamant that the only way to translate the untranslatable was to rewrite it in Russian. A translator had to rewrite the original text as if the author was writing it initially in Russian, thus becoming a co-author of the original text and consequently turning the translated text into a fact of Russian culture.[29]

Hence, the Soviet school of realist translation in the field of children's literature strongly supported the domesticating principle, believing that literary translation was 'high art' and should be treated as such, and promoting the role of translators as creative co-authors of original texts. The principle of the creative translator coincides with Riitta Oittinen's dialogic approach to translation for children. As she declares, a literary translator has visible presence in the translated text: he/she 'does not hide behind the original author but ... steps forward and stands in sight'.[30] In a similar way to translators working during the Soviet period, contemporary Russian translators continue to focus on the aesthetic functions of the translated language and the literary quality of their translations. They are actors who mediate the dissemination of foreign information and, consequently, have agency to introduce new literary forms and stylistic nuances, thus enriching the Russian language, as well as promoting new themes within the field of Russian children's literature.

At the same time, modern Russian translators follow the didactic principle of children's literature, acting as ideological and moral border guards between Russian and English cultures. One would think that, with the demise of the Soviet Union, the influence of ideology on the process of translation would become considerably less. This is true in the context of state ideology: after 1991, many foreign children's books, which had not been accepted by the Soviet state due to censorship, appeared in new uncensored translations. From the general point of view of ideology as a set of norms established by society, however, translated children's literature continues to operate under the influence of mainstream didactic views. Therefore, in the context of policing borders between cultures, modern Russian translators can be seen as actors responsible for filtering and controlling translated literature. Their role is not only to fulfil the didactic purposes of children's literature, including moral issues, but also to ensure the clarity and readability of the Russian language, which for a long time has been one of the principal goals of Russian translation practice.

The views of recognized modern Russian translators working in the field of children's literature – heirs to the traditions of the Soviet school of realist translation – provide context for understanding the roles of translators as creative mediators between cultures as well as creative co-authors. Mikhail Iasnov (b. 1946), a translator of poetry and prose, mainly from French, and a children's author, says that modern Russian translators of children's poetry follow the main principle of the Soviet school of realist translation developed by Chukovsky and Marshak: They retain the rhythm and poetic allusions of the original verse and at the same time make visible their authorial voices in the translated poems, thus becoming co-authors of the new versions of the originals. Irina Tokmakova (1929–2018), a children's poet and a translator of children's literature from English and Swedish, acknowledged that every time she translated she became a co-author of the original text and added words of her own. However, she did not betray the author of the original work and retained the original voice in the translated text. Iuliana Iakhnina (1928–2004), a translator from French and Norwegian who translated a few children's books, adhered to the principle of greater freedom while translating for children. She said that it was necessary for translators to know their own national folklore in order to find similar associations and allusions.[31]

From these statements it is clear that the tendency to promote the domesticating principles of translation within the field of translated children's literature continues nowadays. However, there are views advocating for a balance between domestication and foreignization. Russian translators Alexander Livergant (b. 1942) and Viktor Golyshev (b. 1937), who both translate English-language literature, sum up the key principles which Russian translators are expected to follow: foreign authors should sound in Russian as if it were their own language; and translation should remain a fact of Russian literature, bearing in mind that elements of foreignness will still be present in the translated text. Irina Gurova (1924–2010), a translator and editor of English-language literature, including books written for children, stated that the Soviet school of realist translation went too far in its rejection of foreignization. Her method consisted of recreating the stylistic nuances of the original in the translated text by means of the Russian language, so Russian readers would gain an impression from the translated text that is similar to the aesthetic effect created for readers of the original. Nina Demurova (b. 1930), a translator of English-language literature, including several children's books, explains her approach to the translation of *Alice's Adventures in Wonderland*: 'I devised a new method so readers would understand the wordplay and the grotesque of the book, but at the same time I aimed at avoiding Russification.' Olga Varshaver (b. 1959), a translator of American and British children's literature, sees translators acting as interpreters of different cultures, focusing on preserving the contextual essence of the original and paying less attention to the form of the original text.[32]

These views resonate with the idea proposed by Emer O'Sullivan and Maria Nikolajeva, according to which translated children's texts seek a balance between domestication and foreignization. However, the domestication principle is stronger, or in André Lefevere's terms, it is a 'naturalised' translation. As Viktor Golyshev concludes, there was one main characteristic of the Soviet school of literary translation: in their work translators had to focus on 'Russian literary classics and the pure Russian language of the end of the nineteenth century and the beginning of the twentieth century'.[33] It is possible to explain the Russian inclination to domesticate foreign literature by the fact that imperial Russia and the Soviet Union aimed to Russify other peoples and nations across the empire. Vera Tolz points to Russification as a strategy for developing the idea of Russian national identity by quoting Nikolai Danilevskii, an advocate of the Slavophile ideology, who hailed 'the assimilating power ... of the Russian people, which converts the aliens with whom it comes into contact into Russian flesh and blood'. Tolz indicates that the Russian language and culture were the unifying force for creating a single nation through cultural assimilation in the Russian Empire and the Soviet Union.[34] Therefore, by analogy to this cultural assimilation of peoples, foreign literature can be viewed as having been accommodated within Russian culture with the Russian language and literature as the main influences on the domesticating translation strategies. By following the ideological goal of cultural assimilation it becomes less likely that foreign culture-specific elements will be more pronounced in translated literature in Russia, especially children's literature, where demands to domesticate are strong.

As the above shows, Russian translators have been an integral part of the translation process in Russia since the early days of the young Soviet Republic. Being active proponents of theoretical and practical ideas about literary translation, they certainly played a role in the selection of foreign titles for translation. For a better understanding of how the selection process took place and who the main actors in this field were, it is important to turn first to the discussion about what kind of knowledge about English culture and literature was accessible to Soviet translators and how this knowledge informed their ideas on what kinds of foreign books could be offered to readers.

The general public did not enjoy free access to literary works, documentary sources and reference materials about England. Being unable to see original foreign books, Soviet readers had little chance to understand what had been amended or excluded in translation. Very few could read foreign books in the original language, which in any case were mostly kept in libraries within departments of special storage ('spetskhran' in Russian). Nadezhda Ryzhak in her report on the history of the spetskhran of the Russian State Library (which was known as the Lenin State Library of the USSR from 1925 until 1992) points out that the spetskhran did not officially exist and in reality was a separate library within the main collection. By 1987 the stock of the spetskhran in the Russian State Library amounted to '27,000 Russian books, 250,000 foreign books, 572,000 issues of foreign journals' (in 1988 the spetskhran was closed down and its stock was opened to the public). For censorship reasons, the data on the restricted books was only recorded in the manual catalogue card archive and was never published. According to Ryzhak, only postgraduate researchers and academic scholars could get access to the spetskhran books and materials and they had to show official letters issued from the academic institutions which employed them.[35] According to Maurice Friedberg, there was restricted and unequal access to foreign books at the All-Union State Library of Foreign Literature. Readers could not borrow any books and certain books were kept on-site and on limited view inside the library only. In order to ask the librarian for a photocopy of a book in a foreign language kept in spetskhran, a professional translator had to provide a contract with a publisher for a translation of this book, otherwise he/she was allowed only to study the item on the premises.[36]

All of this clearly points to serious difficulties in accessing foreign materials but not to an actual lack of foreign books in Soviet libraries. The All-Union State Library of Foreign Literature regularly issued bibliographical guides to major works of foreign literature held by the library and also subscribed to major foreign periodicals. For example, according to the bibliographical guides providing information on foreign books in original languages deposited in the library between 1941 and 1986, works of the following English authors who wrote for children and young adults were kept in stock and not fully represented in Russian translation in the Soviet Union:

- 17 original books by Eleanor Farjeon acquired between 1921 and 1979;
- 51 original books by Walter de la Mare acquired between 1916 and 1983;
- 45 original books by C. S. Lewis acquired between 1938 and 1979;
- 28 original books by J. R. R. Tolkien acquired between 1956 and 1983;
- 19 original titles of collections of English folk and fairy tales acquired between 1895 and 1979.[37]

In the wider world, foreign books might have been in the private collections of the translators, or bought abroad, or found in second-hand book shops, although, according to Blium, the content of second-hand book shops was also under censorship in the Soviet Union.[38]

At the same time, several British children's books were published in the original language by the Progress publishing house (e.g. Kenneth Grahame's *The Wind in the Willows*, published in 1981) or as reading books in English for secondary school pupils or university students studying the English language (e.g. Michael Bond's *A Bear Called Paddington* published in 1977; Eve Garnett's *The Family from One End Street* published in 1973; and Arthur Ransome's *Swallows and Amazons* published in 1980). However, Soviet readers would be unlikely to access these books, as their print runs were not substantial. Nina

Demurova prepared an anthology of British children's literature which was published in 1965 by the Leningrad educational publishing house. It included extracts from a few classic texts, including *Peter Pan and Wendy*, *The Wind in the Willows*, *The Jungle Book*, *Winnie-the-Pooh*, *Alice's Adventures in Wonderland*, as well as folk tales, nursery rhymes, poems by Edward Lear, Lewis Carroll, R. L. Stevenson, Rudyard Kipling, A. A. Milne, Walter de la Mare and others.

Although a lot of research has been done in the field of Soviet censorship in literature since 1991, it is still not easy to obtain information on a particular translated book and in what way it was censored. It is difficult to access the list of banned foreign books, especially given that a year before it was closed down Glavlit ordered the destruction of part of its archived documents on censorship dating back ten years or more, including copies of circular letters, data on passages in texts to be amended or cut, correspondence on censorship with local authorities and memos by censors.[39] However, according to data from early publications of the original texts kept at the Russian State Library of Foreign Literature, which nowadays can be obtained via the library's electronic catalogue,[40] it is safe to assume that many original British children's books might have been kept in spetskhran library departments during the Soviet period. It also seems likely that literary translators, who were quite often literary translation scholars, for example, K. Chukovsky, N. Demurova, T. Ozerskaia, N. Volzhina, I. Tokmakova, B. Zakhoder, G. Ostrovskaia and Iu. Kagarlitskii, were given access to these books and tried to introduce them to Soviet readers. For example, Boris Zakhoder first learnt about *Winnie-the-Pooh* (a picture of the bear and a couple of quotes from verses) in 1958 in a library where he was browsing through the English children's encyclopaedia, deciding then to find the original in order to translate it.[41]

Although in general, Soviet culture existed in self-willed isolation, official communication with other cultures did not cease entirely, like cultural contacts between the Soviet Union and Britain that without doubt made an impact on the promotion of translated British literature. As the Soviet Union severely limited access to the outside world, a clear and detailed picture of foreign cultures was impossible. Border closures, which started in the 1920s, led to the impossibility of travelling abroad for the majority of the population, excluding of course the inner circle of the political elite. Interactions such as cultural and professional exchanges and even international correspondence became impossible for most ordinary people. These restrictions continued for four decades until they were eased in the 1960s, when Khruschev was in power and the possibility of contact with the outer world returned. So, cultural interaction between Britain and the Soviet Union was given a new chance after the conclusion of Anglo-Soviet Cultural Agreements, starting from 1959. Since then the volume of cultural contacts has varied according to political relations between the Soviet Union/post-Soviet Russia and Britain. Cultural exchanges were reduced in times of acute political crises and renewed after relations improved. Towards the end of Soviet Russia, the year 1987 saw an increase in cultural contacts due to the Soviet Union's efforts at improving relations with the West.[42]

Officially, cultural links between the Soviet Union and Britain were supported on the Soviet side by the USSR–Great Britain Society, which was founded in April 1958 and had branches in various cities. It supported cultural contacts between the Soviet Union and those British organizations and individuals who promoted friendship, cross-cultural understanding and cultural cooperation with the Soviet Union. It also assisted the process of translating books from and into English and Russian in both countries and organized different Soviet–British exchanges between officials and specialists. For example, in 1967 the Society received writers Charles Percy Snow and Pamela Hansford Johnson, as well as professors of English studies from the University of Birmingham and the University of London. The Society also organized a visit from a British children's theatre group, led by Lady Elwyn-Jones (Pearl Binder) and Marjorie Lynette Sigley, who were both artists, writers and promoters of youth theatre, to children's theatres in Moscow and Leningrad.[43]

In the Soviet Union, not all writers and translators were able to take part in cultural exchanges organized by the USSR–Great Britain Society and its umbrella organization – the Union of Soviet Societies for Friendship and Cultural Contacts with Foreign Countries. It was expected that Soviet writers would have ideologically correct political views and would engage with Soviet themes in their books so as to be able to participate in international exchanges. For example, one Soviet writer, who visited Britain in the 1980s during the first writers' exchange between the Union of Writers of the Soviet Union and the British Council, was the unknown Valerii Stepanovich Rogov. He was in Britain to collect material for his novel on the history of relations between Soviet and British trade unions.[44] However, there was another category of writers and translators who benefited from international cultural contacts. These were state prize-winning writers and established translators – those who were accepted by the Soviet system as members of the Writers Union of the Soviet Union – for example, such prominent children's writers and translators as Samuil Marshak, Korney Chukovsky, Sergey Mikhalkov, Lev Kassil', Agnia Barto, Boris Zakhoder. They were able to go abroad and had access to the extensive library of resources of foreign literature which were off-limits to the general public, influencing decisions made about the selection of foreign books for translation. For example, Tatiana Kudriavtseva, a leading Soviet/Russian translator of American, English and French literature and an editor of *Inostrannaia literatura* journal from 1962 to 1983, travelled widely in Europe and the United States, conducting research for her translations and finding new foreign books for the journal. She also met personally with contemporary foreign writers.[45]

Britain conducted its cultural relations with the Soviet Union through the British Council and the Great Britain–USSR Association, a government-funded organization established in 1959 which organized official cultural contacts between Soviet and British writers. British cultural links with the Soviet Union were also supported by the following three non-government British societies, sympathetic towards the Soviet Union: the Society for Cultural Relations with the USSR (SCR), founded in 1924, the British–Soviet Friendship Society, founded in 1946, and the Scotland–USSR Society, formed in 1945.[46] When the wider Soviet audience is taken into account, British attempts to promote knowledge across the vast Russian territory about contemporary Britain and its culture were not widely supported by the Soviet Union. As John Morison explains, British attempts to promote cultural activities and understanding between Soviet and British people were 'impeded by a plethora of Soviet restrictions, for instance, on travel within the Soviet Union ..., on the access of Soviet citizens to ... information [about Britain]'.[47] Even in the later 1980s when the Soviet Union was seemingly more open to the West, British–Soviet cultural contacts were still closely controlled by the Soviet Union.

The majority of Soviet readers were not acquainted with information about contemporary British culture and literature, whether it was provided by the Soviet Union or through British channels. This information existed but was available only to a limited number of Soviet citizens (certainly, party and government officials and, most probably, translators and publishers were among them). For example, the two British editions – *Britanskii soiuznik* [The British Ally] and *Angliia* [England] – that were published in Russian were not the kind of editions that one could easily buy at a regular Soviet newsagent. *Britanskii soiuznik* was a weekly newspaper published by the British Ministry of Information and printed in the Soviet Union between 1942 and 1950. The paper wrote about military and cultural collaboration between Britain and the Soviet Union, educational and informative materials about contemporary English culture, the daily life of the English people and published works of British writers. By 1946 the weekly circulation of the paper was fifty thousand copies, most of which were sold by subscription to Soviet party and state bodies with only fourteen thousand copies sold by retail, mostly in Moscow (ten thousand copies) and a few other cities.[48] *Angliia* was a quarterly magazine published by the British Government, printed in Britain and distributed in the Soviet Union in major cities by subscription and retail between 1962 and 1993. Similar to *Britanskii soiuznik*, *Angliia* covered contemporary British cultural life in Britain, wrote about different parts of Britain and published works by British writers.

Occasionally *Britanskii soiuznik* and *Angliia* published articles about British children's literature. For example, *Britanskii soiuznik* told its readers about Arthur Ransome, whose works were not favoured by Soviet censorship, in its 1946 article 'Knigi dlia detei' [Books for children] published in issue 31; about A. A. Milne's *Winnie-the-Pooh* in 1947 in the article 'Detskaia biblioteka' [Children's library] that appeared in issue 16; and in 1950 about Enid Blyton in the article 'Detskaia pisatel'nitsa poluchaet 50 000 pisem' [A children's author receives 50,000 letters] in issue 16. It also published a translation of Beatrix Potter's tale *The Tailor of Gloucester* (1947, issue 24), a translation of the second chapter from Milne's *Winnie-the-Pooh* called 'In which Pooh goes visiting and gets into a tight place' (1948, issue 52) long before the first official translation of the book was printed and a short extract from Henry Williamson's *Tarka the Otter* in English (1950, issue 27). As another example, in 1969 in volume 2 *Angliia* magazine published a translation of a short extract from J. R. R. Tolkien's *The Hobbit* (also long before the book's first official translation appeared) and an in-depth article 'Liubimye detskie knigi' [Favourite children's books] featuring popular British fantasy stories, such as Tolkien's *The Hobbit*, C. S. Lewis's *The Lion, the Witch and the Wardrobe*, E. Nesbit's *Five Children and It*, Mary Norton's *The Borrowers*, as well as Arthur Ransome's *Swallows and Amazons* and Williamson's *Tarka the Otter*, all of which had not been translated by that time.[49] Therefore, both periodicals can be seen as channels providing additional information to individuals involved in the translation process about British books that could be introduced to the Soviet readership.

Despite the limited mobility and reduced cultural interaction between the Soviet Union and the West, Soviet translators did not exist in a vacuum and were not completely cut off from the real foreign world. Therefore, they were able to make informed decisions about what kind of books could and should be translated. Moreover, the leading Soviet literary translators knew about the existence of British children's classics and contemporary children's books and most probably it was due to them that these books were finally translated during the Soviet period.

It is important to remember that, being aware of ideological conventions, Soviet translators had to guard translated literature against any ideologically incorrect elements penetrating from the West. This was done firstly through the choice of books for translation. For example, in his speech at the Soviet Writers Congress in 1934, Marshak raised awareness of not letting bourgeois and idealistic books, such as those written by Lidiia Charskaia before the October Revolution of 1917, appear in the Soviet literary system.[50] He was an advocate of Socialist Realism and clearly expressed his views on ideology in translation: 'A translator doesn't distance himself from the ideological struggle and is not free from ideological responsibility' and 'a good translator inevitably reflects his epoch and himself in his translations'.[51] This demand also applied to the selection of foreign books for translation. At the same time, there was an additional view based on an artistic approach. For example, the following principle of choosing original authors for translation was suggested by Chukovsky who promoted this idea among fellow translators: the choice should be based on genuine interest, an appreciation of the foreign author, devotion and a feeling of creative affinity for the author, as well as the desire to make sure the work would be enjoyed by readers of the receiving culture.[52]

Renowned writers and translators played a significant role in the decision-making process regarding the selection of foreign children's books for translation. From the very beginning of the Soviet period the utmost importance was placed on what kind of books could be chosen. Maxim Gorky made great efforts to breathe new life into translated children's literature within his World Literature project. His activities were supported at the governmental level by Anatoly Lunacharsky, who opened the door to a large number of foreign books written for children to enter the new Soviet literary environment. In 1919–20 under Gorky's leadership, Chukovsky, as a member of the Anglo-American section of the board of experts overseeing the selection of English-language books for translation, made a list of foreign children's books to be translated. This was not taken into consideration by the state publishing house for children's literature in its complete form until the 1960s, as revealed in Chulovsky's essay about Gorky. Not many books from this list were published between the 1920s and the 1940s though a few exceptions were allowed for popular classics, such as Walter Scott's *Ivanhoe* and Jonathan Swift's *Gulliver's Travels*.[53]

Obviously, the wealth of knowledge possessed by translators and authors about British literature was not sufficient to be presented as the sole justification for what kinds of foreign books to translate. The final decisions were taken by the official authorities but translators, critics and publishers guided by the demands of censorship did have an impact on this process. For example, as a translator, literary critic and the official figure looking after the Leningrad children's literature publishing house, Marshak stated in an article published in 1933 in the newspaper *Literaturnyi Leningrad* [Literary Leningrad] that some works by the 'talented' writers of children's poetry A. A. Milne and Walter de la Mare should be translated into Russian, 'though, obviously, not very many'.[54] Marshak's words point to self-censorship as an understanding of the impossibility that certain works could be authorized for translation and publication by official bodies. Considering the situation with censorship, it is clear that the final word regarding the demand for translation came from the state authorities and the Communist Party during the Soviet period.

The general rules for deciding what kind of books written for children could be published were set by the resolution 'O pechati' [On printed works] adopted in May 1924 by the Thirteenth Congress of the Russian Communist Party of Bolsheviks. This resolution proclaimed that children's literature had to be created under the close scrutiny and guidance of the Communist Party, the sole aim of which was to strengthen class, international and labour education.[55] The role of the official voice and action of the Party was given to the People's Commissariat of Enlightenment, described by the Russian acronym, Narkompros, and headed by Lunacharsky (between 1917 and 1929). Narkompros had several sections, among which were two bodies looking after children's literature: the main censorship body Glavlit and the State Publishing House, known by the acronym Gosizdat (1919–30). Gosizdat had a children's literature branch that also published foreign children's literature in translation.

For a short period in the 1920s during several years of the NEP (New Economic Policy) private publishing houses and two other state publishing houses – Molodaia gvardiia and Zemlia i fabrika – had some degree of liberty to select translated foreign books for publication. However, this situation changed when in September 1933 the Central Committee of the Communist Party issued the resolution 'Ob izdatel'stve detskoi literatury' [On the publishing house for children's literature] establishing Detgiz – the State Publishing House for Children's Literature. This resolution also set the main directions for the cardinal improvement of the state regulation of books published for children, so control could be concentrated in the hands of Detgiz. One of the main objectives set for Detgiz as a priority task was the publication of new editions of the best foreign children's classics, such as '*Robinson Crusoe, Gulliver's Travels*, Jules Verne's [novels], etc'.[56] These titles, together with works by Rudyard Kipling, Walter Scott and Charles Dickens, were mentioned as books planned for publication by

Detgiz in 1936-7 in the report of the head of Detgiz G. E. Tsypin.⁵⁷ The activities of Detgiz were administered and controlled by Narkompros according to the decisions and resolutions issued by the Party and the government (from 1946 to 1963 these functions were transferred to the Ministry of Education).⁵⁸

The tendency to wield the overwhelming power of state bodies over the selection of books for translation continued during the Thaw (roughly 1954-68) and until the end of the Soviet period. In 1963 Detgiz was renamed as Detskaia literatura and placed under the authority of the State Committee for Publishing (Goskomizdat) which also controlled other state publishing houses responsible for printing foreign children's literature in translation, such as Molodaia gvardiia, Malysh, Progress, Mir, Raduga. The state publishers' decisions were also influenced by the opinions of the committee for children's literature of the Union of Soviet writers and the opinions of literary critics writing about children's literature published in the newspaper *Literaturnaia gazeta* and the journal *Detskaia literatura*.

The foundations for selecting appropriate translations were still laid down by the ideological context of the epoch. A speech by the Soviet literary translator Tatiana Kudriavtseva about the Soviet translations of A. J. Cronin, delivered in 1961 at the meeting of the Moscow section of the Writers Union (the section of criticism, literary studies and literary translation) and the Foreign commission dealing with modern British literature in Russian translations and its criticism, exemplifies the situation: she discussed how British literature was supposed to be translated and what was expected from the British writer and the Soviet translator from an ideological point of view. Kudriavtseva stressed that the decision for the selection of books for translation had to be based on what the Communist Party considered as literature suitable for Soviet readers. She also explained why Cronin was a suitable choice: 'Cronin is a realist writer . . . . In his writing he deeply sympathises with the ordinary people. . . . Cronin is a good average writer who exposes the shady side of bourgeois society.'⁵⁹ Still, despite this statement, which reflected the official ideological position, the Thaw period brought about slight changes. As Marshak mentioned in his letter to the Union of Soviet writers in 1960, the selection of foreign children's books for translation was sometimes based on random choice, financial circumstances, translators' proposals and even the personal preferences of editors.⁶⁰

The overall situation altered in the 1990s with the advent of political changes in Russia. After the demise of the Soviet Union, more possibilities emerged for cross-cultural activities between Russia and the outer world. As a consequence, Russian translators became free to work with a vast amount of information about the West which for a long time was almost closed to them. They also got wider access to travel abroad and were able to participate in translators-in-residence programmes. All this, together with the vast resources on the internet, has enabled translators to learn about new or neglected books and offer them to publishers to be considered for translation. Moreover, the presence of a new commercial ideology meant that the market imposed its own constraints on translation activity. Consequently, commercially successful books are sure to be translated but there are still certain limitations as to what kind of books could be chosen, mostly based on didactic considerations.

3

Translation of British children's literature in Russian context: Responses to political and cultural changes

This chapter continues to dissect the world of translated children's books by putting Russian translations of British children's literature into their historical and cultural context. It draws on Itamar Even-Zohar's polysystem theory to identify distinctive trends in the translated texts during the contrasting Soviet and post-Soviet periods. He regards translated literature as an active system operating within a literary polysystem of the receiving culture. Within the translated literature system appropriate works are selected for translation depending on the influence of ideological, political, social and literary conventions at a given historical moment. The principles governing the selection of original texts for translation correlate with the accepted conventions and prevailing themes in the receiving literature.[1] Even-Zohar's approach makes it possible to demonstrate that Russian translations of British children's texts can be seen not as an arbitrary group but as a corpus that has been created under the influence of ideological and cultural factors. The choice of British children's books for translation was driven by the dynamics of themes in Russian children's literature as well as the ideological constraints imposed on translation in the form of censorship and translation and literary norms that were prevailing during the Soviet and post-Soviet periods.

Hence, the Russian translations analysed in this chapter were divided into two major groups: the Soviet period (1918–91) and the post-Soviet period (1991–2017).[2] This decision is based on the shifting position of Russian children's literature in the literary polysystem. As Marina Balina and Larissa Rudova explain, Russian children's literature held a central position in the Soviet Union because of the important role it played in creating Soviet identity, whereas after

1991 it became peripheral and lost its key status.³ The discussion in each group starts with a brief overview of the political and cultural dynamic prevalent in Russian society and how it affected the choice of British children's books for translation. Afterwards, within each group, the main translated titles that held dominant positions in the translated market are identified and the question of why this was the case is answered.

The corpus of all British children's books used for the analysis was initially rather large, so I decided to include only those books that fell into the category of canonical works and classics of children's literature that contained depictions of Englishness to various degrees. The question of canon in British children's literature is a rather controversial issue and there is no definitive agreement on a canonical list of important titles. However, David Rudd offers four forms in which the establishment determines canons of children's literature (which are lists containing the most important books of a culture): critical texts, anthologies, syllabuses and literary prizes.⁴ Canonical books are timeless and universal, but unstable, as they can lose their status due to changes in literary preferences. Classics are also timeless, but they have a more stable nature, or, as Maria Nikolajeva suggests, they are authored by established writers, included in textbooks and numerously reprinted.⁵ Hence, drawing on these views, I have referred to the following main sources for compiling the list of British children's books for the analysis, which is given in Appendix 2 'Canon and classics of British children's literature': Anne H. Lundin's *Constructing the Canon of Children's Literature: Beyond Library Walls and Ivory Towers*, Perry Nodelman's 'A Tentative List of Books Everyone Interested in Children's Literature Should Know' and three British book awards (Carnegie Medal, Costa Children's Book Award and Guardian Children's Fiction Prize).⁶

The prevailing themes in British children's literature (including books accepted as literature suitable for children), published between the late-Victorian period and the Second World War, were as follows. The late-Victorian and Edwardian periods offered adventure stories depicting Englishmen in challenging situations. The themes of heroism, patriotism and empire also found their way into fiction written for children (or accepted as children's literature) contributing to the romanticizing of Englishness. British children's literature of this period also offered versions of nostalgia for idyllic Arcadia, visions of an English past with elements of fantasy and expressions of silliness. It also treated such themes as family, home and the adventures of middle- and upper-class children at school and during holidays. Although British children's literature published between the two world wars continued to explore the major themes of the Edwardian period, it is mostly characterized by the retreat from memories of the threat of war and social changes. This was achieved by delving into the fantasy genre.

Having compared the corpus of British children's literature and the corpus of Russian translations of British children's literature that appeared synchronically during the first half of the Soviet period, I noticed that the Russian translations did not respond to the prevailing themes of British children's literature. Most of the titles appeared in translation considerably later, with only several books being translated during the Thaw period. The reasons for this can be found in the differences in sociopolitical demands for suitable themes in Britain and the Soviet Union during the period as well as Soviet censorship that determined the selection of books for translation. Throughout the whole Soviet period there was a marked difference between the corpus of British texts and the Russian translations. In selecting original titles for translation, Soviet translators and publishers did not entirely base their choices on the prevailing themes in British children's literature. On the contrary, the selection of original books generally consolidated the formation, development and promotion of Soviet themes in the Soviet children's literary polysystem. Hence, the English themes served as point of departure, or inspiration, rather than an example to follow and reproduce in the receiving literature. The English themes resonated with the ideological demands of the translated literature and through them the Soviet rhetoric was promoted in books offered to Soviet readers.

Two major tendencies emerge in the Soviet period: active translation of old and modern classics and the less widespread translation of contemporary books. In both cases works had to meet strict ideological demands, which in turn determined a preference for themes in British children's literature that did not conflict with Soviet ideology. This case validates Even-Zohar's claim that the principle of selecting original texts for translation correlates with the accepted themes in the receiving literature. Within the Soviet children's literature system the translated children's literature underwent shifts from a central position during the 1920s and the Thaw period, when it responded to innovatory ideas of Soviet children's literature, to the peripheral position between the 1930s and the mid-1950s as well as during the Stagnation period and the late-Soviet period, when it complemented and strengthened Soviet children's literature. During the post-Soviet time decisions to select books for translation were not influenced by state ideology. They were generally determined by commercial demands rather than prevailing themes of national discourse.

Soviet period: From 1918 to 1991

Historical and cultural context of Russian children's literature

With the advent of Russia's October Revolution of 1917, the utopian myth of a perfect world began to take shape, and with it came the birth of a new kind of citizen, capable of building a Socialist society like never before, his mind and body a tabula rasa. Of course, this new creation – Soviet man – would have to be educated completely afresh and this is where literature came into play.

From the early days of the burgeoning Soviet state until the end of Stalin's reign children's literature was used as an ideological vehicle for propaganda, promoting the idea of the necessity of socialist creative labour and playing an important role in the process of educating the working class and in the formation of a positive image of the new Soviet identity. To construct this new hero, it was deemed essential to erode the old traditions, beginning with the books containing pre-revolutionary bourgeois religious, mystical, and middle-class attitudes and features. Nadezhda Krupskaia, who was the deputy People's Commissar for Enlightenment, warned in 1927 that pre-revolutionary children's literature failed to provide suitable information for Soviet children. Her words clearly reflect the official sentiments of the 1920s regarding Soviet children's literature: 'An old book must be remade, it must be "Sovietized" . . . in such way that, along with the entertaining material, [it] would provide as well the ideology that we must provide and want to provide.'[7]

However, the importance of the ideological and didactic functions of Russian children's literature was not a completely new Soviet phenomenon. It was imposed on children's literature long before 1917 by the two very influential nineteenth-century literary critics Vissarion Belinsky and Nikolay Dobrolyubov. Their ideas were suitably applied by Soviet literary critics, theorists and writers to the national and translated literature, whether it originated in the past or the present.[8]

The first decades were marked by strict control of literature that was offered to children and young adults. The state determined the publishing policy regarding national and translated children's literature. It also supported children's literature by forwarding the published books to Soviet libraries and schools and promoting them among Soviet readers. The prevailing ideological norms in the form of the state cultural policy and censorship, which were introduced in the early 1920s and strengthened later, were the essential tools with which state control over children's literature was implemented. The principal goals of Soviet cultural policy involved the class war against internal and external enemies which meant protecting the interests of the working classes, transforming culture into an instrument of socialism by abandoning bourgeois values and ideals and democratizing arts and education, thereby making them more accessible to the working classes and the poor.[9] These aims were pronounced in 1924 at the Thirteenth Communist Party Congress in a resolution, according to which children's literature was to become truly Soviet in concept, controlled and supervised by the Communist Party aiming to enforce the principles of class consciousness, internationalism and education through labour.[10] Moreover, the educational reforms of the 1920s, which had a direct bearing on children's literature, were focused on new educational and didactic principles: patriotism, internationalism, collectivism and class solidarity.[11] School teaching programmes were ordered to abandon religious and bourgeois prejudices and focus instead on understanding of the goals of the revolution and the new Soviet state.

State control over children's literature also manifested itself in the campaign that started in the mid-1920s against the fairy tale and the fantasy genre. The most radical literary scholars considered fairy tales as books that harmed children's fragile minds, taught superstitions and mysticism, and obscured the materialist view of the world. Fairy tales were associated with pre-revolutionary Imperial Russia. They expressed the ideals of the pre-revolutionary ruling classes, had a tendency to amuse children with nonsense, sensations and tricks, and displayed a petty-bourgeois mentality, promoting mysticism, religion and distorted reality. They also contained features such as magic, fantasy, animism and anthropomorphism that were officially pronounced as idealism and hence rejected by the Soviet ideological doctrine. Certainly, according to Soviet ideology, pre-revolutionary fairy tales and fantasy books were unable to follow the main objective of creating a new Soviet man. However, despite attacks on folk and fairy tales in the 1920s, this genre remained popular among Russian child readers,[12] revealing an interesting contradiction between what the state ideology demanded and what the reader actually wanted.

It was not until the mid-1930s that fairy tales and fantasy books were rehabilitated after being brought back to readers thanks to the strong support of the key Soviet literary figures Maxim Gorky and Samuil Marshak. However, their content and moral message had to be guided by Soviet rhetoric, a process which instigated the birth of the Soviet utopian fairy tale. This focus on a negative past versus a wonderful present and future became the rising theme in the literature of the 1930s. The utopianism of the early Soviet years influenced the association of children with the promise of a better future and the transition through hardship to a beautiful fairy tale land began to dominate literature for adults and children in the mid-1930s.[13]

From the 1930s onwards, ideological constraints were tightened. The Sovietization of children's literature started with the adoption of the Central Committee Resolution 'On the Improvement of Press for Children and Youth' in 1932 and the establishment of full control over children's literature via the state publishing house Detskaia literatura that was set up the following year, in 1933. Books for children were expected to be of a high ideological and literary quality. Class struggle, nationalism and patriotism were the dominant Soviet rhetoric in the 1930s. Moreover, the mid-1930s and the 1940s witnessed a stronger politicization and militarization of Soviet society. As a consequence of this tendency, children's literature produced an increased number of titles that responded to military themes. In the first half of the 1940s, official Soviet rhetoric was focused on the role of the Russian people in the war effort and turned the years of the Second World War into the veneration of righteous war and victory. This attitude dominated in the media where the official line reinforced a national theme of patriotism and the heroic fight against enemies. During this period, children's literature promoted ideas of the importance of the war effort and consolidated the will for victory among readers. This bellicose theme was mythologized in books written for children during the post-war period: children and young adults, as main characters, were portrayed as heroes who devoted and sacrificed their lives for their motherland.[14]

As the dynamics of changing historical and political factors in the early Soviet society shows, Soviet writers had to address several politically correct themes when writing for children between 1918 and the end of 1940s. The October Revolution and the new Soviet reality, the Civil War, national heroism and the contextualization of the Second World War were all politicized as themes, as was the class struggle, industrialization and collectivization, patriotism and socialist moral principles. At the same time, these themes covered such social problems as the misfortunes of orphans, the hard life of children in other countries, the troubled childhood in pre-revolutionary Russia and the life of the young Soviet pioneers as builders of a new idyllic socialist society. These themes also had to be reflected in children's books created in such genres as the school tale, adventure stories, science fiction, Soviet fairy tales and fantasy, and popular science books.

Compared to the 1940s, the next decade saw distinctive changes in the cultural life of the country and censorship of literary works became relaxed to some extent, especially after the death of Stalin in 1953. During the Thaw period children's literature became more diverse. Soviet children's writers got a chance to experiment more with themes and literary styles.[15] The Thaw brought about changes in literature for children in the same way that literature had changed for adults. Children's books which had been out of print in the 1930s underwent selective rehabilitation: for example, works that contained elements of silliness written by Kharms, Oleinikov and Vvedensky, who belonged to the OBERIU group.[16] Also adventure stories, fantasy novels, science fiction, stories for girls and humorous novels became a revived trend in Thaw children's literature.

In the 1950s and 1960s heroic child characters were replaced by children who faced problems at school and at home. School novels taught children how to make the right moral choices by using teachers as role models. Between the 1920s and the Thaw, the theme of family did not play any significant role in Soviet children's literature. It was replaced by the school theme which reflected the role of class teams and children's ideological organizations (pioneers) as important links in Soviet children's upbringing. During the Thaw period, the role of family was restored in children's literature and by generally promoting positive values and personal growth, both novels and school and family tales created an idealistic view of the world of Soviet children.[17] However, despite the political and cultural changes during this period, the political and historical themes that covered the Revolutionary period – the cult of Lenin and the Second World War – maintained their solid position in books 'that remained faithful to the prescribed formulas of Socialist Realism', as Marina Balina and Larissa Rudova emphasize.[18]

The focus on these themes and genres remained unchanged during the years of stagnation (1969–85), a period which did not bring any major developments or new restrictions in Soviet children's literature. Changes in themes and genres started appearing towards the end of the Soviet Union. The last years of perestroika (1986–91) ushered in more liberated views on religion and saw a revived interest in the pre-revolutionary literary heritage. From the early 1980s, tastes among children and young adults shifted from a culture promoted by the state ideology towards popular culture, and Soviet literary characters lost their heroic appeal to children and young adults.[19] This prompted calls for more realistic characters that could reflect the spirit of the epoch, relating to real life and the interests of young people.

Despite this, the ideological message of Soviet children's literature was still solid. Patriotism was one of the major ideological themes actively promoted by the Soviet State among its people, and children's literature was seen as a suitable means for developing patriotic feelings among children. The national theme of patriotism in literature in general was closely connected with the historical past of Russia, especially with the themes of labour and war heroism. At the same time, Soviet patriotism was influenced by the anti-imperialist discourse, as explained in an article in *Detskaia literautura* in 1985 covering the importance of the theme of patriotism in books published by Malysh publishing house:

> One of the aims of a patriotic upbringing is to teach citizens to respect other nations, to teach them to be proud of their nation and to share the pain of nations driven into the abyss of misfortune by imperialism. Books about solidarity with people from other countries are also necessary for promoting Soviet patriotism and proletarian internationalism.[20]

British children's books selected for translation into Russian

During the period from 1918 to the early 1950s, political changes instigated new principles that determined how foreign books were to be selected for translation. Official state ideology and the major themes reflecting the national rhetoric were interconnected. This period is characterized by the predominance of politicized themes in translated literature. At the same time, slight changes in the political climate brought about the appearance of several original books that contained elements of nonsense and so-called bourgeois values. The corpus of British children's books translated during this period clearly reflects the political and cultural changes in Soviet society. The themes, which appear in British texts, are strengthened in Russian translations. They include anti-religious and revolutionary ideas, class struggle, war and the fight for independence. Also included are empire and patriotism, the hardships of the poorest classes and orphans, as well as discourses of the fantastic and of silliness. At the same time, looking at this corpus from the point of view of how Englishness is represented, the themes in the selected British texts clearly point to the prevalence of two groups of manifestations of Englishness in Soviet translations: political and ideological associations as well as features of English national character that are expressed in the form of the discourses of the fantastic and silliness.

The first decade of this period provides the most intense dynamic in the English books that were offered for translation. All the titles translated between 1918 and 1930 can be divided into two major groups. On the one hand, they were those that reflected the politically correct themes promoted for a new Soviet country, such as heroism, the class struggle, the fight for independence, patriotism and socialist moral principles. On the other hand, there were those literary works that contradicted the early Soviet ideology and contained elements of so-called bourgeois values, such as the spirit of courageous colonizers, adventurous boarding school boys, sentimentality, as well as fantasy, adventure and nonsense. Clearly, these books were overlooked by the state but they were cast into oblivion for decades when this short-lived freedom ended in the early 1930s. How did such different books co-exist within the emerging landscape of ideologically adjusted Soviet children's and young adult literature?

The main themes popularized in translation in the first decade were connected with political and social rhetoric: brave and hard-working characters, heroes who fought for independence and wanted to overthrow a corrupt social order to bring happiness to society, the life of orphans under the capitalist system and narratives focused on exposing and satirizing the capitalist system. The books that fall under this category are classics and considered as the canon of British children's literature. They include adaptations for children of the major novels of Charles Dickens which first appeared in print in 1918 and then were reprinted throughout the Soviet period. Robert Louis Stevenson's *Treasure Island* was offered to Soviet readers as two different reprints of the pre-revolutionary translations in 1918 and 1926. An adaptation for children of Daniel Defoe's *Robinson Crusoe* was offered in 1922, which was edited by Korney Chukovsky in 1929 and followed by reprints of this edited adaptation during the Soviet period. Jonathan Swift's *Gulliver's Travels* was also adapted for children. In 1918 the adaptation for young children was published by Sytin, a private publisher. In 1931 a new retelling of Gulliver's adventures for young children was created by two translators from Marshak's Leningrad team, Tamara Gabbe and Zoia Zadunaiskaia, and published by Molodaia Gvardia (later this version was reprinted by Detgiz in 1935 and then subsequently reprinted throughout the Soviet era). Another adaptation of *Gulliver's Travels* for older children was produced by Valentin Stenich and published by Detgiz in 1935, although this version was never reprinted during the Soviet period – Stenich was arrested and executed in 1938. The adaptation for older children was reintroduced by Detgiz to readers again in 1946 when a new version in Boris Engel'gardt's translation appeared (it was subsequently reprinted throughout the Soviet era). Books by these four authors were relatively safe to offer to Soviet readers as they met the demand for major political and social themes that Soviet children's literature was expected to contain. What is more, *Robinson Crusoe* and *Gulliver's Travels* were included in a new canon of children's classics by critics highlighting their specific ideological context.[21] Moreover, both books enjoyed great print run numbers throughout the Soviet period, making them one of the most popular reads in British children's literature.

Two of the following titles that resonate with Soviet ideological themes are not classics nor have a canonical status in Britain but they were included in the canon of translated literature by the Soviet authorities. They are James Greenwood's *The True History of a Little Ragamuffin* and Ethel Lilian Voynich's *The Gadfly*. Although not initially written for child readers, both books were accepted as literature suitable for children and young adults. *The Gadfly*, a novel originally written in 1897, is forgotten now in the English-speaking world. However, it has enjoyed great popularity in Russia since its first appearance in Russian translation by Z. Vengerova in 1898 and afterwards in retranslation by M. Shishmareva in 1910. Both pre-revolutionary translations were republished in 1918–19 and subsequently reprinted until a new Soviet retranslation by N. Volzhina appeared in 1945 (which was subsequently reprinted numerous times during the Soviet period).[22] Set in Italy and concerned with the Italian nationalist uprising of 1840s, the novel depicts young English people in the midst of the unsuccessful revolutionary events, including commonly represented traits, such as drinking tea, melancholic character and reserve. As the novel developed anti-religious and revolutionary ideas, which resonated with major Soviet themes in literature, it is little wonder that it had experienced such enormous popularity during the Soviet period. It also has not been out of print since the demise of the Soviet Union – the last publication was in 2011. One possible explanation is that it is a commercially safe classic, easily recognizable by the Russian reader: two Soviet film adaptations and music from Dmitry Shostakovich (*The Gadfly Suite*) must have also contributed to its popularity.

If the Soviet translation of *The Gadfly* contributed to the development of the discourse of war and the fight for independence, then the Soviet translation of *The True History of a Little Ragamuffin* perfectly addressed the hardships of the poorest classes in Victorian Britain. It also repeated the historical trajectory of *The Gadfly* in the Soviet Union. Originally written in 1866 and initially an adult text, not particularly known during the nineteenth century in Britain and forgotten today, this book had become a children's classic, achieved its canonical status in the Soviet Union and is still in publication now. Nina Demurova's article published in 1979 in the journal *Detskaia literatura* provides a good explanation why this book appealed to the Soviet ideology: 'It is the first realistic work fully dedicated to the children of "the bottom" of a capitalist city.'[23] Written in the style of *Oliver Twist*, it is a sentimental story of the hardship of an impoverished child, Jimmy, who runs away from home, lives in the slums of Victorian London and joins its gangs. The book was known to children in pre-revolutionary Russia. During the Soviet period it was retold by A. Annenskaia and K. Chukovsky in

1926 and then by T. Bogdanovich and K. Chukovsky in 1929 (the 1929 version was regularly reprinted during the Soviet period).[24] They adapted this book for children and significantly changed the ending of the story. In their version Jimmy leaves the gang and finds a job at a factory, thus becoming a member of the working class. In the original, Jimmy is put into prison then goes to Australia and upon his return to England starts helping homeless children.[25]

The main themes popularized in translation over this period were connected with political rhetoric: heroes who fought for independence and wanted to overthrow a corrupt social order to bring happiness to society, as well as the life of orphans under the capitalist system. The latter was addressed in Frederic Marryat's *Jacob Faithful* (1834) translated in 1927, the adaptation for children of Henry Fielding's *The History of Tom Jones, A Foundling* (1749) which appeared in abridged translation in 1931.[26] The revolutionary theme of the fight for freedom and a better life for the oppressed class, which echoes the spirit of the early Soviet times, was also well covered in the stories of Robin Hood. Translations and retellings of stories and popular ballads about Robin Hood appeared between 1919 and 1928: a volume of ballads about Robin Hood edited by Nikolai Gumiliev with a foreword by Maxim Gorky was published by Vsemirnaia literatura publishing house in 1919, then the ballads were translated for children by V. Rozhdestvensky in 1926 and Escott Lynn's novel *Robin Hood and His Merry Men* was retold by A. Krivtsova and edited by Evegny Lann in 1928.[27] This English heroic outlaw was popular in the Soviet Union and undoubtedly chimed with state ideology. The ideological topicality of the Robin Hood stories for the new Soviet state can be found in the words of Maxim Gorky who wrote the foreword to the 1919 translation of the ballads: 'Folk ballads portray Robin Hood as an indefatigable enemy of the Norman oppressors and a defender of poor people.'[28] Taking into account this image of Robin Hood, the reason for selecting Robin Hood ballads and stories becomes obvious – the connotation with the image of the young Soviet working class fighting for its freedom and breaking ties with the capitalist world.

In addition to this, the theme of class struggle in the context of the clever poor and the tyrannical rich was reflected in the translation of the English folk ballad *King John and the Bishop* first printed in the seventeenth century.[29] The first translation of this ballad was produced in 1918 by Samuil Marshak (who promoted English folk ballads and children's folk songs in the early Soviet culture). It was published in the provincial newspaper *Utro iuga* under the title of *Korol' Dzhon i episkop* [King John and the bishop]. The second revised version was called *Korol' i pastukh* [The King and the Shepherd] and published as a separate book in 1926 by Raduga publishing house. (Raduga was the leading private publisher specializing in children's literature in the Soviet Union in the 1920s and Marshak was its literary editor.) The translation was revised again and published under the same title in 1936 in the first volume of the children's magazine *Kostior*. This final third revised version was printed in 1937 and 1940 by the Detizdat publishing house. (The 1940 version was subsequently reprinted during the Soviet and post-Soviet periods.) Although this ballad is not considered as a text written for children in the world of English literature, it was positioned in the Soviet Union as children's reading. The ballad is set in Medieval England and tells the story of King John – a collective folk image of an English king – and the Bishop of Canterbury, who was rich and powerful. The king suspects the bishop of treason and gives him three questions to answer. The desperate bishop asks a shepherd for help. The clever shepherd offers to swap places with the bishop, goes to the king, answers his questions and saves the bishop. Marshak created a distorted image of an unjust king, which corresponds to stereotypical Soviet perceptions of the capitalist West and suits the Soviet anti-royal and anti-religious rhetoric. The bad king captures the image of the ruling class in Russia before the 1917 October Revolution and the clever shepherd mirrors the image of the Soviet ruling class of workers and peasants. Hence, Marshak recreates the image of clever English commoners – he praises wit, resourcefulness and the common sense of the shepherd who says that a fool may help a wise man who is in trouble. In the original the shepherd's words go as follows: 'a fool may learn a wiseman wit' (stanza 13 version B). Moreover, Marshak's version contains no information about the English king being merciful, just and generous. On the contrary, it ends with the praise of the clever and brave commoner shepherd who was not afraid to look the king in the face and save the bishop.[30]

There are two books that can be categorized as holding a neutral position, because they did not respond to the above-mentioned ideological Soviet themes and, being considered as a popular read, they were obviously safe to translate: Rudyard Kipling's *Just So Stories* and *The Jungle Book*. Although Englishness is not portrayed in either book, they still deserve mention as they have been very popular among Russian readers and still hold a significant position in the children's literary polysystem. *Just so Stories* appeared first in 1918 as a reprint of the pre-revolutionary translations and was then retranslated by Korney Chukovsky and Samuil Marshak in 1923 (this retranslation was subsequently regularly republished). *The Jungle Book* (*Izbrannye rasskazy*) was offered to Soviet readers in 1918 in a volume of Kipling's stories which was edited by Ivan Bunin. This was a reprint of the pre-revolutionary translation. In 1926 a new retranslation titled as *Maugli* appeared – it was produced by S. Zaimovskii and subsequently regularly reprinted throughout the Soviet period.

The adventures of a good-natured doctor – the main character in Hugh Lofting's *Doctor Dolittle* – could be the theme that attracted the state publisher Gosizdat to introduce the first book in the series to Soviet young readers. It was first offered in 1924 as *Prikliucheniia doktora Dulitlia* [*Adventures of Doctor Dolittle*] translated by L. Khavkina for older children (the print run was small and it was never reprinted). In 1925 this book was adapted and retold for small children by Korney Chukovsky under the title of *Doctor Aibolit* [Doctor Ouch]. This edition was reworked into a free adaptation in 1936 and then subsequently reprinted throughout the Soviet period.[31] The main character – an English physician from the country town of Puddleby-on-the-Marsh – was turned into a neutral person without any specified nationality living in a fairyland and new Russified characters were added. Hugh Lofting's stories about Doctor Dolittle also inspired Chukovsky to write a long poem of the same name, *Doktor Aibolit*. It is important to note that his Doctor Aibolit had a moralistic purpose, as Chukovsky emphasized in his article *Istoriia moego Aibolita* [The story of my Aibolit], saying that 'the theme of a self-sacrificing act of bravery had to be laid out before small readers at once'.[32]

The second big group of English books circulated between 1918 and 1930 included those that did not follow the Soviet socialist context but had elements of sentimentality, fantasy and nonsense, as well as told stories about adventurous colonizers and boarding school boys. These books were not frequently retranslated, if at all, nor were their print runs particularly large. The possible reasons behind this phenomenon were a certain level of creative freedom experienced by authors and translators and projects focused on educating the masses through publishing new retranslations of major world classics by the state publishing house Vsemirnaia literatura. At the same time, it was most probably a response to a slightly changing political situation. With the introduction of the New Economic Policy (NEP) in 1921, private publishers became more active in the Soviet publishing industry, including those that published translated books: Sytin, Raduga and Svetliachok publishing houses. Considering that the foremost goal of these publishing houses was profit, it is obvious that they would choose titles that were popular among readers and would easily be sold. Two state publishing houses – Molodaia gvardiia and Zemlia i fabrika – also focused their print runs on popular mass literature. As NEP brought about a degree of relaxation in the attitude of the state authorities towards translated literature, pre-revolutionary titles were reprinted and the politically neutral books were translated in the early 1920s.

Despite ideological didacticism and Party control, the early Soviet state actually allowed new ways of creative expression in children's literature. This resulted in literary experiments with the theme of nonsense in the 1920s, for example, by the OBERIU group of writers. In turn, this tendency instigated the appearance of Soviet translations of Lewis Carroll's *Alice's Adventures in Wonderland* and *Through the Looking-Glass* in 1923 and 1924 published by L. D. Frenkel' private publisher; Edward Lear's nonsense poem *The Table and the Chair* translated by Samuil Marshak and published by private companies Brokgaus-Efron and Raduga in 1924 and 1928; and Samuil Marshak's versions of English nursery rhymes published by the state companies Gosizdat and Vsemirnaia literatura between 1923 and 1928.

The response to the uncertain political situation during the early years can also be seen with the emergence of *English Fairy Tales*, collected by Joseph Jacobs. These tales appeared in 1918 and 1921, before the official ban on fairy tales, and included such famous English folk tales as *Jack the Giant Killer, Jack and the Beanstalk, The Three Little Pigs* and *The History of Tom Thumb* (they were printed by private publishers).[33] Almost two decades later, when the theme of fairy tales and the fantastic was allowed by authorities to be used in children's literature again, Soviet children were offered a retelling of *The Three Little Pigs* by Sergey Mikhalkov in 1936, three years after the original animated film had been shown at the festival of American cartoons in Moscow.[34] The book was then reprinted almost every year throughout the Soviet period. The late 1930s editions of this fairy tale used illustrations by Walt Disney, and the first Soviet publication appeared during the same year that Soviet children saw the Walt Disney version of the fairy tale.

The following books, which appeared during the same period and published mostly by private companies, contain the so-called bourgeois values reflecting Englishness associated with the middle class: the spirit of courageous and adventurous colonizers, the spirit of adventurous boarding school boys and sentimentality. The ideas of Empire and patriotism were promoted in Russian versions of Robert Baden-Powell's *Scouting for Boys: A Handbook for Instruction in Good Citizenship* and Rudyard Kipling's volume of short stories *Land and Sea Tales for Scouts and Guides* (also known as *Land and Sea Tales for Boys and Girls*). An adaptation of Baden-Powell's *Scouting for Boys* was offered to Russian readers in 1918 by a private publisher V. A. Berezovsky. Titled as *Iunyi razvedchik: rukovodstvo po skautismu* [A young scout: A handbook for Scouting], it was a revised pre-revolutionary edition of 1916 in which several sections were abridged and other sections were adapted to the Russian cultural tradition of Boy Scouting, serving the purpose of developing ideas of patriotism, social responsibility and pre-military youth training. The first Russian translation of this book appeared in 1909 and was used as an ideological inspiration for forming the Russian Scout movement which had become very popular throughout the country. The 1917 October Revolution brought an end to the Scout associations when they were officially banned in 1922 and the Soviet Pioneer movement was introduced as a replacement. Kipling's *Land and Sea Tales* were translated and privately published in 1924 by Kniga publisher and then reprinted in 1928. Titled as *Prikliucheniia na sushe i na more* [Adventures on land and sea], the book told stories about a Boy Scout camp in England and the way the British lived in their colonies in Africa and India, but was unpopular among young Soviet readers as mentioned in the 1926 official recommendations about new children's books published in the Soviet Union.[35]

The themes of English boarding schools, boyhood and fair competition in sports reflected in Rudyard Kipling's novel *Stalky and Co.* and two Talbot Baines Reed's novels about middle-class schoolchildren were also offered to Soviet readers. *Stalky and Co.* was translated in 1925 and privately published by Novella publisher under the title *Shal'naia kompaniia* [An intrepid gang]. The translation of Reed's novel *The Fifth Form at St Dominic's* was offered to young Soviet readers by Vremia publishing house in 1926 as *Piatyi klass svobodnoi shkoly* [The fifth grade of a free school]. His other novel *The Willoughby Captains* was translated before the Revolution and was titled as *Starshiny Vil'baiskoi shkoly* [Captains of Willoughby school]. This edition was reprinted by a private publisher Russkoe knizhnoe izdatel'stvo in 1919 and then again reprinted by the state publishing house Gosizdat in 1925. The theme of adventures was addressed in R. M. Ballantyne's *The Coral Island* which appeared in translation in 1927, and in Frederick Marryat's *Masterman Ready, or the Wreck of the Pacific* and *Mr. Midshipman Easy* which was offered in 1927 and 1928. All three were reprinted versions of the pre-revolutionary translations published by the state publishers Zemlia i fabrika and Molodaia gvardiia. Moreover, distorted reality and sentimental features found their ways to young Soviet readers in two translated books: J. M. Barrie's prose version of the play *Peter Pan* which appeared in 1918 (published by Detskaia kniga) and a 1918 reprint of the pre-revolutionary translation of Frances Hodgson Burnett's *Little Lord Fauntleroy* (published by Knebel').

All the above books from the second group were just a minor example overlooked by the state. The short-term freedom ended in the early 1930s and these English titles, which appeared throughout the first decade after the October Revolution, were cast into oblivion for several decades, except for Reed's *The Willoughby Captains* that was retranslated in 1946 and published by Detgiz.

The period starting from the 1930s until the early 1950s can be characterized as years of severe restrictions imposed on the translation of children's literature, as a culture of suspicion and hostility towards foreigners dominated the country. As a result, British children's literature was hardly represented in Soviet translations. Nevertheless, there were books that met the demand for major political and social themes expected to be covered in children's literature – they were translated in the 1930s and were subsequently reprinted and retranslated throughout the Soviet period. These books included Robert Louis Stevenson's *Treasure Island,* which was retranslated by Nikolai Chukovsky in 1935; Walter Scott's *Ivanhoe* (reprint of the pre-revolutionary translation in 1936) which was positioned as books for older children and young adults; as well as H. G. Wells's *The Invisible Man* and *The War of the Worlds* (translated in 1935 and 1936). Arthur Conan Doyle's stories about Sherlock Holmes were also offered to readers. One story, *The Adventure of the Blue Carbuncle*, was translated by V. Stenich and published by Detizdat in 1937; then several stories about Holmes were retranslated by N. Voitinskaia and published by Molodaia gvardiia in 1946 and by M. and N. Chukovsky and published by Detgiz in 1945. The novel *The Hound of the Baskervilles* was translated by N. Volzhina and published by Detgiz in 1948 and then it was included in the volume of stories about Holmes in 1956.[36]

This period also saw the appearance of a group of reprinted popular classics, including Lewis Carroll's *Alice's Adventures in Wonderland* and nursery rhymes that were translated in the 1920s, as well as translations of the English folk ballads and songs and A. A. Milne's poem *The King's Breakfast* from his volume *When We Were Very Young* which underwent subsequent reprints during the Soviet period. Two volumes of English folk ballads and songs were published in the early 1940s: *Angliiskie ballady i pesni* [English ballads and songs] translated and reprinted in 1941 and 1947, and *Ballady i pesni angliiskogo naroda* [Ballads and songs of the English people] translated in 1942.[37] It is no coincidence that these translations appeared during the Second World War. The Soviet patriotic theme was strengthened by translating folk ballads and poems focused on patriotic Englishness. Moreover, the collaboration between the Soviet Union and Britain during the war most probably influenced the appearance of English folk ballads in Soviet translation. The afterword to the 1942 edition of *Ballady i pesni angliiskogo naroda* says that this book contains poems glorifying the devotion to homeland and ballads telling a story of Robin Hood who was described as 'a merciless enemy of all oppressors of the people, a true friend of the humiliated and the dispossessed'.[38]

Readers were presented with a similar patriotic rhetoric in the adaptation of R. L. Stevenson's poem *Heather Ale: A Galloway Legend* (1890), which was retold by Samuil Marshak. It was first published in 1941 in the literary journal *Krasnaia nov'* (volume 2) and later reprinted in a volume of English ballads in 1944.[39] The adaptation was very popular in the Soviet Union and reprints of the poem in various editions appeared regularly throughout the Soviet period; it was also included in the school curriculum on literature in the Soviet Union and is still read in modern Russia. Also in 1946 Marshak translated Milne's poem *The King's Breakfast*, in which, by adding nuances to the image of the king, Marshak represents him as a tyrant.[40] Moreover, several English nursery rhymes appeared in Marshak's translation in 1944–5. The popularization of nursery rhymes, which can be seen as an obvious expression of national identity through folk art, considerably influenced the creation of the image of Englishness in Russian translations. At the same time, it raised the national spirit in the post-war Soviet Union.[41]

The second half of the 1940s had seen two more translations that do not fit the general corpus: Talbot Baines Reed's *The Willoughby Captains* (retranslated in 1946) and John Meade Falkner's *Moonfleet* (translated in 1949). Regarding *The Willoughby Captains* (an English boarding school story), Catriona Kelly explains this phenomenon by the fact that official Soviet propaganda sometimes allowed occasional but selective contacts with foreign culture that was considered to be progressive.[42] As for Falkner's *Moonfleet*, translation of this novel appeared in the *Britanskii soiuznik* weekly newspaper in 1949 (issues 26–40). Given the limited circulation of *Britanskii soiuznik* among the general public, this attempt to introduce a popular adventure classic to Soviet readers resulted in a translation that was not widely noticed by Soviet readers.

After the 1940s, the next decade saw the easing of ideological restrictions. The changed political climate of the 1950s created the intention to develop cultural ties between Britain and the Soviet Union and, consequently, to introduce English culture to Soviet readers. Party control over publishing houses and literary journals was relaxed, leading to less control over the ideological and class meanings of foreign literature. As Soviet home and foreign policy was liberalized to a certain extent, the 1950s and 1960s saw the emergence of demand for new sources of information – domestic and foreign. A new section of foreign literature was created in the publishing house Detskaia literatura in 1955. Moreover, the Moscow Youth festival in 1957 contributed to the inflow of cultural information into the Soviet Union from the West. Partly as a consequence of these changes, new translated children's books started to appear from the late 1950s. However, the number of books translated from English representing new themes and genres was limited.

Despite the fact that in the Soviet Union translated literature had to represent ideological values, the selection of foreign books for translation was not solely ideology-driven. Sometimes books were chosen on a random basis. Soviet publishers and children's literature critics did not receive up-to-date information about contemporary foreign children's literature and did not know which books were the best, as a Soviet scholar and critic of children's literature Irina Cherniavskaia emphasized in 1970 in the journal *Detskaia literatura*.[43] However, Soviet literary critics and translators knew about several emerging names in twentieth-century British children's literature, though this awareness did not make it possible for the books to be translated. For example, Cherniavskaia mentioned Mary Norton and Kenneth Grahame as the best representatives of English fantasy literature, but their books were not translated in the Soviet Union until 1980 and 1988, respectively.[44] Two other articles published in 1979 in *Detskaia literatura* provided information on British children's writers whose books were not translated during the Soviet period. Maria Nikolajeva discussed Edith Nesbit's and Mary Norton's fantasy books as well as Philippa Pearce's *Tom's Midnight Garden* praising them as books worth reading.[45] In contrast to Nikolajeva, Irina Tokmakova criticized the books of Alison Uttley, Lucy M. Boston and Ted Hughes, labelling them as reading that lacked 'motifs that are common to all mankind and able to unite people but not separate them' and consequently not particularly suitable for Soviet readers.[46] In his letters to the publishing house Detskaia literatura, which appeared in the same journal in 1972 posthumously, Korney Chukovsky recommended publishing Frances Hodgson Burnett's *Little Lord Fauntleroy* and *The Little Princess* instead of *The Secret Garden* that was scheduled for publication, claiming that Burnett's books were 'humanistic books inspiring a feeling of sympathy for the weak'.[47] This means that there was a plan to publish *The Secret Garden*, but for some reason it did not happen. Most probably, official reservations about retranslating this book or reprinting its pre-revolutionary translation were based on the book's sentimental and mystical nature: the Soviet critic of children's literature, Evgenii Brandis stated, for example, that *The Secret Garden* 'permeated with covert mysticism'.[48]

Considering the ideological context prevailing during the Soviet period, the time was not right for the books of Burnett and Nesbit to be offered to Soviet readers. However, the relaxed political and cultural atmosphere in the 1950s instigated the appearance of other books that explored themes of adventure, family, magic and silliness. These themes found a considerable response in the Soviet cultural context. During the 1960s and 1970s new translations of English classics (written between the late-Victorian period and the Second World War) were added to the group of popular classics reprinted during the Soviet period. These books, which create an image of idealized England, include English folk tales, Lewis Carroll's *Alice's Adventures in Wonderland* and *Through the Looking-Glass*, Beatrix Potter's *The Tale of Mrs. Tiggy-Winkle*, A. A. Milne's *Winnie-the-Pooh* and several poems from *When We Were Very Young* and *Now We Are Six*, J. M. Barrie's play *Peter Pan* and the novel *Peter and Wendy*, P. L. Travers's novels about Mary Poppins, Edward Lear's *Nonsense Songs* (selected poems) and J. R. R. Tolkien's *The Hobbit*. The 1980s saw the appearance of new translations of Rudyard Kipling's *Puck of Pook's Hill* and *Rewards and Fairies* (in 1984) and Kenneth Grahame's *The Wind in the Willows* (in 1988), which would go on to be actively reprinted and retranslated during the post-Soviet period, and *The Reluctant Dragon* (1986). In 1978 Soviet child readers were offered a retelling of Walter de la Mare's selected nonsense poems for children (these poems also had elements of fantasy). This translation was reprinted several times during the post-Soviet period.[49] In addition to this, Henry Williamson's *Tarka the Otter*, which offers poetic descriptions of the Devonshire landscape, was translated in 1979. This translation was not republished and only reappeared during the post-Soviet period.[50]

Demand for these books was driven by the Soviet urban intelligentsia – those parents who wanted to buy new books for their children because they were no longer satisfied with the traditional Soviet children's offering, as the Russian cultural studies scholar Igor' Iakovenko explains. He adds that new translations and the retellings of famous foreign authors appeared as a response to this new demand.[51]

One of the best examples of this new tendency in the Soviet world of translated children's literature is A. A. Milne's stories about *Winnie-the-Pooh* (1926–8), by far the most widely known and loved in Russia among translated British children's books. The Russian translation of this book appeared only in 1960 owing to the effort and enthusiasm of Boris Zakhoder and the Detskii mir publishing house. Zakhoder first offered his translation to the Detgiz publishing house but the manuscript was rejected because the original was considered to be too American.[52] The Detgiz editorial view of *Winnie-the-Pooh* goes some way towards explaining why Milne's children's books were neglected for some time in the Soviet Union. Most probably his work was considered sentimental, something that was not favoured by early Soviet ideology. Milne's writings for children followed the traditions of the nonsense poetry of Edward Lear and there was a certain level of official antagonism towards foreign traditions of silliness in Soviet children's literature at the end of the 1920s and during the 1930s (see my discussion earlier). Thus it is hardly surprising that translations of Milne's works written for children only appeared closer to the Thaw period when ideological restrictions on published children's literature became more relaxed.

Nevertheless, Russian *Winnie-the-Pooh* was a big success among readers and quickly became a fixture in Russian culture.[53] In Zakhoder's translation, Milne's stories about the English bear and his friends retain the feeling of playfulness of the original. Nonsense elements, such as invented words, rhymed words, and alliteration, together with playful language, as markers of Englishness, are all present in Zakhoder's version. Although the translator retold Milne's *Winnie-the-Pooh* and introduced changes to the original text by amending and cutting its content in some parts, the original tone and style of the book is noticeable. Zakhoder masterfully dealt with the challenging play on words, respecting the original style but at the same time accommodating the original within the conventions of the Russian language. He preserved the rhythmic patterns of Milne's poetry, added witty twists to his own Russian nonsense words and recreated cultural allusions by putting these new elements in familiar contexts so Russian readers would easily understand the new meanings. For example, in chapter four ('in which Eeyore loses a tail and Pooh finds one') Milne plays on the words 'customary procedure' with the nonsensical 'Crustimoney Proseedcake' to show the silliness of Pooh, who is a 'Bear of Very Little Brain, and long words Bother' him (p. 45). Zakhoder recreates this pun in a mirror-like manner in such a way that the sound pattern remains similar to the original, turning it into 'обычная процедура' [usual procedure, 'obychnaia protsedura'] and nonsensical 'Бычья Цедура' ['bych'ia tsedura'] (p. 31).[54] In careless Russian speech, the combination of sounds in 'obychnaia' might become fused and a child can be heard to say 'bych'ia', although the word 'бычья' means 'ox-like'. It is the combination of a meaningful word 'бычья' and a non-existent word 'цедура' that recreates the nonsensical effect in Zakhoder's translation yet at the same time does not sound too alien.

Positive reviews, which appeared after Zakhoder's version was first published, especially noted that the translator had taught the English bear how to speak good Russian and that the book had found the key to the hearts of many readers. The article by S. Kanevsky, representing a department of international book exchange at the Lenin State Library, was printed in 1968 in the newspaper *Literaturnaia gazeta* and indicated that the Russian version had quickly become very popular among Soviet readers: the 1965 edition published by Detskaia literatura publishing house amounted to 100,000 printed copies, which flew off the shelves.[55] Moreover, the years 1969, 1971 and 1972 saw the appearance of the animated films *Vinni-Pukh* [*Winnie-the-Pooh*], *Vinni-Pukh idiet v gosti* [*Winnie-the-Pooh pays a visit*] and *Vinni-Pukh i den' zabot* [*Winnie-the-Pooh and a busy day*] based on the script co-written by Zakhoder and the film's director Fyodor Khitruk, which made the English bear part of Russian cultural life.

Carroll's *Alice's Adventures in Wonderland* and *Through the Looking-Glass* were retranslated by Nina Demurova in 1967 as a response to the Russification that had dominated the world of Russian translations of Alice's adventures (at the time Demurova's version appeared, several translations already existed). She avoided Russian connotations and modern expressions, and instead successfully preserved the style, tone and cadence of Carroll's surreal story of 10-year-old *Alice* and recreated authorial nonsense and humour in a Russian context. Like the original, her translation was aimed at a dual audience and addressed older children. In 1974 *Alice's Adventures in Wonderland* was retranslated by Boris Zakhoder. His version addressed younger children and was a free adaptation, which won acclaim, although he revealed that he faced difficulties in tackling the fantastical tale, which went on to inspire generations of English artists with its richly layered style and fascinating puzzles.[56] Zakhoder retold Carroll's story by integrating his own version into Russian culture. If Demurova preserved Alice's image as a charming Victorian girl, then Zakhoder's Alice resembled an active and clever Soviet child. He added more emotional expressions, used modern colloquialisms and his puns had allusions to the Russian language and culture. A few years later, in 1977, another retranslation was offered to younger children – by Aleksander Scherbakov – that was similar to Zakhoder's in terms of translation decisions. As shown in Chapter 2 of this book, the strategy of translating original texts so that they conform to the receiving culture was popular among Soviet translators who worked with children's literature, especially taking into account literary and translation norms that very often required translators to domesticate original texts and make them conform to the ideological demands of the time. All three versions were popular, received praising reviews and were reprinted several times during the Soviet period.

Although the books, which appeared in translation in the 1960s–1970s, introduced new themes for Soviet culture, they still had to express ideological values. This precondition was often met by means of highlighting the ideological context in forewords and afterwords to the published translations. It is important to note that children's literature in the Soviet Union faced fewer ideological restrictions compared to adult literature. Therefore, translators, editors and publishers had more scope to manoeuvre in translating and publishing foreign books.

For example, it seems obvious that the theme of fighting evil, as seen from the Soviet point of view, offered a suitable opportunity for introducing to Soviet readers the first Russian translation of Lewis's *The Lion, the Witch and the Wardrobe* (1950) in 1978. The preface to the translation ably illustrates the ideological context of the Soviet time into which this fantasy was accommodated: 'It is not difficult to guess that the White Witch personifies fascism in all its manifestations. Simply speaking, evil can be defeated only by people of good will who are brave and honest and who come to the aid of each other unselfishly.'[57] Hence, this book is an illustrative example of how ideology played a key role in the selection of books for translation. Moreover, the religious discourse of the original was intentionally excluded by censorship. As Russian translator Olga Bukhina explains, the censor removed all Christian connotations: 'A Godfather became an uncle, Christmas ... was changed into the New Year, and all mentioning of the great Emperor-beyond-the-sea was eliminated from the text.'[58]

The same tendency can be observed with Tolkien's *The Hobbit* that was translated by N. Rakhmanova in 1976. Although Rakhmanova's translation is the first official Russian version, there was an initial attempt to introduce *The Hobbit* to Soviet readers. A short abstract and a brief explanation about the book were published in the magazine *Angliia* in 1969.[59] The first translation of *The Hobbit* was abridged and Rakhmanova suggested that the editor and the censor made amendments to the translated text. She did not know about *The Lord of the Rings* and possible allusions it contained to the opposition between the Socialist East and the capitalist West.[60] It seems likely that the assumed political allusions (both in *The Hobbit* and *The Lord of the Rings*) were the reason for only presenting *The Hobbit* to Soviet readers in the 1970s. It is stated in the book blurb to the first publication of *The Hobbit* that it is about 'the destructive power of money, about the struggle between the good and the evil'.[61] These words point to the accordance of the book's themes with the Soviet ideological rhetoric. The first book of *The Lord of the Rings* trilogy – *The Fellowship of the Ring* (1954) – was only translated in 1982 and positioned as a book for older children and young people. Initially a shortened version, it was later revised and offered to Soviet readers in 1989 in its full version.[62] In the same year, Soviet readers saw the revised version of *The Hobbit*. The advent of political changes of the early 1990s brought new full versions of both Tolkien's works and Lewis's *The Chronicles of Narnia*, and they have proved to be among the most popular English titles that have been reprinted in different retranslations between 1991 and 2017.⁶³

As with translated fantasy books, translations of English folk tales and ballads had to be contextualized ideologically in order to be published during the Thaw period. According to the Soviet publishing house Malysh, national folk tales and ballads promoted patriotic feelings among young readers.⁶⁴ This statement can be equally applicable to foreign folklore – it can demonstrate patriotic discourse in reference to a foreign country and this discourse can subsequently be projected by readers onto their own culture. The theme of patriotism is expressed in ballads about Robin Hood that were retranslated by Ignatii Ivanovskii in 1959. Ivanovskii's translation was afterwards frequently reprinted during the Soviet and post-Soviet periods. As in previous years, the image of Robin Hood had not lost its ideological topicality during Soviet times. As Ivanovskii recalled, it was an official demand by the editor that the translated ballads be put into social context. Hence the translator was required to provide an introductory ballad that would cover social themes. As a solution to this problem, Ivanovskii wrote a new ballad himself in which Robin Hood was depicted as a character who robbed the rich, helped the hungry and did not have mercy on priests. In Ivanovskii's words, this introductory poem was favoured by the authorities responsible for ideological issues within Soviet children's literature.⁶⁵

Additionally, the following books have elements that are deemed ideological within the context of Soviet ideological thinking and this might have been a reason for their selection for translation during the 1960s and the 1970s. Henry Rider Haggard's *King Solomon's Mines*, *Fair Margaret* and *The Lady of Blossholme* were translated in the late 1950s. As Brandis emphasized in 1980, Haggard 'truthfully recreated the atmosphere of the late Middle Ages and depicted the moral decay of the feudal elite'. The reason for the delay with translation of these books is trivial: Lenin denounced categorically Haggard's sociopolitical book *Rural England: Being an Account of the Agricultural and Social Researches Carried Out in 1901 and 1902* published in 1906.⁶⁶ Geoffrey Trease's three historical adventure novels – *Cue for Treason* (1940), *Comrades for the Charter* (1934) and *Missing from Home* (1937) – were translated in 1960. According to Brandis's categorization, these books portray the history of the peasant and working-class movements in England.⁶⁷ Although these books were not republished, Trease's other historical adventure novel *The Hills of Varna* (set in the Balkans with a main character who is English) has proved to be more popular with Soviet and Russian publishers. Trease's socialist views and connection to the Society for

Cultural Relations with the USSR (SCR) gained for *The Hills of Varna* a privileged position in the Soviet canon of children's literature. Eric Knight's *Lassie Come-Home* (translated in the 1960s) was probably chosen for translation because the dog Lassie is owned by a family of an English miner. William M. Thackeray's *The Rose and the Ring* (1854), translated in 1970, is a satirical fantasy tale which criticizes the monarchy and high society.

Although the following British texts first appeared in print after 1945, it is necessary to mention them in order to understand the general pattern in the field of translated British children's literature during the second half of the Soviet period. These books complete the general image of Englishness that was presented to Soviet readers.

As a counter to ideological discourse, the 1970s and the 1980s saw the appearance of translated fantasy stories that were published once only and then reprinted in the post-Soviet period: Eleanor Farjeon's *The King's Daughter Cries for the Moon* from *The Little Bookroom* (1955), Alison Uttley's *Sam Pig* (written between 1939 and 1965), Michael Bond's *A Bear Called Paddington* (1958), Mary Norton's *The Borrowers* (1952), selected tales by Joan Aiken from *A Necklace of Raindrops and Other Stories* (1968) and Richard Adams's *Watership Down* (1972). This list also includes Robert Graves's volume of nonsense poems *The Penny Fiddle: Poems for Children* (1960) that was translated in 1965 only and is out of print nowadays. Three books focusing on the social problems and moral choices faced by real teenagers covering social themes were also translated. Cecil Day Lewis's school adventure novel set in post-war Britain *The Otterbury Incident* (1948) appeared in Russian translation in the 1970s. Nina Bawden's *Kerrie's War* was translated in 1984 and never reprinted and Sue Townsend's *The Secret Diary of Adrian Mole, Aged 13¾* was translated in 1989 and afterwards retranslated in 2001.[68]

Additionally, several translated books became popular during the second half of the Soviet period. However, their popular status in the Soviet Union did not match their lesser standing in Britain, for example, Leila Berg's novels about the adventures of ordinary English children, the 1950 novel *The Adventures of Chunky*, written and translated in 1959, and *Little Pete Stories* that appeared in England in 1952 and were translated into Russian in 1956 and reprinted in 1981. These books were popular during the Soviet period and their print run ended with the demise of the Soviet Union. Donald Bissett's selected fairy tales for small children, written between the 1950s and the 1970s and in a playful form presenting Englishness, were first translated in the 1960s and then reprinted throughout the Soviet and post-Soviet periods. Gerald Durrell's 1974 fantasy novel *The Talking Parcel* about the adventures of two English children in a magical land was translated in 1981 and afterwards reprinted during the post-Soviet period. It is important to note that Leila Berg, Donald Bissett and Gerald Durrell were favoured by the Soviet authorities as they were sympathetic towards the Soviet Union. Moreover, Berg and Bissett were involved in the activities of the SCR Writers Group promoting Soviet children's literature.[69] Durrell visited the Soviet Union in the 1980s and made a documentary about Russian wildlife.

As with the corpus of British children's books translated during the first half of the Soviet period, British texts translated between the mid-1950s and 1991 also reflect political and cultural changes in Soviet society. However, the pattern in the translated texts is different. The themes from the British texts, such as adventure and family as well as discourses of the fantastic and silliness, were further developed in Russian translations. At the same time, ideological values continued to be addressed in themes which have clear political connotations: the negative implications of capitalism, class struggle, anti-religious ideas and the fight for independence. Also included are empire and patriotism, as well as social issues around young people. At the same time, looking at this corpus from the point of view of how Englishness is represented, it emerges that the themes in the selected British texts still point to the prevalence of political and ideological associations of Englishness in Soviet translations. However, cultural associations of Englishness and features of English national character expressed through the discourses of the fantastic and silliness noticeably start to play an important role in Soviet translations too.

Post-Soviet period: From 1992 to 2017

Historical and cultural context of Russian children's literature

The cultural and political atmosphere in Russia underwent considerable changes after the break-up of the Soviet Union. As Rosalind Marsh explains, Russian pre-revolutionary and émigré literature and philosophy were regarded highly and Soviet values seemed no longer significant; moreover, Russian culture was no longer disconnected from the world culture.[70] Cultural and political changes inevitably had an impact on Russian children's literature, which lost its dominant position and shifted to the periphery of the country's literary system. After 1991 the situation regarding state control of children's literature changed drastically: political ideology and censorship gave way to market forces (commercial success and readers' demand). The publishing market has experienced a reorientation from a culture that was focused on political and patriotic values and Socialist Realism during the Soviet era to the popular commercial culture that dominated the 1990s and 2000s. Although the aesthetic value of children's literature also played a significant role during the Soviet period, nevertheless, commercial reasons meant less attention was given to aesthetics in children's books in the 1990s.

As a result, the first decade of the post-Soviet period saw the prevalence of popular fiction for children that included the children's detective and mystery novels, fantasy books, fairy tales, children's horror stories, comics and playful works. The dominance of popular fiction over thought-provoking realist literature instigated the appearance of fresh themes. Russian modern children's detective novels of the 1990s and the 2000s promoted new middle-class values, and the demand for the children's detective genre increased among the growing middle-class families of post-Soviet Russia.[71] Popular Soviet genres, such as the school novel, realist stories, moralistic tales and ideological poems, were superseded by fantasy and a playful literature based on absurd and inventive language which was also highly influenced by the English tradition of nonsense which led to the appearance of the eccentric hero.[72] The themes of family life, religion and the historical past of pre-revolutionary Russia and the ideologized Soviet Union were also popular. Since the end of the 2000s Russian children's literature started engaging with controversial historical themes such as painful memories of Stalin's era and the Second World War. More recently, the 2010s have brought slow responses to contemporary social themes such as class and regional differences, unemployment, poverty and family conflicts.[73]

British children's books selected for translation into Russian

As post-Soviet children's literature faced social and political changes, translated literature helped in the search for new names and themes. The greater openness of Russia to the West in the post-Soviet period has led to the saturation of the children's literature market with translated books. In the 1990s especially, there was a great demand for translated literature. As Ben Hellman notes, by the year 2000 translations amounted to 'around half of all children's titles'.[74] Between 1991 and 2017 the selection of British children's books for translation reflected changes in the cultural and political climate in Russian society. Ideological censorship has been replaced by the needs of the publishing market: preference has been given to those books that are commercially safe and sell well. These undoubtedly include the classics of children's literature.

During this period the following English themes that appear in the original texts are fully represented in translation: patriotism, empire, historical past, religion, school, family and home. Also included are adventures, detective stories and mystery, as well as discourses of fantasy and of silliness. These are the themes that are equally present in Russian and British children's literature. During the post-Soviet period a considerable emphasis was given to cultural associations of Englishness, although all three groups of manifestations of Englishness are present in Russian translations. Nostalgia for the past seems to be dominant and expressed in the recreation of the image of 'good old England'. If, during the Soviet period, the image of 'good old England' had political connotations, then during the post-Soviet period its representation resonates with the idealization of the Russian past.

Several new translated titles from the list of British books published between the late 1860s and 1945 appeared after the break-up of the Soviet Union. They included new titles that were not translated before as well as retranslations and reprints of the pre-revolutionary editions of books by Burnett and Nesbit, new translations of C. S. Lewis's *The Chronicles of Narnia*, J. R. R. Tolkien's *The Hobbit* and *Roverandom*, Lewis Carroll's *The Haunting of the Snark* and both tales about Alice's adventures, T. S. Eliot's *Old Possum's Book of Practical Cats* and Spike Milligan's selected nonsense poems.[75] At the same time, the list of popular Soviet translations of British children's classics and books accepted as literature suitable for children, which were discussed in the previous sections in this chapter, did not undergo any major changes during the post-Soviet period and titles from this corpus have been constantly reprinted.[76]

The post-Soviet period has seen a remarkable revival of the themes of historical past and religion. The 1990s' renewed interest in pre-revolutionary Russia points to a nostalgic attitude towards life before 1917. Therefore, the example of retranslations and reprints of pre-revolutionary editions of Burnett's and Nesbit's novels as well as new retranslations of Grahame's *The Wind in the Willows* shows that translated literature about mythologized life in the late-Victorian and Edwardian England contributed to the promotion of the theme of nostalgia for the mythologized Russian pre-revolutionary past. For example, the topicality of Burnett's *Little Lord Fauntleroy*, *The Little Princess* and *The Secret Garden* was emphasized in an article that appeared in *Detskaia literatura* journal in 1993. The author of the article stressed that the main characters of Burnett's idyllic novels were indispensable for Russian children who lived 'in the unkind world' of the early 1990s. The mythologized Englishness of *Little Lord Fauntleroy* is particularly highlighted in this article: 'Thus Cedric Errol is back – a little lord from a big magical kingdom, which we could not visit at the right time. This kingdom populated by princesses, lords and fairies was created by Frances Hodgson Burnett.'[77] What this article implies is that depictions of mythologized late-Victorian and Edwardian England resonated with the nostalgic feelings for the idealized past of Tsarist Russia that had been erased from official cultural memory during the Soviet period.

As a response to nostalgia for Imperial Russia before the Revolution, English books published from the Edwardian period through to the end of the Second World War together with such books as the fantasy tales of Eleanor Farjeon and J. R. R. Tolkien, which refer to the past with nostalgic sentiments, were translated, retranslated and reprinted in the post-Soviet period. At the same time, the nostalgic feeling for the mythologized past was strengthened by the republished sentimental novels of Lidia Charskaia who wrote mostly about the adventures of middle-class and upper-class girls in Tsarist Russia. These novels had regained their popularity in Russia during the 1990s. Also, the renewed interest in the Russian Orthodox religion in a changed Russian society could have been the reason for translating Victorian sentimental fiction for children, which often contained moralistic messages. For example, Georgiana M. Craik's novel for girls *Cousin Trix and Her Welcome Tales* written in 1868 was published in Russian translation by the Russian Orthodox Church publishing house Izdatel'stvo Sretenskogo monastyria in 2013.[78] Another example is Charlotte Mary Yonge's moralistic and sentimental novel *Countess Kate* which first appeared in England in 1862 – it was translated into Russian in 1865, shunned during the Soviet period and reprinted again in 2015.

Since 1991, many popular modern British classics dealing with Englishness to some extent have been translated, including fantasy novels by celebrated authors such as Nina Bawden, Roald Dahl, Alan Garner, Eva Ibbotson, Diana Wynne Jones, Penelope Lively, Michael Morpurgo, Terry Pratchett, Philip Pullman and J. K. Rowling. The theme of contemporary English children and their problems is represented in Russian translations of the books written by David Almond who is also a prize-winning author.[79] A considerable volume of books belonging to English popular fiction for children has been translated, among which are children's detective stories, thrillers, mystery books and teenage girl stories. For example, Enid Blyton's *The Famous Five* and *The Secret Seven* immediately appeared after the demise of the Soviet Union and have proved to be very popular.

In modern Russia, foreign books for translation are no longer selected according to the ideological demands of the state. Instead, publishers are guided by the publishing market expectations and the commercial success of foreign books. For example, the Russian translation of Chris Riddle's book *Goth Girl and the Ghost of a Mouse* (2013) was commissioned by the publishing house AST because Chris Riddle illustrated Neil Gaiman's books which are popular among Russian readers.[80] Also the translation of Elizabeth Goudge's *The Little White Horse* (1946) was commissioned to complement the 2009 release of the fantasy film *The Secret of Moonacre* based on this book. Philippa Pearce's *Tom's Midnight Garden* (1958) was selected because the author's name was mentioned by Philip Pullman upon receiving a readers' award in 2007 (Pullman was voted by readers as their favourite winner of the Carnegie medal).[81]

Several books that portray Englishness have never been translated into Russian during the Soviet and post-Soviet periods, leaving the representation of Englishness to Russian readers as incomplete. Among them are two books that are deeply rooted in the discourse of the fantastic: *The Midnight Folk* (1927) and *The Box of Delights* (1930) by John Masefield. Social changes in British society brought about the emergence of the theme of working-class families. For example, Eve Garnett's *The Family from One End Street* (1937) has never been translated either (it only appeared in English as a textbook for students in 1973). This book has a clear social purpose as the author depicts episodes in the everyday life of English children from a working-class background. Another notable absence is the theme of resilience in English national character during the Second World War, which was explored in three books that were published in the 1940s – Kitty Barne's *Visitors from London* (1940), Noel Streatfield's *The Children of Primrose Lane* (1941) and Mary Treadgold's *We Couldn't Leave Dinah* (1941). Again, these books have never been translated during the Soviet or post-Soviet periods.

To sum up, my analysis of the selected books for translation has drawn a broad picture of the representation of Englishness in the Russian cultural context. Emphasis is given to political and ideological associations of Englishness connected with such themes as class difference, heroism, imperialism and historical past. Clearly, the selection of British children's books during the Soviet period followed the ideological demands of the time and Englishness appears to be politicized. Despite a level of contemporary and historical knowledge about England among Soviet translators and publishers (as I argued in the previous chapters), still, in general, during the Soviet period it was for the most part original books judged to be ideologically correct and that had been written by ideologically suitable authors which were the ones chosen for translation.

It is obvious that during the first half of the Soviet period the choice fell on those original books that were in accord with a recurring ideological motif of a new hero for a new Soviet country. Starting from the Thaw years, the desire to read new foreign books and find out about life in the West resulted in the appearance of more translated books. Broadly speaking, from looking at the selected English titles only (and not at texts in details), it appears that the mythologized image of England that suited the Soviet ideological discourse had an impact on the choice of books for translation. On the one hand, throughout the whole Soviet period there is a focus on the myth of heroic England where poor people stand up for freedom and oppose the rich and the powerful. On the other hand, there is a negative myth of capitalist and imperialist England where the life of the working class is hard. This myth is generally emphasized through the translated books published between 1918 and the beginning of the Thaw. At the same time, capitalist England is presented in a good light, mostly by choosing the original books focused on motifs of family and home, fantastic adventures and some aspects of silliness. These motifs are part of the literary image of 'dobraia staraia Angliia' [good old England] that often appears in the British children's books written between the Edwardian period and the Second World War. Taking into account the social and political contexts in which these books were translated, it logically follows that the image of good old England in Soviet translations would be affected by ideology, as I will show in the second part of this book.

Following the political changes of 1991, the Soviet ideological context of translated literature lost its utmost importance. As a consequence of this, lots of British children's books have been translated in order to fill the void caused by ideological restrictions imposed on the translated literature through censorship. Most of the British children's books written between the Edwardian period and the Second World War have been translated. In these translations, images of the idealized 'good old England' prevail; quite often such images are underpinned by the nostalgic vision of the past of England and Russia.

The larger contextual picture presented in this chapter justifies my choice of translated books for further detailed analysis. I have singled out the following books from the list of English titles that have been translated, retranslated and reprinted during the Soviet and post-Soviet periods – and that are the most representative in terms of having examples of Englishness:

- J. M. Barrie's novel *Peter and Wendy*;
- Kenneth Grahame's novel *The Wind in the Willows*;
- Rudyard Kipling's novels *Puck of Pook's Hill* and *Rewards and Fairies*;
- A. A. Milne's poem 'The King's Breakfast' from the volume *When We Were Very Young*; and poem 'King Hilary and the Beggarman' from the volume *Now We Are Six*;
- P. L. Travers's novels *Mary Poppins*, *Mary Poppins Comes Back* and *Mary Poppins Opens the Door*.

These books are the most popular choices by publishers currently available in print. Moreover, most of these books are included in the list of translated foreign books compiled by the Russian State Library and recommended for purchase in school libraries.[82]

4

J. M. Barrie's *Peter Pan*: Censoring images of the British Empire and Edwardian class society

Translating themes of empire and class, as political and ideological associations of Englishness, contained in J. M. Barrie's novel *Peter and Wendy* (1911) and the play *Peter Pan* (1928), forms the subject of this chapter.[1] It starts with a discussion of the history behind the creation of the translations, focusing on the Soviet ideological interpretation of Barrie's literary output and the role that censorship played in the translation of Peter Pan's adventures. Afterwards, it examines how Soviet translators manipulated representations of empire and class in an ideological context. The analysis focuses on the image of Hook as an English gentleman belonging to the gentry, who is presented as a personification of the heroic and upper-class nature of the idealized British Empire, and on the image of the Lost Boys as the courageous defenders of the British Empire. Both images have distinctive traits of English national character that are lost in the Soviet translations due to the influence of state ideology. The analysis demonstrates that the original representations of empire and class were toned down in the translations produced during the Soviet period as it would not have been ideologically correct to give a full account of Barrie's thoughts on the themes of class divisions and empire. It also shows that character-building and didactic functions are important markers that indicated the suitability of the play and the book for Soviet readers.

The first Russian translation of Barrie's tale of the boy who never grew up was published in 1918 and called *Prikliucheniia Pitera Pana* [The Adventures of Peter Pan].[2] It was a translation of the prose version of the play *Peter Pan* (first performed in England in 1904) and it went largely unnoticed by Russian readers and critics as it appeared at a most unsuitable time, just after the Revolution. There was little chance for such a story to be presented to a large audience of young Soviet readers and their parents at this time, because of the widespread campaign in the 1920s and 1930s against fairy tales as well as fantasy and nonsense literature driven by fears that they could turn children into idealists who might have a distorted perception of the real world.³ Moreover, the 1930 *Literaturnaia entsiklopediia* [Literary Encyclopaedia] characterizes Barrie as 'an author of sentimental fairytale books written for children .... Detached from real life and restricted by narrow and individualistic limits, Barrie idealises reality in his works, thus siding ideologically with the most conservative part of the petty bourgeoisie'.⁴ These factors, together with the sentimentality and middle-class essence of the original novel *Peter and Wendy* and the play *Peter Pan*, made it unlikely that either work would have appeared before the Thaw. It was not until the end of the 1950s when the translators Nina Demurova and Boris Zakhoder attempted to interest Soviet publishers in Barrie's fantasy. They both started translating Barrie's works at the same time: Demurova translated the novel and Zakhoder translated the play. Even though they might not have known each other in the late 1950s, this coincidence points to an understanding that it was possible to have stories about Peter Pan in the Soviet cultural milieu.⁵ Moreover, the more relaxed attitude to Barrie is demonstrated in the 1962 encyclopaedia entry on him, the ideological tone of which was considerably downplayed compared to the 1930 edition:

> Barrie ridicules bourgeois theory about the natural inequality of people. The play *Peter Pan* (1904) is a moving fantastic story about a boy who has never grown up .... At times Barrie complied with petty bourgeois tastes overusing sentimentality, but he could combine the plausible with the fantastic and the crudely humorous description of daily life with romantic intrigue.⁶

Demurova first found out about *Peter and Wendy* in 1956 when she bought the book from a street vendor in India while working as an interpreter for a small cultural delegation from the USSR. She had her translation ready by 1957 but it was rejected by a publisher and ignored for ten years. According to her, the editor's policy against elements of fantasy and burlesque in children's literature was the main reason for rejection. However, Demurova did not give up all hope. She read her translation to her friends, relatives and their children. Eventually *Peter and Wendy* delighted Soviet readers in the same way it had a home audience, but only in 1968, when Demurova was finally contracted by Detgiz publishing house.⁷

While negotiating the conditions with Detgiz in 1968, Demurova pointed to the classic status of the original book which in fact was an essential element for positive decisions on many translated works in the Soviet Union. However, while discussing omissions with Demurova, the censor pointed to serious issues in the original that were considered inappropriate for Soviet children. The book described a flying boy, a nanny dog and a 10-year-old girl cleaning the house. Moreover, as Demurova explains, the censor disliked Captain Hook's ponderings over his identity as a gentleman and insisted on removing this word from the translated text, as Soviet children were not aware of this concept.[8] In order to protect her translation from the suggested changes, Demurova asked Korney Chukovsky for help. He suggested to the publishing house that the character of the little housemaid should stay in the book – Soviet children needed to know about the exploitation of child labour in England. This ironic suggestion saved the translation and the book was published. However, the word 'dzhentlmen' was not included. Demurova acknowledged that she acted as self-censor and removed 'a few lines which, [she] was certain, would never be permitted to appear in a Soviet children's publication'. These lines, which refer to the theme of the British Empire, are discussed later in the chapter. In the end, the book was published by Detgiz in 1968 'with minimal cuts' and an acknowledgement that the book was slightly abridged.[9] Demurova's translation received a favourable review in 1969 in the literary journal *Novyi mir*. The reviewer praised her work, emphasizing that the perfectly translated fairytale would be a wonderful addition to the already existing books offered to young readers. This brought attention to the fact that Barrie's novel had been left unnoticed by Soviet publishers for so long and that Detskaia literatura publishing house had not published enough copies to satisfy possible demand for the translation.[10] Unfortunately, Demurova's version was not reprinted after the first edition, and only in 1987 and then again in 1992 were Russian readers offered a full edition of the Russian *Peter and Wendy* without any omissions.[11]

Demurova's translation was not reprinted between 1968 and 1987. Instead, in 1981, Soviet children were offered a new translation of the novel called *Piter Pen* [Peter Pan]: it was an abridged version retold by Irina Tokmakova. As she recalls, the Detskaia literatura publishing house asked her to translate the story about the adventures of Peter Pan (she translated *Peter and Wendy*). Believing that the language of the original book was 'a bit too ponderous' to produce a faithful translation, Tokmakova suggested to the publishing house that she would retell the original, abridge it 'slightly' and use more colloquial Russian language. She admitted that she became the co-author of the Russian version of *Peter and Wendy* but emphasized that essentially her translation remained the novel *Peter and Wendy* originally written by Barrie.[12] If Demurova openly pointed to the role of the editor as a censor and to her own role as a self-censor in the process of translating *Peter and Wendy*, then Tokmakova did not admit any awareness of the necessity to censor the original text. However, Tokmakova's role as a co-author can be considered as an act of self-censorship in terms of deciding what was stylistically and contextually suitable for Soviet child readers. For example, she omitted episodes in which Peter Pan was unsympathetic towards others, and the author's thoughts about life and death.

The play *Peter Pan* was first presented to Soviet readers in 1966: an extract from the second act was published in the journal *Detskaia literatura*.[13] Zakhoder started working on this play in the late 1950s, as evidenced by his officially submitted application of 3 May 1959 for a stage adaptation of Barrie's play *Peter Pan*.[14] In this application Zakhoder emphasized the patriotic message of the play, stating that children 'refused to betray their friends and their homeland'. He also accentuated the character-building and didactic function of the play: 'the play addressed many serious issues, important for children, in a playful and interesting manner – such as a mother's love and true friendship, attitudes to girls, courage and cowardice'. At the same time, Zakhoder highlighted the novelty of *Peter Pan* for the Soviet audience, saying that it was about play and reality, about the fantastic and the real.[15] These were substantial reasons for allowing *Peter Pan* to be performed on stage. This performance was officially endorsed in 1960 by the Glavlit stamp on the first draft of Zakhoder's translation.[16] However, it was not until 1966 that the play appeared in a journal publication and was performed by the Young People's Theatre of Riazan and then by the Central Children's Theatre in Moscow in 1968. The full-text translation of the play called *Piter Pen* was published as a book in 1967 by the department responsible for the distribution of dramatic works within the Administration for the Protection of Author's Rights (VUOAP). The edition's print run was a mere 150 copies. The publication was reprinted in 1971 by Iskusstvo publishing house and titled *Piter Pen, ili Mal'chik, Kotoryi Ne Khotel Rasti* [Peter Pan or the boy who did not want to grow up] with illustrations by May Miturich-Khlebnikov.

In the epilogue to the 1971 edition Zakhoder pointed to his modifications in the translated play and how he tried to convey the spirit of the original text so that Soviet readers of the 1970s would understand:

> The translator tried to be as close, or rather, faithful, to the original as possible. But the translator allowed himself small liberties. These liberties were brought about by the translator's wish to be faithful to the author and to be understood by the (youthful!) spectator of today. (p. 126)

This statement does not clearly reflect Zakhoder's awareness of the necessity to self-censor the text, but rather the existence of liberties, with which he approached the text. Obviously, this statement points to the translator's presence in the text. Nevertheless, it can be assumed that self-censorship might have played a certain role in making a decision about what was contextually suitable for Soviet child readers.

In the case of all three translations, censorship and self-censorship corresponded to the themes of empire and class, as political and ideological associations of Englishness. The original novel and the play contain implicit hints to empire and more obvious allusions to the class differences deeply embedded in the English national character, two themes which are interconnected. Edwardian literature praised such traits of national character as physical strength, courage and prowess as suitable qualities for builders and defenders of the British Empire. In light of the above, it seems that Demurova, Tokmakova and Zakhoder were well aware of the Soviet ideological conventions and toned down the original in the versions they produced during this period. Clearly, it would not have been ideologically correct to give a full account of Barrie's thoughts on class divisions and empire, as exemplified in the following examples of Soviet translations.

The character of Captain James Hook is an illustrative representation of the theme of class difference. He is an Etonian and belongs to the English gentry. Peter Hollindale explains that 'Hook's Etonian reminiscences ... are full of sharp-edged comedy for those familiar with the English public school system.'[17] There are several scenes in the novel and the play in which Barrie speaks ironically about Hook's position at the top of the British class system. In the novel, in Chapter 5 'The Island Come True', Barrie says of him,

> He was never more sinister than when he was most polite, which is probably the truest test of breeding; and the elegance of his diction, even when he was swearing, no less than the distinction of his demeanour, showed him one of a different cast from his crew. (p. 115)

Tokmakova omits this passage. Demurova conveys the essential meaning of the passage: the Russian Hook (Джеймс Крюк [Dzheims Kriuk] in Russian) behaves properly, his diction is elegant and his manners are noble. However, Demurova is not as exact as Barrie in showing Hook's former high position within society. Her Hook is 'не ровня своим подчиненным' [not an equal to his subordinates]; however, Barrie's Hook is 'one of a different cast from his crew' (p. 51).

In the play, in Act II 'The Never Land', Barrie depicts Hook as follows:

> He is never more sinister than when he is most polite, and the elegance of his diction, the distinction of his demeanour, show him one of a different class from his crew, a solitary among uncultured companions. (pp. 27–8)

In a similar way to Demurova, Zakhoder stays faithful to the original and retains such characteristics of Hook as politeness, elegant diction and manners. However, by describing Hook as only 'он резко отличается от остальных' [he is vastly different from the others] and 'одинок среди своих некультурных приспешников' [a solitary among his uncultured accomplices] (p. 47), he considerably downplays the fact that Hook's position in society is much higher than that of his crew, by rewriting Barrie's description of Hook as 'one of a different class'.

Hook's upper-class upbringing is alluded to in the novel in the following examples. In chapter 14 'The Pirate Ship', Barrie says that other pirates were 'socially so inferior to him' and that Hook

> had been at a famous public school; and its traditions still clung to him like garments, with which indeed they are largely concerned. Thus it was offensive to him even now to board a ship in the same dress in which he grappled her, and he still adhered in his walk to the school's distinguished slouch. But above all he retained the passion for good form. Good form! However much he may have degenerated, he still knew that this is all that really matters. (p. 188)

Demurova conveys Barrie's ironic description of Hook as a representative of the upper classes, concerned about looking good and behaving according to set rules in society, whereas Tokmakova only generally refers to Hook's upper-class upbringing and omits the details. Moreover, Tokmakova considerably tones down the class difference between Hook and the pirates, thus failing to show his social superiority, and mistakenly turns Hook's fixation with propriety into concern about being physically fit. This misunderstanding prevented Tokmakova from showing Hook's dramatic end. Barrie draws the attention of his readers to the importance for Hook of doing everything right according to the rules set by the gentry. Moreover, in chapter 15 'Hook or Me This Time' Barrie shows some sympathy towards Hook, which in its turn points to the importance of class traditions as part of the English national character:

> What sort of form was Hook himself showing? Misguided man though he was, we may be glad, without sympathising with him, that in the end he was true to the traditions of his race. . . . his mind was no longer with them; it was slouching

in the playing fields of long ago, or being sent up for good, or watching the wall-game from a famous wall. And his shoes were right, and his waistcoat was right, and his tie was right, and his socks were right. James Hook, thou not wholly unheroic figure, farewell. (pp. 203–4)

Tokmakova omits the whole passage and only translates its last sentence. Even this sentence is transformed in her version: 'Джеймс Крюк, с этой минуты переставший быть героической личностью, прощай навсегда!' [Dzheims Kriuk, who ceased to be a heroic person from this moment, farewell forever!] (p. 164). On the contrary, there is something heroic about Hook in the original text. Barrie's Hook is a gentleman who is true to the traditions of his social class. This is exactly how Demurova portrays him in the example above. However, she domesticates activities typical for English public schools in Edwardian England (playing fields, being sent up for good, rugby played against a brick wall) to the point where in her version it looks as though Hook was a graduate of a Soviet school: 'Он шёл, сутулясь, по спортивной площадке своей далёкой юности, его вызывали к директору, он болел за футбольную команду своей славной школы' [He was slouching along the sports ground of his faraway youth, he was being summoned to the principal of his school, he was supporting the football team of his famous school.] (p. 137). It was no accident that she chose this strategy, as her translation solutions were most likely dictated by the demands of the time and if done otherwise, her translation would not have been published, as Demurova points to differences in opinion between her and the book's editor on the subject of English public schools and Hook as a representative of their traditions.[18]

Barrie's portrayal of Hook as an eccentric pirate was successfully visualized in the Russian illustrations by May Miturich-Khlebnikov in Zakhoder's translation and by Ilya Kabakov in Demurova's translation, helping readers to generate the meaning embedded in the original and translated texts. In the original text, Barrie describes Hook as a smartly dressed man who smoked two cigars at once. Miturich-Khlebnikov displays Hook as a self-important pirate, just as readers would expect him to be (Figure 1). Moreover, in another illustration (as can be seen on page 8 in Zakhoder's translation) a similar-looking Hook is drawn smoking two cigars. The visual representations of Hook created by Ilya Kabakov in Demurova's translation are scattered throughout several illustrations without appearing as a full portrait: readers are only given a hint as Hook is either almost hidden in the background or drawn in a full-back position. Still, in these pictures Hook can be identified as a typical pirate captain from the

Figure 1 Hook. Illustration by May Miturich-Khlebnikov in J. M. Barrie, *Piter Pen, ili Mal'chik, Kotoryi Ne Khotel Rasti*, translated by Boris Zakhoder (Moscow: Iskusstvo, 1971), p. 48. May Petrovich Miturich-Khlebnikov © DACS 2019.

old times. All the attributes of piracy are there in Hook's visual depiction in both translations and they complement the verbal portrayal. His attire creates allusions to the typical dress of a pirate captain: a doublet or a coat and breeches, stockings, thigh-high boots and hats. At the same time, the Russian pictures

Figure 2 Jolly Roger. Illustration by Ilya Kabakov in J. M. Barrie, *Piter Pen i Vendi*, translated by Nina Demurova (Moscow: Detskaia literatura, 1968), p. 120. Ilya Kabakov © DACS 2019.

evoke an image of men's styling from the sixteenth and seventeenth centuries. In the original text Hook's costume is associated with the time of Charles II when everyday gentleman's clothing consisted of a wig, coat, waistcoat, knee breeches and square-toed shoes. This is how Hook is depicted in the English illustration by Francis Donkin Bedford that appeared in the first edition of *Peter and Wendy* in 1911: he is a fashionable imperious gentleman-pirate (Figure 3). Hence, the visual representation in the original text and the translated versions complement Barrie's description.

The Russian illustrators also display Hook as a comic hero who can at times be deeply sinister but the exaggeration of evil traits in his visual appearance tends to make readers perceive him as a pompous pirate and evoke laughter rather than fear. In the original text, Barrie describes Hook as a deathly pale man with blue eyes, which flicker with red lights when he is plunging his hook into his victims, with long dark curls looking like evil black candles. The illustration

Figure 3 Hook and Peter Pan. Illustration 'This man is mine!' by Francis Donkin Bedford in J. M. Barrie, *Peter and Wendy* (New York: Charles Scribner's Sons, 1911). Illustration copyright © A.E.H. Bedford 2019. Used with permission.

by Miturich-Khlebnikov (Figure 1) merges Barrie's description of Hook into one image. Although drawn in black, red and grey (but with blue eyes, to follow the original text), Hook looks pompous and comic, as his attire creates associations with a flamboyant pirate captain. At the same time, the shape of this villain in black and red makes it appear more comic than frightening. As this image of Hook is also on the front page, the illustrator effectively uses Hook's visual portrayal to introduce readers to this character from the beginning of the story and to amplify the textual narrative created by Zakhoder. As for Demurova's translation, Ilya Kabakov does not focus his attention on the evil image of Hook. However, in one of the illustrations the malevolent nature of Hook as a terrifying pirate is emphasized by the illustrator. As shown in Figure 2, the sharp corners used in the outline of the ship and the two flags with the skull and crossbones as a symbol of the Jolly Roger create an aura of fear – these elements complement the textual representation of Hook in the original and translated texts. Both Russian illustrations considerably differ from the English one in the style and visual narrative. In his detailed drawing, capturing the mood of the scene, Bedford depicts Hook as a scary-looking character: his bitter facial expression, devilish eyes and threatening posture imply that he won't have mercy on the children (Figure 3).

In the scene describing Hook's final moment, Barrie says that Hook provokes Peter Pan to behave badly. Hook needs this provocation to be convinced that Peter is not a gentleman, and to Hook's satisfaction, Peter proves him right. Demurova faithfully conveys this scene and shows the main pirate as a man anxious to look like a gentleman until the last minute of his life:

> Стоя на фальшборте, он оглянулся на Питера, легко скользящего по воздуху, и знаком предложил ему бить не кинжалом, а ногой. Питер так и поступил – он пнул Крюка ногой. Сбылась страстная мечта капитана.
>
> – Невоспитанный мальчишка! – закричал он радостно и упал в море.
>
> [Standing on the bulwark he looked over at Peter easily gliding through the air, and invited him with a gesture to kick but not to stab. And Peter did so – he kicked Hook. The greatest dream of the captain had come true. 'Ill-bred little boy!' he cried happily and fell into the sea.] (p. 137)

On the contrary, this scene in Tokmakova's version is expressed differently, as she presents Hook as a villain:

> Стоя на фальшборте, Крюк видел через плечо подлетавшего к нему Питера. Выждав момент, пират нагнулся, и Питер, вместо того чтобы ударить кинжалом, лягнул его. Наконец-то злодей добился своего.
>
> – Плохая форма! – воскликнул он глумливо и, довольный, отправился к крокодилу в пасть. [Standing on the bulwark, he saw over his shoulder that Peter flew up to him. When the moment was right, the pirate bent down, and Peter kicked him instead of stabbing him. At last the villain had got his own way. 'It's bad form!' he cried jeeringly and went content to the crocodile mouth.] (p. 165)

Zakhoder offers a third interpretation of the end of Hook in the play (in Act V Scene 1 'The Pirate Ship'):

Питер . . . сидит на бочке, играя на своей свирели. Это может удивить кого угодно, кроме Крюка. Схватив мушкетон, он в отчаянии бьет прикладом – не по Питеру, а по бочке; она катится по палубе, а Питер преспокойно сидит в воздухе, продолжая играть. Рассудок пирата помрачился. Крюк, запевая студенческую песню «Гаудеамус игитур», карабкается на поручни и бросается в воду, где навстречу ему гостеприимно раскрывается пасть крокодила. [Peter . . . is sitting in a barrel playing upon his svirel. This may surprise anyone but Hook. After grabbing a blunderbuss, he strikes with the gun stock in despair – not at Peter but at the barrel; it is rolling across the deck, and Peter is sitting calmly in the air still playing upon his svirel. The pirate's mind became clouded. Singing the student's song *Gaudeamus Igitur*, he is climbing up the bulwarks and prostrates himself into the water, where the crocodile is opening his mouth hospitably towards him.] (p. 104)

Barrie says, seeing that Peter Pan is not afraid of Hook: 'the great heart of HOOK breaks. That not wholly unheroic figure climbs the bulwarks murmuring "Floreat Etona", and prostrates himself into the water, where the Crocodile is waiting for him open-mouthed' (p. 73). Not only does Zahoder turn a heartbroken Hook into the insane pirate Dzheims Kriuk, but he also creates a different impression of Hook's upper-class background. In his version, Hook's last words are not the schools' motto 'May Eton flourish', but they are words from the students' anthem 'Gaudeamus Igitur', widespread and known in Russia. These words signify that Dzheims Kriuk was an educated man. At the same time, this song signifies a connection with the educated circles of Soviet society. Therefore, by accommodating this scene within the context of Soviet culture, Zakhoder still conveys the original meaning: Dzheims Kriuk stands high in the social hierarchy.[19]

In these examples from the novel and the play Barrie points to the importance of protecting 'the stability of British order' by conforming to customs, being conservative in behaviour and maintaining 'good form', as Rashina B. Singh notes.[20] These traits add nuances of upper-class distinctiveness to the English national character. The stability of the British order means the stability of the British Empire. Therefore, allusions to empire are linked to the portrayal of the English national character: in the original texts the character of Hook implicitly personifies the heroic and upper-class nature of the idealized British Empire. Allusions to empire are only partially conveyed in Demurova's translation, whereas Tokmakova and Zakhoder remove any hints to empire in Hook's character. Moreover, 'the dreams of empire' and 'the cult of boyhood' are coupled in Barrie's novel and play about Peter Pan, as Singh explains. She clarifies that boyhood crystallizes such masculine traits as strength, courage, prowess and 'yearning for adventure', which were supposed to be used for serving the Empire.[21]

Courage and valour, as distinct traits of the English national character placed within the context of empire, are shown in the walking the plank scene (chapter 14 'The Pirate Ship' of the novel and Act V scene 1 'The Pirate Ship' of the play). Like Hook, the Lost Boys personify the heroism of the English people who were an important part of the British Empire. In both original texts the boys are waiting to be executed by the pirates – they are about to walk the plank. Hook tells the boys that two of them could become cabin boys. The boys think of joining the pirates and ask if they would still be considered 'respectful subjects of the King', to which Hook says they would have to swear 'Down with the King!', but the boys refuse and shout 'Rule Britannia!' After that Wendy encourages them to 'die like English gentlemen' (pp. 191–2).

In translations by Demurova and Zakhoder the original heroic, imperial and patriotic nuances are transformed into a general image about the importance of being loyal to one's own homeland. Demurova said of her translation of 1968 that she had to reformulate these passages, otherwise the book's publication would have been compromised: 'With the sinister shadow of Glavlit over us, I could not help realizing that if those lines were read by the editor the book would be rejected outright.'[22] She changes 'Shall we still be respectful subjects of the King?' into 'А родиной нашей останется Англия?' [Will England still be our homeland?]; 'You would have to swear "Down with the King!"' into 'Придется вам отречься от своей родины!' [You would have to renounce your homeland!]; 'Rule Britannia!' into 'Да здравствует Англия!' [Long live England!]; and 'our sons will die like English gentlemen' into 'вы умрете, как подобает англичанам' [you will die like Englishmen] (pp. 191–2 in Barrie and p. 125 in Demurova). Consequently, Demurova self-censored the original text and considerably downplayed Barrie's original message. Zakhoder followed Demurova's steps and changed the original meaning in his translation. In his version the boys are worried if they would still be Englishmen, they refuse to curse their homeland forever and Wendy encourages the boys to die as true loyal sons of England. Moreover, there is no 'Rule Britannia' exclamation in the original play but only a note that the boys sing the National Anthem.

ДЖОН: Погоди-ка. А мы останемся англичанами?
КРЮК: Вам придется навеки проклясть родину!

ДЖОН:	(величественно) Тогда я не согласен!
МАЙКЛ:	И я не согласен!
[JOHN:	Hold on. Will we still be Englishmen?
HOOK:	You will have to curse your homeland forever!
JOHN:	(grandly). Then I don't agree!
MICHAEL:	And I don't agree!] (p. 95)
and	
ВЕНДИ:	Дорогие мальчики, я скажу вам то, что сказали бы ваши настоящие матери. Слушайте: «Мы надеемся, что наши сыновья умрут как верные сыны Англии.» [WENDY: Dear Boys, I will tell you what your real mothers would have told you. Listen: 'We hope our sons will die as true loyal sons of England.'] (p. 96)

Unlike Demurova and Zakhoder, Tokmakova removed all nuances and provided only a simplified version of the original message. In her story Wendy's words go as follows: 'Если нашим детям суждено умереть, пусть они умрут мужественно и гордо' [If our children were fated to die, let them die courageously and proudly] (p. 152). So, Tokmakova omitted the original passage in which the boys refuse to betray their King and shout 'Rule Britannia'. Therefore, she prevented her readers from perceiving the full image of empire as an ideological association of Englishness. Although she retained Wendy's words, in her version Wendy does not appeal to the boys' sense of Englishness but instead gives them a general encouragement – to die as brave and proud boys.

Tokmakova's translation has not been revised since its first edition and is still published with cuts. As mentioned above, Demurova brought out her full uncut translation in 1987. Her translation was published by the Pravda publishing house in a volume of translated English fantasy stories and fairy tales that was not primarily aimed at child readers. In the same year, the same publishing house reprinted Tokmakova's translation. Between 1981 and 2017 there has been a notably larger amount of reprints of Tokmakova's translations compared to Demurova's translations. Zakhoder's translation was reissued in 1992 only and remained unchanged. Thus, readers' perception of the image of Englishness depends on which translated version they choose. From Tokmakova's translation of the novel especially, and Zakhoder's translation of the play to a lesser extent, Russian readers would not understand that Hook belonged to high society, that it was important for him to be perceived as a member of the gentry and that the actions of Hook and the boys are linked to the context of the British Empire. Consequently, essential elements of Englishness – the themes of class society and empire – are lost in two translations produced during the Soviet period due to the influence of current state ideology and censorship.

5

Translating Rudyard Kipling's duology about Puck: Empire, historical past and landscape

This chapter focuses on the translation of themes of empire, historical past and rural idyll as ideological and cultural associations of Englishness in Rudyard Kipling's *Puck of Pook's Hill* (1906) and *Rewards and Fairies* (1910).[1] It demonstrates that images of empire and historical past were manipulated in an ideological context in the Soviet translation and that images of rural idyll were reimagined and partially Russified in both Soviet and post-Soviet translations. Particular attention is paid to the Soviet period, looking at how the translator as self-censor and the editor as a censor interfered with the final version of the translated text, thus modifying the representations of Englishness. Kipling's England (empire and historical past) was not fully represented in the Soviet translation due to such ideological factors as censorship, including self-censorship, and Soviet publishing policy, as well as the translator's own perception of Russian and English cultures in the core text and paratext, which resulted in a modified image of Englishness. Hence, numerous omissions were necessary to ensure the book's approval for publication. In contrast to the Soviet translation, post-Soviet retranslations did not have significant modifications and consequently did not change the image of empire and historical past initially portrayed in the original texts. Moreover, the chapter shows that images of English landscape are accommodated within the Russian cultural and literary context – they undergo creative transformations in Soviet and post-Soviet versions with translators adding allusions to Russian literature and culture (and state ideology is not involved in the representation of these images).

Kipling's patriotic discourse and his emphasis on the importance of historical continuity as valuable examples to follow were equally important for Soviet and post-Soviet translations and consequently contributed to the publication and reception of Kipling's fantasy stories about Puck in Soviet and post-Soviet Russia. Therefore, it is useful to trace the history of both original books in Russia to understand why it took so long during the Soviet period to select them for translation.

Kipling's poetry and prose first appeared in translation in Russia in the 1890s. Although at that time the imperialist nature of his writings was emphasized by Russian critics, nevertheless, his work was praised for its literary originality and creativity. Attitudes to Kipling in the Soviet Union were also ambivalent. On the one hand, there were negative views of the imperialist and racist position. As the Soviet literary critic Evgenii Brandis emphasized, Kipling had conservative views and promoted the ethos of British imperialism.[2] Although the tsarist empire was dismantled, Kipling, as a poet of empire, was not consigned to oblivion by the October Revolution of 1917. His poetry and prose (although not everything, only what suited Soviet ideology) had been translated in the Soviet Union, on the premise that his work contained universal human values such as 'duty and selfless dedication to a noble cause', praise for technology and progress, and the use of ordinary people as main characters, as Katharine Hodgson explains.[3]

Kipling was presented to Soviet readers selectively. Those books and poems which manifested his strong conservative and imperialist views were not translated. However, translations of his works written for children and adults before 1902, such as Indian novels, *The Jungle Book*, *Just So Stories* and popular poems, were reprinted and retranslated during Soviet times. After 1991 interest in Kipling's works was revived in Russia and many of them were republished or newly translated. Kipling's two volumes of fantasy stories about Puck – *Puck of Pook's Hill* and *Rewards and Fairies* – were first translated in 1916. However, they were forgotten for most of the Soviet period and only retranslated closer to the end of the Communist era. A substantial explanation of this fact can be found in a Soviet publication of the late 1950s – in an article written by T. Motyleva. She referred to both books about Puck calling them 'two volumes of historical legends'. In her view, medieval England was shown conventionally in the context of decorative heroism. Motyleva added that Kipling idealized the British monarchy and, according to him, this idealization should strengthen young people's allegiance to the throne, belief in the divine role of England to conquer and rule other parts of the world. Motyleva concluded that both volumes of Kipling's stories about Puck were artificial, sentimental and boring.[4]

The first Soviet abridged version of Kipling's *Puck of Pook's Hill* and *Rewards and Fairies*, translated by Aleksei Slobozhan, was published in 1984 and then revised in 1992. Slobozhan researched Kipling's poetry and found that his stories about Puck had not been translated in the Soviet Union, notwithstanding the popularity of Kipling among Soviet readers. While preparing a translation proposal for the publishing house he emphasized that Kipling's stories about Puck taught readers love of a native land and appreciation of its past, something which would resonate with Soviet readers. He knew that *Puck of Pook's Hill* was translated in 1916 by Anna Enkvist and that this translation was not republished during the Soviet period.[5] As the pre-revolutionary editions were hardly circulated in the Soviet Union, it is safe to conclude that Slobozhan discovered Kipling's stories about Puck and made them available, though in abridged form, for Soviet readers. However, in order to introduce the books to a Soviet audience, Slobozhan had to make sacrifices in the form of alterations. The reason for doing this was based on textual conflicts arising from censorship, Soviet publishing policy and the translator's and his editor's perceptions of England and the Soviet Union. The translator had to find a balance between wanting to translate Kipling's books and finding a way to have them published.

Slobozhan's translation was titled *Mech Vilanda: Skazki Staroi Anglii* [Weland's Sword: Tales of Old England]. Both original books were combined into one with only a selection of chapters presented in the Russian translation: four out of the original ten in *Puck of Pook's Hill* and three translated chapters out of the original eleven in *Rewards and Fairies*. According to Slobozhan, the reason for omitting chapters was based on the publishing house policy: the size of the collection of stories was limited. He was free to choose the chapters for his translation and the censor was not involved in the selection process. As Kipling's stories describe the history of England and, in Slobozhan's opinion, Russian readers would not know much about the past of England, he chose chapters about events with which Russian readers would be familiar. These chapters were divided into three logical groups: stories about fairies (*Weland's Sword*, '*Dymchurch Flit*' and *Cold Iron*); stories about the Roman invasion of Britain (*A Centurion of the Thirtieth*, *On the Great Wall* and *The Winged Hats*); and stories about universal themes such as ancient people (*The Knife and the Naked Chalk*), as well as astrology and plague (*A Doctor of Medicine*).[6]

In a letter to the editor of the *Kipling Journal* in 1989, Slobozhan alluded that the publisher (as part of the literary translation process) acted as a censor. He said that '[u]nfortunately, in some cases, while translating the stories, I had to make a kind of adaptation because the publishers had their own ideas about children's literature, and I was forced to yield to compromises'.[7] According to Slobozhan, changes to the translated text were made by the editor who decided to exclude references to supernatural forces. The editor also omitted frequent references to god and empire. In the editor's view, empire alluded to the Soviet Union and was seen as a possible implicit criticism of the Soviet Union being a continuation of the Russian Empire, so the Roman chapters were also considerably reduced, compared to the original.[8] These are the three areas, affected by censorship, in which political and ideological associations of Englishness manifest themselves through the themes of empire and the historical past.

Empire and historical past

The stories included in both books deal with the survival of the past into the present. In these stories two children – Dan and Una, who live in Sussex, – meet with Puck on Midsummer Eve and Midsummer Day. Puck, an English mythological fairy or Robin Goodfellow in *A Midsummer Night's Dream*, is referred to as Faun or Pan. Puck explains that he is the last of the People of the Hills, who started as gods before descending into this world. He leads both children in a series of extraordinary historical adventures set during the flint and iron ages, the time when Britain was governed by the Roman Empire, at the time of invasions of Britain by the Saxons, the Vikings and the Normans, as well as during the reign of kings Henry VII, Henry VIII and Charles I, Queen Mary I, Queen Elizabeth I and the Napoleonic Wars.

In both books, Kipling creates his own version of the myth of Englishness as 'Merry England' through the idealization of England's historical past and by populating his stories with fictitious characters. In the novel *Puck of Pook's Hill* in the first chapter 'Weland's Sword' Kipling focuses on the exclusiveness of Englishness, saying that the ancient gods left the English land because 'they could not get on with the English for one reason or another' (p. 14). As Sarah Wintle points out, in the last chapter 'The Treasure and the Law' of *Puck of Pook's Hill* he extends the notion of Englishness and modifies its exclusiveness 'by making a Jew instrumental in the formulation of Magna Carta'. Moreover, by telling the story of how the Magna Carta was signed, Kipling proposes that England will become 'a promised land of freedom for everybody'.[9] Hence, this chapter is a celebration of English liberty. In *Rewards and Fairies* the imaginative portrait of historical Englishness includes many references to the theme of Christianity, as well as leadership and the heroic English character.

Kipling's line of narrative about the English past given in *Puck of Pook's Hill* is lost in Slobozhan's translation. By omitting the Norman stories, the chapter 'Hal o' the Draft' and especially the culminating chapter 'The Treasure and the Law', it offered a distorted original message about the transformation of historical Englishness from exclusiveness to racial mixing. At the same time, by not translating all the chapters of *Rewards and Fairies* and omitting frequent references to Christianity, Slobozhan did not reproduce the completeness of the historical portrait of England.

However, despite the fact that Slobozhan's 1984 version of the original was abridged, the general idea of Kipling's patriotic discourse was preserved in his translation. In a letter about *Puck of Pook's Hill* addressed to Edward Bok, the editor of the American magazine *Ladies' Home Journal*, in which several stories from this book were published in 1906, Kipling stated that history rightly understood meant 'love of one's fellow men and the lands one lives in'.[10] In the preface to his 1984 translation, Slobozhan stressed the significance of devotion to the native land and veneration of its past. He also accentuated the importance of the connection between English national character and the past of England, the importance of the continuity of generations in English culture, the allusions linking the original texts to other literary sources, as well as the heroism and self-sacrifice of the English.[11] Thus, overall, Slobozhan succeeded in recreating Kipling's general theme of the English national past and patriotism.

As an important part of the idealized historical narrative of 'Merry England', Kipling tells imaginary stories of Old England when fairies and gods populated the land. Hence, in the chapters 'Dymchurch Flit', 'Cold Iron', 'A Doctor of Medicine' and 'The Knife and the Naked Chalk' the theme of the historical past is interwoven with elements of the fantastic, folklore and mysticism. Slobozhan kept the chapters 'Cold Iron', 'The Knife and the Naked Chalk' and 'A Doctor of Medicine' in his translation which was published in 1984. However, the chapter 'Dymchurch Flit' was removed from the draft by the editor, according to Slobozhan. The reason for doing that was straightforward. As a tale about fairies – 'people of the hills' – who left England forever, which was set around the time of the Dissolution of the Monasteries in the sixteenth century during the rule of Henry VIII, this chapter had too many references to mysticism. This put it clearly against the Soviet atheist ideology in relation to children's literature. In the chapter 'A Doctor of Medicine' Nicholas Culpeper explains how he stopped the plague in a Sussex village by using astrology to wipe out the rats. There is only one omission in this chapter, referring to the theme of religion. However, a considerable difference between the Soviet translation and the subsequent retranslation can be found in the translator's commentary, in which Slobozhan states that Kipling mocks astrology and explains to his readers that it is a false teaching which misleads people.[12]

Empire is another major theme that refers to political and ideological associations of Englishness. It manifests itself in the three chapters about the

Roman invasion of Britain in *Puck of Pook's Hill*: 'A Centurion of the Thirtieth', 'On the Great Wall' and 'The Winged Hats'. These chapters are a story about a Roman legionary named Parnesius, who was born into a family of assimilated Romans and lived in the later days of Roman Britain during the fourth century. It was a time when the borders of the empire were threatened by the intrusion of barbarians and when internal political rivalry destabilized the country. Parnesius is stationed on Hadrian's Wall on the northern border of the empire and witnesses the fall of the general Magnus Maximus, the commander of Britain. In Kipling's portrayal in these chapters, a strong empire meant good local administration and respect for the traditions of other peoples who lived in the empire, as well as the idea that constant struggles for power could threaten stability.

According to Slobozhan, the Soviet editor imposed quite a lot of omissions, because there were allusions to the Soviet Union regarding power and empire.[13] Kipling depicted the fragility of the formerly powerful Roman Empire and hinted at possible consequences for ambitious emperors who forget about their people. Therefore, in a way, allusions to the fragility of empire could have prompted the editor to suspect an implicit reference to the Soviet Union which could have been considered a prediction of possible doom. Allusions of this kind were most probably not permitted, especially in children's literature. Moreover, the editor's excessive caution can be explained by the existing allegorical similarity in late Soviet poetry between the ideologies of the Roman Empire and the Soviet Union, as, for example, can be seen in the poems of Joseph Brodsky.[14] The metaphorical depiction of empire frequently emerged in Brodsky's verse and his portrayal of ancient Rome evoked the stagnation of the empire, which, as Emily Lygo notes, 'recalls specifically the USSR under Brezhnev'.[15] Although the Soviet Union never officially referred to itself as an imperial power (the concept of empire in Soviet understanding was applicable only to the capitalist West), implicit references to the Soviet state as an empire emerged in Soviet society in the 1970s and the 1980s. As Petr Vail' and Aleksandr Genis argue, by the end of the 1960s the change in political ideologies (from communism to friendship of the peoples) revived responses to the idea of empire in Soviet culture, which were expressed in withdrawing oneself from the life of the destructive empire in order to survive.[16] Considering the circumstances, in which ideological demands played a significant role, and with ideas circulating among the Soviet intelligentsia that empire had a destructive force (in reference to the Soviet Union), it is possible that the Soviet censor/editor might have become sensitive to literary allusions connected with this imperial theme.

As a consequence of the editor's intervention in the final translated text, the theme of empire became less vivid in Slobozhan's translation and consequently lost its original message. In the following examples, by employing the theme of empire, Kipling accentuates the particular traits of English national character – liberal-mindedness and respect for the traditions of other peoples. However, the Soviet translation represents Kipling's view of Englishness rather differently: Kipling's Englishness becomes manipulated due to the influence of Soviet political ideology.

In the chapter 'A Centurion of the Thirtieth' Kipling gives a description of Bath (Aquae Sulis) as a cosmopolitan place in Roman Britain. Parnesius, who is the protagonist in this story, says that Bath is a city where

> you meet fortune-tellers, and goldsmiths, and merchants, and philosophers, and feather-sellers, and ultra-Roman Britons, and ultra-British Romans, and tame tribesmen pretending to be civilised, and Jew lecturers, and – oh, everybody interesting. (p. 87)

This example refers to Kipling's admiration of the British Empire as a place that attracted diversity and solidarity. In this context Kipling's views on the theme of empire strengthen Englishness and develop its concept further in the book. In Kipling's idealistic view, Englishness encompasses respect for personal liberties, tolerance and traditions of newcomers. However, '[U]ltra-Roman Britons, and ultra-British Romans' and 'Jew lecturers' are omitted in Slobozhan's 1984 translation. It is possible that the Soviet editor noticed allusions to nationalism and a likely connection to anti-Semitic attitudes in the late Soviet Union. One would not expect that these two issues would be mentioned in Soviet children's literature. Therefore, the symbolic allusion to empire as a constructive element of Englishness is lost in Slobozhan's 1984 translation and the influence of ideological conventions is clear.

In the next example, also taken from the chapter 'A Centurion of the Thirtieth', Parnesius and his father are talking about the later years of the Roman Empire in the fourth century, when it was divided into two halves – the eastern and the western. Parnesius's father ponders over the reason why it happened and Parnesius comments on his father's thoughts: 'and to listen to him you would have thought Eternal Rome herself was on the edge of destruction, just because a few people had become a little large-minded' (pp. 89–90). On the one hand, it might seem that the presence of liberal-minded people could lead to the fall of the empire. However, Kipling implies that 'large-minded' people could become an asset to empire, and it is that feature of the English national character that makes it so distinctive. In Slobozhan's translation only the first part of this extract (about the fall of the empire) is retained and the reason that might lead to the fall of the empire is omitted: 'Тут он стал вспоминать события минувших веков, и по его словам выходило, что Вечный Рим находится на грани падения' [Then he started recollecting the events of the bygone centuries, and by listening to his words one would have thought that Eternal Rome was on the edge of falling] (p. 69). Most probably, the Soviet editor drew parallels with the Soviet Union and assumed that the allusion was too clear: the presence of liberal-minded people might lead to the destruction of the Soviet empire. Again, as in the previous example, Kipling's view of Englishness is lost in the Soviet translation.

In a final example, in the chapter 'On the Great Wall', Parnesius draws caricatures of the life of the general Magnus Maximus's soldiers stationed on Hadrian's Wall. Maximus dislikes the caricatures and says that people used to be punished for laughing at soldiers of the Roman Empire:

> 'Not long since', he [Maximus] went on, 'men's names were sent up to Caesar for smaller jokes than this.' . . .
>
> 'I was speaking of time past', said Maximus, never fluttering an eyelid. 'Nowadays one is only too pleased to find boys who can think for themselves and their friends'. (pp. 106–7)

In this extract Kipling draws attention to freedom of speech, which is another feature in his version of English national character. This extract is also removed from Slobozhan's translation so that Soviet and modern Russian readers would not be exposed to the portrayal of Parnesius as a brave and 'large-minded' ancestor of the future heroes of the British Empire idealized by Kipling. Once again, it is possible that the Soviet editor was wary of the evident allusion to the suppressed freedom of speech and the powerful Caesar-like leader in the Soviet Union, which resulted in this censored alteration in Slobozhan's translation.

Slobozhan's 1984 translation was reviewed in the journal *Detskaia literatura* in 1986. The reviewer said that the stories about Puck familiarized Soviet readers with the complex history of England and let them understand how English national character was formed.[17] It follows from my analysis that a full portrait of Kipling's idealized England is not reflected in Slobozhan's translation due to such ideological factors as censorship and the Soviet publishing policy. However, the numerous omissions were necessary to ensure the book's approval for publication, as Slobozhan emphasized.[18] At the same time, it is necessary to note that the translator's presence is apparent in the translated text – it is expressed through self-censorship and the translator's own perception of Russian and

English cultures in the core text and paratext, which resulted in the modified image of Englishness.

Slobozhan edited his translation for the version published in 1992. This time it was called *Skazki Paka* [Fairy tales of Puck], and all the cuts, changes and substitutions that occurred in the Soviet translation were restored in the new edition. The 1992 version contained edited chapters from the 1984 translation, newly translated poems and the '*Dymchurch Flit*' chapter. Although the new edition was still a shortened version of the original two volumes, the meaning of Kipling's idealized Englishness was restored. However, for a full acquaintance with the original texts and the full picture of England, Russian readers would have to refer to the two retranslations which were both first published in 1996 by Grigorii Kruzhkov (*Pak s volshebnykh kholmov* [Puck of the magic hills] and *Podarki fei* [Presents from fairies]) and by Irina Gurova (*Pak s kholmov* [Puck of the hills] and *Nagrady i fei* [Rewards and fairies]), or to the translation of *Puck of Pook's Hill* by Anna Enkvist (*Staraia Angliia* [Old England]) which first appeared in 1916 in pre-revolutionary Russia and was republished after 1991.[19] Translations of Enkvist, Krizhkov and Gurova did not have significant modifications and consequently did not change the nature of the themes of empire and historical past as political and ideological associations of Englishness initially portrayed in the original texts.

The theme of empire was expanded in the illustrations included in the Soviet edition (Slobozhan's translation with illustrations by Alexander and Valery Traugots) and the post-Soviet publication (translation by Kruzhkov with illustrations by Sergei Liubaev) by bringing to life the time period and distant cultural setting in the three chapters that tell the story of the Roman invasion of Britain. Kipling's characterization of the Roman legionaries as brave citizens of a strong empire is retained in illustrations as much as possible. The visual in the translated stories adds to the storytelling by presenting extra details about the Roman legionaries, thus considerably expanding the theme of empire in Slobozhan's translation and supporting it in Kruzhkov's translation. Portraits of characters are drawn by both illustrators in the style of profiles engraved on Roman coins. These types of profiles, easily recognizable to readers, are likely to create associations with the Roman period in English history. Both illustrators depict legionaries wearing full armour, helmets and sandals, carrying shields, swords and javelins. An important detail in both illustrations is the eagle standard of a Roman legion, symbolizing imperial rule.

Both illustrators immerse readers in the world of the brave Roman warriors – ancestors of courageous Englishmen – created by Kipling. Alexander and

Valery Traugots do it through the use of expressive black contour lines, grey and terracotta colours, valiant-looking en face and profile images of two legionaries in the foreground (see the picture drawn by Traugots of the legionaries in chapter 'Krylatye shlemy' in Rudyard Kipling, *Mech Vilanda:Skazki staroi Anglii* [Leningrad: Detskaia literatura, 1984] on page 77). Sergei Liubaev uses a black and white palette showing the fearless figures of a cohort of legionaries (as shown in Figure 4). Both illustrators help readers to imagine character types of the bygone era, thus transposing them from the everyday world into the realm of imaginary England. The symbolic visual depiction of the Roman Empire also acts for readers as the image of the other. In this case, both illustrations complement the translated text by creating an effect of foreign presence, reminding readers that they are dealing with translation of a story written about a different culture and people. These attributes make both illustrations interesting and add more meaning to the representation of empire as an ideological association of Englishness. The edition translated by Gurova used the original illustrations created by Harold Robert Millar in 1911. The picture 'Hail, Cæsar!' interpreting one of the scenes in the Roman chapters (Figure 5) has all the details described above. Traugot, Liubaev and Millar interpret Kipling's story in a similar way, thus shaping readers' knowledge about the origins of the British Empire. The only difference is the time period in which all three pictures were created. Millar's drawing exists within the world of Edwardian fantasy, whereas the visual language in both Russian illustrations is modern, thereby Traugot and Liubaev create a contemporary visual metaphor of imperial England.

Both before and after the 1917 Revolution, the ideological and cultural context in Russia made it possible for Kipling's works to appear in translation. His patriotic discourse and his emphasis on the importance of historical continuity as valuable examples to follow are equally important for Soviet and post-Soviet translations. As mentioned earlier, Slobozhan's Soviet translation implicitly appeals to Russian national identity. The post-Soviet retranslations by Kruzhkov and Gurova were first published at a time when Russia was actively searching for a new national idea to unite the nation. In the 2010s, when these retranslations were reprinted, patriotic discourse was no less important, with the political rhetoric in Russia emphasizing the notion of national identity and a sense of national pride. Ideas of empire are also applicable to the translations in both periods. Although the theme of empire in connection with the Soviet Union was problematic for Soviet publications, it seems that from the 1990s the theme of empire as part of Englishness might have contributed to the promotion of a new Russianness. As Rosalind Marsh emphasizes, by the late 1990s the search for a

Figure 4 The Roman legionaries. Illustration by Sergei Liubaev in Rudyard Kipling, *Pak s Volshebnykh Kholmov*, translated by G. Kruzhkov and M. Boroditskaia (Moscow: RIPOL klassik, 2011), p. 180. Illustration copyright © 1996 Sergei Liubaev. Used with permission.

new Russianness and 'the propagation of patriotic values had now entered the mainstream of Russian culture and political thinking'.[20] From the general point of view, the post-Soviet translations can be seen as supporting Russia's modern imperial rhetoric in the context of the idealization of a strong empire. Hence, to some degree, Englishness and Russianness, as concepts, both contributed to the

Figure 5 'Hail, Cæsar!' Illustration by Harold Robert Millar in Rudyard Kipling, *Puck of Pook's Hill* (London: Macmillan and Co., Limited, 1911), p. 200. Public domain.

publication and popularity of Kipling's fantasy stories about Puck in Soviet and post-Soviet Russia.

English landscape

In contrast to the themes of empire and historical past, state ideology did not form part of the representation of English landscape in Kipling's duology about

Puck, which has a strong sense of 'Merry England'. Both books are set in the South and North of England. The real geographical names of locations were retained in most of the cases in all Russian translations. Moreover, Grigorii Kruzhkov and Aleksei Slobozhan visited England and saw the places that Kipling used as settings for both books. Still, Kipling's duology about Puck are fantasy stories and the author created his own idealized portrayal of the English landscape. In general, the overall image of the countryside was conveyed in all the Russian translations. However, there were nuances added by the translators and these alterations are most pronounced in the following three examples.

First, in both books Puck is presented as the oldest thing in England, a spirit of the wilderness. In the late Victorian and Edwardian children's literature the role of this spirit was given to Pan who, as an ancient Greek pagan god from Arcadia, symbolized a literary Pagan god and acted as a personification of the English countryside.[21] Puck tells the children about the connection between England's landscape and history and teaches them to love their land. All four translators retain the detailed depiction of Puck as an English fairy in their texts, and also keep the literary references connected with this character. Moreover, Slobozhan tells his readers about Puck in the foreword to the translated text (p. 8), whereas Kruzhkov explains who Puck is in the endnotes to the translated text, which is an illustrated commentary (p. 323). When Puck is referred to as Faun or Pan (chapters: 'A Centurion of the Thirtieth' and 'On the Great Wall') Slobozhan (p. 281) and Kruzhkov (p. 346) explain in the translator's commentary that he is a woodland deity in Roman and Greek mythology; Anna Enkvist and Irina Gurova provide no explanation.

However, in the original and translated texts Puck represents different mythological universes of Russian and English cultures. In both Kipling's books the two main characters Dan and Una meet Puck on Midsummer Eve and Midsummer Day. At the beginning of *Puck of Pook's Hill* Puck says:

> Then what on Human Earth made you act *Midsummer Night's Dream* three times over, *on* Midsummer Eve, in the middle of a Ring, and *under* – right under one of my oldest hills in Old England? (p. 8)

Enkvist finds a neutral way of rendering 'Midsummer Eve': 'накануне дня в середине лета' [on the eve of the day in the middle of summer] (p. 170). Slobozhan translates it in his text as: 'именно в иванов день' [right on St. John's day] (p. 21) and adds a translator's commentary in the endnotes to the book explaining that St. John's day is a summer solstice ancient celebration when the so-called magical powers are especially strong (p. 275). Kruzhkov renders

'Midsummer Eve' as 'в канун колдовской Купальской ночи' [on the eve of the magic Kupala night] (p. 25) and adds an explanation earlier in the text saying that it is the night when all the miracles happen in Shakespeare's play *A Midsummer Night's Dream* (p. 23). Gurova translates it as 'в канун Ивановой ночи' [on the eve of St. John's night] (p. 396). In *Rewards and Fairies* Slobozhan, Gurova and Kruzhkov translate 'Midsummer Day' as 'Иванов день' [St. John's day].

Hence, Slobozhan, Kruzhkov and Gurova create a specific allusion to Russian culture – the celebration of Ivan Kupala. The motif of the Kupala or Ivanov (St. John's) night as a Slavic pagan celebration was used by the Russian writers Konstantin Paustovskii, Nikolai Gogol, Ivan Bunin and the Russian poet Sergei Esenin. It also brings to mind evocations of the Kupala celebrations (dances and songs) in the drama *Finist – Iasnyi Sokol* (Finist, the Bright Falcon) written by Nikolai Shestakov, based on the Russian folk tale of the same name. It was made into a popular children's fantasy film first shown in 1975. The Ivan Kupala celebration is related to the summer solstice and St. John's day and involves Slavic Pagan rituals connected with water, bonfires and different magic herbs (including fern, which is supposed to flower during that night and make any wish come true).

Thus, in this example, the Russian translators successfully create the image of Puck associated with the spirit of the wilderness and retain the historical context of the Arcadian image of this character as a distinctive feature of Edwardian literature. At the same time, regardless of whether the translated text was produced during the late Soviet or the post-Soviet period, the translators Russify the representation of Puck by adding their perceptions of Russian culture. As a result, this points to a reimagined vision of the English landscape in Russian translations.

In the second example, in *Puck of Pook's Hill*'s chapter 'On the Great Wall', which takes readers to fourth-century Britain and talks about the defence of Hadrian's Wall against the Picts, the main characters talk about the Roman soldiers burning the heather that the Picts grow. Allo, the Pict, says: 'How can we make our holy heather-wine, if you burn our bee-pasture?' (p. 108). Kruzhkov translates 'holy heather-wine', which is closely connected with the image of the landscape from the original text, as 'священное вересковое пиво' [holy heather ale] (p. 198), Enkvist – as 'святое вересковое вино' [holy heather wine] (p. 255), Gurova – as 'священное вересковое вино' [holy heather wine] (p. 500). Slobozhan conveys the heather wine as 'чудесный напиток, вересковый мёд' [wonderful drink, heather mead] (p. 182) and creates a literary allusion to the Soviet translation of R. L. Stevenson's poem *Heather Ale: A Galloway Legend* (1890) produced by

Samuil Marshak in 1941. It is notable that through this intertextual link readers are referred to another classic work of British literature, well known to child and adult readers, in which the translator recreates the image of the Scottish landscape and the courageous character of the Picts. Therefore, the stereotyped vision of British culture based on translated literature (that heather mead used to be a popular drink in the North of Britain) might have influenced Slobozhan's decision to refer to the existing literary image of 'heather wine'.

The third example is the Russian portrayal of Hobden the Hedger and Tom Shoesmith (Hobden's dead friend whose identity Puck uses to conceal himself) representing countryfolk and appearing in the most folkloric chapter 'Dymchurch Flit'. The images of both men are integrated into the English landscape and, in the case of this particular chapter, into the eerie landscape of Romney Marsh in the south-east of England. Kipling uses dialect to demonstrate the connection of Ralph Hobden and Tom Shoesmith to rural England and to show the class distinction between countryfolk and the children of the gentry – Dan and Una. Tom Shoesmith tells a tale about fairies, or Pharisees in the Sussex dialect, who flitted out of England in the 1530s – at the time of the Dissolution of the Monasteries. According to the folk tale, the fairies' departure was prompted by the great suffering they experienced through religious conflicts. Feeling discontent, they crowded on Romney Marsh ready to be carried over the sea to France in a boat by the Widow Whitgift's two sons, who were blind and dumb and were chosen so they could not tell about what they had seen.

Translation of dialect is a problematic issue for translators, especially when the cultures of the original and translated texts are rather distant from each other, as in the case with Russia and England. V. S. Vinogradov, a Russian scholar of literary translation, argues that regional variations of two different languages will never be equivalent. Therefore, content losses can be compensated for in two ways: by using a vernacular language of the receiving culture, which can be considered a substitution of the original dialect, or by using the standard literary language of the receiving culture and explaining the context. As Vinogradov suggests, in both cases translators should aim not to Russify their translations too much.[22] In the Russian versions translators used both strategies: the English regional dialect is either represented via the use of Russian vernacular language or standard literary language. Hence, partial Russification or generalization is inevitable in translation of English dialect into Russian. Consequently, the representation of class issues as part of the image of countryfolk is toned down towards partial Russification.

For example, vernacular words and phrases as markers of the southeastern English dialect that Kipling uses in the conversation between Hobden and Tom Shoesmith as well as in Tom Shoesmith's narrative include the following: *I belieft 'em, ain't, 'tween, an' a deal o' conjurin', d'ye do, fancy-talkin', 'thout it dyin', dunno, no more'n you, the sort o' man I be, do ye, won'erful, nigromancin'*. Russian translators did not always offer corresponding equivalents in Russian vernacular for all of these. On the one hand, they followed the strategy of choosing the standard literary language for the translation of the Sussex dialect. At the same time, as a compensation strategy Enkvist, Slobozhan, Gurova and Kruzhkov used Russian colloquial words and phrases in other parts in this chapter, where they sounded more logically appropriate: запамятовал [slipped my mind], наверняка [happen], не зналась [didn't know him from Adam], эт-точно [bang on], надули [made a monkey of], неужто [straight up?], ну-ну [blimey], долгонько [long], всегошеньки [at all], аж [even], коли вам невдомек [little ye know], иль [or], башка [noggin], не худо [not bad], помирать [to kick the bucket], из каковских я буду [the sort o' man I be], тамошний народ [that lot], то-то и оно [spot on].

This dual strategy applied to translation of dialect is clearly seen in the following example. While talking about his wife with Tom Shoesmith, Hobden says: 'Twas a passel o' no-sense talk . . . about Pharisees' (p. 150).

Slobozhan and Enkvist preferred the standard literary language: 'Она все повторяла набор каких-то бессмысленных фраз о . . . феечках' [She kept repeating some meaningless phrases about . . . little fairies] (Slobozhan, p. 106) and 'Ее занимали нелепости; она говорила . . . о фаризиях' [Absurdities occupied her mind; she was talking about farizies] (Enkvist, p. 294). Whereas Kruzhkov and Gurova favoured the Russian vernacular words 'околесица', 'толковать', 'несусветица' in 'Она порой заводила всякую околесицу . . . толковала об эльфантах' [Sometimes she was talking a load of tosh . . . talking about elves] (Kruzhkov, p. 275) and 'Несусветица всякая . . . про фейков' [Some sort of gibberish . . . about fairies] (Gurova, p. 544). As for fairies, all four translators also create a new word based on the root or meaning of fairies/elves to imitate the Sussex dialect word 'Pharisees' for fairies.

The nuances, discussed above, added by the Russian translators to their representations of English landscape act as evidence of the reimagined portrayal of England. This happens through recreating a broader image of Englishness that often becomes partially Russified. The adapted version of Kipling's good old England evokes images of Russianness in the readers' mind. When Russian translators Russify their translated texts, they bring Englishness closer to Russianness. As a result of this, the borders between Russian and English cultures become less obvious, which can be regarded as a gain, or a positive effect, in translation. On the one hand, child readers are not alienated from the foreign text they are reading, and on the other hand, they are made aware of the existence of a different culture, which England is for them.

6

A. A. Milne through Soviet eyes: Translating silliness and traditions

This chapter examines how Englishness is translated in A. A. Milne's poems *The King's Breakfast* from the collection *When We Were Very Young* (1924) and *King Hilary and the Beggarman* from the collection *Now We Are Six* (1927), focusing on the discourse of silliness, as an expression of features of English national character, and the theme of traditions.[1] As Milne's children's books only appeared closer to the Thaw period when ideological restrictions on published children's literature became more relaxed, the analysis starts by looking at who played an important role in introducing the books to Russian readers. Afterwards, the discussion moves to Soviet translations of both poems and demonstrates that, although the atmosphere of playful silliness is recreated in the translation of *The King's Breakfast* and *King Hilary and the Beggarman*, still there are added ideological nuances that modify the original image of Englishness. In doing this, the translators follow the prevailing Soviet ideology that was expressed in negative stereotypes of the capitalist West, thus making both poems ideologically appropriate for Soviet readers.

Although widely known in Russia as the author of the stories about *Winnie-the-Pooh*, Milne's other two famous works – books of poetry for children *When We Were Very Young* (1924) and *Now We Are Six* (1927) – were not fully translated until the post-Soviet period. However, several poems from both books appeared during Soviet times. Milne's poetry was introduced to Soviet children by Samuil Marshak who translated several poems included in Milne's volumes *When We Were Very Young* and *Now We Are Six*. There is good reason for this: English nonsense literature was rated highly by Marshak. In his article 'Skazka krylataia i beskrylaia' [Imaginative and unimaginative fairy tales] Marshak characterized Milne's poems and stories as 'fantastical fairy tales'.[2] He also mentioned Milne in his letter to Eduard Gol'derness, a Russian poet and translator, saying 'I very much love the merry children's poetry of England. I think Milne . . . was the last person who represented it.'[3]

The poem *The King's Breakfast*, from the volume *When We Were Very Young*, considered in this analysis, was first translated in 1946. It was published in a volume of Marshak's selected translations which was not aimed at children.[4] The translation was entitled *Ballada o korolevskom buterbrode* [Ballad about the king's bread and butter]. Afterwards, in 1965, the poem was included in a book called *Korolevskii buterbrod* [The king's bread and butter] and comprised seven poems from A. A. Milne's book *When We Were Very Young*. That was the time when Soviet children first saw it. The other poem to be analysed in this section – *King Hilary and the Beggarman* from the volume *Now We Are Six* – was translated by the Russian poet and translator Nonna Slepakova. It first appeared in the children's magazine *Kostior* in 1968 and later in 1987 was included in the translation of *Now We Are Six* called *Ia byl odnazhdy v dome* [Once I was in the house].

On the book jacket of *Korolevskii buterbrod* readers were told that Marshak had produced a free translation preserving the distinctive intonations and rhythms of the original poems. These intonations and rhythms (e.g. using repetitions, matching sound with rhythm, creating puns and imitating physical movements with the pattern of the verse) are an important part of the discourse of silliness that is a characteristic feature of all the original poems in both Milne's books. The other significant part of the discourse of silliness is hilarious nonsense, the use of humour, distorted representations and playful mockery. *The King's Breakfast* contains all these important features. According to Patricia Parker, Milne creates an image of 'a most unkinglike king' in this poem that inspires nothing but charm.[5] Milne transforms the King into a humorous figure with whom children can identify: the King does not want to 'settle for marmalade instead of butter just to make things easier for everyone else' and thinks that 'his day is ruined', as Anita Wilson and Humphrey Carpenter say in their analysis of this poem.[6]

On the one hand, Marshak recreates the atmosphere of silliness in his translation, but at the same time, he adds Soviet ideological nuances. Marshak's translation of *The King's Breakfast* is an illustrative example of how ideology relates to the construction of the image of Englishness in the Soviet cultural environment. Marshak, as a translator, is ambivalent. He is interested in England and he also follows the prevailing Soviet ideology that was expressed in negative stereotypes of the capitalist West.

Considering the position of Marshak in the Soviet literary establishment, it is possible that changes were dictated by the spirit of the time. Being an active advocate of Socialist Realism, Marshak reflected the general ideological demands of the time in his popular poems for children. He praised Soviet patriotism and feats of heroism, satirized the petty bourgeois, adding his share to the collective creation of a negative image of the Western capitalist world. Two of the poems *Mister Tvister* (1933) and *Kto on?* [Who is he?] (1938) exemplify his response to the contemporary ideology. In these poems Marshak used the stereotypical image of a rich American thinking in terms of the capitalist world and contrasted this image to the just world of the socialist Soviet Union.

Taking into account Marshak's quote mentioned in Chapter 2 in this book – that good translators must reflect the current era in their translations – the following two examples, referring to Marshak's 1920s versions of English nonsense poetry, provide a bigger picture of the translation process of which Marshak was an integral part. In these examples the textual and the visual narratives come into play together. Moreover, the visual elements extend the translated words, not only imitating the aura of playful silliness of both poems but also ensuring that the storyline as a whole is fit within the boundaries of ideological correctness. Edward Lear's poem *The Table and the Chair*, retold by Marshak, was published in 1924 by the Leningrad private publishing house Brokgaus and Efron. The well-known Russian/Soviet painter Boris Kustodiev was commissioned to create the visual image of Lear's poem. It is a lively and abundantly illustrated book, thanks to Kustodiev, who, as a member of the pre-revolutionary Mir Iskusstva [World of Art] circle, created his drawings in the grotesque and playful manner recreating the nonsensical spirit of the original. As Marshak's retelling was considerably Russified, so the illustrator managed to achieve the same effect: Kustodiev used different character types and details of everyday life peculiar to pre-revolutionary Russia. However, a prominent feature alluding to Soviet Russia after the Civil War (which ended in 1922) was embodied in one of his drawings. As Figure 6 demonstrates, the central part of the illustration is taken by the table and the chair running away from the crowd led by a Red Army soldier brandishing a sabre. It was exactly as Marshak urged: the necessity to respond to the ideological demands of contemporary times.

The 1927 publication of Marshak's free adaptation of the English nursery rhyme *The Three Jovial Huntsmen* with illustrations by Randolph Caldecott was not devoid of ideological influences either. Called *Tri zverolova* [Three hunters], the book was published by the state publishing house Gosizdat and illustrated by the awarded Russian/Soviet illustrator Vladimir Konashevich.

Figure 6 The adventures of the Table and the Chair. Illustration by Boris Kustodiev. The title page in Samuil Marshak, *Prikliucheniia stola i stula. Nebylitsa po Edvardu Liru* [The adventures of the Table and the Chair. A tale based on Edward Lear's poem] (Leningrad: Brokgaus and Efron, 1924). Cotsen Children's Library, Department of Rare Books and Special Collections, Princeton University Library. Public Domain.

Being a member of the Mir iskusstva movement, he foregrounded salient decorative and theatrical features in his illustrations. His visual interpretation intensified the playful and ironic tone of Marshak's words in this nursery rhyme. At the same time, the illustrator offered a new interpretation of the poem, replacing the original fox huntsmen with an African, an English and

Figure 7 Three hunters. Illustration by Vladimir Konashevich in Samuil Marshak, *Tri zverolova* [Three hunters] (Leningrad: Gosizdat, 1927), p. 1. Cotsen Children's Library, Department of Rare Books and Special Collections, Princeton University Library. Illustration copyright © 1927 Vladimir Konashevich, heirs. Used with permission.

a Russian hunter. The stereotyped image of these three hunters becomes an independent element of the visual narrative, as shown in Figure 7, fulfilling an ideological function of children's literature. The Englishman is drawn as an eccentric explorer wearing a pith helmet and smoking a pipe. The allusion in the portrayal of the English hunter to the British imperialist past can also be considered as topical, taking into account the stormy political relations throughout the 1920s between Britain and the Soviet Union based on mutual distrust and heated disagreement.

At the same time this stereotyped image can be considered as a visual element that strengthens the absurdist nature of the original text and its translation. As Marshak faithfully transferred the nonsense effect of the original poem to his translation, so did Konashevich in his illustration. He visually mirrored Marshak's poetic nonsensical message: co-existence of the three absolutely different figures that would have nothing in common in terms of common sense proves the absurd nature of this scene. Interestingly, the author of a satirical article published in Literaturnaia gazeta at that time misunderstood this visual stunt: he criticized Marshak's poetry and accused Konashevich of conveying an idea of 'anti-internationalism and imperialism' in his illustrations to *Tri zverolova*.[7]

Marshak's literary work reflected ideological and cultural changes in Soviet society. Parallels between the historical context and the shifting nature of Marshak's literary activity are drawn by Ben Hellman:

> In the twenties Marshak was part of the avant-garde culture; in the thirties, as Socialist Realism became the literary norm, his poems about the transformation of the country and feats of heroism played an active part in pushing children's literature in a new direction. After World War II, Soviet patriotism with all its insignia dominated his works, leading to the author's crowning as poet laureate.[8]

Marshak held an influential position in the field of Soviet children's literature – from 1924 until 1938 he headed the Leningrad branch of the state publishing house for children's literature (Izdatel'stvo detskoi literatury – Detizdat). The Leningrad branch of Detizdat was dismantled in 1937. The children's writers working for it, who were Marshak's colleagues (the Marshak group), were arrested and some of them executed.[9]

The destruction of Detizdat was initiated by its political editor and censor D.I. Chevychelov who informed against the Marshak group accusing them of being traitors, regardless of the fact that Marshak was considered an authority in the children's literature world. In the report dated 9 October 1935 he wrote about the 'abnormal state of affairs' in Detizdat, blaming several female writers for being 'our hidden enemies'.[10] In the second report dated 2 November 1937 he openly acted against Marshak by urging to 'finally unmask the sabotage publishing activity of Marshak's group and Marshak himself' and to 'free the publishing house of all alien and suspicious people and to eliminate effects of the sabotage activity as soon as possible', stressing that under Marshak's guidance, the Leningrad branch of Detizdat 'eradicated political-educational Bolshevik content'. By sabotage activity in the field of children's literature he meant not publishing enough books that were focused on Soviet and current political themes, introducing new children's writers who were 'alien and hostile' to the Soviet people (e.g. N. Oleinikov), who wrote anti-revolutionary works (e.g. Belykh and Panteleev), and advocating the restoration of the monarchy (e.g. Vvedensky and Kharms).[11]

Chevychelov's report achieved its goal: Marshak ceased to be the editor in the Leningrad branch of Detizdat and moved to Moscow in 1938. (Later, in 1941, Chevychelov became the director of the Leningrad branch of Detizdat and stayed in this post until 1959.) Marshak evaded purges aimed at him and his literary circle. There is no clear recorded evidence as to exactly how he managed to survive. According to his grandson, Alexandr Marshak, children's literature saved Marshak from the political purge. By 1937 he was already a widely popular children's author with his name known to basically every Soviet family. So it would not have been easy for the authorities to find justification for accusing him of anti-Soviet activities and arresting him. Moreover, Stalin liked Marshak and rated him as a good children's writer. He personally crossed out Marshak's name from the list of people to be executed.[12] Lydia Chukovskaya claims that there was 'no order from above' to crush Marshak in 1937 and further turbulent years.[13] Instead of being arrested, in 1939 Marshak was awarded with a state reward – the Order of Lenin. So, throughout the 1930s Marshak became 'a responsible and reliable Soviet writer', whose writing was 'ideologically charged', as Hellman observes.[14] This explains the prolific volume of poetic works, translations and literary criticism he created, which went in line with Soviet ideology. He, of all people, knew the rules under which Soviet society operated. There was a forced necessity to keep in step with the times, as superior officials gave orders to publish ideologically correct books.[15]

In the translation of *The King's Breakfast,* Marshak created an image of a good-hearted eccentric king, but at the same time he pointed to typical characteristics of monarchs, according to Soviet ideology, such as tyranny and foolishness. Considering that Marshak was an advocate of the principles of ideological responsibility that were paramount for Soviet translators, his move to make the end of the poem ideologically appropriate in his translation is understandable. It is not the whole poem that underwent changes, only a few nuances. However, these translated nuances modify the theme of silliness.

The King wants to have some butter for his 'Royal slice of bread', but upon hearing that it would be better to use marmalade instead, he sobs and whimpers:

'Nobody,'
He whimpered,
'Could call me
A fussy man;
I only want
A little bit
Of butter for
My bread!' (p. 58)

Afterwards, when the Queen brings butter to him, the King becomes hilariously happy – he bounces out of bed and slides down the banisters – and exclaims:

Nobody,
My darling,
Could call me
A fussy man –
BUT
I do like a little bit of butter for my bread! (p. 59)

The King in Milne says that he is not 'a fussy man'. The word 'fussy' reflects the playful mockery that is part of the discourse of silliness in the original text. In both examples in Marshak's translation this feature is modified. In the original poem, the King whimpers and refuses to be called 'fussy', whereas in the translated text he sighs and does not want to be called 'capricious':

– Еще никто, –
Сказал он, –
Никто меня на свете
Не называл капризным…
Просил я только масла
На завтрак мне подать!
['Yet no one,' he said, 'No one has ever called me capricious …. I only asked to be served butter for breakfast!'] (p. 4)

As follows from the examples from the original and the translated texts, Milne's King insists on the particular way he wanted his bread-and-butter, whereas Marshak's King is guided by a whim (he suddenly changes his mind and behaviour about what he orders, something that Marshak emphasizes) which points to a slight negative connotation in presenting the King's image. At the end of the original poem, the King again insists that he cannot be called a 'fussy man'. However, in Marshak's translation the King says 'тиран и сумасброд' [a tyrant and a madman/unbalanced person]:

Никто не скажет, будто я
Тиран и сумасброд,
За то, что к чаю я люблю
Хороший бутерброд.
['…No one will say that I am a tyrant and a madman because I like to have a good bread and butter with my tea.'] (p. 7)

In this case, by turning the King into 'a tyrant and a madman', the discourse of silliness transmits political ideology, reflecting the spirit of the time. It could be considered a minor detail that readers might not even notice but it refers to a certain ideological concept that would most probably be useful to add to ensure the book was published. The addition might seem a trivial detail at the end of the poem, but still it transmits the message that the image of the King can be linked to the stereotypical image of tyrannical Western monarchs.

The state ideology of the Soviet Union is apparent from a review of Marshak's translation published in 1966 in the journal *Detskaia Literatura*. The reviewer, Iurii Koval', concluded that kings were never kind, they sat on thrones, hoarded gold, tormented their subjects and brandished their swords; nobody liked them because they were tyrants and despots. Koval' goes on to say that there was a king who did not want to be called a tyrant, that all he wanted was bread and butter. He called him a nice king and reminded the reader of another merry King Cole, saying that both characters were given a Russian voice by the same translator – Samuil Marshak.[16] This review is important in order to understand why Marshak added ideological connotations to the King's image. Moreover, the Russian translation scholar Efim Etkind mentioned Marshak's translation in his critical essay 'Dlia malen'kikh chitatelei' [For small readers]. He stressed that the original discourse of silliness was preserved in Marshak's translation. Etkind emphasized that Marshak added an important nuance, which consisted of mocking a lazy king, who did nothing, and contrasting the king to the useful cow, who produced the butter that was, eventually, served up to the King.[17]

Hence, there are two ways of looking at Marshak's King: either he is lazy, as Etkind describes him, or he is a nice king who does not want to be called a tyrant, a king who could be associated with the image of 'Merry England'. It depends on the reader how this image is perceived. At the same time, it might be equally suggested that Marshak added 'a tyrant and a madman' to fit with the rhythm of the verse. Illustrations in the book *Korolevskii buterbrod* (1965) do not reflect the implicit political discourse and only convey connotations of silliness used by Milne to create the King's image.

The visual narrative of the Soviet illustration shows the King happily sliding down the banister of a grand staircase, wearing his crown and clutching a mace and sceptre (see the picture drawn by Evgenii Meshkov of the King in Samuil Marshak, *Korolevskii buterbrod* [Moscow: Detskaia Literatura, 1965] on page 7). This reflects the story told by means of the original E. H. Shepard's drawing, which presents the King dancing merrily (Figure 8). The playful silliness of both the King and the whole poem is emphasized in the Soviet drawing. It is through the use of this and other illustrations in the translated book that the representation of the tyrant king is toned down. So, one cannot

Figure 8 The King's Breakfast. Illustration by Ernest Howard Shepard to *The King's Breakfast* in A. A. Milne, *When We Were Very Young* (London: Egmont, 2016), p. 59. Line illustrations by E. H. Shepard © The Shepard Trust. Colouring of the illustrations by Ernest H. Shepard and Mark Burgess © 1989 Egmont UK Limited and ©The Shepard Trust. Reproduced with permission from Curtis Brown Group Ltd on behalf of The Shepard Trust. The illustration provided by Egmont UK Ltd and printed with permission.

but ask how this seemingly lively king could ever fume over being called a tyrant.

However, if Marshak's King is perceived as a lazy monarch, then it is safe to assume that the addition of the words 'a tyrant and a madman' met the demands of current political ideology. His translation demonstrates his view that the current epoch should be reflected in translation and that Soviet translators were expected to bear ideological responsibility. Hence, it was inevitable that there would be elements of Soviet ideology in Marshak's translation, particularly considering his poem *Mister Twister* and his views on translation. Nevertheless, it does not diminish the place of Marshak's version of *The King's Breakfast* in Russian culture. His version has been popular since its appearance and subsequently republished in various editions while Milne's original poem has never been retranslated.[18]

It is noteworthy that Marshak's translations of the English folk ballad *King John and the Bishop* (the final version was published between 1936 and 1940)[19] and *The King's Breakfast* (the translated text was first published in 1946) appeared within a decade and carried a similar implicit message about stereotypical tyrant kings who lived in the Western world. Marshak's decision to add nuances to the image of his King is not coincidental: his portrayal of the King as a tyrant and a madman/unbalanced man reflects the existence of such an image in Soviet children's literature, theatre and cinema.

An illustrative example of a Soviet translation which fits into the ideologically interpreted representation of English tyrant kings and enslaved but clever common people is Geoffrey Trease's play for children *The Dragon Who Was Different* (1938).[20] This play was translated by Natalia Konchalovskaia in 1939 under the title *Drakon, kotoryi ne pokhozh na drugikh* [The dragon who was not like the others] and was allowed to be performed in Soviet children's theatre groups. L. Dirik, a political editor/censor from Glavrepertkom (the state department controlling both theatrical repertoire and performances), issued a report that authorized the performance of the play. This report particularly stressed that the play told the story of a greedy tyrant king who fooled his people and of a small poor boy whose courage and determination helped his fellow oppressed subjects to overthrow the monarch.[21] A decade later, an image of the foolish king Topsed (reverse of Despot [despot]) was coined in Vitalii Gubarev's fantasy novel *Korolevstvo krivykh zerkal* [The kingdom of crooked mirrors] – a dystopian Soviet fairy tale hinting at the negative essence of the capitalist world. The novel was published in 1951, turned into a play in 1952 and then adapted into a very popular fairy-tale film under the same name in 1963. The film *Korolevstvo krivykh zerkal* was directed by Aleksandr Rou and produced at Gorky Film Studio.[22]

The portrayal of the King as a tyrant was further developed in the Soviet animated film *Korolevskii buterbrod* [The king's bread-and-butter], based on Marshak's translation. It was directed by Andrei Khrzhanovskii and released by Soiuzmul'tfil'm in 1985. In this version the silliness of the original poem was turned into an ideological parody: the 'fussy' king was presented as a tyrant and the royal household was shown as foolish. To achieve this result, the director applied elements of grotesque and irrationality in his retelling of Milne's poem, such as the King jogging and skateboarding around his kingdom, an army of sleuths following him around, courtiers pandering to the King's every whim and medals being awarded to those who brought him butter. The animated film demonstrates how a playful poem for children was turned into an ideological parody aimed at a dual audience (adults and children). This parody can even be read through the lens of early 1980s Soviet society. In a way, the playful effect of the original poem was retained; however, the original features of silliness were transformed into the subversive narrative, alluding to the pompous and preposterous nature of the stagnant Soviet establishment.

Milne's poem *King Hilary and the Beggarman,* from *Now We Are Six,* is another illustrative example of how minor ideological nuances were introduced and how the original impression of Englishness was altered in the Soviet translation. Playful silliness is expressed in the poem's narrative: King Hilary, just like a small child, excitedly anticipates the various Christmas gifts that might appear at his door and dismisses his arrogant Lord Chancellor who refuses to do what the King wants. Hence, Milne calls him 'Proud Lord Willoughby, Lord High Chancellor' (p. 70). In the translated poem under the title *Korol' i brodiaga* [The king and the vagrant], the Lord Chancellor was described as a proud Lord Chancellor Antony Chvansler (p. 44). The translator Nonna Slepakova used play on words to emphasize the arrogance of the Lord High Chancellor: the Russian adjective 'чванливый' [conceited] was transformed into an English-sounding surname 'Chvansler' alluding to vanity and snobbishness.

Moreover, the illustration to the 1968 publication, when the translation first appeared in the Soviet children's magazine *Kostior,* had recognizable tropes characteristic of Soviet rhetoric – a smart and daring pauper versus a foolish rich man (as can be seen on the picture of the King, Lord Chvansler and the Vagrant drawn by Kira Savkevich in Nonna Slepakova, *Korol' i brodiaga,* in the children's magazine *Kostior,* December 1968, on page 45). In this case, the illustrator not only recreated the end scene from the textual narrative but also created a new value by means of the modified visual narrative. In the original poem Milne gives the central role to the King who suggests to the Beggarman that he throws out the Lord Chancellor and takes his place instead. The Soviet illustration has the Beggarman (the Vagrant in Slepakova's translation), facing the reader, positioned next to the throne and confidently kicking the Lord Chancellor. The King is drawn with his back to the reader and the dynamic action in this scene is shifted to the Beggarman. The publication of the original poem does not have a drawing illustrating this particular final scene. However, E. H. Shepard depicts a conversation between the King and Lord Chancellor in which the powerful Lord Chancellor visually dominates the timid King (Figure 9).

Milne's poem has a Christmassy spirit and can also be seen as an example of the theme of English traditions. Milne starts the poem by saying 'Of Hilary the Great and Good they tell a tale at Christmas time' (p. 70) and focuses the attention of his readers on a Christmas stocking, which is to be filled with presents, as is traditional in English Christmas celebrations. In the 1968 translation, Nonna Slepakova omitted any reference to the Christmas theme. She substituted the

Figure 9 The King and the Lord Chancellor. Illustration by Ernest Howard Shepard to *King Hilary and the Beggarman* in A. A. Milne, *Now We Are Six* (London: Egmont, 2016), p. 71. Line illustrations by E. H. Shepard © The Shepard Trust. Colouring of the illustrations by Ernest H. Shepard and Mark Burgess © 1989 Egmont UK Limited and ©The Shepard Trust. Reproduced with permission from Curtis Brown Group Ltd on behalf of The Shepard Trust. The illustration provided by Egmont UK Ltd and printed with permission.

first two lines of the original poem with a neutral version just saying that the story being presented to her readers had been told repeatedly (p. 44). Also she recreated the recurring Milne's line 'to put in my stocking' referring to various gifts brought by visitors to the King (p. 70) into a new version – her King wants various gifts to be put at his royal feet (pp. 44–5).

The omission of references to Christmas celebrations in the 1968 translation is not surprising. It was standard practice in Soviet censorship not to allow religious themes in children's literature. Hence, in Slepakova's 1968 translation readers would not be able to understand why the king was so anxious to see who was waiting at the door and why he expected presents. The original theme of Christmas tradition is lost and the new Soviet version instead conveys a new meaning – a king who just wants presents without the explanatory nuances that specifically connect this poem to Christmas. Slepakova's 1968 version was included in the book *Ia byl odnazhdy v dome* [Once I was in the house], which was published in 1987, and the changes referring to the theme of Christmas were retained. *King Hilary and the Beggarman* was retranslated in 1992 by Nina Voronel' and the original spirit of Christmas was returned in the new post-Soviet version.[23]

7

Framing P. L. Travers's *Mary Poppins* in ideological and cultural contexts: Translating features of English national character

This chapter considers the translation of features of English national character which include the discourses of silliness and the fantastic and the trope of the English governess, as represented in P. L. Travers's books about Mary Poppins: *Mary Poppins* (1934), *Mary Poppins Comes Back* (1935) and *Mary Poppins Opens the Door* (1943).[1] The discussion starts with the history of the original texts in Russia to see why it took so long for them to be selected for translation during the Soviet period. An understanding of the historical and political context enables a deeper analysis of the representations of Englishness, asking why they were treated ideologically in Soviet translations and whether subsequent changes in the translations and retranslations followed after the fall of the Soviet Union. Afterwards I analyse how ideological nuances were introduced by the Soviet translator and demonstrate that the fantastic content in *Mary Poppins* is treated ideologically. The supernatural elements of the original text are toned down and more attention is devoted to character-building and didactic function in the translated text. When cultural and historical contexts are taken into account, it is to be accepted that certain culture-specific elements would be treated ideologically in the Soviet translation. The Soviet translation had to respond to external circumstances (determined by cultural and political changes) so that it could be published.

If, in the examples referring to the discourse of the fantastic, features of English national character are treated ideologically in the Soviet translation, then representations of the discourse of silliness and elements in the image of Mary Poppins as the English governess tend towards Russification in both Soviet and post-Soviet translations. The Soviet translation strategy was influenced by the necessity for the translated text to sound as if it was originally written in

Russian and to recreate a similar aesthetic and emotional effect by sacrificing faithfulness to the original. Thus, accommodating the impressions created by the original work within the context of Russian children's literature meant that the original text would inevitably be Russified. In comparison to the Soviet translation, the post-Soviet translations offer stories about Mary Poppins that are closer to the original texts. The image of the post-Soviet Mary Poppins was not changed through ideology, although it was also partially Russified.

Soviet readers were first introduced to the *Mary Poppins* books in 1968. The Soviet version was called *Meri Poppins* [Mary Poppins] and consisted of two parts (*House № 17* and *Mary Poppins Comes Back*) with a mention on the title page that the translation was abridged.[2] Boris Zakhoder, the first translator of the *Mary Poppins* books, did not have the originals and had to borrow them from the library. He mentioned in his letter to Pamela Travers in 1969 that, strange as it may seem, he did not own any of her books and that he had used library copies in order to produce his translation.[3] P. L. Travers sent all her *Mary Poppins* books to Boris Zakhoder by the end of 1969 (the first four books of the series), as he mentioned in his reply to her.[4] This correspondence points to my supposition that the original books were not freely accessible to the general public and might have been on a censor's list as titles not allowed for circulation. The reason why Mary Poppins was not translated into Russian for so long was perhaps revealed by Travers herself when she suggested in an interview given to *The New Yorker* in 1962 that the Soviet authorities might consider Mary Poppins 'a bourgeois institution':

> My great hope is to have her translated into Russian . . . . I know we don't have any copyright agreement with Russia, but I say to my agent, 'Never mind. Leave her around where the Russians can steal her.' We haven't left her around enough yet. I suppose the authorities would take her *au pied de la lettre* – they'd say a nursemaid was a bourgeois institution – but the children would understand her.[5]

A narrow circle of people might have known about the existence of Mary Poppins as a literary character after the Disney film *Mary Poppins* was shown at the Fourth Moscow International Film Festival in July 1965. The title of the book and the name of the author appeared in the opening credits and an attentive viewer could have spotted that the movie was based on the books about Mary Poppins. Although the Disney film was screened as an out-of-competition film, it was a hit with the festival audience.[6] However, it was not shown in Soviet cinemas afterwards. In the 1980s people could find it only on pirated videotapes and only after the demise of the Soviet Union did the Disney *Mary Poppins* become available to the general public.

Another reason for failing to introduce books about Mary Poppins to Soviet readers might be explained by Travers's negative views about the Soviet Union. In 1932 Travers went to the Soviet Union to see Leningrad and Moscow and published a book about her journey in 1934 (before she wrote *Mary Poppins*), which was called *Moscow Excursion*.[7] This book was immediately reviewed in the *New York Times* and called 'impertinent and gay'; it was mentioned that Travers found the way the Soviet Union presented itself appalling and that the Soviets would probably denounce her as a 'class enemy'.[8] Travers depicted the Soviet Union as a depressing society and noted '[t]he drabness, the universal grey, the complete sameness of the people'.[9] According to Sheila Fitzpatrick, Travers toured the Soviet Union to understand its politics but had little sympathy beforehand or on her return to England.[10] Travers's lack of sympathy towards Soviet society is explicitly demonstrated in the book's introduction: 'In a world rocking madly between Fascism and Communism the writer prefers the latter form of tyranny if the choice must be made.'[11] As discussed in Chapter 3 of this book, the 1930s saw severe restrictions on the circulation of foreign literature in the Soviet Union. Censorship control was strengthened amid fears of intervention by international capitalism in the USSR; and foreign mass media, as well as literature were considered a great force for the promotion of ill feeling towards the Soviet Union.[12] This is the most logical explanation why the foreign publication of Travers's *Moscow Excursion* might have affected the possibility of her *Mary Poppins* books being translated in the Soviet Union.

According to the correspondence between Travers and Zakhoder, it was the famous Soviet children's poet Sergey Mikhalkov who met Travers in Switzerland at the end of the 1960s and told her that her books had been translated into Russian.[13] The Soviet *Mary Poppins* immediately became very popular among Soviet adult and child readers, as Zakhoder's letters to Travers show. Zakhoder wrote in his letter to Travers in 1969 that the print-run of ten thousand copies was instantly sold out in Moscow and that there were favourable reviews, including one in the literary journal *Novyi mir*.[14] In the 1970s the translation was adapted for a radio show and for the stage, the script of which was also written by Zakhoder. Moreover, updated versions of the play have been performed in theatres around the country since 1991. In 1983 Mary Poppins appeared on Soviet TV screens in the film *Meri Poppins, do svidania*. It immediately became a hit and has been very popular since its first broadcast. At the same time, Mary Poppins was turned into a household name in modern Russia – babysitter agencies, cafés, family fun centres and even a fashion label are all called after the famous nanny.

Zakhoder regretted in his letter to Travers that his translation was abridged – fifteen chapters only from the first, the second and the third books – and mentioned that he was not able to obtain the fourth book.[15] In the preface to the first edition Zakhoder promised Soviet children that they would meet with Mary Poppins again and that the story would be continued. Unfortunately, he did not keep his promise and the omitted chapters have never been recovered in the subsequent reprints of Zakhoder's translation.[16] Although two retranslations appeared in the 1990s (by Marina Litvinova and Igor Rodin), Zakhoder's translation is considered a canonical text in Russian culture and is well positioned in the Russian children's literature market.[17]

In a letter to Travers in July 1969 the director of the Detskaia Literatura publishing house K. Piskunov explained why the Russian translation was abridged (quoted from the Russian original and its English translation, which was enclosed with the official letter sent to P. L. Travers):

> Сокращение отдельных глав было обусловлено не только трудностями их перевода, но и большим желанием издать одновременно обе части, а детям младшего возраста, на кого рассчитана эта книга, мы избегаем давать книги большого объема.
>
> [Abridgement of separate chapters was necessary partly owing to difficulties of translating and the desire to publish both parts at the same time and because for the younger children for whom this book is intended we do not like and avoid giving bulky books.][18]

He also said that it was uncertain whether B. Zakhoder would continue the translation of the next books about Mary Poppins and whether Detskaia Literatura would be able to revise the current translation. This letter points to the prevailing ideological conventions in Soviet literature written for children. At the same time, it signals the presence of censorship, although this matter is not clearly expressed in the correspondence. It is possible that self-censorship and editorial decisions could have somehow influenced Zakhoder's opinion, to a certain extent, on how to construct the image of the English nanny in a way that Soviet child and adult readers of the late 1960s would accept, understand and like; and why certain chapters should not be included into his version, thus modifying the original structure of Travers's books and the hidden message contained in them.

The first three books, *Mary Poppins* (1934), *Mary Poppins Comes Back* (1935) and *Mary Poppins Opens the Door* (1943), have elements of myth and are structured as myth – the interconnected chapters are repeated and everything returns, but in a modified manner.[19] In Zakhoder's translation the books' original structure is modified, thereby distorting Travers's intention to create the books in the form of myth. Travers was not happy about the new structure of the stories in Zakhoder's translation and pointed out in a letter to Zakhoder that 'the books are written in a definite rhythm and the stories should be read in their proper sequence'. She also added that she had 'always thought that Russian readers would like it as they have a great sense of humour and poetry', as she discovered when she went to Russia in the 1930s.[20] Unfortunately, the Soviet readers who could not obtain the original texts (as well as the Russian readers nowadays who prefer Zakhoder's translation) were not aware of the original narrative and Travers's intention to create the original in the mythic form.

Zakhoder omitted one of every pair of repetitive chapters. It is difficult to know whether there was too much of the untranslatable in these chapters from the point of view of Zakhoder and the editor of Detskaia literatura publishing house, or whether there were ideological reasons for the omissions. In the first book, *Mary Poppins,* Zakhoder excluded the chapters 'The Day Out', 'Bad Tuesday', 'The Bird Woman' and 'Christmas Shopping'. It is possible that the chapters 'The Day Out' and 'Christmas Shopping' were omitted because they contain lengthy descriptions of Mary Poppins's clothes and of what the characters bought as their Christmas presents in, as Travers says, 'the Largest Shop in the World' (p. 151). Also the chapter 'Christmas Shopping' refers to Christmas as a religious celebration. From the point of view of Soviet ideology, both chapters might have looked like propaganda for religion and consumerism in the West, which might have been thought unsuitable for Soviet children.

The chapter 'Day Out' might have been left out because it echoed the chapter 'Bad Wednesday' from the second book that was translated. Both chapters show a slipping from reality into an imaginary world through a portal to the unreal: in the first book Mary Poppins goes into the coloured-chalk picture drawn on the pavement by her friend Bert the Match-man and goes on an outing with him; in the second book Jane finds herself in the past inside the antique Royal Doulton bowl after she accidentally cracks it. It is difficult to guess why the chapter 'The Bird Woman' was excluded because it does not contain any lexical difficulties for translation, nor does it have any ideologically sensitive allusions to religion, mysticism or the bourgeois style of life. The chapter 'Bad Tuesday' corresponds to the chapter 'Bad Wednesday' from the second book. Also the chapter 'Bad Tuesday' contained stereotyped representations of Africans, Chinese, Eskimos and American Indians, which was considered inoffensive when the book was first published (but accusations of racism appeared later, in the 1970s, and Travers was forced to replace the stereotyped ethnic characters, which caused offence in the United States, with exotic animals in the revised 1981 edition). It is highly likely that the Soviet censor would never allow a book with racial content for publication. Most probably these were the reasons for omitting the chapter 'Bad Tuesday'.

In the second book, *Mary Poppins Comes Back*, Zakhoder left out the chapters 'Topsy-Turvy', 'The New One', 'Robertson Ay's Story', 'The Evening Out' and 'Nellie-Rubina'. The chapters 'Topsy-Turvy' and 'Laughing Gas' (included in the first book) have the same pattern – the children and Mary Poppins go to see her relatives; therefore, the appearance of another surreal adventure might have been the reason for omitting the chapter 'Topsy-Turvy' from the translation. However, by neglecting this chapter the translator denied his readers the opportunity to find out that the Royal Doulton bowl (which got broken in the translated chapter 'Bad Wednesday') was mended by Mary Poppins's cousin Mr Turvy. The other chapters from the second book not included in Zakhoder's translation might not have been thought suitable for Soviet children because of their allusions to religion, existential and spiritual ideas widely incorporated by Travers throughout the whole series of books. (Travers was interested in fairy tales, mythological literature, mysticism and spiritualism.)[21] The chapter 'Nellie-Rubina' might have been left out because it alludes to Noah's Ark as a Biblical topos or because it echoes the chapter 'Mrs Cory' included in the translation. The chapter 'The New One' repeats the translated chapter 'The Twins' from the first book, but it also has the newborn Annabel saying that she came from 'the Dark where all things have their beginning': 'I am earth and air and fire and water . . . I come from the sea and its tides . . . It was a long journey' (p. 105). The chapter 'The Evening Out' has a similar pattern to the translated chapter 'Full Moon' from the first book but at the same time it questions the nature of existence and contemplates the universe in a spiritual way. Finally, in the chapter 'Robertson Ay's Story' the silly king is mocked by all his subjects but his jester, the Dirty Rascal, teaches him to be true to himself and do what he wants. This chapter might have been deemed unsuitable because of its individualistic approach to life but it is also safe to say that Zakhoder might have decided to substitute this chapter with the translated chapter 'The Cat That Looked at the King' from the third book *Mary Poppins Opens the Door*.

It appears that ideological norms (in the form of self-censorship) played a partial role in the process of choosing which chapters to translate. At the same time, it is important to take into account the counterargument of Alexandra

Borisenko, who proposes that in order to avoid repetitions and to make the Russian translation a more interesting read, Zakhoder chose his favourite chapter from two repetitive ones.[22] A similar opinion is expressed by Galina Zakhoder (Zakhoder's widow):

> Pamela Travers often exploits the same [literary] devices. In one chapter [characters] are flying under the ceiling, in another chapter – they are flying in some other way. And the narration in these parts loses its pace. Boris omitted passages of such a kind. I think Travers got angry when she found out the truth. It appeared to me that she felt that Zakhoder was right, that is why she was angry.[23]

This view is feasible and can be explained by Zakhoder's possible misunderstanding of the peculiarities of the narrative structure of the *Mary Poppins* books. It also points to the presence of the translator's co-authorial voice based on his own literary preferences.

The books about Mary Poppins contain elements that refer to the discourse of the fantastic so it is useful to consider how this is defined. There are four categories of the fantastic, according to Farah Mendlesohn: 'the portal-quest, the immersive, the intrusive, and the liminal'. In the portal-quest readers are encouraged to go into the fantastic; in the intrusion fantasy the fantastic becomes part of the fictional world; in the liminal fantasy the magic is elusive; and there is no escape for readers in the immersive fantasy.[24] This classification works across children's fantasy and helps analyse its narrative. The examples of the portal and the intrusion are the most widespread categories in children's fantasy. In the former a protagonist enters a fantastic world through a portal. In the intrusion fantasy, as Mendlesohn explains, the fantastic repeatedly breaks into the real world creating horror and/or amazement.[25] These two categories can also be interconnected: the portal fantasy can use elements of the intrusion fantasy and vice versa. Both categories are illustrated by the *Mary Poppins* books: the protagonists find themselves in the fantastic world with the aid of different portals.

Travers casts Mary Poppins as the supernatural Mother Goddess, connecting her image with the discourse of the fantastic. Travers herself continually emphasized that the character of Mary Poppins was drawn from myth and fairy tale and that she was 'either the Mother Goddess or one of her creatures'.[26] In the context that is used by Travers, myth stands for a story involving supernatural elements and echoes of fantasy and fairy tales. The fantastic and daily life interact in P. L. Travers's stories about Mary Poppins. Mixing the two contrasting phenomena is an English literary tradition. This interaction is highlighted by Colin Manlove: the Mary Poppins books create a portrait of a governess to a middle-class English family and also a fairy who uses her magical powers to change the ordinary domestic lives of the children into fantastic adventures.[27] Moreover, Staffan Bergsten notes that Travers mixes obvious fact and pure fantasy, as well as punning allusions to old themes and motifs. In his words, the *Mary Poppins* books have 'features of the fantastic tale and of nonsense literature but they are also strongly rooted in an historically and sociologically identifiable reality'.[28] The character of Mary Poppins is entrusted with a dual role. As Giorgia Grilli explains, being a governess, Mary Poppins introduces the children to the world of proper behaviour and discipline, thus preparing for entry into society, instructing them on what the social group to which they belong demands from individuals. At the same time, she offers magical experiences and acts as 'provocateur', showing a path to a subversive world in which the protagonists experience extraordinary possibilities.[29]

In an interview with Richard R. Lingerman for *The New York Times* in 1966, Travers confirmed that her *Mary Poppins* books can be characterized as 'very English' and she wondered how 'so English a book could have attained world popularity'.[30] In one of the interviews with Jane L. Mickelson, given between 1985 and 1988, Pamela Travers talked about the Russian translation of *Mary Poppins* and stressed that she could not read Russian and therefore did not have 'any idea what they [the Soviet translator and the Soviet publisher, and presumably the Soviet editor/censor] have Mary Poppins saying'. She joked about the absurdity of the idea that the Soviets might have made Mary Poppins pronounce all sorts of propaganda.[31] In reality there was no propaganda in Zakhoder's rewriting of the *Mary Poppins* books. Generally, Zakhoder retained many of the fantastic elements of the originals – his Mary Poppins takes the children on amazing adventures in the world of the supernatural that exists in Mary Poppins's England. As a character, Mary Poppins represents the discourse of the fantastic, because she is the portal between the supernatural and existential knowledge and the real world. However, Zakhoder changed the nuances in Mary Poppins's representation, thus altering the discourse of the fantastic expressed in Mary Poppins's character.

The fantastic invokes, in Dorothea von Mücke's words, 'mystery, occult knowledge, or laws that encompass the supernatural'.[32] The fantastic genre provides children's writers with the opportunity 'to deal with important psychological, ethical and existential questions', as Maria Nikolajeva points out.[33] So, by using the discourse of the fantastic, Travers speaks to her readers about existential matters. In the chapter 'Full Moon' from the first book, Mary Poppins exposes the children to the supernatural when her birthday falls on the full moon and is celebrated in the zoo. Travers turns the existing world upside down: the animals are free and people are put in cages. However, the world is harmonious. The culmination of the party is the great chain which is formed by animals who dance around Mary Poppins – all together and united. Through the words of a king cobra, the Hamadryad, Travers communicates her existential ideas to the readers:

> We are all made of the same stuff, remember, we of the Jungle, you of the City. The same substance composes us – the tree overhead, the stone beneath us, the bird, the beast, the star – we are all one, all moving to the same end. Remember that when you no longer remember me, my child. (p. 147)

Zakhoder translates this passage as:

> …все – и вы в городах, и мы в джунглях – сделаны из одного и того же вещества. Из того же материала – и дерево над нами, и камень под нами; зверь, птица, звезда – все мы одно и идем к одной цели. Помни это, дитя, когда ты уже не будешь помнить обо мне.
>
> [… all of us – you of cities and we of the jungle – are made of the same stuff. Of the same substance – the tree overhead us, the stone beneath us; the beast, the bird, the star – we are all going towards one aim. Remember that, child, when you no longer remember me.] (p. 74)

Zakhoder changed the meaning of the original phrase 'we are all one, all moving to the same end' that has existential connotations. In Travers's articulation it symbolizes death and rebirth – the inevitable end of everything and subsequent reincarnation; especially taking into account the symbolic circular dance which follows the wise words of the king cobra. One would not be able to decode the original's symbolism in Zakhoder's translation. His version plays down the original and offers a general careful phrase that 'we are all going towards one aim'. Although his rendering of the dance covers all the details, it is doubtful that readers would be able to guess which 'aim' is meant in the translated book.

It is noteworthy that the chapter 'Full Moon' was retained in Zakhoder's translation, although the example mentioned above sounds too thought-provoking for Soviet children's literature. By drawing on this example, I suggest that the demands of Soviet censorship were not particularly strong in relation to translated children's literature. At the same time, I assume that the supernatural in this example was modified in Zakhoder's translation, because it sounded too idealistic and ambiguous for a book offered to Soviet children. Therefore, it was either not approved by a censor due to its idealism or was self-censored by Zakhoder. In any case, all the omitted chapters that have portrayals of the supernatural, along with the altered nuances of the supernatural in the chapter 'Full Moon', do not contribute to the creation of the overall image of Mary Poppins in translation as the fantastic Mother Goddess that opens the door to the world of the mystical England.

As Russian readers venerate canonical translations (many comments on online forums and online bookshop sites point to this) and there is a widespread opinion that canonical translations should not be challenged, most probably publishers prefer the canonical translation of *Mary Poppins* books produced by Zakhoder. This means that the distorted image of the books as a representation of the discourse of the fantastic is likely to persist. That is, unless Russian readers decide to read the books in English or choose the new translations produced in the 1990s by Marina Litvinova and Igor Rodin who retained the original mystical structure of Travers's books. Both Litvinova and Rodin preserve Travers's mystical message from the chapter 'Full Moon' of the first book about 'all moving to the same end': 'все движется к одному концу' [all is moving to one end] in Litvinova's translation (p. 137) and 'Все . . . в свой час рождается, живет и в свой час умирает' [all is born in its own time, lives and dies in its own time] paraphrased by Rodin (p. 106).

Another illustrative example of how the fantastic content is treated ideologically can be found in Zakhoder's translation of the chapter 'The Cat that Looked at a King' from the third book, *Mary Poppins Opens the Door*. In the original chapter Mary tells the children a story about a king who thought a lot and did not look after his kingdom:

> You must not think the King meant to be unkind. Indeed, it seemed to him that his subjects were luckier than most, for hadn't they a King who knew practically everything? But while he was busy gathering knowledge his people grew poorer and poorer. Houses fell into ruin and fields went untilled, because the King needed all the men to help him in his thinking. (pp. 56–7)

Zakhoder translated this passage. However, in the play and in the book he added a whole paragraph of new information which can be considered as hidden satirical allusions to the Soviet way of life.[34]

> А все женщины страшно сердились. Им казалось, что вся королевская ученость – чушь и пустяки. Ведь никакими сведениями не накормишь ребенка, рассуждали они, и тем более не заплатишь данными за квартиру!

Даже свинопасы и пастушки были недовольны и роптали. А если вы припомните, что обычно они счастливейшие люди на свете (ведь они знают, что все они – заколдованные принцы и принцессы), тогда вы поймёте, как плохо шли дела в Королевстве.

[And all women were terribly angry. It seemed to them that all the knowledge that the king had was nothing but nonsense and trifles. You see, knowledge will not feed a baby, they thought, and certainly, information will not pay for a flat! Even swineherds and shepherdesses were unhappy and quietly complained. And if you remember that they are usually the happiest people in the whole world (because they know that they are enchanted princesses and princes), then you will understand how bad things were in the kingdom.] (p. 137)[35]

By contrast, the post-Soviet translation produced by Rodin makes no alterations in the chapter 'The Cat that Looked at a King', thus preserving the original meaning of the text (pp. 491–2).

The role of Mary Poppins as the magical 'provocateur' connecting reality with the supernatural and the fantastic Mother Goddess is reduced in Zakhoder's translation by the alterations that he made. What is important is that Zakhoder puts more emphasis on the character-building and didactic role of Mary Poppins as a character, two key areas in Soviet children's literature that were seen as important factors for the socialization of Soviet children. However, it is important to note that, notwithstanding these changes, Zakhoder preserved the playful and adventurous spirit of the original books. This was emphasized in the 1969 review of *Mary Poppins,* in which Zakhoder's translation was characterized as a book 'full of captivating and marvellous adventures and wonders' addressed to those readers who never ceased to remember their childhood.[36]

The tendency towards toning down the supernatural elements and devoting more attention to the character-building and didactic function in the Soviet translation can be explained by the general ideological demands prevalent in Soviet children's literature. As discussed in Chapter 2 in this book, adherence to the principles of Socialist Realism demanded a truthful and historically accurate reflection of reality, as well as an educational and character-building role for children's literature. Another important factor in this process is highlighted by Borisenko who reminds us that 'Soviet mass culture put forward a very strong concept of a happy, sunny, carefree childhood.'[37] Such an idea of an ideal childhood seems to underlie the choices about how to translate literature for Soviet children.

My supposition about the importance of the character-building function and didacticism in Zakhoder's translation is supported by two sources relating to the play *Mary Poppins*. Based on Zakhoder's translation of *Mary Poppins* books, this play was adapted for the stage by Zakhoder together with Vadim Klimovskii. It was first performed in 1976 in the Ermolova Moscow Theatre and then aired on television in 1979. A short review of the TV play accentuates its character-building and didactic function:

> Lots of miracles happen in P. Travers' book *Mary Poppins*. This book was turned into a cheerful play with lively rhymes and songs by B. Zakhoder and V. Klimovskii. . . . The play is primarily addressed to children, and it will also spark the interest of adults because it is about the importance of being patient, considerate towards others and responsive to the needs of everyone and everything around us.[38]

Moreover, the first performance of the play was discussed at a meeting in the Ministry of Culture's department of theatre in 1976. According to the shorthand report of this meeting, the principal message of the play ties together three important concepts: kindness, joy and generosity. The play is aimed at educating children who are theatre audiences of the future. This report also states that the play emphasizes the changes in the attitudes of the children – Jane and Michael – towards their parents: At the end of the play the children no longer think that their mother is unkind. As Zakhoder pointed out during the discussion, it was important that in the finale Mary's pedagogy proved to be successful – that the children would change from being disobedient, when Mary Poppins first met them, to good, when she was leaving them.[39]

Illustrative examples of character-building and didacticism in Zakhoder's translation can be found in the fifth and the sixth acts of the play, which are based on the chapters 'The Cat that Looked at a King' from the third book and 'West Wind' from the first book. In the fifth act of the play Zakhoder adds a new conversation between Jane and Mary Poppins at the end. The original text does not have this conversation and Zakhoder's translation does not have it either. Jane tells Mary Poppins that she now knows who she is and is praised for starting to behave and think sensibly:

> ДЖЕЙН (вдруг). Мэри Поппинс! Можно, я посмотрю Вам в глаза?
> МЭРИ (наклонилась над Джейн). Что же ты там увидела?
> ДЖЕЙН. Я не сумею рассказать, Мэри Поппинс. Но, мне кажется, я теперь тоже знаю, кто я такая!
> МЭРИ (вдруг ласково положила руку на голову Джейн). Наконец-то Джейн, ты становишься большая!'

[JANE (suddenly). Mary Poppins! May I look into your eyes?
MARY (bending over Jane). What have you seen in them?
JANE. I won't be able to tell, Mary Poppins, but I think I now know who I am!
MARY (suddenly putting her hand gently on Jane's head). Finally, Jane, you are growing up!][40]

In the last chapter of the first book, 'West Wind', Mary Poppins is parting with the children:

Then she put one hand lightly on Michael's head and the other on Jane's shoulder. 'Now', she said, 'I am just going to take the shoes down for Robertson Ay to clean. Behave yourselves, please, till I come back'. (p. 167)

In the last act of the play this scene goes as follows:

МЭРИ (осмотрев комнату). Ну, так. (Кладет руку на голову Майкла, другую на плечо Джейн). А теперь я пойду отнесу туфли вниз, пусть Робертсон Эй их почистит. Ведите себя как следует до моего возвращения. Майкл! Будь хорошим мальчиком! Джейн! Позаботься о Майкле. Ты теперь большая!

[MARY (having looked around the room). Well, there. (Putting one hand on Michael's head and the other on Jane's shoulder). And now I am going to take my shoes down. Let Robertson Ay clean them. Behave yourselves properly until I come back. Michael! Be a good boy! Jane! Take care of Michael. You are a grown-up girl now!][41]

Unlike the play, Zakhoder's translation of the book does not contain the phrase about Jane who, as Mary Poppins thinks, has become a grown-up girl ('You are a grown-up girl now!') and, therefore, can take care of her brother. In the translated book Mary Poppins only says 'Ведите себя как следует до моего возвращения' [Behave yourselves properly until I come back] (p. 79). The Russian phrase 'как следует' [properly] adds an ideological and didactic nuance to the original utterance, turning the English Mary Poppins's request into the Russian Mary Poppins's instruction. Travers's Mary Poppins pronounces nearly the same words but the ideologically stressed word 'properly' does not exist in the original text. As for two other Russian translators, both Rodin and Litvinova translate this passage as 'behave yourselves well': in Rodin's version it goes as 'Ведите себя, пожалуйста, хорошо, пока я не вернусь' [Behave yourselves well, please, until I come back] (p. 120); and Litvinova interprets it as 'Ведите себя хорошо, пока меня не будет' [Behave yourselves well while I am away] (p. 157).

From the above examples it becomes obvious that in the Soviet play Mary Poppins plays a more accentuated didactic and character-building role, compared to the original and the translated book. Consequently, the image of Mary Poppins as the fantastic Mother Goddess is given an ideological interpretation in line with the Soviet tradition of educating children by means of using literature, theatre, cinema and the fine arts. In the original books the journey that Mary Poppins has prepared for the children does not just merely turn them from badly behaved children into good ones, but this journey has a more existential nature. With Mary Poppins's help, the children experience the fantastic world that exists beyond their reality, as highlighted in the third book when Mary Poppins is parting with the children for good: '"Now, be good children!" she said quietly. "And remember all I have told you"' (p. 200). She has given them new knowledge about the world around them and the one inside them. The fantastic events that happen to the children beyond their real world are psychologically fulfilling, as emphasized in Grilli's study of the *Mary Poppins* books. Mary Poppins steers the children towards mystical experiences, from which they emerge, and their understanding of themselves and of the outer world becomes much deeper and more complete.[42] It would be misleading to treat the *Mary Poppins* books as pedagogical narrative only; on the contrary, Travers's writing for children has a dual nature:

> Travers ... aims to liberate her readers from all overly strict and reductive pedagogical claims, from a very specific civilization process and its standards, and from narrow-mindedness in general. Yet at the same time, ... she believes that, in order to grow and develop as authentically as possible, certain lessons must be learned and certain rules must be respected, or at least recognized. [These lessons] are the ones of Life, rather than those of the specific society we find ourselves living in.[43]

Grilli's point supports my suggestion that in the books about Mary Poppins the supernatural aspect, which is part of the fantastic narrative, exists on equal terms with the character-building narrative. With the reduced amount of chapters, Travers's existential message, encoded for her English-speaking readers (that life could be perceived differently and not as prescribed by the society in which one lives), is unlikely to be received in its full extent in Zakhoder's translation and would not have been welcome in the Soviet Union.

If, in the examples referring to the discourse of the fantastic, features of English national character are treated ideologically in the Soviet translation, then the representation of the discourse of silliness has a different tendency in both Soviet and post-Soviet translations – it is Russified. In the following examples from the original chapter 'The Cat that Looked at a King', silliness is represented in a form of playful absurdity and through allusions to English fairy tales and nursery rhymes. In the first example, the King says to the Cat:

> My court is composed of the Very Best People. Jack-the-Giant-Killer digs my garden. My flocks are tended by no less a person than Bo-Peep. And all my pies contain Four-and-Twenty Blackbirds. (p. 59)

Here Travers resorts to wordplay on the themes of the English fairy tale *Jack the Giant Killer* and two English nursery rhymes *Little Bo Peep* and *Sing a Song of Sixpence*. By placing characters from English folklore familiar to English readers into the new fantastic environment, she creates a nonsensical effect in her text.

In Zakhoder's translation (both the play and the book) playful silliness is accommodated within the Russian cultural and literary context:

> При моем дворе одни только Сливки Общества! Джек-Потрошитель Великанов ухаживает за моим садом! Мои стада стережет не кто иной, как Мальчик-с-пальчик! И в каждом моем пироге ровнехонько Сорок семь Сорок!
>
> [Only the cream of society are at my court! Jack-the-Giants-Ripper looks after my garden! My flocks are guarded by no less a person than the Thumb-sized boy! And all my pies have exactly Forty seven magpies!] (p. 139)[44]

Zakhoder uses allusions to the English folk tale *Jack the Giant Killer*. This fairy tale was translated in 1957 as *Джек – Победитель Великанов* [Dzhek the Giant's Conqueror], so it seems that it would have been known to Soviet child readers. At the same time, Zakhoder uses a familiar fairy-tale character – 'Мальчик с пальчик' [the Thumb-sized boy] – instead of Bo Peep from the *Little Bo Peep* nursery rhyme. On the one hand, this character can be recognized as an English folklore character Tom Thumb. On the other hand, it belongs to Russian fairy tales. Moreover, Zakhoder refers to Marshak's free translation of the English nursery rhyme *Sing a Song of Sixpence*.[45] Hence, it can be assumed that in this example, Zakhoder accommodated the passage from the original text within the boundaries of Russian culture (if the Thumb-sized boy is approached as belonging to a Russian fairy tale) and, at the same time, reminded his readers of existing translations of English material.

Rodin translates this passage in the following way:

> Мой двор – это сливки общества! Сад стережет Джек-Победитель Великанов! Овец пасет никто иная как малютка Мэри. А в каждом моем пироге запечено ровно 22 вороны!

[My court has the cream of society! Jack-the-Giants-Conqueror guards my garden! My sheep are tended by no less the person than the Little Mary! And exactly twenty two crows are baked in each of my pie!] (p. 493)

As can be seen from the above translation, like Zakhoder, Rodin also refers to the Russian translation of *Jack the Giant Killer*. At the same time, Rodin introduces new literary, culture-specific material in his version: he provides his translation of *Sing a Song of Sixpence* and calls it *Королевский пирог* [the King's pie] as well as substituting *Little Bo Peep* with another popular nursery rhyme *Mary Had a Little Lamb* by translating it as *Малютка Мэри* [Little Mary] (pp. 599–600). Hence, compared to Zakhoder, Rodin stayed more in line with the original allusions and wordplay.

In the next example Travers alludes to other popular English nursery rhymes – *Hey Diddle Diddle* and *A Frog He Would A-wooing Go* – in which she again creates a playful nonsensical effect. The Cat tells the Cow that there was no point in jumping over the Moon, because there could be something else for her to do. The Cat also tells the Frog that he should have listened to his mother and not got married at all. Zakhoder chooses popular Russian nursery and counting rhymes as a replacement. The English frog from the original text that courted the mouse becomes the Russian toad that hopped accidentally into the tsar's house ('царский дом').⁴⁶ In this case, Zakhoder combines two popular Russian counting rhymes into one, and in his version the toad finds itself in the tsar's house, so that 'царь' [tsar] becomes a key word signifying Russianness. The English cow that jumped over the Moon is turned into the Russian nanny goat with big horns that wanted to butt the disobedient children. This nanny goat is a character from a well-known Russian nursery rhyme *Idiet koza rogataia* [A nanny goat with big horns is coming] widely used by Russian parents to playfully scare their disobedient children.⁴⁷

Both examples demonstrate that Zakhoder's version reflects the tendency to naturalize English culture in Russian translation. Moreover, in the case of the nanny goat, he adds a disciplinary message to his translation and straightaway questions the importance of this message by calling it 'чепуха' [nonsense]: 'И вдруг ей [козе] показалось, что действительно совершенно незачем бодать малых ребят! Впервые в жизни она поняла, что занимается просто чепухой.' [And suddenly it seemed to her [the Nanny Goat] that there was no need to butt the little children! For the first time in her life she understood that what she did was nonsense] (pp. 146–147). Here Zakhoder contradicts himself, alluding to his uncomfortable feelings towards didacticism. On the one hand, he emphasized the importance of the didactic approach when discussing the play about Mary Poppins (as shown above), and at the same time, he implied that it was pointless to use the Nanny Goat to intimidate disobedient children as there were other methods to deal with them. In contrast to Zakhoder, Rodin provides his own translations of both English nursery rhymes which stay faithful to the original text (pp. 502–3).

Although in the above examples the strategies of translation vary, in the following example Zakhoder and Rodin adhere to the same strategy – accommodation of the content to a Russian context. Both translators tone down the original text; and, consequently, the nuances that allude to the English tradition of village celebrations are lost. In the original, Travers writes:

> The King commanded his subjects … to put up Maypoles and dance around them; to get out Merry-go-rounds and ride them; to dance and feast and sing and grow fat and love one another dearly. (p. 73)

Both translators omit 'dancing around Maypoles' and substitute this tradition with 'пир на весь мир' [a feast of feasts] (in Zakhoder, p. 147) and 'большой пир' [a great feast] (in Rodin, p. 503), which evoke associations with a Russian saying 'пир на весь мир' [a feast of feasts]. This saying is very often used in Russian fairy tales as a culmination of a hero's victory over numerous hardships.

It was emphasized in the 1969 review of Zakhoder's translation that *Mary Poppins* had a deep and thought-provoking meaning in terms of the way that ordinary things and ordinary people could turn out to be miraculous. Nevertheless, the book remained an amusing and exciting fairy tale.[48] What the review does not mention is that the existential content is attenuated in Zakhoder's translation. Certainly, one possible explanation is that Zakhoder's version was abridged; therefore, the connection between the existential and the fantastic regarding features of English national character in his translation was not obvious. Reaction to the demands of the time is an important factor in understanding Zakhoder's translation choices. It was important to consider educational and character-building functions in translated books in general. Hence, taking into account the fact that Russian fairy tales are often didactic, in this case it can be suggested that Zakhoder's version is accommodated within the Soviet ideological context. As it may be supposed that Zakhoder did not support Soviet ideology enthusiastically, most probably the way he conveyed features of English national character – in the form of the discourse of the fantastic and parts of the discourse of silliness – was a necessary requirement for his translation to be published. Most probably, such a situation was voluntarily accepted by Zakhoder. Therefore, it seems that it was inevitable that certain elements pertaining to expressions of English national character were treated ideologically in the Soviet translation of stories about Mary Poppins.

Still, censorship and ideology were not the only decisive factors in Zakhoder's translation. His own authorial voice played an important role and was determined by literary norms that set up the rules of the game – how to write and translate for Soviet children. Hence, there was the necessity for the translated text to sound as if it was originally written in Russian and to recreate a similar aesthetic and emotional effect by sacrificing faithfulness to the original in transferring certain details and nuances. Thus, accommodating the impressions created by the original work within the context of Russian children's literature meant that parts of the original text would inevitably be Russified. In comparison to Zakhoder's version, the post-Soviet translations offer stories about Mary Poppins that are closer to the original text. The image of the post-Soviet Mary Poppins is not changed through ideology, although it is also partially Russified.

This strategy of partial Russification was applied by all three Russian translators to create an image of the Russian Mary Poppins as an English governess representing the idealized way of life of the middle classes. She is undoubtedly the most typical and popular governess in British children's literature. Under her supervision children are expected to acquire good manners, become well-behaved and disciplined. She is an impeccable governess whose favourite book is *Everything a Lady Should Know*. Giorgia Grilli describes Mary Poppins as someone who is 'almost always mute, breaking her silence only to issue orders, call into line or reprimand the children with all the severity normally associated with the figure of the governess'.[49] In her interview with Richard R. Lingerman for *The New York Times* in 1966, Travers admitted that the books about Mary Poppins were set in a relatively realistic depiction of the England of the 1930s.[50] The literary image of Mary Poppins in the translations of Zakhoder, Rodin and Litvinova corresponds to the one created by Travers. The Russian Mary Poppins is also elegant, she loves her image in the mirror and the description of her clothes is conveyed fully. The severity of her character in the three Russian translations accords with the portrayal drawn by Travers. The Russian Mary Poppins also grins, sniffs, frowns and seldom smiles; she is stern and sometimes arrogant but full of surprises. However, there are elements that are Russified in the image of Mary Poppins constructed in all three translations.

For example, in the chapter 'Full Moon' in the first book Michael wants to know 'what happens in the Zoo at night, when everybody's gone home'. Mary Poppins uses an English proverb for her answer: 'Care killed a cat' (p. 130).

Zakhoder and Rodin translate Mary's answer as 'много будешь знать, скоро состаришься' [if you know too much, you get old sooner] (p. 62 and p. 93, respectively). It is a well-known Russian proverb and is used for a reply when one doesn't want to answer a question, whereas Litvinova uses calque for the first example – 'забота кота убила' [care killed a cat], which does not have a similar connotation in Russian culture (p. 119). In the second example, in the chapter 'West Wind' Mary Poppins says: 'trouble trouble and it will trouble you!' (p. 167). In this example Travers plays on the meaning of the English and American proverb 'Never trouble trouble till trouble troubles you'. Zakhoder finds a Russian equivalent of this proverb and his Mary Poppins pronounces the Russian proverb instead: 'Не буди лиха, пока оно спит!' [do not wake sorrow up while it is sleeping] (p. 79). According to Slavonic myths, лихо [likho] is a one-eyed evil spirit bringing misfortune and sorrow. Similar to Zakhoder, Rodin finds another Russian proverb: 'от добра добра не ищут' [one does not expect more good deeds from something good that has already happened] (p. 120). Litvinova applies a popular Russian saying: 'не зови беду – накличешь' [do not look for more ill fortune, you might bring it] (p. 156).

In the third example, at the end of the chapter 'Full Moon' Mary Poppins says: 'Me? A quite orderly person who knows that early to bed, early to rise makes a man healthy, wealthy and wise?' (p. 150). Zakhoder translates Mary's words as: 'Я, воспитанная девица, которая знает, что полагается, а что – нет?' [Me? A well brought-up young woman who knows what is supposed to be done and what is not?] (p. 76). In this case the translator finds a neutral way to translate the English proverb. However, the word 'девица' evokes an old-fashioned image of an unmarried young Russian woman (stress on 'и') or Russian folklore expressions 'красна девица', 'девица-красавица' (stress on 'е'). In contrast to Zakhoder, Rodin renders Mary's words as 'ни одна воспитанная и уважающая себя особа не станет ...' [not a single well brought-up and self-respecting woman would not do ...] (p. 108) and Litvinova translates it as 'Я, уравновешенная, добропорядочная особа?' [Me, a good-tempered and right-minded woman?] (p. 141). Both versions recreate the lady-like arrogant behaviour, thereby reproducing the traits of Mary Poppins's character presented in the original.

If the textual representation of Mary Poppins is partially Russified, then her visual image created by Gennady Kalinovsky for the Soviet editions of Zakhoder's translation is set in a different time period. The textual content in the original text represents people and events from the England of the 1930s, as mentioned above. The illustrations created by Mary Shepard to the first edition in the early 1930s were used by Travers to emphasize this particular time. Shepard's illustrations show a nanny whose appearance was based on a little Dutch doll that Travers showed to Shepard during one of their disagreements.[51] As Travers explained, her stories about Mary Poppins were set in at a time when a middle-class family could afford a full-time nanny for their children. Hence, it is highly likely that Mary's clothes and accessories would be what a typical English nanny of that time was expected to wear: a midi length buttoned-up cut coat with a belted waist, a flat hat, sensible Mary Jane shoes and a ladylike bag.[52] Shepard's pictures offer a faithful interpretation of what Travers described in textual form (Figure 10).

Figure 10 Mary Poppins. 'On sailed the curious figure, its feet neatly clearing the tops of the trees'. Illustration of Mary Poppins by Mary Shepard in P. L. Travers, *Mary Poppins Comes Back* (London: HarperCollins, 2018), title page (first publication in 1935). Copyright © 1935 and renewed 1963 by P. L. Travers. Reprinted by permission of Houghton Mifflin Harcourt Publishing Company and by permission of HarperCollins Publishers Ltd © Mary Shepard 1935.

In the 1985 interview to Jane L. Mickelson, Travers disapprovingly commented on the illustrations in the 1968 Soviet edition created by Gennady Kalinovsky: '[t]hey drew her as a little match-stick type of figure; wispy and not quite real.'[53] In her letter to B. Zakhoder, Travers emphasized that she could not understand why the illustrations in the Soviet translation looked so different from the original Mary Poppins drawn by Mary Shepard.[54] Notwithstanding Travers's comments, the 1968 Kalinovsky illustrations created a similar effect. What unites them with the original illustrations is that Shepard and Kalinovsky both use vibrant black line drawings to perfectly capture a recognizable visual image of the famous English nanny. Similar to Shepard, Kalinovsky recreated the dynamic character of Mary Poppins through the use of clearly traced lines for details and black-and-white palette, faithfully following Travers's textual portrayal of her protagonist. However, when it comes to the visual interpretation of details in Mary Poppins's image, differences in illustrations in the original and translated texts are rather noticeable.

Kalinovsky's portrayal of Mary Poppins – a non-naturalistic interpretation, angular, distorted and out of proportion with sharpened facial features – creates the illusion of a certain historical milieu from which Mary Poppins comes – the 1960s. These illustrations reflect the artistic vision of the period in which they were produced, establishing what the work represented to the 1960s generation of readers who, most probably, would feel comfortable with this kind of rendering. He draws a female figure from their time wearing a knee-length coat with its straight cut, recalling Western and Soviet fashion patterns of the early 1960s. As the books are full of dancing, Mary Poppins often appears with turned-out feet in first or fourth position. On Shepard's illustration from the second book *Mary Poppins Comes Back* in Figure 10, when Mary returns to the Banks children from the clouds at the end of a kite string, she is shown floating in the sky as if she is dancing, with her feet turned out. This is an important feature of Mary's overall image as a theatrical figure who dances a lot in many stories. Illustrating the same scene in the 1968 edition, Kalinovsky only captures Mary's body movements in her normal nanny mode (as can be seen in the first chapter of the second part of Zakhoder's translation – in P. L. Travers, *Meri Poppins* (Moscow: Detskaia literatura, 1968) on page 119). His Mary is not a dancing sorceress but a practical, serious and stern nanny, looking after the children in a business-like manner. Being a prim and proper lady, she stands rigid and upright, frowns and pouts, not letting herself smile. Kalinovsky updated his illustrations of Mary Poppins for the new version translated by Marina Litvinova in 1996. New illustrations show Mary as a more contemporary figure, occasionally half smiling, and even standing with her feet turned-out in the third balletic position, although she is still prim and proper (as can be seen in Chapter 7 of Litvinova's translation – in P. L. Travers, *Meri Poppins s Vishnievoi ulitsy* (Moscow: Rosmen, 2012) on page 84).

Hence, Kalinovsky's illustrations are directed to the didactic and moralistic principle upon which the overall image of Russian Mary Poppins created by Zakhoder is based, thus reinforcing the translator's didactic message. However, it is only one side of Mary Poppins's visual representation. Having created illustrations to Russian translations of Lewis Carroll's *Alice's Adventures in Wonderland* and *Through the Looking-Glass* and Jonathan Swift's *Gulliver's Travels*, Kalinovsky was fully aware of the demands that English fantasy stories posed for illustrators, although he was not completely satisfied with his representation of Mary Poppins claiming that initially he imagined Mary's character differently.[55] Notwithstanding Kalinovsky's negative remarks about his visual interpretation of Travers's books, his illustrations in Russian books about Mary Poppins demonstrate a successful visual transfer of both the original spirit of foreignness and the fantastic from English to Russian culture. The atmosphere of magical transformations is recreated through the ornate style of Kalinovsky's drawing and attributes of foreignness are conveyed through the constructed visual image of the English nanny that enhances Russian versions of Travers's textual portrayal.

Alongside Kalinovsky's illustrations in the 1990s and 2000s, there have appeared other variations of Mary Poppins's image interpreted by several illustrators: Olga Dmitireva, Vladimir Gal'diaev, Ekaterina Lopatina and Vadim Chelak. By far the most popular of them in the last decade are the pictures created by Vadim Chelak for Zakhoder's translation reprinted by the publishing house Rosman. Also, another illustrator worth mentioning, who created the most recent pictures of Mary for the same reprint of Zakhoder's translation, is Kseniia Shafranovskaia. Their visual interpretations are closer to Travers's description of the famous English governess. They both recreate the atmosphere of the idyllic England of the 1920s–1930s and Mary's look suggests that she is a nanny from that particular period, as Travers intended. Their Mary wears a midi-length coat with buttons, a flat hat or a bonnet, Mary Jane shoes or low-cut boots, and she has an umbrella and a big lady-like bag (Figures 11 and 12). There is no trace of didacticism in the image of Mary created by the two illustrators. Their Mary is real, friendly, gentle and more smiling (unlike Kalinovsky's Mary) and yet she is the magical nanny with supernatural powers who transfers the children to the world of merriment and fantasy.

Figure 11 Mary Poppins. Illustration by Vadim Chelak in P. L. Travers, *Meri Poppins vozvraschaetsia*, translated by B. Zakhoder (Moscow: Rosman, 2011), p. 19. Illustration copyright © 2011, ROSMAN Publishing House. Used with permission. The illustration provided by ROSMAN Publishing House and printed with permission.

In the case of the illustrations by Kalinovsky, Chelak and Shafranovskaia, the Soviet and post-Soviet representations of Mary Poppins, in both visual and word form, build a bridge for Soviet readers and modern Russian readers so that their imagination could breathe foreign air. Indeed, as mentioned in Chapter 3 in this book in reference to new Russian translations that appeared in the 1960s, the overall image of a magical English nanny created in 1968 by Zakhoder and Kalinovsky, although corrected with the view to express didactic values, met demand from the Soviet child and adult readership for a new literary protagonist. As the books with Kalinovsky's illustrations were offered to readers in the post-Soviet period, together with the new pictures created by Chelak and Shafranovskaia, including pictures by other illustrators, all these versions open the door to magical adventures in 'Merry England' and beyond, loved by readers of all ages in modern Russia.

Figure 12 Mary Poppins. Illustration by Kseniia Shafranovskaia in P. L. Travers, *Meri Poppins*, translated by B. Zakhoder (Moscow: Rosman, 2018), p. 119. Illustration copyright © 2018, ROSMAN Publishing House. Used with permission. The illustration provided by ROSMAN Publishing House and printed with permission.

8

Re-imagining Kenneth Grahame's *The Wind in the Willows*: Images of mythical rural England and the English way of life

In this chapter, the analysis centres on the translation of cultural associations of Englishness and features of English national character that relate to the literary myth of 'Merry England', or 'good old England' in its Russian equivalent, in Kenneth Grahame's *The Wind in the Willows* (1908).[1] The main idea is based on the premise that Russian representations of England – as a rural idyll, as the land of gentlemen and as the cosy English home – are re-imagined and partially Russified irrespective of whether the translated texts appeared during the Soviet or post-Soviet periods. Similar to the representation of landscape in Russian translations of Kipling's *Puck of Pook's Hill* and *Rewards and Fairies*, state ideology is not involved in forming the picture of Englishness in *The Wind in the Willows*. On the contrary, there is a strong appeal of the myth of 'Merry England' which may well have informed the decision to select the original book for translation.

Before moving to the analysis of the translated texts, a few words are needed to explain the reasons why translation of Grahame's book was delayed almost until the end of the Soviet period. The analysis is divided into two sections. The first examines Russian representations of images of the mythologized English countryside and the second analyses Russian representations of images of mythologized home and national character. The analysis in the first section demonstrates that representations of rural Englishness in the translated texts are subjective and different from the way they appear in the original. Particular attention is paid to the influence of images of the Russian landscape from Russian literature on reconstructing depictions of mythical rural England in the translated texts. Russian translators tend to Russify images of idyllic England to some extent, though they do not seek to accommodate their texts fully within the context of Russian culture. Hence, rural England is depicted as an idyllic Arcadia and an Edenic garden, as well as a mysterious place unfamiliar to Russian readers.

The discussion in the second section demonstrates that the original images of the idyllic English home in the translated texts show a tendency towards generalization and partial Russification. As a result, the recreated picture evokes an analogy to Russian home in Russian readers' minds. At the same time, simplified descriptions of the English home appear in those translations that are aimed at younger children. However, elements of foreignness and faithfulness to historical detail appear in later retranslations, which are aimed at older children. As for the portrayal of England as an idealized land of gentlemen, these images are less lifelike in the translations published in 1988 and the early 1990s compared to the original depictions, while elements of Russification are also present. Later retranslations stay closer to Grahame's portrayal of the idyllic lifestyle of the English, thus reconstructing the original representation.

The Wind in the Willows was almost unknown to pre-revolutionary Russian and Soviet child and adult readers. The book was not translated until 1988 – just three years from the end of the Soviet Union – and, although there were two Soviet publications in the original language, copies of both editions were limited. An extract from the book was included in Nina Demurova's anthology of British children's literature published by the Leningrad educational publishing house in 1965 and the complete annotated text was released by the Progress publishing house in 1981. One can only speculate why this famous book had not reached readers in Soviet Russia in translation. Most likely, it was restricted after criticism of its obvious social subtext by Marxists, leaving it untranslated until the final days of the Soviet Union. Maria Nikolajeva and Kathryn Graham refer to Marxist criticism of the scene in which weasels and stoats, as the unnamed inhabitants of the Wild Wood, seize Toad's ancestral home, Toad Hall.[2] In addition, Peter Hunt, Neil Philip and Peter Green explain the social symbolism disguised in the novel.[3] They contrast the Wild Wooders – an evil proletariat, the vulgar masses – with riverbankers – protagonists who lead luxurious lifestyles and form a privileged circle of leisured landowners. This social context alone might have been enough to warrant rejection of the book in the Soviet Union, but there were other aspects, such as Mole's escape from monotonous workdays into the hedonistic life of 'messing about in boats', as the famous quote from Kenneth Grahame went, plus allusions to paganism and a description of Christmas celebrations, which also ran counter to official Soviet ideology.

Moreover, as mentioned in Chapter 3 in this book, the scope of Soviet children's literature was rather limited due to ideological and political factors; therefore, a protagonist in Soviet children's books was expected to be disciplined and hard-working and follow ideas of patriotism, proletarian internationalism and atheism. These criteria contradicted the values and ideas of *The Wind in the Willows*, whose heroes think and act independently, enjoy life in abundance, value friendship, worship a demigod and protect their comfortable existence from intruders. Western writers were expected to share communist values in order to be presented to Soviet readers. Kenneth Grahame's fears that social revolution would destroy the structure of English class society, as stressed by Peter Green,[4] meant there were plenty of reasons for the book's absence from the Soviet world of children's literature.

The first Russian translation was done by Irina Tokmakova in 1988, just before the fall of the Soviet Union, and was later reprinted several times. There have been eight subsequent retranslations and two retellings between 1988 and 2017. Four of these retranslations are worthy of attention, as they are currently the most widely available on the Russian literary market: by Vladimir Reznik (1992), Mikhail Iasnov and Aleksander Kolotov (1993), Leonid Iakhnin (2002), Viktor Lunin (2011). Other remaining versions can be found in libraries and second-hand online sales, although availability is limited.

Landscape – Translating the unfamiliar

The Wind in the Willows captures the unique spirit of the late-Victorian and early Edwardian era as the high point of the British Empire faded into history. The story is set in a pastoral idyll and tells about the friendship and adventures of four animals – Mole, Rat, Badger and Toad – who behave and live like humans and belong to the world of the male middle classes living from independent means. The Edwardian context of *The Wind in the Willows* is very important. According to Deborah Cogan Thacker, the novel was shaped by the early part of twentieth-century society.[5] It appeared during the *fin de siècle* and was influenced by the author's dreams and fears, which were deeply imbedded into the narrative. *The Wind in the Willows* is a nostalgic dream about life in the English countryside of the late Victorian and Edwardian time that Grahame saw passing away, 'as cars, railways, socialism (and possibly feminism) changed the landscape literally and figuratively'.[6] Rural life was being slowly eroded by the developing towns and cities and everything they gave rise to. Most probably, the appearance of the car, travelling at speeds of up to twenty miles per hour by 1903, was one of the most disturbing elements to those who enjoyed the quiet pleasures of rural life in a small English village.[7] And Kenneth Grahame was one of them, inevitably depicting England as a mythical idyllic Arcadia. Grahame's portrayal demonstrates a vision of the quintessential English countryside that contains such distinctive elements as hedgerows, heathland, the open road and rolling hills. The mythologized England as a rural pastoral idyll in Grahame's depiction, containing such distinctive elements as river, flowers, grass and meadows, has a sense of peacefulness, pleasance and delight. Though familiar to English readers, these concepts are not widely recognized in Russian culture; therefore, it is interesting to see how Russian translators dealt with this problem.

To accurately consider Grahame's depiction of the English rural landscape, it is useful to start with the image of the road. As a trope, the road 'connects distant places, often crossing vast tracts of land in order to do so' and helps travellers to learn about the surrounding landscape, as Jane Carroll explains.[8] Moreover, authors often use the high road trope as a means to depict their native land and show its socio-historical diversity, as Mikhail Bakhtin indicates.[9] So, in the second chapter, 'The Open Road', Toad tries to convince his friends Mole and Rat to travel with him in his new gypsy caravan by describing what they might see during their journey along the English road: 'The open road, the dusty highway, the heath, the common, the hedgerows, the rolling downs!' (p. 19). The Russian translations go as follows:

- Tokmakova: 'Широкие просёлки, пыльные большаки, вересковые пустоши, равнины, аллеи между живыми изгородями, спуски, подъёмы!' [Wide country lanes, dusty highways, the heather wasteland, the plains, the walks between hedges, descents, ascents!] (p. 46);
- Reznik: 'Широкие дороги, пыльные просёлки, здоровье, простота, луга, пригорки!' [Wide roads, dusty country lanes, health, simplicity, the meadows, the hillocks!] (p. 21);
- Iasnov and Kolotov: 'Широкая дорога, пыльные шоссе, луга, поля и холмы' [The wide road, dusty highways, meadows, fields and hills] (p. 21);
- Iakhnin: 'Прямые дороги, шумные шоссе, луговины, рощицы, волны холмов!' [Straight roads, noisy highways, small meadows, copses, the waves of hills!] (p. 43);
- Lunin: 'Дальняя дорога, пыльный большак, степи, пастбища, горы и долины!' [The faraway road, the dusty highway, steppes, pastures, mountains and valleys!] (p. 35).

The passage from the original text exemplifies the idyllic image of the English countryside common in Edwardian literature and recognizable nowadays. All the elements of the road trope in this passage are major features that signify the Englishness of the English landscape. Grahame first mentions that the story is set in England only at the end of chapter VI ('Mr. Toad'). Nevertheless, English readers are left in no doubt about the setting: images of the rural landscapes of Berkshire, the river Thames and the Cornish river Fowey are used by Grahame to construct lyrical depictions of the imagined landscape which serves as the backdrop to *The Wind in the Willows*.[10] Most probably, Russian readers will not find it very easy to recognize scenes set in an English rural environment. As will be shown further, Russian translators conveyed the original texts' evocation of the landscape and in doing so formed the image of Englishness for the Russian readers.

'The open road', with its sense of a main country road, does not appear to pose any difficulty for translators. However, the metaphorical meaning of 'the open road' as an endless road is also a historical allusion to a popular Edwardian anthology of poetry and prose about open air travelling – *The Open Road, A Little Book for Wayfarers* (written in 1899) compiled by E. V. Lucas.[11] Moreover, according to Seth Lerer, Edwardian readers imagined 'the open road' as a symbol of freedom and adventure.[12] Only Lunin creates an image of the faraway road, which partly preserves the historical message of the original text. All other translators choose a generalized image of a wide road. As for 'the dusty highway', Ford Madox Ford in his book *The Heart of the Country* (1906), part of the trilogy of England and the English, gives an impressionistic view of the highways of Edwardian England: 'level, white and engrossed beneath the sky . . ., the great highways run across the green islands' and describes them as 'singularly deserted' 'except for the automobiles, which as yet have done little to change the face of the country'.[13] Therefore, Iakhnin's decision to translate 'the dusty highways' as 'шумные шоссе' [noisy highways] seems misleading from a historical point of view. At the same time, the decision of Tokmakova and Lunin to render 'the highway' by the Russian vernacular word 'большак' [bol'shak], which signifies 'a wide country road, as opposed to country by-roads and lanes',[14] points to the Russification of the image of the highway in the original text.

Considering Gideon Toury's view that translations are 'facts of target cultures', which should be studied within the context of receiving cultures,[15] I will refer to examples from Russian literature to inform my understanding of the translation decisions employed by the Russian translators and to reveal their presence in the translated texts. My idea of drawing on the literature of the receiving culture is based on the views of Soviet translators Maria Lorie (1904–92) and Nikolai Liubimov (1912–92), who both stress the importance for Russian translators of reading Russian writers either of the same historical period or genre. This would enable translators to find new possibilities in the Russian language for conveying style and content of the original.[16]

The usage of the Russian word 'большак' [bol'shak] in the depiction of a Russian road can be found in a number of literary works written between 1870 and 1930. Ivan Bunin in a miniature called *Muravskii shliakh* [Muravskii trail] (1930) describes a country road as: 'Летний вечер, ямщицкая тройка, бесконечный, пустынный большак … Много пустынных дорог и полей на Руси …' [The summer evening, the coachman's troika, the endless deserted bol'shak … There are many deserted roads and fields in Russia …].[17] Mikhail Prishvin in his autobiographical novel *Kashcheeva tsep'* [Kashchey's chain] (1953) writes: 'В это время на большак с проселочных дорог выехало много деревенских подвод, растянулись длинною цепью, и это стало – обоз' [Meanwhile, lots of peasants' carts drove onto the bol'shak from country paths, they stretched out as a long chain and it all became a caravan].[18] Ivan Turgenev evokes the image of a country road in the short story *Rasskaz otsa Aleksseia* (1877): 'На шестой версте от города – вижу: шагает он по большаку. Я его догнал, соскочил с телеги' [Six versts from the town – I see him striding down the bol'shak. I drove up to him and jumped off the cart].[19] Hence, drawing on these examples, it is possible to assume that the existing literary images of the Russian country road might have inspired the two translators (Tokmakova and Lunin) in their creation of the image of the English country road.

The image of the open road contains elements of the open green space: 'the heath', 'the common', 'the hedgerows' and 'the rolling downs'. 'The heath' is only conveyed in the translation of Tokmakova as 'вересковые пустоши' [the heather wasteland]. Reznik, Iasnov and Kolotov, as well as Iakhnin put 'the heath' and 'the common' together and assign it the general meaning of common land, which in their translations is represented by fields, meadows and coppice. Lunin creates a new image for 'the heath' – in his translation it becomes 'the steppe', thereby sending a message to Russian readers that his imagined English landscape resembles something more of a Russian nature (a steppe) than an English one (a heathland).

The steppe and the field evoke images of the Russian landscape as an extensive boundless open land. The steppe is considered a symbol of freedom in Russian culture and the field evokes the image of a plain or an expanse of land devoid of trees. The English landscape imagined by Iasnov/Kolotov and

Lunin is transformed into a partly Russified countryside. On the one hand, the meadows and fields denote the image of a generalized landscape which can be found in many countries. On the other, the fields and steppe can evoke images of the Russian landscape in the minds of Russian readers. So, again, it is useful to consider the use of these two images in their Russian cultural and literary context.

The Russian historian of the late nineteenth century Vasilii Kliuchevskii said: 'The forest, the steppe, the river – these, one might say, are the fundamental elements of Russian nature in its historical significance.'[20] The vastness of the steppe and the field, as the key elements of Russian landscape, is broadly represented in Russian prose and poetry, for example, in the writings of Anton Chekhov, Ivan Bunin, Ivan Turgenev and Alexander Blok. Anton Chekhov's short novel *The Steppe*, written in 1888, depicts the steppe as 'широкая, бесконечная равнина' [a vast, endless plain] and 'Сжатая рожь, бурьян, ... дикая конопля – всё, побуревшее от зноя, рыжее и полумертвое' [the cut rye, the wild steppe grass, the spurge, the hemp – all turned brown under the hot sun and half dead].[21] Petr Viazemsky – who greatly influenced the development of Russian landscape poetry[22] – starts his poem *The Steppe*, written in 1828: 'бесконечная Россия словно вечность на земле' [boundless Russia like eternity on earth] and his steppe is vast, barren and as hot as a fiery sea.[23] The heat and boundlessness of the steppe is pictured in Ivan Bunin's poem *Kamennaia baba* [The stone idol] (1906).[24] The feeling of joy and vastness evoked by the Russian steppes is conveyed in Ivan Turgenev's 1852 collection of short stories *Zapiski okhotnika* [*A Sportsman's Notebook*] in chapter IX 'Kassyan from fair springs':

> And then, beyond Kursk, come the steppes, the steppe-country, the surprise of it, the joy to your heart, the spaciousness of it, the blessing of God! Why, the steppes run, so they say, right to the warm seas, where lives the Gamayun bird with the sweet voice.[25]

The image of endless Russian fields as a typical Russian landscape is found in Sergei Esenin's poem *Glianu v pole, glianu v nebo...* [I look at the field, I look at the sky...] written in 1917: 'Гляну в поле, гляну в небо – | И в полях и в небе рай. | Снова тонет в копнах хлеба | Незапаханный мой край' [I look at the field, I look at the sky – there is heaven in the field and in the sky. And again my unploughed country is drowned in sheaves of wheat].[26] Bunin depicts endless Russian fields in the novel *Zhizn' Arsen'eva* [*The Life of Arseniev*] (1939) in the following way: 'Зимой безграничное снежное море, летом – море хлебов, трав и цветов ... И вечная тишина этих полей' [In winter – the boundless sea of snow, in summer – the sea of wheat, grass and flowers … And the eternal stillness of these fields].[27] Similarly, Ivan Turgenev recreates the image of endless fields [раздольные поля] in the closing chapter 'Forest and Steppe' of *A Sportsman's Notebook*.[28] In Vladimir Nabokov's novel *Mashen'ka* [Mary] (1926) the main character Ganin recalls his past life in Russia and his fond memories of his love for Mashen'ka are set against the vast fields of Russian landscape in late summer: 'the broad fields, already harvested' [просторы скошенных полей].[29] These examples from literary works create a sense of the breadth and expanse of the Russian landscape. While reading descriptions of landscape in translated English literature, Russian readers might visualize the vastness of the Russian landscape, which may shape the way the image of Englishness is constructed in their imagination.

'The hedgerows' are represented only in Tokmakova's translation – as 'walks between hedges', the other translators decide to leave out this important element of English rural landscape. For a better understanding of why the decision to omit the word 'hedge' turns the image of the English open road into just 'any road', it is helpful to look at the depiction of hedgerows in the English literature of the Edwardian period. For example, Ford Madox Ford in *The Heart of the Country* devotes a whole chapter to English roads. In his view, hedges are inherent elements of English roads, as well as 'the essential first note' of the English pastoral countryside. He describes hedgerows as 'riotous with dog-rose, odorous with elder in blossom, along which the nefarious but beloved bramble will carry the delighted eye [of a traveller] from briony to briony'.[30] In the minds of English readers, hedges are much more than simply foliage bordering the side of the road. In fact, the etymology of the word 'hedge' can be traced to Saxon settlers who used the word 'haga' for defining the hedge, as 'haga' was their name for the fruit of the hawthorn tree.[31] Perhaps omitting the word 'hedge' in four Russian translations diverts the reader's attention from the presentation of Englishness per se towards a generalized image of any landscape, be it English or Russian.

As for 'the rolling downs' – an essential feature pointing to the setting of the novel in the South of England – Tokmakova and Lunin misrepresent the original landscape, thus leaving their readers with a generalized image of any countryside. Other translators are closer to the original image of 'the rolling downs' which they render as 'hills'. Therefore, it is obvious that the Russian translators create a modified image of the rural English landscape and lean towards generalization and partial Russification as strategies for conveying Englishness. The Edwardian literary picture of the rural idyll masterfully portrayed by Grahame in the above examples is hardly recognizable in the Russian translations.

The next two examples recreate a sense of pleasure connected with the image of England as a pastoral idyll. At the beginning of the first chapter 'The River Bank', Mole leaves his underground home in search of sunlight, finds himself enjoying 'the delight' of the English spring as he explores the world above his burrow:

> Hither and thither through the meadows he rambled busily, along the hedgerows, across the copses, finding everywhere birds building, flowers budding, leaves thrusting – everything happy, and progressive, and occupied. (p. 6)

The Russian translators do not attempt to recreate Grahame's text stylistically, missing the gently undulating rhythm which foregrounds the author's adoring and nostalgic contemplation of English nature. However, they convey the key lexical elements of the original extract (the meadows, the hedgerows, the copses) that symbolize the southern English countryside, thereby introducing Russian readers to the beauty of the landscape from the very beginning of the book. Two translators pay no attention to transferring the word 'hedgerow' and translate it as 'fence' [изгородь] (Reznik, p. 3) and 'prickly bushes' [кусачие кусты] (Iakhnin, p. 10) which in a way is closer to the concept of 'hedgerow'. Three other translators preserve the concept of 'hedgerow' in their translations (Tokmakova, p. 8; Iasnov and Kolotov, p. 6; and Lunin, p. 11). Consequently, having introduced only minor modifications to the image of Englishness created by Grahame, the Russian translators picture England as a mythical pastoral idyll and recreate the original sense of delight.

In the third chapter 'The Wild Wood', Mole and Rat spend quiet winter days sitting in the burrow by the fire, remembering beautiful summer days. Grahame creates masterful evocations of the ideal English pastoral summer. By alluding to the protagonists' reminiscences of scenes from the ideal past at the beginning of the extract given below, Grahame creates a sense of nostalgia in his representation of the riverbank idyll, which is reflected in symbolic Arcadian images of the English landscape – the Thames near Cookham.[32] Grahame uses metaphorical literary language by giving the flowers that grow along the riverbank (purple loosestrife, willow-herb, comfrey, dog-rose and meadow-sweet) different roles in the pageant, according to how these flowers start blooming one after another in summer. An important feature added to create the feeling of pleasure is the metaphorical language which Grahame employs to introduce pastoral, medieval romance and fairy-tale allusions. The sense of nostalgia, descriptions of flowers and metaphorical language recreate the image of a mythical, idyllic Arcadia as a manifestation of Englishness and are important for analysing the extracts from the Russian translations. For my analysis I agree with Gillian Avery's view that Grahame might have based his choice of flowers in his description of the riverbank on Richard Jefferies' book about English rural life in *The Life of the Fields* (1884).[33]

The description of the riverbank represents the English idyllic landscape imagined by Grahame (p. 28). Three translators (Reznik, Iakhnin and Lunin) clearly retain the sense of nostalgia for the idyllic past by constructing the following emotions:

- 'Каким дивным кажется прошлое, когда вдруг найдешь время оглянуться на него!' [How wonderful the past seems when you find time to look back at it!] (Reznik, p. 34);
- 'Да, как вспомнишь, то были счастливые деньки!' [Oh, when one remembers, those were the happy days!] (Iakhnin, p. 66);
- 'Какой богатой, какой наполненной была каждая глава их воспоминаний!' [How abundant and full of life was every chapter of their memories!] (Lunin, p. 49).

Tokmakova decides to apply a more neutral approach to conveying nostalgic emotions about the past: 'О, лето было роскошной главой в великой книге Природы, если внимательно в нее вчитаться' [Oh, summer was a lush chapter in the great book of Nature, if one attentively reads oneself into it] (p. 69). Iasnov and Kolotov omit the whole passage from their translation. As for the personification of the meadow-sweet, the pastoral, medieval romance and fairy-tale motifs are retained in all four translations. And finally, four of the five types of flowers – purple loosestrife, comfrey, dog-rose and meadow-sweet – are represented in the Russian translations. The willow-herb flower is translated by Reznik (p. 34), Iakhnin (p. 66) and Lunin (p.49) as 'иван-чай' [ivan-chai], which is a Russian common name for this flower. It creates an association with Russian culture, unlike the botanical name – 'кипрей' [kiprei] which is used in the translation of Tokmakova (p. 69). All of these flowers grow on riverbanks in both Russia and England. However, Reznik does not mention that the whole scene is set on a riverbank and, consequently, fails to recreate the original image. Although the translators introduce one Russified element in this extract, it can be concluded that they recreate Grahame's evocations of the ideal English pastoral summer and, consequently, demonstrate the vision of rural England as a mythical idyllic Arcadia.

The last two examples illustrate the representation of the spirit of wilderness associated with the mystical English rural landscape. The way Grahame personified Pan was typical for Edwardian fiction: an ancient Greek pagan god from Arcadia who played a central role in the way nature was imagined.³⁴ This representation goes in line with the general trend in late-Victorian and Edwardian children's literature: The role of the spirit of wilderness manifested through a figure or a person and closely linked with landscape was often given to Pan who represented a literary Pagan god.³⁵ But this Pan, as a personified spirit of English landscape in both original and translated texts, actually represents different mythological universes in Russian and English cultures. Bearing in mind that the myth of Englishness in the original texts is developed from the borrowed Greek myth of Arcadia, I will demonstrate that in the translated text this myth is altered with added elements of Slavic mythology.

According to the mythological tradition in English literature, midsummer night is the most likely time that Pan would appear. In the opening of the lyrical seventh chapter 'The Piper at the Gates of Dawn' Grahame points to midsummer night:

> Though it was past ten o'clock at night, the sky still clung to and retained some lingering skirts of light from the departed day; and the sullen heats of the torrid afternoon broke up and rolled away at the dispersing touch of the cool fingers of the short midsummer night. (p. 72)

All five Russian translators fail to notice the allusion to the significance of the night and they deal with the translation of 'the cool fingers of the short midsummer night' in the following way: Tokmakova as 'прохладными пальцами июльской ночи' [by cool fingers of the July night] (p. 190); Reznik as 'прохладных ладошек июльской ночи' [cool small palms of the July night] (p. 102); Iasnov and Kolotov as 'прохладных пальцев ночи' [of the cool fingers of the night] (p. 85); Iakhnin as 'прохладной ладошки летней ночи' [of the cool small palm of the summer night] (p. 189); Lunin as 'прохладные пальцы короткой летней ночи' [cool fingers of the short summer night] (p. 124).

In the translations of Reznik, Yakhnin, Iasnov and Lunin, Pan is an ancient Greek pagan god from Arcadia who protects shepherds and herdsmen, flora and fauna, and a popular character in the art of late-Victorian and Edwardian England, 'the satyr, who is both man and beast' and 'demigod' (77).³⁶ Moreover, in the translations of Iakhnin and Lunin the image of Pan is backed up by illustrations, which help Russian readers to identify him as a demigod. However, in the translation of Tokmakova he is just an apparition. Tokmakova's image of Pan does not have any religious connotation, and it is not supported by any illustration. Tokmakova offers a generalized depiction of Pan by calling him 'друг и помощник' [the friend and helper] and 'тот, который играл на свирели' [the one who played the pipe] (pp. 202–5). Unlike the other translators, whose texts were published after 1991 and who could adhere to the context of this mystical and lyrical chapter, Tokmakova's decision to simplify the image of Pan can be explained by the prevailing atheist ideology in the Soviet Union and norms in literature that restricted references to, or the use of, religious material.

Moreover, there is another distinctive feature that points to the Russification of Pan's image. Grahame's Pan plays the pan-pipes. In all of the translations the pan-pipes appear as 'свирель' [svirel] and 'дудочка' [dudochka] (both mean 'a simple wooden pipe' in English). Mikhail Vrubel's painting *Pan* (1899) could be used for reference to pan-pipes – an instrument consisting of several pipes bound together, which means 'флейта Пана' [the flute of Pan] in Russian. At the same time, Pan can be shown playing a double flute. The Russian word 'svirel' is used in connection with the image of Pan. However, more often, especially for those who do not know Greek mythology, the word 'svirel' evokes an old Russian folk instrument made of wood, similar to a single or double flute. For example, such flute is played by Lel', the son of the Slavic pagan goddess of spring and love Lada. This in turn brings to mind the evocations of Alexander Ostrovsky's play *Snegurochka* [The Snow Maiden: A Spring Fairy Tale] (1873) and the opera of the same name composed by Nikolai Rimsky-Korsakov (1881). Therefore, the decision to translate the 'pan-pipe' as 'svirel' or 'dudochka' points towards the Russification of this image.

Hence, the recreated image of the English landscape reflects the way the Russian translators see English nature. They portray England as an idyllic Arcadia and a mysterious land unfamiliar to Russian readers, who are offered a partially Russified version of the English countryside. This partial Russification leads to a re-imagined image of Englishness in the Russian versions. This image has the power to evoke a vision of the Russian landscape with its vast steppe and fields as well as Russian folklore (svirel). By adding elements of Russian culture translators re-imagine the symbolic and idyllic image of the English countryside of the Edwardian period, which is recognizable nowadays as a manifestation of Englishness of the English landscape (the open road, the heath, the common, the rolling downs, the hedgerows) and offer it as a new myth of Englishness to Russian adult and child readers.

The idyll of English home and the world of gentlemen

The late-Victorian and Edwardian authors who wrote for children often resorted to images of the English cosy home and close-knit family to portray the idealized domestic England, evoking feelings of nostalgia for the Golden Age. This literary portrayal of the idyllic English home reflected the world of upper-, middle- and lower-middle classes, quite often depicting the stately houses of the aristocracy and country houses of the middle class. In the following example Grahame describes Mole's dwelling, called 'Mole End' (in chapter V 'Dulce Domum') which symbolizes the lifestyle of the lower-middle class during late-Victorian and Edwardian England. As Peter Hunt says, Mole's home is 'little England, Thomas Hardy at his most benign, with a skittle-alley, carol-singers, home-made produce from the village shops, and ale in the cellar'.[37] According to Seth Lerer, Mole's home is decorated 'in the fashions of the late Victorian period', thus representing 'an ideal of the aesthetic', in which Grahame 'synthesized a world of perceptions'.[38] Grahame included into the description of the courtyard in front of 'Mole End' elements characteristic to the era, such as a garden seat, a roller, wire baskets with ferns, plaster statuary, a skittle-alley and a small round pond (pp. 53–4). All of these elements are conveyed in translations by Tokmakova (pp. 140–1), Reznik (pp. 71–2), Iakhnin (pp. 139–40) and Lunin (p. 93). However, Iasnov and Kolotov simplified their version by excluding the garden seat, the roller and the skittle-alley from their portrayal (pp. 62–3).

Grahame mentions that Mole had plaster statues of 'Garibaldi, and the infant Samuel, and Queen Victoria, and other heroes of modern Italy' in brackets hanging outside on the walls of his house (p. 54). According to Hunt, this description refers to a joke, by which Grahame commented 'on the lower-class Victorian fashion for plaster statues'.[39] Moreover, Lerer explains that images of Garibaldi and the Queen were in lots of English homes due to their popularity in the country, and the infant Samuel was 'a favorite image of Victorian piety'.[40] Therefore, it seems important to convey the detailed description of the statues in translations in order to reflect the spirit of the late-Victorian and Edwardian era. However, Tokmakova omits the names of the statues and instead generalizes them as 'гипсовые статуэтки' [plaster statuettes] (p. 142). Yakhnin mentions Queen Victoria only and substitutes other names with a general expression 'гипсовые скульптуры, изображавшие знаменитых героев, принцев' [plaster statuary depicting famous heroes, princes] (pp. 139–40). M. Iasnov and A. Kolotov omit the infant Samuel, add Count Cagliostro and use Spain instead of Italy (p. 62). Only Lunin (p. 93) and Reznik (p. 72) are consistent in their translations: they retain all the names of the statues and thus represent the particular interior of an English home of the late-Victorian and Edwardian time. The approaches of Tokmakova and Iakhnin can be explained by the prevailing universal norm of simplification of translated children's literature. At the same time, taking into account that both translations are aimed at younger children, it seems possible that in choosing their approaches Tokmakova and Iakhnin might have resorted to their own opinions about the scope of historical knowledge of their assumed readers and how well they could cope with unknown information in the translated text.

The celebration of Christmas at Mole's home is another distinctive feature of late-Victorian and Edwardian domesticity. In the original text the field-mice 'go round carol-singing regularly at this time of the year' (p. 56). Tokmakova simplifies the image of Christmas festivities by turning it into a general celebration: 'Они в это время года ходят по домам и поют песни' [they go around, visit homes and sing songs] (p. 148). Iakhnin renders it as 'всегда на Рождество ходят по домам и поют свои песенки' [they always on Christmas go around, visit homes and sing their songs] (p. 146). Iasnov and Kolotov translate it as: 'Они каждый год ходят здесь и поют рождественские баллады' [They go around here every year and sing Christmas ballads] (p. 65). Lunin conveys this passage as: 'Они всегда появляются в это время года, чтобы спеть рождественский гимн' [they always appear at this time of the year to sing a carol hymn] (p. 95). Unlike previous translators, Reznik introduces elements of Russification: 'Под Рождество они ходят по домам и поют особые песни, – вроде колядок' [On Christmas Eve they go around and sing special songs – something like koliadka] (p. 74). He uses koliadka – a traditional Russian Orthodox Christmas celebration song – for conveying the idea of carol-singing.

The field-mice sing 'one of the old-time carols ... at Yule-time' (the carol is given in the original text) (pp. 56–7). Tokmakova translates it as 'старинная песня ... в декабре' [an old song in December] and omits the Christmas carol in her version (pp. 149–50). In all other post-Soviet translations it is conveyed that the field-mice sing a Christmas song for celebrating Christmas (Iakhnin, pp. 147–8; Iasnov and Kolotov, pp. 65–6; Reznik, pp. 76, 78; and Lunin, p. 96). Also all post-Soviet translators include the Christmas carol, rendering it in verse form. At the end of the celebration the field-mice leave the Mole and the Rat with 'wishes of the season' (p. 59). Tokmakova and Reznik generalize this expression by presenting it as 'пожелания' [greetings] (p. 155) and 'праздничные пожелания' [festive greetings] (p. 80), respectively. Iasnov and Kolotov domesticate this phrase and present it as 'новогодние пожелания' [New Year greetings] (p. 69). The connotation of Christmas is retained in the translations by Iakhnin as 'пожелать хорошего Рождества' [to wish a merry Christmas] (p. 155) and by Lunin as 'пожелали хозяевам веселого Рождества' [wished hosts a merry Christmas] (p. 100). It is clear from the above examples that

Tokmakova, whose version of *The Wind in the Willows* was published in 1988, omits any reference to Christmas. Therefore, her version becomes generalized and simplified. In contrast to her, the post-Soviet translations convey the celebration of Christmas in full and from their translations the target readers can grasp the idea of Christmas festivities in late-Victorian and Edwardian England. Tokmakova's choice can be explained by the influence of Soviet ideological policy and norms prohibiting references to religion. By contrast, after the fall of the Soviet Union, religion became popular, thereby bringing translations of Christmas celebrations closer to the original, though with elements of Russification in one post-Soviet translation.

The Wind in the Willows has one of the most widely known personifications of the English gentleman in children's literature. As Peter Green notes, 'the River-Bankers: Rat, Mole, Badger, Otter, and their friends form a close-knit community of leisured landowners who observe an extremely strict code of responsible behaviour'. The River-Bankers symbolize the middle and upper classes of the English establishment of the late-Victorian and Edwardian era. Being gentlemen by birth and/or social status, the main characters lead a life of 'one unending holiday, boating, tramping round the countryside, eating enormous meals, and getting caught up in occasional adventures'.[41]

In the first chapter of the novel Mole pronounces the famous motto that symbolizes the idyllic lifestyle of the English gentleman: 'there is nothing – absolutely nothing – half so much worth doing as simply messing about in boats' (p. 7). As Lerer explains, the phrase 'messing about' first appeared in the 1880s and connoted 'pleasant time wasting'.[42]

Tokmakova translates this extract as 'нету дела, которым и вполовину стоило бы заниматься, как попросту – попросту – повозиться с лодкой' [there is nothing half so much worth doing as simply – simply – being busy with a boat] (p. 14). In the version by Reznik it goes as follows: 'нет абсолютно ничего, что стоило хотя бы половину обыкновенного катания на лодке' [there is absolutely nothing half so much worth doing as simply going boating] (стр. 5). Iasnov and Kolotov resort to the following solution: 'нет в мире ничего, хотя бы наполовину сравнимого с прогулками на лодках' [there is nothing in the world half so much comparable to boating] (p. 8). Iaknin interprets this extract as 'ничего, абсолютно ничего нет такого, чем стоило бы заниматься, как просто-напросто болтаться в лодке' [there is absolutely nothing worth doing as simply idling around in a boat] (p. 15). Finally, Lunin renders it as 'Ничто, абсолютно ничто не может и вполовину сравниться со сладостным ощущением безделья в лодке!' [Nothing, absolutely nothing can be compared to the delightful feeling of lazing away in a boat!] (p. 14).

Only two translations accord with the original connotation of this phrase: Iakhnin translates it as 'болтаться в лодке' [to idle around in a boat] (p. 15) and Lunin renders it as 'безделье в лодке' [lazing away in a boat] (p. 14). Three other translations generalize the original by offering their readers new versions, such as 'повозиться с лодкой' [to be busy with a boat] (Tokmakova, p. 14); 'катание на лодке' [going boating] (Reznik, p. 5); and 'прогулки на лодках' [boating] (Iasnov and Kolotov, p. 8). Therefore, these translations fail to emphasize the status of the main characters as gentlemen of leisure. Hence, Grahame's depiction of the idyllic lifestyle of the country gentleman is made less vivid in the translations produced in 1988 and the early 1990s and reconstructed in later retranslations.

J. R. R. Tolkien wrote briefly about *The Wind in the Willows* in the drafts to his essay *On Fairy Stories*: 'Except for the character of Mr Toad . . ., the animals in *The Wind in the Willows* live enchanting lives by the River-bank and have enchanting adventures.'[43] This 'enchanting' and indolent pastime of 'messing about in boats' was artfully recreated in Ernest H. Shepard's illustrations which, as widely acknowledged, best capture the spirit of Englishness in the story. They first appeared in the thirty-eighth Methuen edition in 1931 and since then have become identified with *The Wind in the Willows* and with Englishness (e.g. they were used by the English Tourist Board to represent the National Heritage in the 1980s, as Peter Hunt notes[44]). Shepard's illustration in Figure 13 contributes much to readers' visualization of Grahame's description of the scene in which Rat tells Mole about his blissful life on the river. Both characters are drawn gliding in a boat down the river against the backdrop of an idyllic river landscape.

These important details are not presented in the illustration to the 1988 edition of the translation by Tokmakova (see the picture drawn by Sergei Denisov of Rat and Mole in the first chapter of Kenneth Grahame, *Veter v ivakh* (Moscow: Detskaia literatura, 1988) on page 20) nor is it present on Reznik's illustration, of Rat and Mole, in the first chapter of his translation (see Kenneth Grahame, *Veter v ivakh* (St. Petersburg: Assotsiatsia "VEK", 1992) on page 12). Denisov used yellow background, thus evoking pleasant dreams of a happy sunny day in spring or summer. He also put various images into bubble shapes, symbolizing Rat lost in reverie about his wonderful life on the river. This way, the illustrator managed to recreate the original impression of the scene but missed the important detail which is the surrounding nature. Reznik illustrated his translation himself. His portrayal of Grahame's story in the form of a colourful comic strip offered a humorous

Figure 13 Mole and Rat enjoy the delights of life on the river. Illustration by Ernest Howard Shepard in the first chapter and on the front cover in Kenneth Grahame, *The Wind in the Willows* (London: Egmont, 2012). Line illustrations copyright © E. H. Shepard. Colouring of the line illustrations copyright © 1970, 1971 by E. H. Shepard and Egmont UK Limited. Reproduced with permission of Curtis Brown Group Ltd on behalf of The Shepard Trust. The illustration provided by Egmont UK Ltd and printed with permission.

interpretation of the various adventures of the main characters. He showed Mole and Rat in a boat with the blue river around them. In Reznik's interpretation, Mole wants to lead a life filled with excitement, just like his newly found friend Rat does (the speech bubbles on the drawing say 'I want it' and 'Ha! Ha!'). Similar to the 1988 illustration by Denisov, Reznik partially recreated the original context of this scene through the depiction of Rat's emotions but excluded elements of landscape. Hence, the absence of the pictorial narration of landscape in both Russian illustrations robs the original textual representation of its embedded Englishness, thus considerably modifying its appeal to Russian readers.⁴⁵

Tokmakova's version was also published with new illustrations created by Vadim Chelak (see Kenneth Grahame, *Veter v ivakh* [Moscow: Labirint, 2014] on page 15). Unlike the illustrations in the Soviet editions, Chelak's pictures capture the pastoral atmosphere of idyllic England with which the book was synonymous. The 'messing about in boats' episode is faithfully reproduced, complete with typical rowboat gliding gracefully past a grassy, tree-lined riverbank. For modern Russian readers of Tokhmakova's interpretation, this richly illustrated edition offers a reassuring view of 'Merry England'.

The atmosphere in *The Wind in the Willows* can be viewed as clubby in the manner of English gentlemen's clubs. The animals relax by the fire chatting and spend time eating, drinking and smoking. In the first chapter, when the Rat and the Mole meet and become friends, they have a delicious lunch, later joined by the Otter, and during this meal the Mole and the Otter become friends. In the fourth chapter, after being lost in the cold and snowy wild wood, the Rat and the Mole find comfort and security in the Badger's kitchen, where they find the best fire in the woods and an ample supper, and where in the morning they have breakfast, slowly turning into lunch together with the Badger and the Otter. In the fifth chapter, in Mole's modest home, the Rat and the Mole share a Christmas supper with field mice who sing carols. In the ninth chapter the Rat invites his new friend, the Sea Rat, to lunch during which he listens to the Sea Rat's stories about voyages to foreign places. In the eleventh chapter over an evening meal the Rat, the Mole, the Badger and the Toad devise a plan about recapturing Toad Hall, after it was seized by weasels, ferrets and stoats. They start their culminating adventure with a simple meal in the eleventh chapter and celebrate their victory first with a supper full of delicacies and later with a banquet for all the animals in the twelfth chapter.

In all of the above scenes Grahame gives detailed descriptions of the meals the animals have. Often these meals include the delicacies peculiar to the late-Victorian and Edwardian time and to the middle- and upper-class environment of that era, which contemporary English readers should be able to recognize. For this reason, it is a fairly difficult task for modern translators to convey foreign food elements for Russian readers enjoying the book a century later. Moreover, Russian food culture is different from English cuisine, especially of the late-Victorian and Edwardian period. As the following example demonstrates, elements of Edwardian meals as connotations of middle- and upper-class living were partially accommodated within the Russian cultural context. Hence, it is more likely that the Rat and the Mole's picnic will be associated by Russian readers as lunch containing food familiar to them and not as lunch that had foodstuffs popular during the time when Grahame wrote his novel.

During the picnic in the first chapter Rat and Mole have the various foodstuffs in the luncheon basket which is reminiscent of the late-Victorian picnic – a favourite social activity of English middle class. The original goes as follows:

'There's cold chicken inside it', replied the Rat briefly; 'coldtonguecoldhamcoldbeefpickledgherkinssaladfrenchrollscresssandwichespottedmeatgingerbeerlemonadesodawater –.' (p. 8)

The Russian translators render this passage in the following way:

- Tokmakova: 'Жареный цыпленок, – сказал дядюшка Рэт коротко, – отварной язык-бекон-ростбиф-корнишоны-салат-французские булочки-заливное-содовая ...' ['Fried chicken,' said uncle Rat briefly, 'boiled tongue-bacon-roast beef-cornichons-salad-French rolls-meat in jelly-soda water'] (p. 16);
- Reznik: 'Там охлажденный цыпленок табака, – кратко ответил Крыс, – языкветчинаговядина (маринованные), салаткорнишоныфранцузс киебулочки, крэссэндвичитушеные, пивоводылимонад ...' ['There are cooled fried chicken tabaka, replied Rat briefly, 'tonguehambeef (marinated), saladcornichonsFrenchrolls, braisedcresssandwiches, beerwaterlemonade'] (p. 6);
- Iasnov and Kolotov: 'Там внутри салат, маринад, кока-кола, лимонад, – деловито отвечал Крыс, – цыплята табака, кусочек языка, свиная отбивная, бублики, рогалики, шоколадные пирожные, земляничное мороженое ...' ['There inside are salad, marinade, coca-cola, lemonade,' replied Rat in a business-like manner, 'chicken tabaka, a piece of tongue, pork steak, bubliki, rogaliki, chocolate slices, strawberry ice cream ...'] (p. 10);
- Yakhnin: 'Холодный завтрак, - откликнулся мистер Крысси и затараторил без передышки. – Холодныйязыкхолоднаяветчинахо лоднаяговядина, а еще огуречныйсалатбутербродныйсалатвсяки йдругойсалат, ну и там фруктово имбирносодовыйлимонад и ...' ['Cold breakfast,' answered mister Kryssi and gibbered without rest. Cold tonguecoldhamcoldbeef, and also cucumbersaladsandwichsaladallkindsofot hersalad, and also fruitandgingerandsodawaterlemonade and ...'] (p. 17);
- Lunin: 'Жареные цыплята, – затараторил Рэт, – отварной язык-свиной окорок-говядина-маринованные огурчики-салат-французские булочки-сэндвичи-мясо в горшочке-имбирное пиво-лимонад-содовая ...' ['Fried chickens,' jabbered Rat, 'boiled tongue-ham-beef- pickled gherkins-salad-French rolls-sandwiches-meat in a pot-ginger beer-lemonade-soda water ...'] (p. 16).

It is notable that the presentation style of the original is conveyed to a certain extent in all translations. Even though Iasnov and Kolotov do not put several words together, like others do in order to create the visual effect of Rat talking very fast, they still recreate Grahame's style through rhyming pairs of foodstuffs. However, when it comes to conveying the historical context of this extract by representing elements of Rat's Victorian picnic hamper, the translators are not so consistent in choosing their solutions. Rat has leftovers of roast chicken and roast beef. Both Tokmakova and Lunin translate 'cold chicken' as 'жареный цыпленок' [roast or fried chicken]. Reznik and Iasnov/Kolotov render 'cold chicken' as 'цыпленок табака' [chicken tabaka] meaning a Georgian dish of pan-fried chicken seasoned with garlic. Lunin and Iasnov/Kolotov use plural instead of singular, thus making the Rat's basket even bigger. Yakhnin renders it as 'холодный завтрак' [cold breakfast], which might imply any kind of food. Roast chicken and fried chicken tabaka, which can be eaten hot or cold, are very popular meals in Russia, as they were in the Soviet Union. Therefore translating 'cold chicken' as 'fried chicken tabaka' can lead to associations of a recognizable Russian dish.

Although cold boiled tongue is not a widespread food in modern Britain, Russians consider it a delicacy and it is a food item identifiable more with the Soviet period. Tokmakova translates 'cold beef' as 'ростбиф' [rostbif, 'roast beef'], which is an accepted foreign name of the typically English dish 'roast beef', but usually served hot in Russia. Thus Tokmakova gives a foreign hint to her translation of this food item. At the same time, she renders 'potted meat' as a typical Soviet/Russian dish 'заливное' [meat or fish in aspic] which is a type of hors d'oeuvre mainly eaten in winter and quite often on New Year's Eve. Typically it is boiled chicken, beef or fish with carrots, black pepper and garlic (or without) covered with broth with gelatin, left in the refrigerator to cool down and eaten cold. Unlike potted meat, it is not a preserved food. Yakhnin and Reznik omit 'potted meat' and Lunin translates it as 'мясо в горшочке' [meat in a pot], which is another popular Russian dish that is cooked in a pot in the oven (meat and usually vegetables). But in the original text this food item refers to the meat preserved in a sealed jar and represents a typical preserved food item of the Victorian and Edwardian periods. Tokmakova omits 'sandwiches' altogether, whereas Yakhnin uses a Russian equivalent 'бутерброд' [buterbrod, 'sandwich'], which can be an open sandwich or bread and butter, and thus an opposite of English sandwich. Lunin and Reznik use a modern loan word version of this word 'сэндвич' [sendvich, 'sandwich'] thus creating a foreign feel for their translations. Iasnov and Kolotov omit 'sandwiches' and 'potted meat' and substitute them with sweet dishes typical of Russian cuisine: they introduce 'bubliki' (a Russian version of bagels), 'rogaliki' (crescent rolls), 'chocolate slices' and 'strawberry ice cream'.

Having considered all the above examples from *The Wind in the Willows* and their corresponding translations it would be wrong to say that all that Russian readers see are the Russified Rat, Mole, Badger and Toad. Quite the contrary, all five Russian translators skilfully recreate the mythical image of the English landscape, and the idyll of home and the world of gentlemen. However, there are nuances which cannot be overlooked and these nuances point to the solid presence of Russianness in the created images of rural England and the English way of life. It is an unavoidable process, if one takes into account the fact that translated children's literature in Russia, as generally accepted, is aimed at making translated texts facts of the receiving culture. As an outcome of this process, Russian children might create familiar images of Russian culture-specific elements while reading about England, rather than trying to imagine how things exist in England, a country which seems strange and mysterious to them. Certainly, it would be easier for children to imagine an unknown land by making associations with their native landscape and way of life they know so well. However, when they visit England, they might be surprised that the land looks very different from the one they imagined.

It is important to remember that children's literature plays an educational and aesthetic role and that translated children's books teach readers about foreign cultures. If educational purpose is the principal aim of translators, it seems that it would be better not to mix the two different landscapes and ways of life of England and Russia. However, as far as subjectivity in the representation of Englishness is concerned, and aesthetic concerns are taken into account, it is very likely that the representation of England will be influenced by elements specific to Russian culture. This is especially true if the translated text is supposed to be read as if it was initially written in the Russian literary language, which is the dominating norm of the country's traditional approach to translation.

Conclusion

The representation of Englishness in Russian translations of British children's classics published in Soviet and modern Russia reflects the spirit of the times, the political mood in Russian society and Russian stereotypes of England; it is also informed by Russian traditions of literary translation. The book does not argue that Englishness is completely different in Russian translations compared to the originals; only certain elements are modified, and that is the area of focus for this study. Having said this, the whole picture consists of separate elements; therefore, it can be concluded that Englishness is altered in Russian translations of British children's classics. Russian responses to examples of Englishness diverge from the way the images are represented in the original texts. This can be explained by the dual role that ideology played in the field of children's literature in the Soviet Union and modern Russia: in the case of the Soviet Union it was ideological doctrine and censorship; in the case of modern Russia, commercial interests and revived patriotic views. Political changes induced Russian translators to adjust to varying ideologies in their representation of Englishness. The areas of emphasis in the translated texts are in line with the themes that are made ideologically appropriate in Soviet children's literature (as shown in Chapter 3). To some extent Soviet stereotyping of the capitalist West affected the translation and censorship of the original texts. It is also possible that existing images of Englishness in children's literature written in Russian during the Soviet period influenced and complemented the representation of Englishness in the translated texts.

In all the examples there were external circumstances to which translators were forced to respond, so that their translations could be published. As I have shown in the examples from the Russian translations, both ideological norms and censorship over literary translation contributed to the creation of a modified image of Englishness, expressed generally in the translated texts produced during the Soviet period. This has led to my suggestion that Englishness can also be seen in this context as a propaganda tool for various political ends beneficial to Soviet ideology and to modern Russian imperial and patriotic discourses. Clearly, the entire texts are not changed through ideology, but those elements that are adapted under the influence of ideology contribute to the creation of a Soviet vision of the original texts. With the end of the Soviet Union and the appearance of subsequent retranslations, the Russian image of Englishness shifted closer to its original meaning. But not everything was updated: some of the first translated versions considered in my analysis are still published with cuts. In addition, there are new retranslations and revised translations, in which all the censored parts have been restored. Therefore, it can be concluded that Englishness, affected by ideology, being a distinct feature of the Soviet time, is still presented to readers in modern Russia. So, today's readers opening Zakhoder's *Mary Poppins* or Tokmakova's *Peter Pan* or *The Wind in the Willows* will encounter a patchy version of Englishness.

The Soviet practice of Russifying original texts by following prevailing ideological norms dwindles after 1991 with moves to a more faithful representation of the original text. But it was not solely censorship that caused Englishness to be modified in the Soviet translations. Ideology aside, literary norms and conventions, setting the rules of how to translate for children, stimulated creative decisions in Soviet translations. The same tendency can be observed in modern Russian translations: Englishness undergoes creative transformations with Russian cultural and literary traditions influencing the translation process. In both cases – with ideology (which means translators' own and popular perceptions of England, including Soviet stereotypes of it as capitalist West) and Russian cultural and literary traditions involved – Russian translators reimagine the image of 'Merry England' and turn it into the Russian vision of 'dobraia staraia Angliia' [good old England]. It is an adapted portrayal of the original mythologized 'Merry England' that evokes images of Russianness in Soviet and post-Soviet readers' minds. The idealized image fits well into the Soviet literary and ideological framework; nevertheless, it has continued through to the present day.

It is safe to say that the combination of limited Soviet knowledge about England and the ideological constraints exerted by the state influenced, to some extent, the creation of an imaginary England. What could not be experienced in reality was recreated with the help of the imagination. Elements forbidden from appearing in translated texts – such as religion, allusions to the Soviet empire, sentimentality – led to changes in the translated versions of the original books. Caused by historical and political circumstances, these modifications prompted the distortion of the original material and the re-imagining of stories.

Roland Barthes theorizes that contemporary mythologization is socially determined and should be seen as an inverted reflection of an idea which is taken from its original context and reshaped in line with the view of current ideology; subsequently, the new ideological content of this idea becomes 'natural' or, in other words, 'Common Sense, Right Reason, the Norm, General Opinion'.[1] Taking Barthes's view into account, it can be concluded that by changing the original content of Englishness through ideology, Soviet translators create a Soviet myth of Englishness. It is shaped by the demands of Socialist Realism in Soviet children's literature – the educational, moralistic and character-building functions – as well as Soviet stereotypes of capitalist England. Based on the doctrine of Socialist Realism, Soviet ideology was 'political and attempted to displace actual reality with a surrogate ideal realm that did not exist in the world of daily experience'.[2] Equally, in the field of translated children's literature, Soviet translators were compelled to create images of foreign countries in an ideologically constrained environment. In the case of England, the image of the country was an idealized one. As for post-Soviet Russia, although translators are not controlled by the state, the dominance of commercial ideology means that the market imposes its own constraints on translation activity. Commercially successful books are sure to be translated and the popular myth of 'dobraia staraia Angliia' [good old England] is a marketable concept.

The image of England as an imaginary country in Soviet and post-Soviet understanding is supported by Alexei Yurchak's concept of the imaginary West in his study of late Soviet society.[3] He argues that the West was imagined by Soviet people and proposes a concept of 'a Soviet imaginary "elsewhere" that was not necessarily about any real place'. This place was created in the minds of Soviet people simply because 'the real West could not be encountered'. Therefore, he looks at the Soviet version of 'elsewhere' as 'the Imaginary West'.[4] Yurchak concludes that between the 1950s and the 1980s 'the entity of the Imaginary West emerged as an internal "elsewhere" of late Soviet culture and imagination'.[5] Several key translated children's books appeared at that time too, which contributed to the creation of the discourse of an imaginary 'elsewhere'. The concept of the imaginary England coincides with the concept of the mythologized England. Yurchak demonstrates that the West was imagined by Soviet people; in other words, the conception of the West did not correspond to the real place. It was a dream about the West, an illusion. As I have shown, the image of England in Russian translations is mythologized. Considering the didactic and educational role of children's literature, it seems that it is easier and safer to introduce children to a myth of England, which includes stereotyped images of the country familiar to children and adult readers.

The modified image of Englishness, unearthed in my analysis of Russian translations of children's literature published during the Soviet and post-Soviet periods, is in many ways similar to the stereotyped image of 'dobraia staraia Angliia' (which is positive and negative) generally accepted in Russian culture. First, as I have shown in Chapter 1, it is an image that appears in both Soviet and modern Russian non-fiction (for adults) and fiction (for children) which offers two contrasting sets of opinions: on the one hand, England is positively portrayed as an idyllic land; on the other hand, it is a country in which negative aspects, such as inequality, the hardship of the English working class and the country's imperialist past, prevail.

Secondly, the stereotyped image of England, which has positive and sometimes negative tones, still appears in modern Russian society in spite of the recent openness to the rest of the world. Popular modern-day perceptions of English life and Englishness can be readily found reported among Russian digital media publications.[6] The most common views are the following: the English are polite and they preserve their traditions; they are snobbish, prim and proper; and they talk about the weather and have a peculiar sense of humour (which the Russians call 'тонкий английский юмор' [subtle English humour]). An English gentleman is reserved, wears a smoking jacket, or a tweed jacket, and a bowler hat; he carries an umbrella and smokes a pipe. It always rains in England – or Foggy Albion, as the Russians still often call the country – and is populated by gentlemen and ladies who like their five o'clock tea, eat porridge for breakfast and leave without saying goodbye. At the same time, England is sometimes thought of as a mystical land with haunted castles where knights fought for freedom. Undoubtedly, there are many reasons to assume that such a heavily stereotyped image of England has been formed under the influence of the media, television, cinema and literary works. For example, Vladimir Posner's documentary *Angliia v obschem i v chastnosti* [*England in General and in Particular*], shown on Russian television in January 2015, is a good demonstration of Russian myths about England. All the elements of mythologized Englishness are present in the film. It constructs an image of 'Merry England', a country of tradition built on the class system. It also attempts to describe certain aspects of the English national character, not least based on the widespread Russian stereotyped perceptions of the English, such as privacy, the 'stiff upper lip', eccentricity, self-irony, absurdity and a peculiar sense of humour; to this can be added tolerance, as well as the tendency to complain, apologize for everything and not to draw attention to oneself.[7]

In both cases, whether it is critical or complementary, the Russian image of 'good old England' is mythologized and this is how it is presented in the Russian translations analysed in this book. Therefore, the combination of negative and positive sides of this image shows there are clear contradictory views revealing an ambivalence in the way practitioners translated children's literature – there is no consistent trend one way or the other. Of course, the cultural and political connotations of this image depend on the historical and political contexts. A politicized environment affects translated literature, especially children's literature in translation, because it can be used as means of forming an image of and controlling attitudes towards foreigners. And this leads to the emergence of a mythologized image of 'dobraia staraia Angliia' being manipulated in an ideological context. In times of political quiet, ideological connotations of Englishness are given considerably less attention or even none at all. So, during such times the imaginary England in Russian perceptions has cultural connotations of the original idealized image of 'Merry England', though with elements of Russianness.

It is important to mention that stereotyped perceptions of England are also widespread among young Russians. Examples of these are given in Arkadii Kuznetsov's article *Britanskii sled v Rossii. Vstrechaia god Velikobritanii* [Tracing Britain in Russia: towards the year of Britain in Russia]. According to this article, Russian upper-form students have associated English culture over the last twenty years with the following: red double-decker buses, Big Ben, the Tower, the Queen, Parliament, gentlemen, five o'clock tea, porridge, fog and rain, football, as well as Winston Churchill, William Shakespeare, Agatha Christie and Sherlock Holmes.[8] The popular Russian stereotyped vision of England as a foggy and a treacherous Albion is highlighted in Alexei Gromyko's monograph on images of Russia and England. Gromyko mentions that the Russians see England in terms of centuries-old traditions and consider the English to be arrogant, conservative and practical minded. He also reminds us of the stereotypical sayings widespread in Russia that characterize the English, such as 'мой дом – моя крепость' [my home is my castle], 'слово джентльмена' [a gentlemen's word] and 'бремя белого человека' [The White Man's Burden].[9] Similar ideas about English culture were offered in an opinion poll called *Interes k Velikobritanii. Chto rossiiane znaiut o Velikobritanii? I khotiat li pobivat' v etoi strane?* [Interest in Great Britain. What do Russian people know about Britain? Would they like to visit Britain?], produced by the Russian Public Opinion Foundation (Fond Obschestvennoe Mnenie, FOM). The survey was conducted in March 2014 with respondents from cities, towns and villages in Russia. The peculiarity of this poll is that only 2 per cent of those questioned had been to England.[10] This statement points to a mostly stereotyped perception of England and its culture by people who have never seen it in reality.

One further ingredient to be added to the mix of cultural perception is the image of England idealized by Russian translators. This idealization goes towards building the Russian myth of Englishness, which draws on the English myth and then departs from it. The Russian view of the myth of Englishness is modified under the influence of existing positive and negative perceptions of England. It also rests on the translators' individual memories and feelings about England, their wide knowledge and appreciation of English culture. Although Russian translators were under varied pressures, it feels like there was no intention on their part to paint England in an unfavourable light. There was more desire in some cases to reflect positive qualities they admired about the country. It seems clear that, notwithstanding changes in political and cultural relations between Russia and Britain, the translators featured in this book have created their own mythical 'Merry England'. In doing so, they have made an important contribution to the promotion of interest in England and an understanding of the island nation and its people among a wide audience of Russian readers.

Appendix 1: Englishness in Russian literature

1. Englishness in Russian non-fiction

Before 1917

- Korney Chukovsky, *Zagovorili molchavshie: Anglichane i voina* (Petrograd: Izdatel'stvo tovarischestva A. F. Marks, 1916).
- Samuil Marshak, letters 26–30, 32, 43, in *Marshak S. Ia., Sobranie sochinenii v 8 tomakh*, ed. V. M. Zhirmunskii, 8 vols (Moscow: Khudozhestvennaia literatura, 1968–72), viii: *Izbrannye pis'ma*, ed. S. S. Chulkova (1972).
- Samuil Marshak, sketches *Otdykh moriaka* [Sailor's rest], *Lift* and *Rybaki Polperro* [Fishermen of Polperro], in *Marshak S. Ia., Sobranie sochinenii v 8 tomakh*, ed. V. M. Zhirmunskii, 8 vols (Moscow: Khudozhestvennaia literatura, 1968–72), vi: *Stat'i. Vystupleniia. Zametki. Vospominaniia. Proza raznykh let*, ed. S. S. Chulkova and E. B. Skorospelova (1971), pp. 474–91.
- Samuil Marshak, poem *20 iiunia – 7 iiulia* [20 June–7 July], in *Stikhotvoreniia i poemy* (Leningrad: Sovetskii pisatel, 1973), pp. 440–52.
- Sergei Mech, *Angliia. Tret'ie izdanie* (Moscow: Tipo-litograficheskoe tovarischestvo I.N. Kushnerev i Ko, 1914).
- Elizaveta N. Vodovozova, *Kak liudi na belom svete zhivut. Anglichane* (St. Petersburg, [n. pub.], 1897).

Soviet period

- Gerontii V. Efimov, *Na Britanskikh ostrovakh* (Leningrad: Lenizdat, 1967).
- Ilya G. Ehrenburg, *Angliia* (Moscow: Federatsiia, 1931), also published in Ilya G. Ehrenburg, *Sobranie sochinenii v 9 tomakh*, 9 vols (Moscow: Khudozhestvennaia literatura, 1962–7), vii: *Khronika nashikh dnei. Viza vremeni. Ispaniia. Grazhdanskaia voina v Avstrii. Stat'i* (1966), pp. 444–78.

- N. A. Erofeev, *Tumannyi Al'bion: Angliia i anglichane glazami russkikh, 1825–1853 gg.* (Moscow: Nauka, 1982).
- Boris Izakov, *Vse meniaetsia dazhe v Anglii* (Moscow: Sovetskii pisatel'*,* 1965).
- Yuri Nagibin, 'Dva starika', in *Yu. Nagibin. Nauka dal'nikh stranstvii* (Moscow: Molodaia gvardiia, 1982), first published in *Ogoniek*, № 15, 1979.
- Vladimir D. Osipov, *Britaniia 60-e gody* (Moscow: Politizdat, 1967).
- Vsevolod Ovchinnikov, *Korni duba: Vpechatleniia i razmyshleniia ob Anglii i anglichanakh* (Moscow: Mysl', 1980), also published in English translation as V. V. Ovchinnikov, *Britain Observed: A Russian View*, trans. Michael Basker (Oxford: Pergamon Press, 1981).
- Mikhail Ozerov, *Angliia bez tumanov* (Moscow: Detskaia literatura, 1977).
- Konstantin Paustovsky, 'Ogni La-Mansha', in *K. Paustovsky. Sobranie sochinenii v 9 tomakh, volume 7. Skazki. Ocherki. Literaturnye portrety* (Moscow: Khudozhestvennaia literatura, 1983), first published in *Nedelia*, № 47, 1964.
- Marietta Shaginian, 'Progulki po Londonu', in *M. Shaginian. Zarubezhnye pis'ma* (Moscow: Sovetskii pisatel', 1977).
- A. N. Tolstoy, 'Anglichane, kogda oni liubezny', in *'Ia bereg pokidal tumannyi Al'biona . . .': russkie pisateli ob Anglii, 1646–1945*, ed. Olga A. Kaznina, and A. N. Nikoliukin (Moscow: ROSSPEN, 2001), pp. 362–9.
- Liudmila Z. Uvarova, 'Vstrecha na mostu Naitbridzh', in *Sovetskaia kul'tura*, 8 January 1983.
- Larisa Vasil'eva, *Al'bion i taina vremeni* (Moscow: Sovetskaia Rossiia, 1983), first published in *Novyi mir*, № 3–4, 1978.

Post-Soviet period

- Kseniia Atarova, *Angliia, moia Angliia* (Moscow: Raduga, 2008).
- Tat'iana N. Breeva and Liliia F. Khabibulina, *Natsional'nyi mif v russkoi i angliiskoi literature* (Kazan': RITs 'Shkola', 2009).
- *Rossiia i Britaniia. Sviazi i vzaimnye predstavleniia XIX-XX veka*, ed. Apollon Davidson (St. Petersburg: Nauka, 2006).
- *Rossiia i Britaniia. Vypusk 5. Na putiakh k vzaimoponimaniiu*, ed. Apollon Davidson (St. Petersburg: Nauka, 2010).
- *Lingvokul'turnyi Tipazh 'Angliiskii chudak'*, ed. Vladimir I. Karasik and Elena Iarmakhova (Moscow: Gnozis, 2006).

- Mikhail Liubimov, *Gulianiia s Cheshirskim kotom: memuar-esse ob angliiskoi dushe* (St. Petersburg: Amfora, 2001).
- Nina P. Mikhal'skaia, *Rossiia i Angliia: problemy imagologii* (Samara: OOO 'Porto-print', 2012).
- Zurab Nalbandian, *Chaepitie u korolevy: v nachale XXI veka v Britanii* (Moscow: Vremia, 2007).
- Anna Pavlovskaia, *Angliia i anglichane* (Moscow: Moskovskii universitet, Triada, 2004).
- Anna Pavlovskaia, *5 O'Clock i drugie traditsii Anglii* (Moscow: Algoritm, 2014).
- Viacheslav P. Shestakov, *Angliiskaia literatura i angliiskii natsional'nyi kharakter* (St. Petersburg: Nestor-Istoriia, 2010).
- Ekaterina Viazova, *Gipnoz anglomanii. Angliia i 'angliiskoe' v russkoi kul'ture rubezha XIX-XX vekov* (Moscow: Novoe literaturnoe obozrenie, 2009).
- Anton Vol'skii, *Angliia. Bilet v odnu storonu* (Moscow: Eksmo, 2014).

2. Englishness in Russian fiction

Englishness in Soviet and Russian fiction

- Vasily Aksyonov, *Zatovarennaia bochkotara* (1968).
- Mark Aldanov, *Kliuch / Begstvo / Peschera* (1929–32).
- Joseph Brodsky, *Temsa v Chelsi* (1974), *V Anglii* (1977).
- Ivan Bunin, *Brat'ia* (1914).
- Anton Chekhov, *Doch' Al'biona* (1883).
- Fyodor Dostoevsky, *Igrok* (1866).
- Yurii German, *Dorogoi moi chelovek* (1962).
- Ivan Goncharov, *Fregat 'Pallada'* (1858).
- Fasil' Iskander, *Anglichanin s zhenoi i rebenkom* (1974).
- Alexander Kuprin, *Zhidkoe solntse* (1913).
- Evgenii Lann, *Staraia Angliia: istoricheskii roman* (1943).
- Nikolay Leskov, *Levsha* (1881), *Zapechatlennyi angel* (1873).
- Vladimir E. Maksimov, *Zaglianut' v bezdnu* (1986).
- Vladimir Nabokov, *Podvig* (1930–2).
- Vladimir Odoyevsky, *Chernaia perchatka* (1838).
- Valentin Pikul', *Rekviem karavanu PQ-17* (1970).

- Boris Pil'niak, *Staryi syr* (1924), *Otryvki iz 'Povesti v pis'makh', kotoruiu skuchno konchit'* (1924), *Tret'ia stolitsa* (1923).
- Alexander Pushkin, *Baryshnia-krest'ianka* (1831).
- Aleksey Remizov, *Podstrizhennymi glazami*, chapter 'Anglichanin' (1951).
- Mikhail Sholokhov, *Tikhii Don* (1928–40).
- Teffi, *Trubka* (1924).
- Alexey N. Tolstoy, *Petr Pervyi* (1934).
- Leo Tolstoy, *Anna Karenina* (1878).
- Ivan Turgenev, *Dvorianskoe gnezdo* (1859), *Ottsy i deti* (1862).
- Yuri Tynianov, *Smert' Vazir-Mukhtara* (1929).
- Evgeny Zamyatin, *Ostrovitiane* (1917), *Lovets chelovekov* (1918).

Englishness in Soviet and Russian children's literature

- Sergey Aksakov, *Detskie gody Bagrova-vnuka* (Moscow: Gosudarstvennoe izdatel'stvo detskoi literatury, 1962), written in 1858.
- Vasily Aksyonov, *Moi dedushka – pamiatnik* (Kemerovo: Sovremennaia otechestvennaia kniga, 1991), first published in 1970.
- Marina Aromshtam, *Kot Lantselot i zolotoi gorod. Staraia angliiskaia istoriia* (Moscow: Kompasgid, 2014).
- Kir Bulychev, *Angliia: bogi i geroi* (Tver': Izdatel'stvo 'Polina', 1997).
- Aliosha Dmitriev, *Angliiskie dzhentl'meny* (Moscow: Oktopus, 2013).
- Nikolai Garin-Mikhailovsky, *Detstvo Tiomy* (Moscow: Khudozhestvennaia literatura, 1971), written in 1892.
- Mikhail Gershenzon, *Robin Gud* (Moscow: Detskaia literatura, 1966).
- Daniil Kharms, *Plikh i Pliukh* (Moscow, Leningrad: Detizdat, 1937); 'Plikh i Pliukh (poema) (vol'nyi perevod knigi Vil'gel'ma Busha)', in Daniil Kharms, *Chto eto bylo?* (Moscow: Malysh, 1966).
- Vadim Levin, *Glupaia loshad'* (Novosibirsk: Zapadno-sibirskoe knizhnoe izdatel'stvo, 1969).
- Samuil Marshak, *Pochta* (Moscow, Leningrad: Raduga, 1927).
- Dina Rubina, *Dzhentl'meny i sobaki* (Moscow: Eksmo, 2012).
- Zinaida Shishova, *Dzhek-solominka* (Moscow: Detgiz, 1946).
- Vissarion Sisnev, *Zapiski Vikvikskogo kluba* (Moscow: Detskaia literatura, 1980).
- Irina Tokmakova, *Robin Gud* (Moscow: Terra, 1996).

- Andrei Usachev, 'Angliia', in *Moi geograficheskie otkrytiia. Vesielye uchebniki* (Moscow: Samovar, 1994), pp. 30-2.
- Boris Zhitkov, *Maria i Meri* (Moscow: Gosudarstvennoe izdatel'stvo, 1929).
- Boris Zhitkov, 'Urok geografii', in B. Zhitkov, *Rasskazy* (Moscow: Detizdat, 1940), pp. 257-62.
- Lev Zilov, *Mai i Oktiabrina* (Moscow: Mospoligraf, 1924).

Appendix 2: Canon and classics of British children's literature (including books accepted as literature suitable for children), published during the late-Victorian period and 1945

The late-Victorian period

R. M. Ballantyne, *The Coral Island* (1858).
Frances Hodgson Burnett, *Little Lord Fauntleroy* (1886).
Lewis Carroll, *Alice's Adventures in Wonderland* (1865) and *Through the Looking-Glass* (1871).
John Meade Falkner, *Moonfleet* (1898).
Henry Rider Haggard, *King Solomon's Mines* (1886).
Richard Jeffries, *Bevis* (1882).
Charles Kingsley, *The Water-Babies* (1863).
Rudyard Kipling, *Stalky & Co.* (1899).
Edward Lear, *Nonsense Songs* (1871).
George Macdonald, *At the Back of the North Wind* (1871), *The Princess and the Goblin* (1972).
Edith Nesbit, *The Story of the Treasure Seekers* (1899).
Talbot Baines Reed, *The Fifth Form at St Dominic's* (1887), *The Willoughby Captains* (serialized 1883–4).
Anna Sewell, *Black Beauty* (1877).
Robert Louis Stevenson, *Treasure Island* (1883).
H. G. Wells, *The Time Machine* (1895), *The Invisible Man* (1897), *The War of the Worlds* (1898).

The Edwardian period

Robert Baden-Powell, *Scouting for Boys: A Handbook for Instruction in Good Citizenship* (1908).
J. M. Barrie, *Peter Pan in Kensington Gardens* (1906), *Peter and Wendy* (1911).
Hilaire Belloc, *Cautionary Tales for Children* (1907).
Angela Brazil, *The Fortunes of Philippa* (1906).
Frances Hodgson Burnett, *A Little Princess* (1905), *The Secret Garden* (1911).
Arthur Conan Doyle, *The Hound of the Baskervilles* (1902), *The Adventures of Sherlock Holmes* (1892), *The Lost World* (1912).
Kenneth Grahame, *The Wind in the Willows* (1908).
Henry Rider Haggard, *Fair Margaret* (1907), *The Lady of Blossholme* (1909).
Rudyard Kipling, *Kim* (1901), *Puck of Pook's Hill* (1906), *Rewards and Fairies* (1910).
Edith Nesbit, *Five Children and It* (1902), *The Phoenix and the Carpet* (1904), *The Story of the Amulet* (1906), *The Railway Children* (1906), *The Enchanted Castle* (1907), *The House of Arden* (1908).
Beatrix Potter, *The Tale of Peter Rabbit* (1901) and other stories.

1914–45

Kitty Barne, *Visitors from London* (1940).
Enid Blyton, *The Famous Five* (1942–63).
Richmal Crompton, *Just William* series (1922–70).
Walter de la Mare, *Songs of Childhood* (1902), *Peacock Pie* (1913), *Come Hither* (1923), *Broomsticks and Other Tales* (1925), *The Lord Fish* (1933).
T. S. Eliot, *Old Possum's Book of Practical Cats* (1939).
Eleanor Farjeon, *Martin Pippin in the Apple Orchard* (1921) and *Martin Pippin in the Daisy Field* (1937).
Eve Garnett, *The Family from One End Street* (1937).
Norman Hunter, *The Incredible Adventures of Professor Branestawm* (1933).
Eric Knight, *Lassie Come-Home* (1940).
Hugh Lofting, *The Story of Doctor Dolittle* (1920/2).

John Masefield, *The Midnight Folk* (1927), *The Box of Delight*s (1930).
A. A. Milne, *When We Were Very Young* (1924), *Now We Are Six* (1927), *Winnie-the-Pooh* (1926), *The House at Pooh Corner* (1928).
Mary Norton, *The Magic Bed Knob* (1943), *Bonfires and Broomsticks* (1947).
Arthur Ransome, *Swallows and Amazons* (1930).
Noel Streatfield, *Ballet Shoes* (1936), *The Circus Is Coming* (1938), *The Children of Primrose Lane* (1941).
J. R. R. Tolkien, *The Hobbit* (1937).
P. L. Travers, *Mary Poppins* (1934), *Mary Poppins Comes Back* (1935), *Mary Poppins Opens the Door* (1943).
Mary Treadgold, *We Couldn't Leave Dinah* (1941).
Geoffrey Trease, *Bows against the Barons* (1934), *Cue for Treason* (1940).
Alison Uttley, *A Traveller in Time* (1939).
Denys Watkins-Pitchford (BB), *The Little Grey Men* (1942).
Terence Hanbury White, *The Sword in the Stone* (1938), *Mistress Masham's Repose* (1946).
Henry Williamson, *Tarka the Otter* (1927).

Appendix 3: British children's classics (and books considered as reading for children) written between the late-Victorian period and the Second World War that were translated into Russian

1. Mostly reprinted British classics that appeared in Russian translation during the Soviet and post-Soviet periods

List of mostly reprinted British texts that were translated into Russian during the Soviet period

- adaptations for children of the major novels of Charles Dickens.
- retellings of selected English nursery rhymes.
- selected English folk ballads.
- selected English folk tales.
- J. M. Barrie, the play *Peter Pan* and the novel *Peter and Wendy*.
- Lewis Carroll, *Alice's Adventures in Wonderland* and *Through the Looking-Glass*.
- Arthur Conan Doyle, stories about Sherlock Holmes and *The Lost World* (positioned as books for young adults).
- James Greenwood, *The True History of a Little Ragamuffin*.
- Rudyard Kipling, *Just so Stories* and *The Jungle Book*.
- Edward Lear, *Nonsense Songs* (selected poems).
- Hugh Lofting, *The Story of Doctor Dolittle*.
- A. A. Milne, *Winnie-the-Pooh* and *The King's Breakfast* (from *When We Were Very Young*).
- Beatrix Potter, *The Tale of Mrs. Tiggy-Winkle* (only).
- Robert Louis Stevenson, *Treasure Island*.
- P. L. Travers, novels about Mary Poppins.
- Ethel Lilian Voynich, *The Gadfly*.
- H. G. Wells, *The Invisible Man*, *The War of the Worlds* and *The Time Machine*.

List of mostly reprinted British texts that appeared in Russian translation during the post-Soviet period

The books from the previous group and

- Enid Blyton, *The Famous Five*.
- Frances Hodgson Burnett, *Little Lord Fauntleroy*, *A Little Princess* and *The Secret Garden*.
- Kenneth Grahame, *The Wind in the Willows*.
- Rudyard Kipling, *Puck of Pook's Hill* and *Rewards and Fairies*.
- Eric Knight, *Lassie Come-Home*.
- C. S. Lewis, *The Chronicles of Narnia*.
- George Macdonald, *The Princess and the Goblin*.
- A. A. Milne, all poems from *When We Were Very Young* and *Now We Are Six*.
- Edith Nesbit, *The Story of the Treasure Seekers*, *Five Children and It*, *The Phoenix and the Carpet*, *The Story of the Amulet*, *The Railway Children*, *The Enchanted Castle*.
- Beatrix Potter, *The Tale of Peter Rabbit* and other tales.
- Anna Sewell, *Black Beauty*.
- J. R. R. Tolkien, *The Hobbit*.

2. British children's books that were not translated during the Soviet period and appeared in translation in the post-Soviet period

Hilaire Belloc, *Cautionary Tales for Children*.
Enid Blyton, *The Famous Five* and *The Secret Seven*.
Frances Hodgson Burnett, *A Little Princess* and *The Secret Garden*.
Richmal Crompton, *Just William* (series).
Eleanor Farjeon, *Martin Pippin in the Daisy Field* and *Martin Pippin in the Apple Orchard*.
Charles Kingsley, *The Water-Babies*.
Rudyard Kipling, *Kim*.
George Macdonald, *At the Back of the North Wind*, *The Princess and the Goblin* (one fairy tale only was translated in 1986).

Edith Nesbit, *The Story of the Treasure Seekers, Five Children and It, The Phoenix and the Carpet, The Story of the Amulet, The Railway Children, The Enchanted Castle* (only two fairy tales – *Billy the King* and *The Charmed Life* – were translated in 1986).

Beatrix Potter, *The Tale of Peter Rabbit* and other stories (only *The Tale of Mrs. Tiggy-Winkle* was translated in 1958 and subsequently reprinted during the Soviet period).

Arthur Ransome, *Swallows and Amazons* (it was published in English as a textbook for students of English in 1980).

Anna Sewell, *Black Beauty* (it was published in English in 1961 and 1967 as a textbook for students of English).

Noel Streatfield, *Ballet Shoes*.

J. R. R. Tolkien, *Roverandom*.

Denys Watkins-Pitchford (BB), *The Little Grey Men*.

Terence Hanbury White, *The Sword in the Stone*.

3. British texts that were only translated once and not reprinted afterwards during the Soviet period, and then appeared in translation in the post-Soviet period

Robert Baden-Powell, *Scouting for Boys: A Handbook for Instruction in Good Citizenship* (the pre-revolutionary version was reprinted in 1918 only).

J. M. Barrie, *Peter Pan in Kensington Gardens* (translated in 1986).

Frances Hodgson Burnett, *Little Lord Fauntleroy* (the pre-revolutionary translation was reprinted only once in 1918).

T. S. Eliot, *Old Possum's Book of Practical Cats* (only 'Macavity: The Mystery Cat' and 'Old Deuteronomy' were translated in 1959 by S. Marshak and by A. Sergeev 1984, respectively; the whole book was translated after 1991).

John Meade Falkner, *Moonfleet* (translated in 1949 only).

Kenneth Grahame, *The Wind in the Willows* (translated in 1988 only).

Rudyard Kipling, *Stalky & Co.* (translated in 1925 only), *Puck of Pook's Hill* and *Rewards and Fairies* (stories about Puck were translated in 1984).

Eric Knight, *Lassie Come-Home* (translated in 1963 only).

Henry Williamson, *Tarka the Otter* (translated in 1979 only).

4. British texts not translated during the Soviet and post-Soviet periods

Kitty Barne, *Visitors from London*.
Angela Brazil, *The Fortunes of Philippa*.
Eve Garnett, *The Family from One End Street* (only appeared in English as a textbook for students of English in 1973).
Richard Jeffries, *Bevis*.
Norman Hunter, *The Incredible Adventures of Professor Branestawm*.
John Masefield, *The Midnight Folk* and *The Box of Delights*.
Noel Streatfeild, *The Circus Is Coming* and *The Children of Primrose Lane*.
Mary Treadgold, *We Couldn't Leave Dinah*.
Alison Uttley, *A Traveller in Time*.

Notes

1 Introduction

1 Korney Chukovsky, *Vysokoe iskusstvo. Printsipy khudozhestvennogo perevoda* (St. Petersburg: Azbuka-Klassika, 2011), chapter 9 'Perevody prezhde i teper' [Translations in the past and now], pp. 342–3.
2 See more on cultural meanings in Stuart Hall, 'The Question of Cultural Identity', in *Modernity: An Introduction to Modern Societies*, ed. Stuart Hall et al. (Malden, MA: Blackwell, 1996), pp. 595–634 (pp. 611, 613); and Stuart Hall, 'Whose Heritage? Un-settling "the Heritage", Re-imagining the Post-nation', *Third Text*, 13(49) (1999), 3–13 (p. 4).
3 *The Future of Multi-Ethnic Britain: Report of the Commission on the Future of Multi-Ethnic Britain*, ed. Bhikhu Parekh (London: Profile Books, 2000), pp. 15–16 and 19–20.
4 Iain Chambers, *Border Dialogues: Journeys in Postmodernity* (London: Routledge, 1990), p. 27.
5 Jaqueline Simpson and Steve Roud, 'Merrie England', in *A Dictionary of English Folklore* (Oxford: Oxford University Press, 2003), p. 235.
6 I use the English phrase 'Merry England' rather than the equally widespread alternative 'Merrie England' (as per Google Books Ngram Viewer, https://books.google.com/ngrams), as the change in spelling does not alter the connotation of the phrase and the results of Google Scholar search demonstrate that 'Merry England' has been a more popular choice since 2010.
7 The list of British children's books is given in Appendix 2.
8 Rebecca Knuth, *Children's Literature and British Identity: Imagining a People and a Nation* (Lanham: Scarecrow Press, 2012), pp. 9, 127.
9 I. O. Naumova, *Frazeologicheskie kal'ki angliiskogo proiskhozhdeniia v sovremennom russkom iazyke (na materiale publitsistiki): Monografiia* (Kharkov: KhNAGKh, 2012), p. 80.
10 See K. N. Batyushkov, 'Ten' druga', in *K. N. Batyushkov. Polnoe sobranie stikhotvorenii* (Moscow: Sovetskii pisatel', 1964), pp. 170–1; and M. I. Tsvetaeva, 'Ia bereg pokidal tumannyi Al'biona . . .', in *Marina Tsvetaeva. Stikhotvoreniia. Poemy* (Moscow: RIPOL klassik, 2007), pp. 158–9.
11 For example, N. M. Karamzin, P. I. Sumarokov and A. I. Herzen mentioned the depressing nature of English fog and rain. See more on this in Nikolay A.

Erofeev, *Tumannyi Al'bion: Angliia i anglichane glazami russkikh, 1825–1853 gg.* (Moscow: Nauka, 1982), p. 179; and *'Ia bereg pokidal tumannyi Al'biona . . .': russkie pisateli ob Anglii, 1646–1945*, ed. Olga A. Kaznina and A. N. Nikoliukin (Moscow: ROSSPEN, 2001).

12 See more on this in Erofeev, *Tumannyi Al'bion*, pp. 289, 298.

13 For example, Russian Anglophobic views, which are based on Russian political antipathy towards Britain, are discussed in Apollon B. Davidson, 'Obraz Britanii v Rossii XIX i XX stoletii', *Novaia i noveishaia istoriia*, 5 (2005), http://vivovoco.astronet.ru/VV/PAPERS/HISTORY/ALBION.HTM#15 (accessed 16 May 2019), and in Apollon B. Davidson, *Na putiakh k vzaimoponimaniiu*, 19 March 2014 https://histrf.ru/biblioteka/b/na-putiakh-k-vzaimoponimaniiu (accessed 16 May 2019).

14 'Target culture' is understood as the culture of the country into which the language of the original text is translated; 'source culture' stands for the culture of the country where the original text is produced. Gideon Toury, *Descriptive Translation Studies – and Beyond*, rev. edn (Amsterdam: John Benjamins, 2012), pp. 22–3.

15 André Lefevere, 'Mother Courage's Cucumbers: Text, System and Refraction in a Theory of Literature', in *The Translation Studies Reader*, ed. Lawrence Venuti, 1st edn (London: Routledge, 2000), pp. 233–49 (p. 237).

16 Lawrence Venuti, *The Scandals of Translation: Towards an Ethics of Difference* (London: Routledge, 1998), p. 67.

17 Zohar Shavit, 'Translation of Children's Literature', in *The Translation of Children's Literature: A Reader*, ed. Gillian Lathey (Clevedon: Multilingual Matters, 2006), pp. 25–40 (p. 26).

18 Emer O'Sullivan, *Comparative Children's Literature*, trans. Anthea Bell (London: Routledge, 2005), p. 74; Maria Nikolajeva, *Children's Literature Comes of Age: Toward a New Aesthetic* (New York: Garland, 1996), pp. 35–6.
Broadly speaking, when the original text is domesticated, it means that its unfamiliar foreign components are replaced with those known to readers of the receiving culture. In contrast to domestication, the original text which is foreignized in translation introduces its foreignness to readers of the receiving culture so that they can see differences between cultures.

19 Roderick McGillis, *The Nimble Reader: Literary Theory and Children's Literature* (New York: Twayne, 1996), p. 112.

20 Ian Mason, 'Discourse, Ideology and Translation', in *Translation Studies: Critical Concepts in Linguistics*, ed. Mona Baker (London: Routledge, 2009), iii, pp. 141–56 (p. 143).

21 For example, scholarly views on the essence of Englishness are given in Anthony Easthope, *Englishness and National Culture* (London: Routledge, 1999); Krishan Kumar, *The Making of English National Identity*

(New York: Cambridge University Press, 2003); Ina Habermann, *Myth, Memory and the Middlebrow: Priestley, du Maurier and the Symbolic Form of Englishness* (Basingstoke: Palgrave Macmillan, 2010); Rebecca Knuth, *Children's Literature and British Identity: Imagining a People and a Nation* (Lanham, MD: Scarecrow Press, 2012); Jean Webb, 'Walking into the Sky: Englishness, Heroism, and Cultural Identity: A Nineteenth- and Twentieth-Century Perspective', in *Children's Literature and the Fin de Siècle*, ed. Roderick McGillis (Westport, CT: Praeger, 2003), pp. 51–6; and Margaret Meek, 'The Englishness of English Children's Books', in *Children's Literature and National Identity*, ed. Margaret Meek (Stoke-on-Trent: Trentham Books, 2001), pp. 89–100. An analysis of different literary portraits of England and its people created by English writers, who draw on their own perceptions of Englishness, is given in David Gervais, *Literary Englands: Versions of 'Englishness' in Modern Writing* (Cambridge: Cambridge University Press, 1993); Menno Spiering, *Englishness: Foreigners and Images of National Identity in Postwar Literature* (Amsterdam: Rodopi, 1992); and the volume *Writing Englishness 1900–1950: An Introductory Sourcebook on National Identity*, ed. Judy Giles and Tim Middleton (New York: Routledge, 1995). As for Russian studies, there is a wide bibliography on the dialogue between English and Russian culture, as well as the image of Englishness in Russian literature. The major works are the following: Nina P. Mikhal'skaia, *Rossiia i Angliia: problemy imagologii* (Samara: OOO 'Porto-print', 2012); Tat'iana N. Breeva and Liliia F. Khabibulina, *Natsional'nyi mif v russkoi i angliiskoi literature* (Kazan': RITs 'Shkola', 2009); Viacheslav P. Shestakov, *Angliiskaia literatura i angliiskii natsional'nyi kharakter* (St. Petersburg: Nestor-Istoriia, 2010); Erofeev, *Tumannyi Al'bion*; *Lingvokul'turnyi Tipazh 'Angliiskii Chudak'*, ed. Vladimir Karasik and Elena Iarmakhova (Moscow: Gnozis, 2006); *'Ia bereg pokidal tumannyi Al'biona . . .'*, ed. Olga Kaznina and A. N. Nikoliukin.
22 Julian Barnes, *England, England* (London: Vintage Books, 2012), pp. 81–3.
23 Meek, 'Preface', p. xv, and Meek, 'The Englishness of English Children's Books', p. 90, both in *Children's Literature and National Identity*, ed. Margaret Meek.
24 Stuart Hall, 'Whose Heritage? Un-settling "the Heritage", Re-imagining the Post-nation', *Third Text*, 13(49) (1999), 3–13 (pp. 4–5), DOI: 10.1080/09528829908576818 (accessed 18 July 2019); Stuart Hall, 'The Question of Cultural Identity', in *Modernity: An Introduction to Modern Societies*, ed. Stuart Hall, et al. (Malden, MA: Blackwell, 1996), pp. 595–634 (p. 613).
25 Knuth, *Children's Literature and British Identity*, pp. 5–7; and Webb, 'Walking into the Sky', pp. 51–6.
26 *Writing Englishness 1900–1950*, ed. Judy Giles and Tim Middleton, pp. 22–3, 195–6.
27 Easthope, *Englishness and National Culture*, pp. 55–6.
28 Webb, 'Walking into the Sky', pp. 51–6.

29 M. Daphne Kutzer, *Empire's Children: Empire and Imperialism in Classic British Children's Books* (New York: Garland, 2000), pp. xvii, xx.
30 Knuth, *Children's Literature and British Identity*, pp. 5–7.
31 Phillip Mallett, 'Rudyard Kipling and the Invention of Englishness', in *Beyond Pug's Tour: National and Ethnic Stereotyping in Theory and Literary Practice*, ed. C. C. Barfoot (Amsterdam: Rodopi, 1997), pp. 255–66 (pp. 263–4).
32 For a detailed analysis of Englishness through the lens of English fictional and non-fictional writing refer to Elena Goodwin, *'Dobraia Staraia Angliia' in Russian Perception: Literary Representations of Englishness in Translated Children's Literature in Soviet and Post-Soviet Russia* (PhD thesis, University of Exeter, 2017), pp. 63–92.
33 David Matless, *Landscape and Englishness* (London: Reaktion Books, 1998), p. 17; Alun Howkins, 'The Discovery of Rural England', in *Englishness: Politics and Culture 1880–1920*, ed. Philip Dodd and Robert Colls (London: Croom Helm, 1986), pp. 62–88 (pp. 73–4).
34 Howkins, 'The Discovery of Rural England', pp. 73–4.
35 Christine Berberich, *The Image of the English Gentleman in Twentieth-Century Literature: Englishness and Nostalgia* (Aldershot: Ashgate, 2007), pp. 38, 136, 39.
36 Richard R. Marsh, 'The Farmer in Modern English Fiction', *Agricultural History*, 23 (1949), 146–59 (p. 148).
37 Robert Colls, *Identity of England* (Oxford: Oxford University Press, 2002), p. 248, 306.
38 Giorgia Grilli, *Myth, Symbol, and Meaning in Mary Poppins: The Governess as Provocateur*, trans. Jennifer Varney (New York: Routledge, 2007), pp. 122, 127.
39 Ulrike Lentz, 'The Representation of Western European Governesses and Tutors on the Russian Country Estate in Historical Documents and Literary Texts' (Doctoral thesis, University of Surrey, 2008), p. 66.
40 Easthope, *Englishness and National Culture*, pp. 107, 109, 207.
41 Humphrey Carpenter and Mari Prichard, *The Oxford Companion to Children's Literature* (Oxford: Oxford University Press, 2005), p. 380.
42 Ernest Barker, 'An Attempt at Perspective', in *The Character of England*, ed. Ernest Barker (Oxford: Clarendon Press, 1947), pp. 550–75 (pp. 569–70).
43 Colin Manlove, *The Fantasy Literature of England* (Basingstoke: Macmillan, 1999); and Colin Manlove, *From Alice to Harry Potter: Children's Fantasy in England* (Christchurch, NZ: Cybereditions, 2003).
44 Manlove, *The Fantasy Literature of England*, pp. 2, 191, 198–9.
45 Kumar, *The Making of English National Identity*, p. 218.
46 Krishan Kumar, '"Englishness" and English National Identity', in *British Cultural Studies: Geography, Nationality, and Identity*, ed. David Morley and Kevin Robins (New York: Oxford University Press, 2001), pp. 41–55 (p. 53).

47 See Knuth, *Children's Literature and British Identity*, pp. 88, 180, 181, on the image of idealized England.
48 The term 'social practices' is understood as the habitual activities of people within a community which shape everyday life, for example, routine behaviour. Also social practices are performed according to a community's worldview and the perception of the community's sense of identity, for example, formal greetings.
49 For a detailed analysis of Englishness through the lens of Russian fictional and non-fictional writing refer to Elena Goodwin, *'Dobraia Staraia Angliia' in Russian Perception: Literary Representations of Englishness in Translated Children's Literature in Soviet and Post-Soviet Russia* (PhD thesis, University of Exeter, 2017), pp. 93–121.
50 See Nikolay A. Erofeev, *Tumannyi Al'bion: Angliia i anglichane glazami russkikh, 1825–1853 gg* [Foggy Albion: England and the English through Russian eyes, 1825–1853], pp. 5, 7, 22, 30. Erofeev's study has influenced different post-Soviet studies of Englishness produced by the following Russian scholars: Apollon Davidson, Nina Mikhal'skaia, Viacheslav Shestakov, Olga Kaznina, Ekaterina Viazova, Tat'iana Breeva, Liliia Khabibulina and Vladimir Karasik. The main works for the post-Soviet period are given in Appendix 1, part 1.
51 Detailed reviews of representing England in Russian culture in the historical perspective are given in Olga A. Kaznina, 'Angliia glazami russkikh', in *'Ia bereg pokidal tumannyi Al'biona . . .': russkie pisateli ob Anglii, 1646–1945*, ed. Olga A. Kaznina and A. N. Nikoliukin (Moscow: ROSSPEN, 2001), pp. 3–24; Davidson, 'Obraz Britanii i Rossii XIX i XX stoletii'; and Davidson, *Na putiakh k vzaimoponimaniiu*.
52 Korney Chukovsky, *Zagovorili molchavshie: Anglichane i voina* (Petrograd: Izd. tov-va A. F. Marks, 1916), p. 3.
53 N. I. Kareev, 'How Far Russia Knows England', in *The Soul of Russia*, ed. Winifred Stephens, trans. Adeline L. Kaye (London: Macmillan, 1916), pp. 96–101 (pp. 96, 99, 101).
54 See more on this in Anna Vaninskaya, 'Under Russian Eyes: Foreign Correspondents in Edwardian Britain', *The Times Literary Supplement* (26 November 2014), 17–19; and Anna Vaninskaya, 'Korney Chukovsky in Britain', *Translation and Literature*, 20 (2011), 373–92.

Sketches by Samuil Marshak portray England as he saw it when staying there between 1912 and 1914. While studying in London, he went hiking during summer breaks in the South West, recording his impressions of Devon and Cornwall in three sketches *Otdykh moriaka* [Sailor's rest], *Lift* [lift/giving a lift] and *Rybaki Polperro* [Fishermen of Polperro] – all published in the periodical press in 1914 (see Samuil Marshak, *Sobranie sochinenii v 8 tomakh*, ed. V. M. Zhirmunskii, 8 vols [Moscow: Khudozhestvennaia literatura, 1968–72], vi: *Stat'i. Vystupleniia. Zametki.*

Vospominaniia. Proza raznykh let, ed. S. S. Chulkova and E. B. Skorospelova (1971), pp. 474–91). He also documented his walks in Devon and Cornwall in the poem *20 iiunia – 7 iiulia* [20 June–7 July] written in 1913 but published only in 1973 (see Samuil Marshak, *Stikhotvoreniia i poemy* [Leningrad: Sovetskii pisatel', 1973], pp. 440–52). In addition to this, Marshak described aspects of daily life in England, English folklore, landscape and national character in private letters written between 1912 and 1914 (see Marshak, *Sobranie sochinenii v 8 tomakh*, viii: *Izbrannye pis'ma*, letters 26–30, 32, 43).

55 On the influence of British children's literature on Chukovsky's works written for children, see his article 'Kak ia poliubil anglo-americanskuiu literaturu' [How I came to love English and American literature], p. 487, in Chukovsky, Korney, *Sobranie sochinenii v 15 tomakh*, 15 vols (Moscow: Agentstvo FTM, 2012), iii: *Visokoe iskusstvo. Iz anglo-amerikanskikh tetradei*, Ebook, pp. 485–8. On the influence of British children's literature and folk ballads on Marshak's translations and original works written for children, see his article 'O sebe' [About myself], in *Marshak S. Ia., Sobranie sochinenii v 8 tomakh*, ed. V. M. Zhirmunskii, 8 vols (Moscow: Khudozhestvennaia literatura, 1968–72), i: *Proizvedeniia dlia detei*, ed. V. I. Leibson (1968), pp. 5–15.

56 A. N. Tolstoy, 'Anglichane, kogda oni liubezny', in *'Ia bereg pokidal tumannyi Al'biona . . .': russkie pisateli ob Anglii, 1646–1945*, ed. Olga A. Kaznina and A. N. Nikoliukin (Moscow: ROSSPEN, 2001), pp. 362–9.

57 O. S. Vasil'ev, *Sovetskie Pisateli ob Anglii* (Leningrad: Lenizdat, 1984).

58 The main works are given in Appendix 1, part 1 'Englishness in Russian non-fiction'. However, the list is not comprehensive. More publications referring to the pre-Soviet and Soviet periods can be found in two compilations: *'Ia bereg pokidal tumannyi Al'biona ...': russkie pisateli ob Anglii, 1646–1945*, ed. Olga A. Kaznina and A. N. Nikoliukin (Moscow: ROSSPEN, 2001) and O. S. Vasil'ev, *Sovetskie Pisateli ob Anglii* (Leningrad: Lenizdat, 1984).

59 Ilya G. Ehrenburg, 'Angliia', in Ilya G. Ehrenburg, *Sobranie sochinenii v 9 tomakh*, 9 vols (Moscow: Khudizhestvennaia literatura, 1962–7), vii: *Khronika nashikh dnei. Viza vremeni. Ispaniia. Grazhdanskaia voina v Avstrii. Stat'i* (1966), pp. 444–78 (pp. 452, 460).

60 See Anton Vol'skii, *Angliia. Bilet v odnu storonu* (Moscow: Eksmo, 2014); Zurab Nalbandian, *Chaepitie u korolevy: v nachale XXI veka v Britanii* (Moscow: Vremia, 2007); Mikhail Lyubimov, *Gulianiia s Cheshirskim kotom: memuar-esse ob angliiskoi dushe* (St. Petersburg: Amfora, 2015), Ebook; Kseniia Atarova, *Angliia, moia Angliia* (Moscow: Raduga, 2008); Anna Pavlovskaia, *Angliia i anglichane* (Moscow: Izdatel'stvo: Moskovskii universitet, Triada, 2004); Anna Pavlovskaia, *5 O'Clock i drugie traditsii Anglii* (Moscow: Algoritm, 2014).

61 See the list of books in Appendix 1, part 2 'Englishness in Russian fiction'.

62 Boris Zhitkov, *Maria i Meri* (Moscow: Gosudarstvennoe izdatel'stvo, 1929).
63 Vasily Aksyonov, *Moi dedushka – pamiatnik* (Kemerovo: Sovremennaia otechestvennaia kniga, 1991), pp. 133–4. This novel first appeared in the monthly children's magazine *Kostior* in 1970 (issues 7–10). Afterwards it was published by Detskaia literatura publishing house in 1972.
64 Dina Rubina, *Dzhentl'meny i sobaki* (Moscow: Eksmo, 2012).
65 Joseph Brodsky, 'In Memory of Stephen Spender', in *On Grief and Reason: Essays* (London: Penguin Books, 2011), pp. part X, Kindle edition.
66 See the report on the Russian book market in 2017 published by the Russian Federal Agency for Press and Mass Communications: *Knizhnyi rynok Rossii: Sostoianie, tendentsii i perspektivy razvitiia. Otraslevoi doklad. 2018*, ed. V. V. Grigoriev (Moscow: Federal'noe agentstvo po pechati i massovym kommunikatsiiam, 2018), pp. 8, 12, 16.
67 Sergei Dovlatov, 'Perevodnye kartinki', in *Sergei Dovlatov. Sobraniie sochinenii v 4-kh tomakh*, 4 vols (St. Petersburg: Azbuka-klassika, 2005), iv, 328–48, http://www.sergeidovlatov.com/books/perev_kart.html (accessed 18 July 2019).
68 This survey was held by Labirint.ru. For more information see Labirint.ru, 'Vneklassnoe chtenie. Otchet dlia pedagogov i roditelei po resul'tatam vserossiiskogo onlain-oprosa' (May 2013), https://en.calameo.com/read/00046390357ebf9393e1f (accessed 18 July 2019).
69 Alexandra Borisenko, '"The Good Are Always the Merry": British Children's Literature in Soviet Russia', (p. 208).
70 See, for example, the following works researching Russian translations of *Winnie-the-Pooh*: Alexandra Borisenko, 'Pesni nevinnosti i pesni opyta: O novykh perevodakh "Vinni-Pukha"', *Inostrannaia literatura*, 4 (2002), https://magazines.gorky.media/inostran/2002/4/pesni-nevinnosti-i-pesni-opyta.html (accessed 18 July 2019); Alexandra Borisenko, '"The Good Are Always the Merry": British Children's Literature in Soviet Russia', in *Translation in Russian Contexts: Culture, Politics, Identity*, ed. Brian James Baer and Susanna Witt (New York: Routledge, 2018), pp. 205–19; Judith Inggs, 'Translation and Transformation: English-Language Children's Literature in (Soviet) Russian Guise', *International Research in Children's Literature*, 8 (2015), 1–16; Yuri Leving, '"Kto-to tam vsie-taki est' . . .": Vinni-Pukh i novaia animatsionnaia estetika', in *Veselyie chelovechki: kul'turnye geroi sovetskogo detstva*, ed. Il'ia Kukulin, Mark Lipovetskii and Mariia Maiofis (Moscow: Novoe literaturenoe obozrenie, 2008), pp. 245–73; Natalia Smoliarova, 'Detskii "Nedetskii" Vinni-Pukh', in *Veselyie chelovechki: kul'turnye geroi sovetskogo detstva*, ed. Il'ia Kukulin, Mark Lipovetskii and Mariia Maiofis (Moscow: Novoe literaturenoe obozrenie, 2008), pp. 224–44.

See the following works researching Russian translations of *Alice's Adventures in Wonderland*: Nina Demurova, 'Golos i skripka (k perevodu ekstsentricheskikh skazok L'iuisa Kerrolla)', *Masterstvo perevoda*, 7 (1970), 150–85; Judith Inggs, 'Translation and Transformation: English-Language Children's Literature in (Soviet) Russian Guise', *International Research in Children's Literature*, 8 (2015), 1–16; Eleni Karvounidou, 'The Manipulation of Children's Literature: The Russian Translations of "Alice's Adventures in Wonderland" ' (Doctoral thesis, University of Surrey, 2018); V. V. Lobanov, *L'iuis Kerroll v Rossii: annotirovannaia bibliografiia perevodov* (Moscow: Maks-Press, 2000); Mee Ryoung Park, 'A Case Study of Russification in Two Translations of *Alice's Adventures in Wonderland* by Vladimir Nabokov and Boris Zakhoder', *Children's Literature in Education*, 49(2) (2018), 140–60; Fan Parker, *Lewis Carroll in Russia: Translations of Alice in Wonderland, 1879–1989* (New York: Russian House, 1994); Elena Tchougounova-Paulson, 'A history of early and fin de siècle Russian translations of Lewis Carroll's "Alice's Adventures in Wonderland" ', forthcoming.

2 Translated literature in Russia: The 'high art' of realist translation, censorship and key actors within the field

1 The development of Russian theoretical views on literary translation before 1917 is analysed in Vilen Komissarov, 'Russian Tradition', in *Routledge Encyclopedia of Translation Studies* ed. Mona Baker (London: Routledge, 2001), pp. 694–705; and Maurice Friedberg, *Literary Translation in Russia: A Cultural History* (University Park, PA: Pennsylvania State University Press, 1997). Also a brief account of the history of Russian literary translation from the eighteenth century to the Soviet time is given in Mikhail Gasparov's article *Briusov i bukvalism* [*Briusov and Literalism*] first published in *Masterstvo perevoda*, 8 (1971), 88–128 (pp. 108–9) and translated into English in *Russian Writers on Translation*, ed. Brian James Baer and Natalia Olshanskaya (Manchester: St. Jerome, 2013), pp. 132–4.
2 For the history of the Vsemirnaia literatura publishing house, see Maria Khotimsky, 'World Literature, Soviet Style: A Forgotten Episode in the History of the Idea', in *Ab Imperio*, 3 (2013), 119–54.
3 The principles of Socialist Realism were established as the dominant methodology in literature in the 1930s; they were articulated as an official formula of Soviet literature at the First Congress of Soviet Writers of 1934. The broad definition of Socialist Realism in literature was given in the Charter of the Union of Soviet Writers, describing it as 'a truthful and historically accurate depiction of reality in its revolutionary development' aimed at 'the ideological remoulding and educating of the working class in the spirit of socialism' (*Pervyi Vsesoiuznyi S'ezd Sovetskikh pisatelei, 1934: Stenographicheskii otchet* [Moscow: Gosudartstvennoe izdatel'stvo khudozhestvennoi literatury, 1934; repr. Moscow: Sovetskii pisatel', 1990], p. 712).

4 More on the First All-Union Conference of Translators is given in Susanna Witt, 'Arts of Accommodation: The First All-Union Conference of Translators, Moscow, 1936, and the Ideologization of Norms', in *The Art of Accommodation: Literary Translation in Russia*, ed. Leon Burnett and Emily Lygo (Bern: Peter Lang, 2013), pp. 141–84.

5 See more on Al'tman in Andrei Azov, *Poverzhennye bukvalisty: Iz istorii khudozhestvennogo perevoda v SSSR v 1920-1960-e gody* (Moscow: Vysshaia shkola ekonomiki, 2013), pp. 48–50, 52.

6 Ibid., pp. 59–60.

7 Lauren G. Leighton, 'Translation as a Derived Art', *Proceedings of the American Philosophical Society*, 134 (1990), 445–54 (pp. 448, 449).

8 Korney Chukovsky, *Sobranie sochinenii v 15 tomakh*, 15 vols (Moscow: Agentstvo FTM Ltd, 2012), xiii: *Dnevnik (1936–1969)*, Ebook, p. 317.

9 Aleksandr A. Smirnov and M. P. Alekseev, 'Perevod', in *Literaturnaia entsiklopediia*, ed. A. V. Lunacharsky and others, 11 vols (Moscow: Kommunisticheskaia akademiia; Moscow: Sovetskaia entsiklopediia; Moscow: Khudozhestvennaia literatura, 1929–39), viii (1934), 512–32 (p. 512).

10 Igor Motyashov, 'The Social and Aesthetic Criteria Applied in Choosing Children's Books for Translation', in *Children's Books in Translation: The Situation and the Problems*, ed. Göte Klingberg, Mary Ørvig and Stuart Amor (Stockholm: Almqvist and Wiksell International, 1978), pp. 97–103 (pp. 99, 100).

11 Balina and Rudova, 'Introduction', p. 193.

12 Herman Ermolaev, *Censorship in Soviet literature, 1917–1991* (Lanham, MD: Rowman and Littlefield, 1997), p. 10.

13 Arlen V. Blium, *Tsenzura v Sovetskom Soiuze. 1917–1991. Dokumenty* (Moscow: ROSSPEN, 2004) p. 69, dokument № 46 'Tsirkuliari Glavlita ego mestnym organam'.

14 Ibid., p. 100, document № 79 'Dokladnaia zapiska o deiatel'nosti Glavlita'.

15 Arlen V. Blium, *Za kulisami 'Ministerstva pravdy': Tainaia istoriia sovetskoi tsenzury. 1917–1929* (St. Petersburg: Akademicheskii proekt, 1994), p. 194.

16 Arlen V. Blium, *Sovetskaia tsenzura v epokhu total'nogo terrora: 1929–1953* (St. Petersburg: Gumanitarnoe agentstvo 'Akademicheskii proekt', 2000), pp. 14–17.

17 Inna Slobozhan, 'Pugalo, ili byli o sovetskoi tsenzure', in Inna Slobozhan, *A v serdyse moiem – Leningrad . . .* (St. Petersburg: Izdatel'stvo 'Severnaia zvezda', 2013), pp. 102–7 (pp. 102–3).

18 The Soviet/Russian literary translator and literary critic Vladimir M. Rossels quoted in Leighton, *Two Worlds, One Art*, p. 36.

19 Daniil Adamov and Viktoriia Sal'nikova, 'Perevodchik Viktor Golyshev – o Brodskom, tsenzure i idealizatsii 60-kh', *Setevoe izdanie m24.ru* (24 May 2015), http://www.m24.ru/articles/71723 (accessed 18 July 2019).

20 Samantha Sherry, 'Censorship in Translation in the Soviet Union: The Manipulative Rewriting of Howard Fast's Novel *The Passion of Sacco and Vanzetti*', *Slavonica*, 16 (2010), 1–14 (p. 4).
21 Korney Chukovsky, *Vysokoe iskusstvo. Printsipy khudozhestvennogo perevoda* (St. Petersburg: Azbuka-Klassika, 2011), pp. 295, 153, 188.
22 Samuil Marshak, 'O nasledstve i nasledstvennosti v detskoi literature', in *Marshak S. Ia., Sobranie sochinenii v 8 tomakh*, ed. V. M. Zhirmunskii, 8 vols (Moscow: Khudozhestvennaia literatura, 1968–72), vii: *Vospitaniie slovom (Stat'i, zametki, vospominaniia)*, ed. E. B. Skorospelova (1971), pp. 513–41.
23 Samuil Marshak, 'Iskusstvo poeticheskogo portreta', in *Masterstvo perevoda, 1* (Moscow: Sovetskii pisatel, 1959), pp. 245–50 (p. 246), translated into English by Brian James Baer in *Russian Writers on Translation: An Anthology*, ed. Brian James Baer and Natalia Olshanskaya, pp. 90–2 (p. 91).
24 A letter No. 197 to V. S. Rudin, 23 February 1952, in Samuil Marshak, *Sobranie sochinenii v 8 tomakh*, ed. V. M. Zhirmunskii, 8 vols (Moscow: Khudozhestvennaia literatura, 1968–72), viii: *Izbrannye pis'ma*, ed. S. S. Chulkova (1972), pp. 256–61.
25 Efim Etkind, *Poeziia i perevod* (Moscow: Sovetskii pisatel', 1963), p. 354.
26 Samuil Marshak, 'Dom, uvenchannyi globusom. Dve besedy S. Ia. Marshaka s L. K. Chukovskoi', *Novyi mir*, 9 (1968), 158–81 (p. 160); Korney Chukovsky, *Vysokoe iskusstvo*, p. 264.
27 Viktor Lunin, 'Vospominaniia: Zakhoder i dr.', *Vyshgorod: literaturno-khudozhestvennyi obschestvenno-politicheskii zhurnal*, 1–2 (2007), 142–59 (p. 152).
28 Etkind, *Poeziia i perevod*, p. 263.
29 Boris Zakhoder, *'No est' odin poet': neopublikovannoe nasledie v 2-kh tomakh*, 2 vols (Moscow: Gala-Izdatel'stvo, 2008), ii: *Moi tainyi sovetnik*, pp. 267, 295, 305–6; Boris Zakhoder, 'Prikliucheniia Vinni-Pukha (Iz istorii moikh publikatsii)', *Voprosy literatury*, 5 (2002), 197–225 (p. 201).
30 Riitta Oittinen, *Translating for Children* (New York: Garland, 2000), p. 162.
31 For M. Iasnov, see Elena Kalashnikova, *Interview with Mikhail Iasnov 'Perevod – iskusstvo poter'*, Russkii Zhurnal / Krug chteniia, 11 January 2002, http://old.russ.ru/krug/20020111_kalash-pr.html (accessed 18 July 2019); and Mikhail Iasnov, 'Ot Robina-Bobina do malysha Russelia', *Druzhba narodov*, 12 (2004), 190–200. For I. Tokmakova, see Evgenii Kurneshov, *Irina Petrovna Tokmakova predstavliaet knigu 'Piter Pen' Dzh. Barri izdatel'stva 'Moskovskie uchebniki'*, online video recording, YouTube, 31 May 2012, https://www.youtube.com/watch?v=PeA5IpUEzGg (accessed 16 May 2019).

    For Iu. Iakhnina, see Elena Kalashnikova, *Po-russki s liubov'iu: besedy s perevodchikami* (Moscow: Novoe Literaturnoe Obozrenie, 2008), p. 549.
32 For A. Livergant and V. Golyshev, see Nataliia Kienia, *Interview with Viktor Golyshev. 'Esli perevodish' popsu, nechego tseremonit'sia': Viktor Golyshev o*

prilizannykh tekstakh, 'Garri Pottere' i novoiaze, Theory&Practice, 25 February 2015, http://theoryandpractice.ru/posts/10266-golyshev (accessed 18 July 2019); and Azamat Rakhimov, 'Interview with Alexander Livergant: "Perevodchik - professiia smirennaia"', *Nasha gazeta. Shveitsarskie novosti na russkom* 17 December 2014, http://nashagazeta.ch/news/peoples/18739 (accessed 18 July 2019).

For I. Gurova, see Elena Kalashnikova, *Interview with Irina Gurova 'Svoi metod ia nikomu ne rekomenduiu, no sudiat-to po resul'tatu . . .'*, Russkii Zhurnal/ Krug chteniia, 4 December 2002, http://old.russ.ru/krug/20021128_kalash.html (accessed 18 July 2019).

For N. Demurova, see Elena Kalashnikova, *Interview with Nina Demurova: 'Vse proizvedeniia ia perevodila s udovol'stviem'*, Russkii Zhurnal/Krug chteniia, 15 March 2002, http://old.russ.ru/krug/20020315_kalash.html (accessed 18 July 2019); and Kalashnikova, *Po-russki s liubov'iu*, p. 202.

For O. Varshaver, see Ol'ga Varshaver, 'Razmyshleniia o nekotorikh kul'turologicheskikh aspektakh perevoda detskoi literatury', in *Konstruiruia detskoe. Filologiia. Istoriia. Antropologiia. Kollektivnaia monografiia. Trudy seminara 'Kul'tura detstva: normy, tsennosti, praktiki'. Vypusk 9*, ed. M. R. Balina et al. (Moscow: Azimut, Nestor-Istoriia, 2011), pp. 266–82.

33 Anna Narinskaia, 'Interview with Viktor Golyshev: "Ne nado k perevodu otnosit'sia kak k sviatyne"', *Kommersant Weekend*, 48 (12 December 2008), http://www.kommersant.ru/doc/1091063 (accessed 18 July 2019).

34 Vera Tolz, *Russia* (London: Arnold, 2001), pp. 201, 203.

35 Nadezhda Ryzhak, 'Censorship in the USSR and the Russian State Library', in *IFLA/ FAIFE Satellite meeting 11–12 August 2005/Documenting censorship - libraries linking past and present, and preparing for the future* (The Nobel Institute in Oslo, Norway: 11 August 2005), http://www.bibalex.org/wsisalex/faife.htm (accessed 18 July 2019).

36 Maurice Friedberg, 'Soviet Censorship: A View from the Outside', in *The Red Pencil: Artists, Scholars, and Censors in the USSR*, ed. Marianna Tax Choldin and Maurice Friedberg (Boston: Unwin Hyman, 1989), pp. 15–28 (p. 23).

37 *Izdaniia VGBIL: Vyborochnyi bibliograficheckii ukazatel' 1941–1981*, ed. I. P. Kukhterina (Moscow: VGBIL, 1982); *Izdaniia VGBIL: Vyborochnyi bibliograficheckii ukazatel' 1975–1986*, ed. I. P. Kukhterina (Moscow: VGBIL, 1987).

38 See Arlen V. Blium, 'Stat'ia dlia entsiklopedii "Tsenzura"', http://www.encyclopedia.ru/news/enc/detail/46922/ (accessed 18 July 2019).

39 Blium, *Tsenzura v Sovetskom Soiuze. 1917–1991. Dokumenty*, pp. 554–5, documents № 456–457 'Ob archivakh Glavlita'.

40 Electronic catalogue of the Russian State Library of Foreign Literature, https://libfl.ru/ru/item/catalogue (accessed 18 July 2019).

41 Galina Zakhoder, *Zakhoder i vse-vse-vse. Vospominaniia* (Moscow: Zakharov, 2003), p. 183.
42 See more on this in John Morison, 'Anglo-Soviet Cultural Contacts Since 1975', in *Soviet-British Relations Since the 1970s*, ed. Alex Pravda and Peter J. S. Duncan (Cambridge: Cambridge University Press, 1990), pp. 168–92.
43 Moscow, RGALI, 'Materialy obschestva "SSSR–Velikobritaniia": ustav obschestva, spisok chlenov obschestva i sostava pravleniia i dr. (1958–1982 gg.)', f. 1899, op. 1, d. 633, ll. 2, 7.
44 See John C. Q. Roberts, *Speak Clearly into the Chandelier: Cultural Politics Between Britain and Russia 1973–2000* (Richmond: Curzon Press, 2000), p. 157. Writers' exchanges were initiated by article III (2d) of the 1985/87 Cultural Agreement between Britain and the Soviet Union.
45 T. A. Kudriavtseva, *Prevratnosti odnoi sud'by. Zapiski literatora i perevodchika* (Moscow: R. Valent, 2008).
46 The British–Soviet Friendship Society was a successor body to such groups as the Anglo–Soviet Friendship Committee (established in 1940), the Russia Today Society (established in 1934) and the Friends of the Soviet Union (established in 1930): *Routledge Guide to British Political Archives: Sources since 1945*, ed. Chris Cook (London: Routledge, 2006), p. 252. For the Scotland–USSR Society and the SCR see ibid., pp. 380 and 389.
47 Morison, 'Anglo-Soviet Cultural Contacts since 1975', p. 172.
48 Proekt dokladnoi zapiski agitpropa TSK Stalinu I.V. po voprosu o ezhenedel'nike 'Britanskii soiuznik', 13 October 1946, Mezhdunarodnyi fond 'Demokratiia' (Fond Aleksandra N. Iakovleva), http://www.alexanderyakovlev.org/fond/issues-doc/69315 (accessed 18 July 2019).
49 See Phoebe Latham, 'Liubimye detskie knigi', *Angliia*, 2 (1969), 22–9.
50 See more on this in Ben Hellman, *Fairy Tales and True Stories: The History of Russian Literature for Children and Young People (1574–2010)* (Leiden: Brill, 2013).
51 Samuil Marshak, 'Pocherk veka, pocherk pokoleniia', in *Sobranie sochinenii v 8 tomakh*, ed. V. M. Zhirmunskii, 8 vols (Moscow: Khudozhestvennaia literatura, 1968–72), vi: *Stat'i. Vystupleniia. Zametki. Vospominaniia. Proza raznykh let*, ed. S. S. Chulkova and E. B. Skorospelova (1971), pp. 351–4.
52 Chukovsky, *Vysokoe iskusstvo*, p. 261.
53 Korney Chukovsky, 'Gorky', in Chukovsky, Korney, *Sobranie sochinenii v 15 tomakh*, 15 vols (Moscow: Agentstvo FTM Ltd, 2012), v: *Sovremenniki. Portrety i etiudy*, Ebook, pp. 38–76 (pp. 72, 76).
54 See Samuil Marshak, 'Ia pobyval v triekh stranakh' [I have been to three countries], first published in the newspaper *Literaturnyi Leningrad* [*Literary Leningrad*], 5 October 1933, and reprinted in *Zhizn' i tvorchestvo Samuila Iakovlevicha Marshaka. Marshak i detskaia literatura* [*Life and works of Samuil Iakovlevich Marshak.*

Marshak and children's literature], ed. B. Galanov, I. Marshak and M. Petrovskii (Moscow: Detskaia literatura, 1975), pp. 233–5 (p. 234).

55 See the resolution 'O pechati' in *Direktivy VKP(b) po voprosam prosvescheniia*, ed. A. Ia. Podzemskii (Moscow: OGIZ, 1931), pp. 69–74 (p. 71).

56 *O partiinoi i sovetskoi pechati. Sbornik dokumentov* (Moscow: Pravda, 1954), pp. 437–8.

57 Detgiz was renamed as Detizdat in 1936 and then back to Detgiz in 1941. See G. E. Tsypin's report in 'Doklad direktora Detizdata tov. G. E. Tsypina', in *Detskaia literatura*, 1 (1936), 15–17.

58 See more on Detgiz in Olga Simonova, 'Detskaia kniga v fokuse vliianiia (konets 1940-kh – nachalo 1950-kh gg.' [Children's Book as a Subject of Influence Struggle (late 1940s–early 1950s)], in *Detskie chteniia*, 10(2) (2016), 170–89.

59 Moscow, Rossiiskii gosudarstvennyi arkhiv literatury i iskusstva (RGALI), 'Stenogramma ob"edinennogo zasedaniia sektsii kritiki, literaturovedeniia i khudozhestvennogo perevoda Moskovskogo otdeleniia SP RSFSR i Inostrannoi komissii, posviashchennogo sovremennoi angliiskoi literature v russkikh perevodakh i kritike, 1961 g.', f. 631, op. 26, d. 956, l. 87.

60 See Marshak's Letter No. 300 of 8 October 1960 in Samuil Marshak, *Sobranie sochinenii v 8 tomakh*, ed. V. M. Zhirmunskii, 8 vols (Moscow: Khudozhestvennaia literatura, 1968–72), viii: *Izbrannye pis'ma*, ed. S. S. Chulkova (1972), pp. 367–9.

3 Translation of British children's literature in Russian context: Responses to political and cultural changes

1 Itamar Even-Zohar, 'Polysystem Studies', *Poetics Today*, 11 (1990), 7–193 (p. 46).
2 The list of sources used for choosing Russian translations for the analysis in this chapter is given in the Bibliography.
3 Balina and Rudova, 'Introduction' (p. 186).
4 *The Routledge Companion to Children's Literature*, ed. David Rudd (London: Routledge, 2010), p. 153.
5 Nikolajeva, *Children's Literature Comes of Age*, p. 19.
6 See Anne H. Lundin, *Constructing the Canon of Children's Literature: Beyond Library Walls and Ivory Towers* (New York: Routledge, 2004), pp. 68–108; Perry Nodelman, 'Grand Canon Suite, Including "A Tentative List of Books Everyone Interested in Children's Literature Should Know"', *Children's Literature Association Quarterly*, 5(2) (1980), 1–8 (pp. 6–8); and Humphrey Carpenter, Mari Prichard and Daniel Hahn, *The Oxford Companion to Children's Literature*, 2nd edn (Oxford: Oxford University Press, 2015), pp. 659–63.

7   N. K. Krupskaia, 'O detskoi biblioteke i detskoi knige', in *Pedagogicheskie sochineniia v 10-ti tomakh. Tom 8* (Moscow: Izdatel'stvo Akademii pedagogicheskikh nauk, 1957–63), viii (1960), pp. 172–3 quoted in Evgeny Dobrenko, *The Making of the State Reader: Social and Aesthetic Contexts of the Reception of Soviet Literature*, trans. Jesse M. Savage (Stanford, CA: Stanford University Press, 1997), p. 69.
8   Marina Balina, 'Creativity through Restraint: The Beginnings of Soviet Children's Literature', in *Russian Children's Literature and Culture*, ed. Marina Balina and Larissa Rudova (New York: Routledge, 2008), pp. 3–17 (p. 4). See also Svetlana Maslinskaya, '"Nasledstvo i nasledstvennost": evoliutsiia kritiki russkoi detskoi literatury 1910–1920-x godov', *Revue des études slaves*, 88(1–2) (2017), 237–55, for the discussion about the concept of novelty of Soviet children's literature being based on the model of children's literature proposed in the pre-revolutionary critical works.
9   See more in Sheila Fitzpatrick, *The Cultural Front: Power and Culture in Revolutionary Russia* (Ithaca, NY: Cornell University Press, 1992), pp. 93–4.
10 *KPSS v rezoliutsiiakh i resheniiakh s'ezdov, konferentsii i plenumov*, Part I (Moscow: Gosudarstvennoe izdatel'stvo politicheskoi literatury, 1953), p. 867.
11 Balina, 'Creativity through Restraint', pp. 5, 11.
12 For the discussion of the fairy tale and fantasy genre in Russian children's literature in the 1920s see the following: Dobrenko, *The Making of the State Reader*, p. 191; Marina Balina, 'Fairy Tales of Socialist Realism: Introduction', in *Politicizing Magic: An Anthology of Russian and Soviet Fairy Tales*, ed. Marina Balina and others (Evanston, IL: Northwestern University Press, 2005), pp. 105–21 (p. 107); and Catriona Kelly, *Children's World: Growing Up in Russia, 1890–1991* (New Haven, CT: Yale University Press, 2007), p.458.
13 Kelly, *Children's World*, pp. 100–1.
14 Military themes and the portrayal of the Second World War in Russian children's literature in the mid-1930s and throughout the 1940s have been discussed in the following works: Balina, 'Creativity through Restraint', pp. 12–13; Katerina Clark and Evgeny Dobrenko, *Soviet Culture and Power: A History in Documents, 1917–1953* (New Haven, CT: Yale University Press, 2007), pp. 348–9, 478; Larissa Rudova, 'From Character-Building to Criminal Pursuits', in *Russian Children's Literature and Culture*, ed. Marina Balina and others (New York: Routledge, 2008), pp. 19–40 (p. 24); and Ben Hellman, *Children's Books in Soviet Russia: From October Revolution 1917 to Perestroika 1986*, 1991, http://www.helsinki.fi/~bhellman/summary.html (accessed 16 May 2019).
15 See more on this in A. V. Fateev, *Stalinizm i Detskaia Literatura v Politike Nomenklatury SSSR, 1930-e–1950-e gg.* (Moscow: Maks Press, 2007), chapter V 'Reformy i detskaia literatura v 1953–1958 gg', http://psyfactor.org/lib/detlit5.htm (accessed 18 July 2019).

16 Kelly, *Children's World*, pp. 137–9.
17 Balina, 'Creativity through Restraint', pp. 24–5; Evgeny Dobrenko, 'The School Tale in Children's Literature of Socialist Realism', in *Russian Children's Literature and Culture*, ed. Marina Balina and Larissa Rudova (New York: Routledge, 2008), pp. 43–66 (p. 65).
18 Marina Balina and Larissa Rudova, 'Introduction', *The Slavic and East European Journal, Special Forum Issue: Russian Children's Literature: Changing Paradigms*, 49(2) (2005), 186–98 (p. 194).
19 Balina, 'Creativity through Restraint', p. 25.
20 V. Golov, 'Rastit' patriota – internatsionalista', *Detskaia literatura*, 1 (1985), 2–6 (p. 6).
21 For a detailed analysis of a 'Sovietization' of Swift's *Gulliver's Travels*, see Muchael Düring, 'Canon Formation in the Soviet Union: The Case of Swift as an Author of a Children's Classic', in *Canon Constitution and Canon Change in Children's Literature*, ed. Bettina Kümmerling-Meibauer and Anja Müller (New York: Routledge, 2017), pp. 72–84. An illustrative example of the Soviet discussion about the ideological context in *Robinson Crusoe* and *Gulliver's Travels* can be found in Evgenii Brandis, *Ot Ezopa do Dzhanni Rodari: Zarubezhnaia literatura v detskom i iunosheskom chtenii* (Moscow: Detskaia literatura, 1980), pp. 33–46.
22 See Ethel Lilian Voynich, *Ovod*, trans. N. Volzhina (Moscow, Leningrad: Detgiz, 1945).
23 Nina Demurova, 'Malen'kie oborvyshi v bol'shoi literature', *Detskaia literatura*, 7 (1979), 21–33 (p. 30).
24 See James Greenwood, *Malen'kii oborvysh: Povest' dlia iunoshestva*, ed. K. Chukovsky (Leningrad: Kubuch, 1926) and James Greenwood, *Malen'kii oborvysh: Povest'*, retold by T. Bogdanovich and K. Chukovsky (Moscow, Leningrad: Gosizdat, 1929).
25 For more information on the Russian translation of this book, see Nikolajeva, *Children's Literature Comes of Age*, p. 18, and *Zarubezhnye detskie pisateli v Rossii: biobibliograficheskii slovar'*, ed. I. G. Mineralova (Moscow: Flinta, Nauka, 2005), pp. 122–7.
26 See Frederick Marryat, *Prikliucheniia Iakova Vernogo*, ed. M. Levidov (Moscow, Leningrad: Gosizdat, 1927)) and Henry Fielding, *Istoriia Toma Dzhonsa naidenysha: Roman*, ed. N. Kamionskaia (Moscow, Leningrad: Molodaia gvardiia, 1931).
27 See *Ballady o Robin Gude*, ed. N. Gumilev (Peterburg: Vsemirnaia literatura pri Narodnom komissariate po prosveshcheniiu, 1919); *V lesakh Robin Guda*, trans. V. Rozhdestvenskii (Moscow: Raduga, 1926); Escott Lynn, *Robin Hood and his Merry Men* (London: W. & R. Chambers, 1924); and Escott Lynn, *Robin Gud*, trans. A. Krivtsova, ed. Ev. Lann (Moscow, Leningrad: GIZ, 1928).

28 *Ballady o Robin Gude*, ed. N. Gumilev, p. 12.
29 'King John and the Bishop', in *English and Scottish Popular Ballads*, ed. Helen Child Sargent and George Lyman Kittredge (London: George G. Harrap, 1904), pp. 403–14.
30 Samuil Marshak, *Korol' i pastukh. Angliiskaia narodnaia ballada* (Leningrad: Raduga, 1926); Samuil Marshak, *Korol' i pastukh* (Moscow: Detizdat, 1940); 'King John and the Bishop', in *English and Scottish Popular Ballads*, p. 410. After 1991 the ballad appeared only occasionally in Marshak's collections of children's poetry; for example, it was included in Samuil Marshak, *Deti nashego dvora* (Moscow: AST/Astrel', 2008), pp. 240–6.
31 See Hugh Lofting, *Prikliucheniia doktora Dulitlia*, trans. L. Khavkina (Moscow: Gosizdat, 1924); Hugh Lofting, *Doktor Aibolit*, retold by K. Chukovsky (Leningrad: Gosizdat, 1925); and Korney Chukovsky, *Doktor Aibolit. Po G. Loftingu* (Moscow, Leningrad: Detizdat, 1936).
32 Korney Chukovsky, 'Istoriia moego Aibolita', *Literaturnaia Rossiia*, 30 January (1970), pp. 16–17. For a detailed analysis of Chukovsky's adaptation of *Doctor Dolittle*, see Kevin M. F. Platt, 'Doktor Dulitl i doctor Aibolit na prieme v otdelenii travmy', trans. A. Plisetskaia, in *Veselyie chelovechki: kul'turnye geroi sovetskogo detstva*, ed. Il'ia Kukulin, Mark Lipovetskii and Mariia Maiofis (Moscow: Novoe literaturenoe obozrenie, 2008), pp. 80–98; and I. V. Vdovenko, 'Perevod kak "appropriatsiia" teksta. "Aibolit" i "Barmalei"', in I. V. Vdovenko, *Strategii kul'turnogo perevoda* (St. Petersburg: RIII, 2007), http://www.chukfamily.ru/kornei/bibliografiya/articles-bibliografiya/i-v-vdovenko-strategii-kulturnogo-perevoda (accessed 18 July 2019).
33 See Joseph Jacobs, *Angliiskie skazki*, trans. Semyon Zaimovskii (Moscow: Mir, 1918), a reprinted edition of the earlier 1916 translation, and *Dzhek – pokoritel' velikanov*, retold by Korney Chukovsky (Peterburg: Epokha, 1921).
34 The festival of American animated films took place in 1933 and was held at the principal Moscow cinema Udarnik – see https://about.disney.ru/about/history/2/ (accessed 18 July 2019). For the translation of *The Three Little Pigs* see *Tri porosenka. Tekst i risunki studii Val'tera Disneia* [text and illustrations by The Walt Disney Studio], trans. and adapted by Sergey Mikhalkov (Moscow, Leningrad: Izdatel'stvo detskoi literatury, 1936).
35 See *Novye detskie knigi*, vol. IV (Moscow: izdatel'stvo "Rabotnik prosvescheniia", 1926), pp. 91–2.
36 See *Zapiski o Sherloke Kholmse*, ed. K. Chukovsky (Moscow: Detgiz, 1956).
37 *Ballady i pesni angliiskogo naroda*, trans. M. Tsvetaeva, and others, ed. M. Morozov (Moscow: Detgiz, 1942); *Angliiskie ballady i pesni*, trans. S. Marshak (Moscow: Sovetskii pisatel', 1941).
38 *Ballady i pesni angliiskogo naroda*, pp. 62–3.

39 See Samuil Marshak, 'Vereskovyi mied', in Samuil Marshak, *Angliiskie ballady i pesni* (Moscow: Goslitizdat, 1944), pp. 80–4.
40 The translation of this poem is analysed further in this book.
41 *Angliiskie narodnye pesenki*, trans. S. Marshak (Moscow: Detgiz, 1944).
42 Catriona Kelly, '"Malen'kie grazhdane bol'shoi strany": internatsionalism, deti i sovetskaia propaganda', *Novoe Literaturnoe Obozrenie*, 60 (2003), 218–51 (p. 236).
43 I. Cherniavskaia, 'O nekotorykh tendentsiiakh v sovremennoi zarubezhnoi literature', *Detskaia literatura*, 3 (1970), 26–9 (p. 29).
44 Ibid.
45 Maria Nikolajeva, 'U istokov angliiskoi detskoi literatury XX veka', *Detskaia literatura*, 7 (1979), 33–7.
46 Irina Tokmakova, 'Zheleznyi chelovek i velosipedist-prizrak: Kratkie zametki po povodu sovremennoi detskoi literatury v Anglii', *Detskaia literatura*, 7 (1979), 40–4 (p. 43).
47 Korney Chukovsky, 'Tri pis'ma Chukovskogo', *Detskaia literatura*, 4 (1972), 44–5 (p. 44).
48 Evgenii Brandis, *Ot Ezopa do Dzhanni Rodari: Zarubezhnaia literatura v detskom i iunosheskom chtenii* (Moscow: Detskaia literatura, 1980), p. 111.
49 Walter de la Mare, *Sygraem v priatki*, trans. Viktor Lunin (Moscow: Detskaia literatura, 1978).
50 Henry Williamson, *Vydra po imeni Tarka. Ee radostnaia zhizn' i ee smert' v doline dvikh rek*, trans. G. Ostrovskaia (Moscow: Mir, 1979).
51 I. Iakovenko, 'Krizis adekvatnosti: Razdum'ia kul'turologa', *Vestnik Evropy*, 33 (2012), https://magazines.gorky.media/vestnik/2012/33/krizis-adekvatnosti.html (accessed 18 July 2019).
52 Zakhoder, 'Prikliucheniia Vinni-Pukha (Iz istorii moikh publikatsii)', p. 198. Prior to the official book publication, Zakhoder's translation of chapter two 'in which Pooh goes visiting and gets into a tight place' from *Winnie-the-Pooh* appeared in the children's magazine *Murzilka* in 1958 (volume 8, pp. 20–2). However, there were two earlier publications of the same chapter in other translations: in *Murzilka* in 1939 (volume 9, pp. 8–9) and in *Britanskii Soiuznik* in 1948 (issue 52, p. 8).
53 In the first edition as A. A. Milne, *Vinni-Pukh i vse ostal'nye*, retold by B. Zakhoder (Moscow: Gosudarstvennoe izdatel'stvo "Detskii mir", 1960). Afterwards the book was published by Detgiz and Malysh publishing houses under a slightly different title: See, for example, A. A. Milne, *Vinni-Pukh i vse vse vse*, retold by B. Zakhoder (Moscow: Izdatel'stvo 'Malysh', 1970).
54 A. A. Milne, *Winnie-the-Pooh* (London: Egmont, 2004) and A. A. Milne, *Vinni-Pukh i vse vse vse*, retold by B. Zakhoder (Moscow: Izdatel'stvo 'Malysh', 1970).
55 See A. Asarkan, 'Mir Vinni-Pukha', *Novyi mir*, 8 (1961), 269–71; I. Kurbatova, 'Mir geroev Vinni-Pukha', *Detskaia literatura*, 1 (1973), 29–32; S. Mikhalkov,

'Dve udachi', *Literaturnaia gazeta*, 61 (23 May 1961), 3; and S. Kanevsky, 'Novye prikliucheniia Vinni-Pukha', *Literaturnaia gazeta*, 14 (4 March 1968), 12.

56 See Boris Zakhoder, 'Glava nikakaia, iz kotoroi tem ne menee mozhno koe-chto uznat'', in *Lewis Carroll. Prikliucheniia Alisy v strane chudes*, trans. Boris Zakhoder (Moscow: Studiia 4+4, 2012), pp. 9–14 (p. 13).

57 C. S. Lewis, *Lev, Koldun'ia i platianoi shkaf*, trans. G. Ostrovskaia (Leningrad: Detskaia literatura, 1978), p. 2.

58 Olga Bukhina, 'From Narnia to Russia: A History of Translation', *Proceedings of the 33rd IBBY International Congress 'Crossing Boundaries: Translations and Migrations'*, 23–26 August 2012 (2012), http://www.congress2012.ibby.org.uk/transcripts.php (accessed 16 May 2019).

59 This publication can be found in *Angliia*, volume 2 (issue 30), 1969, pp. 30–40.

60 Natal'ia Rakhmanova, 'Vospominaniia', www.kulichki.com/tolkien/arhiv/ugolok/rakhmanova_int.shtml (accessed 18 July 2019).

61 J. R. R. Tolkien, *Khobbit, ili Tuda i obratno. Skazochnaia povest'*, trans. N. Rakhmanova (Leningrad: Detskaia literatura, 1976).

62 J. R. R. Tolkien, *Khraniteli: Letopis' pervaia iz epopei 'Vlastelin Kolets'*, trans. A. Kistiakovskii and V. Murav'ev (Moscow: Detskaia literatura, 1982).

63 For an analysis of numerous Russian translations of both books see Mark T. Hooker, *Tolkien through Russian Eyes* (Zurich: Walking Tree, 2003).

64 Golov, V., 'Rastit' patriota – internatsionalista', p. 3.

65 See Ignatii Ivanovskii, *Ballady o Robin Gude* (Leningrad: Izdatel'stvo detskoi literatury, 1959 and 1963), pp. 5–7; and Ignatii Ivanovskii, 'Fragmenty', *Zarubezhnye zapiski*, 4 (2005), https://magazines.gorky.media/zz/2005/4/fragmenty-2.html (accessed 18 July 2019).

66 Brandis, *Ot Ezopa do Dzhanni Rodari*, pp. 159, 157.

67 Ibid., p. 347.

68 According to the director of the Great Britain–USSR Association John C. Q. Roberts, this book was given as a gift in the mid-1980s to one of his Moscow friends who had close links to Soviet publishing industry and whose teenage daughter was studying English at school. Thus a chance gift led to the book's publication in the Russian translation in 1989. See Roberts, *Speak Clearly into the Chandelier*, pp. 177, 179.

69 Jane Rosen, 'Baba Yaga in Brixton', *SCRSS Digest*, Summer (2014), 13–15 (p. 14).

70 Marsh, *Literature, History and Identity in Post-Soviet Russia*, p. 553.

71 Rudova, 'From Character-Building to Criminal Pursuits', pp. 19, 28, 38.

72 I. N. Arzamastseva and S. A. Nikolaeva, *Detskaia literatura*, 6th edn (Moscow: Academiia, 2009), pp. 475–6.

73 These themes have been promoted by the KompasGid and Samokat publishing houses.

74 Hellman, *Fairy Tales and True Stories*, p. 563.
75 See Appendix 3 part 2 and part 3 for the list of books that were not translated during the Soviet period and only appeared in translation after 1991.
76 See Appendix 3 part 1 'Mostly reprinted English classics that appeared in Russian translations during the Soviet and post-Soviet periods.'
77 Elena Chudinova, 'Vozvraschenie Sedrika Errola. O tvorchestve Frensis Bernet', *Detskaia literatura*, 5 (1993), 31–6 (pp. 36, 31).
78 See Georgiana M. Craik, *Istorii kuziny Triks. Sbornik dlia detei*, trans. A. Berseneva-Shankevich (Moscow: Izdatel'stvovo Sretenskogo monastyria, 2013).
79 See, for example, Russian translations of *Skellig* (1998), *My Name Is Mina* (2010) and *The Boy Who Swam with Piranhas* (2012): David Almond, *Skellig*, trans. O. Varshaver (Moscow: Inostranka, 2004), David Almond, *Menia zovut Mina*, trans. O. Varshaver (Moscow: Azbuka, 2014), and David Almond, *Mal'chik, kotoryi plaval s piran'iami*, trans. O. Varshaver (Moscow: Samokat, 2015).
80 Mikhail Visel, 'Perevod kalamburov, alliuzii, perekodirovka kul'turnykh kodov na materiale, nakoplennom v khode raboty nad perevodom trilogii Krisa Ridella "Lunnaia Ledi Got" (AST, redaktsiia Mainstream, 2013–2015)', paper presented at the International conference *Detskaia literatura kak sobytie* [Children's literature as happening], The State Educational Institution of Higher Professional Education of the City of Moscow, Moscow City Teacher Training University, 11–13 December 2015.
81 Olga Bukhina, who translated *The Little White Horse* and *Tom's Midnight Garden*, told me about both books when I briefly interviewed her at the International conference 'Detskaia literatura kak sobytie' [Children's literature as happening] (The State Educational Institution of Higher Professional Education of the City of Moscow, 'Moscow City Teacher Training University', 11–13 December 2015). See Philippa Pearce, *Tom i polnochnyi sad*, trans. O. Bukhina (Moscow: Samokat, 2011) and Elizabeth Goudge, *Taina lunnoi doliny*, trans. O. Bukhina (Moscow: Zakharov, 2009).
82 A. V. Teplitskaia, et al., 'Tysiacha luchshikh proizvedenii mirovoi khudozhestvennoi literatury v russkikh perevodakh, rekomendovannykh dlia komplektovaniia shkol'noi biblioteki', NIO bibliografii RGB, (2004), https://olden.rsl.ru/ru/s3/s331/s122/d311/ (accessed 18 July 2019).

4 J. M. Barrie's *Peter Pan*: Censoring images of the British Empire and Edwardian class society

1 I will refer further in this chapter to the following texts. English originals: J. M. Barrie, 'Peter and Wendy', in *Peter Pan in Kensington Gardens and Peter and Wendy*

(Oxford: Oxford University Press, 2008), pp. 67–226; and J. M. Barrie, *Peter Pan: a Fantasy in Five Acts* (London: Samuel French, 1977).

Russian translations: J. M. Barrie, *Piter Pen i Vendi*, trans. Nina Demurova (Moscow: Detskaia literatura, 1968); J. M. Barrie, *Piter Pen, ili Mal'chik, Kotoryi Ne Khotel Rasti*, trans. Boris Zakhoder (Moscow: Iskusstvo, 1971); J. M. Barrie, *Piter Pen*, trans. Irina Tokmakova (Moscow: Detskaia literatura, 1981).

References to the original texts and their translations in this chapter are given after quotations in the text.

2   J. M. Barrie, *Prikliucheniia Pitera Pana*, trans. L. A. Bubnova (Moscow: Detskaia kniga, 1918).

3   See more on nonsense and fantasy literature in the early years of the Soviet Union in Brandis, *Ot Ezopa do Dzhanni Rodari*, p. 269; and Lydia Chukovskaya, *V laboratorii redaktora* (Arkhangel'sk: OAO 'IPP "Pravda Severa", 2005), http://www.chukfamily.ru/Lidia/Publ/Laboratoria/glava7.htm (accessed 18 July 2019), chapter 7 'Marshak-redaktor', section 15.

4   'Barri Dzh', in *Literaturnaia entsiklopediia. V 11 tomakh, 1929–1939*, ed. P. I. Lebedev-Polianskii, et al., 11 vols (Moscow: Kommunisticheskaia akademiia, 1930), i (1930), 720–1, http://feb-web.ru/feb/litenc/encyclop/le1/le1-7205.htm (accessed 18 July 2019).

5   Nina Demurova recollected that in 1962 the Detskii mir publishing house had plans to publish the translation and Zakhoder agreed to supervise the edition of Demurova's translation. However, this publishing house could not fulfil its plans as it was banned from publishing foreign literature in the same year. See Nina Demurova, 'Peter Pan in Russia: Or Peter Pan, Korney Chukovsky and the Soviet Censor', in *The Neverland: Two Flights Over the Territory*, ed. Nina Demurova and Chris Routh ([n.p.]: Children's Books History Society, Occasional Paper II, 1995), pp. 19–28 (pp. 20–1).

6   B. A. Gilenson and N. Ia. D'iakonova, 'Barri', in *Kratkaia literaturnaia entsiklopediia*, ed. A. A. Surkov, 9 vols (Moscow: Sovetskaia entsiklopediia, 1962–78, i (1962), 459, http://feb-web.ru/feb/kle/kle-abc/ke1/ke1-4591.htm (accessed 18 July 2019).

7   See Kalashnikova, *Po-russki s liubov'iu: besedy s perevodchikami*, pp. 199–200; and Demurova, 'Peter Pan in Russia: Or Peter Pan, Korney Chukovsky and the Soviet Censor', p. 20.

8   Demurova, 'Peter Pan in Russia: Or Peter Pan, Korney Chukovsky and the Soviet Censor', p. 22; Kalashnikova, *Po-russki s liubov'iu: besedy s perevodchikami*, pp. 199–200.

9   Demurova, 'Peter Pan in Russia: Or Peter Pan, Korney Chukovsky and the Soviet Censor', pp. 24, 26. See also J. M. Barrie, *Piter Pen i Vendi*, trans. Nina Demurova (Moscow: Detskaia literatura, 1968).

10 See S. Sivokon', 'Dzh. M. Barrie. Piter Pen i Vendi. Povest'-skazka. Perevod s angliiskogo N. Demurovoi. Stikhi v perevode D. Orlovskoi. "Detskaia literatura". M. 1968. 160 str.', *Novyi mir*, 10 (1969), 282–3.

11 See J. M. Barrie, 'Piter Pen i Vendi', in *Pochti kak v zhizni*, ed. Iulii Kagarlitskii, trans. Nina Demurova (Moscow: Pravda, 1987), pp. 443–579; J. M. Barrie, *Piter Pen i Vendi*, trans. Nina Demurova (Moscow: Slovo, 1992).
12 Evgenii Kurneshov, *Irina Petrovna Tokmakova predstavliaet knigu 'Piter Pen' Dzh. Barri izdatel'stva 'Moskovskie uchebniki'*, online video recording.
13 J. M. Barrie, 'Dzheims Barri. Piter Pen. P'esa v 5 deistviiakh. Akt 2', *Detskaia literatura*, 12 (1966), 37–8. It was translated by Boris Zakhoder.
14 See Moscow, RGALI, 'Zaiavka B. V. Zakhodera na instsenirovku p'esy D. Barri "Piter Pen"', 1959 g.', f. 2939, op. 2, d. 449.
15 Ibid., ll. 6, 7.
16 Moscow, RGALI, '"Piter Pen" – p'esa v 5 deistviiakh L. Barri. Perevod s angliiskogo B. V. Zakhodera. Pervyi variant', f. 2939, op. 2, d. 446.
17 Peter Hollindale, 'Introduction', in *Peter Pan in Kensington Gardens and Peter and Wendy* (Oxford: Oxford University Press, 2008), pp. vii–xxviii (p. xxii).
18 Demurova, 'Peter Pan in Russia: Or Peter Pan, Korney Chukovsky and the Soviet Censor', p. 23.
19 A discussion of these two examples and others from Barrie's text and the Russian translations of Barrie's *Peter Pan* can be found in Borisenko, '"The Good Are Always the Merry": British Children's Literature in Soviet Russia' in the sections 'Double Reading: The Case of the Two Alices and Two Peter Pans' and 'Good Form and Bad Form: The Case of Captain Hook', as well as in Demurova, 'Peter Pan in Russia: Or Peter Pan, Korney Chukovsky and the Soviet Censor' (pp. 22–3). Examples referring to Hook in the original text and its corresponding translations in both articles inspired me to develop them further, but with a narrower view, in connection with Englishness.
20 Rashna B. Singh, *Goodly Is Our Heritage: Children's Literature, Empire, and the Certitude of Character* (Lanham, MD: Scarecrow Press, 2004), pp. 79–80.
21 Ibid., pp. 150–1.
22 Demurova, 'Peter Pan in Russia: Or Peter Pan, Korney Chukovsky and the Soviet Censor', p. 24.

5 Translating Rudyard Kipling's duology about Puck: Empire, historical past and landscape

1 I will refer further in this chapter to the following texts. English originals: Rudyard Kipling, 'Puck of Pook's Hill' and 'Rewards and Fairies', in *Puck of Pook's Hill and Rewards and Fairies* (Oxford: Oxford University Press, 1993).
   Russian translations: (1) Rudyard Kipling, *Mech Vilanda: Skazki staroi Anglii*, trans. A. Slobozhan (Leningrad: Detskaia literatura, 1984); and Rudyard Kipling,

'Skazki Paka', in *Skazki staroi Anglii*, trans. A. Slobozhan (Moscow: Master, 1992), pp. 10–204; (2) Rudyard Kipling, 'Staraia Angliia', in *Red'iard Kipling. Otvazhnye moreplavateli. Indiiskie rasskazy. Sbornik (biblioteka P. P. Soikina)*, trans. A. Enkvist (St. Petersburg: Logos, 1995), pp. 149–303; (3) Rudyard Kipling, 'Pek s kholmov. Nagrady i fei', in *Rediard Kipling. Polnoe sobranie rasskazov dlia detei v odnom tome*, trans. I. Gurova (Moscow: Al'pha-Kniga, 2009), pp. 391–768; (4) Rudyard Kipling, *Pak s Volshebnykh Kholmov*, trans. G. Kruzhkov and M. Boroditskaia (Moscow: RIPOL klassik, 2011); and Rudyard Kipling, *Podarki fei*, trans. G. Kruzhkov and M. Boroditskaia (Moscow: RIPOL klassik, 2010).

References to the original texts and their translations in this chapter are given after quotations in the text.

2 Brandis, *Ot Ezopa do Dzhanni Rodari*, p. 172.
3 Katharine Hodgson, 'The Poetry of Rudyard Kipling in Soviet Russia', *Modern Language Review*, 93 (1998), 1058–71 (pp. 1061–2).
4 T. Motyleva, 'Kipling', in *Istoriia angliiskoi literatury. Tom 3* (Moscow: Izdatel'stvo AN SSSR, 1958), pp. 256–79 (p. 261).
5 Email correspondence with Aleksei Slobozhan.
6 Ibid.
7 Aleksei Slobozhan, '"Puck" Stories in Russian', *Kipling Journal*, 63 (March 1989), 35–6 (p. 36).
8 Email correspondence with Aleksei Slobozhan.
9 Sarah Wintle, 'Introduction', in *Rudyard Kipling. Puck of Pook's Hill* (Harmondsworth: Penguin Books, 1987), pp. 7–34 (pp. 26, 33).
10 Letter to Edward Bok of 28 July 1905, in *The Letters of Rudyard Kipling*, ed. Thomas Pinney, 3 vols (Basingstoke: Palgrave Macmillan, 2004), iii, p. 189.
11 Aleksei Slobozhan, '"Skazki Staroi Anglii" Red'iarda Kiplinga', in *Red'iard Kipling. Mech Vilanda: Skazki Staroi Anglii* (Leningrad: Detskaia literatura, 1984), pp. 5–12.
12 Rudyard Kipling, *Mech Vilanda: Skazki staroi Anglii*, trans. A. Slobozhan (Leningrad: Detskaia literatura, 1984), p. 282.
13 Email correspondence with Aleksei Slobozhan.
14 This idea was suggested to me by Dr Alexandra Smith during the discussion of my paper based on this section, which was presented at the BASEES 2015 Annual Conference. The title of the paper: 'The story of Rudyard Kipling's *Puck of Pook's Hill* (1906) and *Rewards and Fairies* (1910) in Russia'.
15 Emily Lygo, *Leningrad Poetry 1953–1975: The Thaw Generation* (Bern: Peter Lang, 2010), p. 303.
16 Petr Vail' and Aleksandr Genis, *60-e. Mir sovetskogo cheloveka*, 2nd edn (Moscow: Novoe literaturnue obozrenie, 1998), pp. 282, 290.
17 V. Gopman, 'Red'iard Kipling. Mech Vilanda. Skazki staroi Anglii', *Detskaia literatura*, 1 (1986), 73–4 (p. 74).

18 Email correspondence with Aleksei Slobozhan.
19 As of 2014–18 situation, Kruzhkov's translation is mostly favoured by the Russian publishers, followed by Enkvist's translation. It is less likely to find Gurova's translation and Slobozhan's translation has not been reprinted since 2003.
20 Marsh, *History and Identity in Post-Soviet Russia*, p. 510.
21 Peter Bramwell, *Pagan Themes in Modern Children's Fiction: Green Man, Shamanism, Earth Mysteries* (Basingstoke: Palgrave Macmillan, 2009), p. 38.
22 V. S. Vinogradov, *Vvedenie v perevodovedenie (obshchie i leksicheskie voprosy)* (Moscow: Izdatel'stvo instituta obshchego srednego obrazovaniia RAO, 2001), p. 85.

6 A. A. Milne through Soviet eyes: Translating silliness and traditions

1 The texts I will refer to further in this chapter are the following.
   English originals: A. A. Milne, 'The King's Breakfast', in *A. A. Milne. When We Were Very Young* (London: Egmont, 2016), pp. 55–9; and A. A. Milne, 'King Hilary and the Beggarman', in *A. A. Milne. Now We Are Six* (London: Egmont, 2016), pp. 70–5.
   Russian translations: A. A. Milne, 'Ballada o korolevskom buterbrode', in *Samuil Marshak. Korolevskii buterbrod*, trans. S. Marshak (Moscow: Detskaia literatura, 1965), pp. 2–7; A. A. Milne, 'Korol' i brodiaga', trans. Nonna Slepakova, *Kostior*, December 1968, pp. 44–5; and A. A. Milne, *Ia byl odnazhdy v dome*, trans. Nonna Slepakova (Leningrad: Detskaia literatura, 1987), pp. 73–83.
   References to the original texts and their translations in this chapter are given after quotations in the text.
   Credit/Acknowledgements
   Text by A. A. Milne © Trustees of the Pooh Properties 1924. Reproduced with permission of Curtis Brown Group Ltd on behalf of the Trustees of the Pooh Properties.
   'The King's Breakfast' from WHEN WE WERE VERY YOUNG by A. A. Milne, copyright 1924 by Penguin Random House LLC. Copyright © renewed 1952 by A. A. Milne. Used by permission of Dutton Children's Books, an imprint of Penguin Young Readers Group, a division of Penguin Random House LLC. All rights reserved.
   Extract from When We Were Very Young by A. A. Milne. Text copyright © The Trustees of the Pooh Properties 1924. Published by Egmont UK Ltd and used with permission. Text by A. A. Milne © Trustees of the Pooh Properties 1927.

Reproduced with permission of Curtis Brown Group Ltd on behalf of the Trustees of the Pooh Properties.

'King Hilary and the Beggarman' from NOW WE ARE SIX by A. A. Milne, copyright 1927 by Penguin Random House LLC. Copyright © renewed 1955 by A. A. Milne. Used by permission of Dutton Children's Books, an imprint of Penguin Young Readers Group, a division of Penguin Random House LLC. All rights reserved.

Extract from Now We Are Six by A. A. Milne. Text copyright © The Trustees of the Pooh Properties 1927. Published by Egmont UK Ltd and used with permission.

Quotations from 'Ballada o korolevskom buterbrode' by A. A. Milne, translated by Samuil Marshak. Text copyright © 1965 Samuil Marshak, heirs. Used with permission.

2. Samuil Marshak, *Vospitanie slovom: stat'i, zametki, vospominaniia* (Moscow: Sovetskii pisatel', 1961), p. 33.
3. 'Pis'ma S. Ia. Marshaka E. R. Gol'dernessu, pp. 445–447. Letter No 359, Yalta, 28 September 1962', in Marshak, *Sobranie sochinenii v 8 tomakh*, viii: *Izbrannye pis'ma*, p. 446.
4. See Samuil Marshak, *Izbrannye perevody: Angliiskie ballady i pesni* (Moscow: Gosudarstvennoe izdatel'stvo khudozhestvennoi literatury, 1946), pp. 210–13.
5. Patricia Parker, 'What Comes after Mother Goose?', *Elementary English*, 46 (1969), 505–10 (p. 507).
6. Anita Wilson, 'A. A. Milne's When We Were Very Young and Now We Are Six: A Small World of Everyday Pleasures', in *Touchstones: Reflections on the Best in Children's Literature. Volume Two: Fairy Tales, Fables, Myths, Legends, and Poetry*, ed. Perry Nodelman (West Lafayette, IN: ChLA, 1987), pp. 173–82 (p. 174); Humphrey Carpenter, *Secret Gardens: A Study of the Golden Age of Children's Literature* (London: Allen & Unwin, 1985), p. 199.
7. See D. Kal'm, 'Protiv khaltury v detskoi literature!' [Against cheating in children's literature!], in *Literaturnaia gazeta*, 35 (1929), 2.
8. Ben Hellman, 'Samuil Marshak: Yesterday and Today', in *Russian Children's Literature and Culture*, ed. Marina Balina and Larissa Rudova (New York: Routledge, 2008), pp. 217–39 (p. 217).
9. Among them were Tamara Gabbe (arrested and released in 1937), Alexandra Liubarskaia (arrested in 1937 and released in 1939), Raisa Vasilieva (died in a labour camp in 1938), Nikolay Oleynikov (executed in 1937), Grigorii Belykh (died in a labour camp in 1938), Daniil Kharms (arrested in 1941 and died in a psychiatric ward in 1942). These writers also worked for Ezh (abbreviated from 'Ezhenedel'nyi zhurnal' – the weekly magazine), which was published between 1928 and 1935, and Chizh (abbreviated from 'Chrezvychaino interesnyi zhurnal' – the

extremely interesting magazine), which was published from 1930 until June 1941, as well as Leningrad section of Molodaia gvardia publishing house. See Lydia Chukovskaya, *Procherk*, chapter 'Bespamiatstvo' in Lidia Chukovskaya, *Procherk. Stikhotvoreniia. Sofia Petrovna. Spusk pod vodu* (Moscow: Art-Fleks, 2001), pp. 165–207. See also memoirs of Alexandra Liubarskaia about arrests in the Leningrad branch of Detizdat published in Neva journal: A. I. Liubarskaia, 'Za tiuremnoi stenoi', *Neva*, 5 (1998), 148–72.

10 'Dokladnaia zapiska o polozhenii v Leningradskom otdelenii "Izdatel'stva detskoi literatury pri TsK VLKSM" upolnomochennogo Lenoblgorlita pri Lendetizdate Chevychelova', document № 208, in Blium, *Tsenzura v Sovetskom Soiuze. 1917–1991*, pp. 236–8 (p. 237).

11 'Dokladnaia zapiska o polozhenii v leningradskom otdelenii "Izdatel'stva detskoi literatury" tsenzora Chevychelova', document № 226, in Arlen V. Blium, *Tsenzura v Sovetskom Soiuze*, pp. 262–6 (pp. 265, 264, 263).

12 Aleksander Tregubov, 'Vnuk Marshaka o svoiem legendarnom dede: "V 1937 ego spasli deti"', mk.ru, 4 November 2018, https://www.mk.ru/culture/2018/11/04/vnuk-marshaka-o-svoyom-legendarnom-dede-v-1937-ego-spasli-deti.html (accessed 18 July 2019).

13 Chukovskaya, *Procherk*, p. 170.

14 Hellman, 'Samuil Marshak: Yesterday and Today', pp. 232–3.

15 Chukovskaya, *Procherk*, p. 47.

16 Iu. Koval', 'S. Marshak. Iz A. A. Mil'na. Korolevskii buterbrod. Ris. E. Meshkova. M., izd. "Detskaia literatura", 1965', *Detskaia literatura*, 3 (1966), 51–3. Marshak's translation of the popular British nursery rhyme *Old King Cole was a Merry Old Soul* was first published in the children's magazines *Pioner* in 1937 (№ 7) and *Murzilka* 1941, (№ 7).

17 Etkind, *Poeziia i perevod*.

18 For example, Marshak's translation of *The King's Breakfast* is included in the latest translation of all poems that appear in Milne's *When We Were Very Young*. See A. A. Milne, *Kristofer Robin i vse-vse-vse. Kogda my byli esche malen'kie*, trans. M. Boroditskaia, G. Kruzhkov, S. Marshak, N. Voronel', N. Slepakova (Moscow: AST, 2014).

19 See Chapter 3 in this book.

20 See Geoffrey Trease, *The Dragon Who Was Different: And Other Plays for Children* (London: Muller, 1938).

21 Moscow, RGALI, '"Triz Dzhoffri. Drakon, kotoryi ne pokhozh na drugikh". P'esa dlia detei mladshego vozrasta (22 July 1939–31 July 1939)', f. 656, op.3, d. 2650, l. 3.

22 Vitalii Gubarev, *Korolevstvo krivykh zerkal (povest'-skazka)* (Moscow: Molodaia gvardiia, 1951). This book has been very popular in Russia. For the recent edition see Vitalii Gubarev, *Korolevstvo krivykh zerkal* (Moscow: Makhaon, 2015).

23 A. A. Milne, *Dela korolevskie*, trans. Nina Voronel' (Moscow: Art-Bisnes-Tsentr, 1992), pp. 73–83. The latest translation of all poems that appear in Milne's *Now We Are Six* includes Nina Voronel's translation of *King Hilary and the Beggarman*. See A. A. Milne, *Kristofer Robin i vse-vse-vse. A teper' nam shest'*, trans. G. Kruzhkov, M. Boroditskaia, S. Marshak, N. Voronel' and N. Slepakova (Moscow: AST, 2014), pp. 78–84.

7 Framing P. L. Travers's *Mary Poppins* in ideological and cultural contexts: Translating features of English national character

1 I will refer further in this chapter to the following texts. English originals: P. L. Travers, *Mary Poppins Opens the Door* (London: HarperCollins, 2018); P. L. Travers, *Mary Poppins Comes Back* (London: HarperCollins, 2018); P. L. Travers, *Mary Poppins* (London: HarperCollins, 2008).

   Russian translations: P. L. Travers, *Meri Poppins*, trans. Igor Rodin (Moscow: EKSMO-Press, 2002); P. L. Travers, 'Meri Poppins', in *Vsie o Meri Poppins: skazochnye povesti*, trans. Boris Zakhoder (Moscow: ROSMEN, 2012), pp. 5–82; P. L. Travers, 'Meri Poppins vozvraschaetsia', in *Vsie o Meri Poppins: skazochnye povesti*, trans. Boris Zakhoder (Moscow: ROSMEN, 2012), pp. 83–188; and P. L. Travers, *Meri Poppins s Vishnievoi ulitsy*, trans. M. Litvinova (Moscow: ROSMEN, 2012).

   References to the original texts and their translations in this chapter are given after quotations in the text.

2 However, Zakhoder's translation was first published in the Soviet children's magazine *Pioner* in 1967, issues 3–8.

3 Bloomington, Indiana, Indiana University, The Lilly Library, Lilly Library Manuscript Collections, Travers, P. L. MSS., 2nd letter from B. Zakhoder to P. L. Travers, 1969. Courtesy of The Lilly Library, Indiana University, Bloomington, Indiana.

4 Lilly Library Manuscript Collections, Travers, P. L. MSS., 3rd letter from B. Zakhoder to P. L. Travers, December 1969. Courtesy of The Lilly Library, Indiana University, Bloomington, Indiana.

5 Geoffrey T. Hellman, 'The Talk of the Town: Mary Poppins', *The New Yorker*, 38(35) (20 October 1962), 44, http://www.newyorker.com/archive/1962/10/20/1962_10_20_044_TNY_CARDS_000274309?printable=true&currentPage=all (accessed 18 July 2019).

6 See https://about.disney.ru/about/history/12/ (accessed 18 July 2019).

7 P. L. Travers, *Moscow Excursion* (New York: Reynal and Hitchcock, 1935). This book is translated into Russian: P. L. Travers, *Moskovskaia ekskursiia*, trans. Ol'ga Maeots (St. Petersburg: Limbus Press, 2016).

8 John Chamberlain, 'Books of the Times', *New York Times (1923-Current file)* (8 August 1935), 15.
9 Travers, *Moscow Excursion*, p. 30.
10 Sheila Fitzpatrick, 'Australian Visitors to the Soviet Union: The View from the Soviet Side', in *Political Tourists: Travellers from Australia to the Soviet Union in the 1920s-1940s*, ed. S. Fitzpatrick and C. Rasmussen (Carlton: Melbourne University Press, 2008), pp. 1–39 (p. 24).
11 Travers, *Moscow Excursion*, p. 10.
12 Document № 182 'Iz protokola zasedania kollegii Lenobllita', in Blium, *Tsenzura v Sovetskom Soiuze. 1917–1991. Dokumenty*, p. 203.
13 Lilly Library Manuscript Collections, Travers, P.L. MSS., 1st letter from B. Zakhoder to P. L. Travers, December 1968, and Letter from P. L. Travers to B. Zakhoder, February 1969. Courtesy of The Lilly Library, Indiana University, Bloomington, Indiana.
14 Lilly Library Manuscript Collections, Travers, P.L. MSS., 2nd letter from B. Zakhoder to P. L. Travers, 1969. Courtesy of The Lilly Library, Indiana University, Bloomington, Indiana.
 Zakhoder refers here to the review by S. Sivokon' titled 'P. L. Trevers. Meri Poppins. Sokraschennyi perevod s angliiskogo B. Zakhodera. 'Detskaia literatura'. M. 1968. 240 str.' published in *Novyi mir*, volume 5, 1969, pp. 284–5.
15 The books that Zakhoder translated are *Mary Poppins* (1934), *Mary Poppins Comes Back* (1935), *Mary Poppins Opens the Door* (1943).
16 In 2007 all Mary Poppins stories were published in one volume, which included Zakhoder's translations of the first three books and the new translations of the remaining books by Leonid Yakhnin, Aleksandra Borisenko and Irina Tokmakova. However, the original order of chapters in the first two books (*Mary Poppins* and *Mary Poppins Comes Back*) was not restored and Zakhoder's selection was retained. The third book *Mary Poppins Opens the Door* had chapters initially translated by Zakhoder and newly translated remaining chapters by Yakhnin. See P. L. Travers, *Meri Poppins: skazochnye povesti* (Moscow: ROSMEN, 2012).
17 Marina Litvinova retranslated the first book about Mary Poppins in 1996 and Igor Rodin retranslated the first four books about Mary Poppins in 1994. For information on the canonicity of Zakhoder's translation, see Aleksandra Borisenko, 'Pesni nevinnosti i pesni opyta: O novykh perevodakh "Vinni-Pukha"', and *Zarubezhnye detskie pisateli v Rossii: biobibliograficheskii slovar'*, p. 426. Readers' responses to the 'classic' translation of B. Zakhoder can be found online: http://www.ozon.ru/context/detail/id/4066228/ (accessed 18 July 2019).
18 Lilly Library Manuscript Collections, Travers, P.L. MSS., Letter from K. Piskunov to P. L. Travers, 2 July 1969. Courtesy of The Lilly Library, Indiana University, Bloomington, Indiana.

19 See more on myth in *Mary Poppins* in Grilli, *Myth, Symbol, and Meaning in Mary Poppins*, pp. 2, 26, 48, 51, 64, 76. Also the influence of myth on Mary Poppins' books is analysed in Staffan Bergsten, *Mary Poppins and Myth* (Stockholm: Almqvist and Wiksell International, 1978).
20 Lilly Library Manuscript Collections, Travers, P.L. MSS., Letter from P. L. Travers to B. Zakhoder to, February 1969. Courtesy of The Lilly Library, Indiana University, Bloomington, Indiana.
21 See more about this in Bergsten, *Mary Poppins and Myth*, p. 19, and P. L. Travers, 'Only Connect', *The Quarterly Journal of the Library of Congress*, 24 (1967), 232–48 (p. 241).
22 Alexandra Borisenko, 'Istoriia skazki', in *Trevers Pamela Lindon. Vse o Meri Poppins* (Moscow: ROSMEN, 2012), pp. 628–36 (p. 634).
23 Shaul' Reznik, 'Galina Zakhoder: "Boris ne pozvolial sebia toptat"', interview with Galina Zakhoder', *Lekhaim*, 288 (1 March 2016), https://lechaim.ru/events/galina-zahoder-boris-ne-pozvolyal-sebya-toptat/ (accessed 18 July 2019).
24 Farah Mendlesohn, *Rhetorics of Fantasy* (Middletown, CT: Wesleyan University Press, 2008), p. xiv.
25 Ibid., p. xxii.
26 See Edwina Burness and Jerry Griswold, 'The Art of Fiction No. 63, The Interview with P. L. Travers', *The Paris Review*, 86 (1982), http://www.theparisreview.org/interviews/3099/the-art-of-fiction-no-63-p-l-travers (accessed 18 July 2019). Also Travers talks about the mythical nature of her writings in Travers, 'Only Connect', pp. 240, 247.
27 Manlove, *From Alice to Harry Potter: Children's Fantasy in England*, p. 64.
28 Bergsten, *Mary Poppins and Myth*, pp. 9, 12.
29 Grilli, *Myth, Symbol, and Meaning in Mary Poppins*, p. xvi.
30 Richard R. Lingerman, 'Visit with Mary Poppins and P. L. Travers', *New York Times (1923-Current file)* (25 December 1966), p. A12.
31 Jane L. Mickelson, 'P.L. Travers: 1906–1996', *The Horn Book Magazine*, 72 (1996), 640–4 (p. 641).
32 Dorothea E. von Mücke, *The Seduction of the Occult and the Rise of the Fantastic Tale* (Stanford, CA: Stanford University Press, 2003), p. 2.
33 Maria Nikolajeva, 'The development of children's fantasy', in *The Cambridge Companion to Fantasy Literature*, ed. Edward James and Farah Mendlesohn (Cambridge: Cambridge University Press, 2012), pp. 50–61 (p. 60).
34 As Borisenko notes, it is certain that Zakhoder was not an enthusiastic advocate of Soviet ideology in general – see Borisenko, '"The Good Are Always the Merry": British Children's Literature in Soviet Russia', section 'The Sunny World of a Soviet Child: The Case of Boris Zakhoder'.

35 Also Moscow, RGALI, '"Meri Poppins". Komediia v 2-kh deistviiakh B. Zakhodera i V. Klimovskogo', f. 2949, op. 1, d. 1414, l. 61.
36 S. Sivokon', 'P. L. Trevers. Meri Poppins. Sokraschennyi perevod s angliiskogo B. Zakhodera. "Detskaia literatura". M. 1968. 240 str.', *Novyi mir*, 5 (1969), 284–5.
37 Borisenko, '"The Good Are Always the Merry": British Children's Literature in Soviet Russia', section 'Censorship matters', p. 208.
38 This review was published in the newspaper *Sovetskaia kul'tura* [Soviet culture] of 22 August 1980. See also Moscow, RGALI, 'Zametka o spektakle "Meri Poppins". Gazetnaia vyrezka', f. 2949, op. 1, d. 1418, l. 2.
39 Moscow, RGALI, 'Stenogramma obsuzhdeniia v Upravlenii teatrov Minesterstva kul'tury RSFSR spektaklia "Meri Poppins"', f. 2949, op. 1, d. 383, ll. 3, 4, 22, 25.
40 Moscow, RGALI, '"Meri Poppins". Komediia v 2-kh deistviiakh B. Zakhodera i V. Klimovskogo', f. 2949, op. 1, d. 1414, l. 74.
41 Moscow, RGALI, '"Meri Poppins". Komediia v 2-kh deistviiakh B. Zakhodera i V. Klimovskogo', f. 2949, op. 1, d. 1414, l. 78.
42 Grilli, *Myth, Symbol, and Meaning in Mary Poppins*, p. 16.
43 Ibid., pp. 17–18.
44 Also Moscow, RGALI, ' "Meri Poppins". Komediia v 2-kh deistviiakh B. Zakhodera i V. Klimovskogo', f. 2949, op. 1, d. 1414, l. 64.
45 Marshak's translation is called *Птицы в пироге* [Birds in a pie]. See Samuil Marshak, *Stikhotvoreniia i poemy* (Leningrad: Izdatel'stvo 'Sovetskii pisatel', 1973), 'Ptitsy v piroge', p. 490.
46 This Russian rhyme can be found in M. Iu. Novitskaia and I. Raikova, *Detskii fol'klor* (Moscow: Russkaia kniga, 2002), p. 240.
47 For the nanny goat Russian rhyme see M. N. Mel'nikov, *Russkii detskii fol'klor* (Moscow: Prosvescheniie, 1987), p. 174.
48 I. Bochkareva, 'P. Trevers. Meri Poppins', *Detskaia literatura*, 3 (1969), 62–3.
49 Grilli, *Myth, Symbol, and Meaning in Mary Poppins*, pp. 1, 2, 11.
50 Lingerman, 'Visit with Mary Poppins and P. L. Travers', p. A12.
51 Mickelson, 'P.L. Travers: 1906–1996', p. 642.
52 Lingerman, 'Visit with Mary Poppins and P. L. Travers', p. A12.
53 Mickelson, 'P.L. Travers: 1906–1996', p. 641.
54 Lilly Library Manuscript Collections, Travers, P.L. MSS., Letter from P. L. Travers to B. Zakhoder, February 1969. Courtesy of The Lilly Library, Indiana University, Bloomington, Indiana.
55 See Gennady Kalinovsky, 'Kak sozdaietsia knizhnaia illiustratsiia', in *Panorama iskusstv*, issue 8, ed. Iu. M. Riadchenko (Moscow: Sovetskii khudozhnik, 1985), pp. 15–20; and Marina Baranova, 'Kazhdaiia novaia kniga delaiet menia drugim' [Interview with Gennady Kalinovsky]', *Detskaia literatura*, 7 (1990), p. 66.

8 Re-imagining Kenneth Grahame's *The Wind in the Willows*: Images of mythical rural England and the English way of life

1. I will refer further in this chapter to the following texts. English original: Kenneth Grahame, *The Wind in the Willows* (Oxford: Oxford University Press, 2010).
    Russian translations: Kenneth Grahame, *Veter v ivakh*, trans. V. Reznik (St. Petersburg: Assotsiatsia 'VEK', 1992); Kenneth Grahame, *Veter v Ivakh: Povest'-skazka*, trans. M. Iasnov and A. Kolotov (Saratov: Region. Privolzhskoe izdatel'stvo Detskaya kniga, 1993); Kenneth Grahame, *Veter v Ivakh: Skazka*, trans. I. Tokmakova (St. Petersburg: Azbuka-klassika, 2008); Kenneth Grahame, *Veter v Ivakh*, trans. L. Iakhnin (Moscow: Eksmo, 2010); *Veter v Ivakh: Skazochnaia Povest'*, trans. V. Lunin (Moscow: Makhaon, Azbuka-Attikus, 2011).
    References to the original texts and their translations in this chapter are given after quotations in the text.
2. Maria Nikolajeva, *From Mythic to Linear: Time in Children's literature* (Lanham, MD: Children's Literature Association and the Scarecrow Press, 2000), p. 38; and Kathryn V. Graham, 'Grahame, Kenneth', in *The Oxford Encyclopedia of British Literature*, ed. Scott Kastan (Oxford: Oxford University Press, 2006) Oxford Reference Online, DOI: 0.1093/acref/9780195169218.001.0001 (accessed 19 July 2019).
3. Peter Hunt, *The Wind in the Willows: A Fragmented Arcadia* (New York: Twayne Publishers, 1994), pp. 78–81; Neil Philip, 'The Wind in the Willows: The Vitality of a Classic', in *Children and Their Books: A Celebration of the Work of Iona and Peter Opie*, ed. Gillian Avery and Julia Briggs (Oxford: Clarendon Press, 1989), pp. 299–316 (p. 313); and Peter Green, *Kenneth Grahame 1959–1932: A Study of His Life, Work and Times* (London: John Murray, 1959), p. 246.
4. Green, *Kenneth Grahame 1959–1932*, p. 246.
5. *Introducing Children's Literature: From Romanticism to Postmodernism*, ed. Deborah Cogan Thacker and Jean Webb (London: Routledge, 2002), p. 6.
6. See Adrienne E. Gavin, 'Grahame, Kenneth', in *The Oxford Encyclopedia of Children's literature*, ed. Jack Zipes, Oxford University Press, Oxford Reference Online, 2006, DOI: 10.1093/acref/9780195146561.001.0001 (accessed 19 July 2019).
7. Peter Hunt, 'Introduction', in *The Wind in the Willows*, by Kenneth Grahame (Oxford: Oxford University Press, 2010) pp. vii–xxxii (p. xi).
8. Jane Suzanne Carroll, *Landscape in Children's Literature* (New York: Routledge, 2011), p. 108.
9. M. Bakhtin, 'Formy vremeni i khronotopa v romane: Ocherki po istoricheskoi poetike', in *Voprosy literatury i estetiki: Issledovaniia raznykh let*, ed. M. Bakhtin (Moscow: Khudozhestvennaia literatura, 1975), pp. 234–408, pp. (393–4).

10 See, for example, on Berkshire – Lundin, *Constructing the Canon of Children's Literature*, p. 120; about rivers – Peter Hunt, 'Explanatory notes', in *The Wind in the Willows* (Oxford: Oxford University Press, 2010), pp. 147–70 (p. 148). Also in explanatory notes in Russian, on rivers – A. V. Preobrazhenskaia, 'Kommentarii', in *The Wind in the Willows* (Moscow: Progress, 1981), pp. 315–59 (p. 323).
11 Hunt, 'Explanatory Notes', p. 151.
12 Kenneth Grahame, *The Wind in the Willows: An Annotated Edition*, ed. Seth Lerer (Cambridge, MA: Belknap Press of Harvard University Press, 2009), p. 63.
13 Ford, *England and the English*, pp. 145–6.
14 S. I. Ozhegov, *Slovar' russkogo iazyka*, ed. N. Iu. Shvedova (Moscow: Russkii iazyk, 1991), p. 60.
15 Toury, *Descriptive Translation Studies*, pp. 23, 22 accordingly.
16 Friedberg, *Literary Translation in Russia*, pp. 159, 160.
17 I. A. Bunin, 'Muravskii shliakh', in *Sobranie sochinenii v 9 tomakh*, 9 vols (Moscow: Izdatel'stvo 'Khudozhestvennaia literatura', 1965–7), v: *Povesti i rasskazy 1917–1930* (1966), p. 427.
18 M. M. Prishvin, *Sobranie sochineniiv shesti tomakh*, 6 vols (Moscow: Gosudarstvennoe izdatel'stvo khudozhestvennoi literatury, 1956–7), i: *Kashcheeva tsep'* (1956), p. 80.
19 I. S. Turgenev, 'Rasskaz otza Alekseia', in *Sochineniia. Tom 11. Povesti i rasskazy 1871–1877* (Moscow–Leningrad: Nauka, 1966), pp. 291–304 (p. 303).
20 V. O. Kliuchevskii, *Sochineniia: Kurs russkoi istorii* (Moscow: Politicheskaia literatura, 1956), p. 66, quoted in Ely, *This Meager Nature*, p. 223.
21 A. P. Chekhov, 'Step': Istoriia odnoi poezdki', in *Izbrannye proizvedeniia v 3 tomakh*, 3 vols (Moscow: Khudozhestvennaia literatura, 1970), i, 422–515 (p. 431).
22 Ely, *This Meager Nature*, p. 68.
23 P. A. Viazemskii, *Stikhotvoreniia* (Moscow – Leningrad: Sovetskii pisatel', 1969), p. 332.
24 I. A. Bunin, *Stikhotvoreniia* (Leningrad: Sovetskii pisatel', 1961), p. 258.
25 I. S. Turgenev, *A Sportsman's Notebook*, trans. Charles and Natasha Hepburn (London: The Book Society, 1959), p. 188.
26 S. Esenin, *Stikhotvoreniia. Poemy. Povesti. Rasskazy* (Moscow: EKSMO, 2008), p. 129.
27 I. A. Bunin, *Sobranie sochinenii v 9 tomakh*, 9 vols (Moscow: Izdatel'stvo 'Khudozhestvennaia literatura', 1965–7), vi: *Zhizn' Arsen'eva. Iunost'* (1966), p. 9.
28 I. S. Turgenev, 'Forest and Steppe', in *A Sportsman's Notebook*, trans. Charles and Natasha Hepburn (London: The Book Society, 1959), pp. 391–8.
29 Vladimir Nabokov, *Mary*, trans. Michael Glenny (Greenwich, CT: Fawcett, 1970), p. 86.
30 Ford, *England and the English*, pp. 130–1.

31 Sue Clifford and Angela King, *England in Particular: A Celebration of the Commonplace, the Local, the Vernacular and the Distinctive* (London: Hodder & Stoughton, 2006), p. 224.
32 Tony Watkins, 'Reconstructing the Homeland: Loss and Hope in the English Landscape', in *Aspects and Issues in the History of Children's Literature*, ed. Maria Nikolajeva (Westport, CT: Greenwood Press, 1995), pp. 165–72 (p. 167).
33 Kenneth Grahame, *The Wind in the Willows*, ed. Gillian Avery (New York: Penguin Classics, 2005), pp. 194–5.
34 Grahame, *The Wind in the Willows: An Annotated Edition*, ed. Seth Lerer, pp.148, 156.
35 Peter Bramwell, *Pagan Themes in Modern Children's Fiction*, p. 38.
36 Michael Mendelson, 'The Wind in the Willows and the Plotting of Contrast', *Children's Literature*, 16 (1988), 127–44 (p. 126).
37 Hunt, 'Introduction', pp. vii–xxxii (p. xiv).
38 Seth Lerer, 'Introduction', in *Kenneth Grahame. The Wind in the Willows, an Annotated Edition*, ed. Seth Lerer (Cambridge, MA: Belknap Press of Harvard University Press, 2009), pp. 1–43 (pp. 28, 29).
39 Hunt, 'Explanatory Notes', p. 158.
40 Lerer, 'Introduction', p. 28.
41 Green, *Kenneth Grahame 1959–1932*, pp. 245, 248.
42 *Kenneth Grahame. The Wind in the Willows, an annotated edition*, ed. Seth Lerer (Cambridge, MA: Belknap Press of Harvard University Press, 2009), p. 51.
43 *Tolkien On Fairy-Stories: Expanded Edition with Commentary and Notes*, ed. Verlyn Flieger and Douglas A. Anderson (London: HarperCollins, 2014), p. 97.
44 Peter Hunt, 'Introduction', in *The Wind in the Willows*, p. xxvi.
45 It is important to note that starting from 1992 several reprints of the translation done by Tokmakova used Shepard's original illustrations; Lunin's translation was published with the original illustrations created by Robert Ingpen.

Conclusion

1 Roland Barthes, *Image, Music, Text*, trans. Stephen Heath (London: Fontana, 1977), p. 165.
2 Balina and Rudova, 'Introduction', p. 194.
3 Alexei Yurchak, *Everything Was Forever, Until It Was No More: The Last Soviet Generation* (Princeton, NJ: Princeton University Press, 2006), chapter 5 'Imaginary West: The Elsewhere of Late Socialism', pp. 158–206.
4 Ibid., p. 159.
5 Ibid., p. 162.

6 For example, http://www.km.ru/glavnoe/2006/04/25/kniga/v-anglii-vse-naoborot-antologiya-angliiskogo-yumora (accessed 19 July 2019); and Anna Pavlovskaia, 'Osobennosti natsional'nogo kharaktera, ili za chto anglichane liubiat ocheredi', *Vokrug sveta*, 6 (2003), http://www.vokrugsveta.ru/vs/article/512/ (accessed 19 July 2019).
7 Vladimir Posner, *Angliia v obschem i v chastnosti*, 2015, http://pozneronline.ru/category/ filmy-v-poznera/angliya-v-obshhem-i-v-chastnosti/ (accessed 19 July 2019).
8 Arkadii Iu. Kuznetsov, 'Britanskii sled v Rossii. Vstrechaia god Velikobritanii', *Biblioteka v shkole*, 2 (317) (2014), 57–61 (p. 58).
9 Al. A. Gromyko, *Obrazy Rossii v Velikobritanii: real'nost' i predrassudki* (Moscow: Institut Evropy RAN: Russkii suvenir, 2008), p. 21.
10 FOM, 'Opinion Poll 'Interes k Velikobritanii. Chto rossiiane znaiut o Velikobritanii? I khotiat li pobivat' v etoi strane?' [Interest in Great Britain. What do Russian people know about Britain? Would they like to visit Britain?]' (24 March 2014), http://fom.ru/Mir/11416 (accessed 19 July 2019).

Bibliography

Primary sources

Children's books written in English and their Russian translations

Barrie, J. M., 'Peter and Wendy', in *Peter Pan in Kensington Gardens and Peter and Wendy* (Oxford: Oxford University Press, 2008), pp. 67–226.

Barrie, J. M., *Peter Pan: A Fantasy in Five Acts* (London: Samuel French, 1977).

Russian translations

Barrie, J. M., *Piter Pen i Vendi*, trans. Nina Demurova (Moscow: Detskaia literatura, 1968).

Barrie, J. M., *Piter Pen, ili Mal'chik, Kotoryi Ne Khotel Rasti*, trans. Boris Zakhoder (Moscow: Iskusstvo, 1971).

Barrie, J. M., *Piter Pen*, trans. Irina Tokmakova (Moscow: Detskaia literatura, 1981).

Grahame, Kenneth, *The Wind in the Willows* (Oxford: Oxford University Press, 2010).

Russian translations

Grahame, Kenneth, *Veter v ivakh*, trans. V. Reznik (Saint Petersburg: Assotsiatsia 'VEK', 1992).

Grahame, Kenneth, *Veter v Ivakh: Povest'-skazka*, trans. M. Iasnov and A. Kolotov (Saratov: Region. Privolzhskoe izdatel'stvo Detskaya kniga, 1993).

Grahame, Kenneth, *Veter v Ivakh: Skazka*, trans. I. Tokmakova (Saint Petersburg: Azbuka-klassika, 2008).

Grahame, Kenneth, *Veter v Ivakh*, trans. L. Iakhnin (Moscow: Eksmo, 2010).

Grahame, Kenneth, *Veter v Ivakh: Skazochnaia Povest'*, trans. V. Lunin (Moscow: Makhaon, Azbuka-Attikus, 2011).

Kipling, Rudyard, 'Puck of Pook's Hill', in *Puck of Pook's Hill and Rewards and Fairies* (Oxford: Oxford University Press, 1993), pp. 1–176.

Kipling, Rudyard, 'Rewards and Fairies', in *Puck of Pook's Hill and Rewards and Fairies* (Oxford: Oxford University Press, 1993), pp. 177–409.

Russian translations

Kipling, Rudyard, *Mech Vilanda: Skazki staroi Anglii*, trans. Aleksei Slobozhan (Leningrad: Detskaia literatura, 1984).

Kipling, Rudyard, 'Skazki Paka', in *Skazki syatoi Anglii*, trans. Aleksei Slobozhan (Moscow: Master, 1992), pp. 10–204.

Kipling, Rudyard, 'Staraia Angliia', in *Red'iard Kipling. Otvazhnye moreplavateli. Indiiskie rasskazy. Sbornik (biblioteka P. P. Soikina)*, trans. A. Enkvist (Saint Petersburg: Logos, 1995), pp. 149–303.

Kipling, Rudyard, 'Pek s kholmov. Nagrady i fei', in *Red'iard Kipling. Polnoe sobranie rasskazov dlia detei v odnom tome*, trans. I. Gurova (Moscow: Al'pha-Kniga, 2009), pp. 391–768.

Kipling, Rudyard, *Podarki fei*, trans. G. Kruzhkov and M. Boroditskaia (Moscow: RIPOL klassik, 2010).

Kipling, Rudyard, *Pak s Volshebnykh Kholmov*, trans. G. Kruzhkov and M. Boroditskaia (Moscow: RIPOL klassik, 2011).

Milne, A. A., 'The King's Breakfast', in *A. A. Milne. When We Were Very Young* (London: Egmont, 2016), pp. 55–9.

Milne, A. A., 'King Hilary and the Beggarman', in *A. A. Milne. Now We Are Six* (London: Egmont, 2016), pp. 70–5.

Russian translations

Milne, A. A., 'Ballada o korolevskom buterbrode', in *Samuil Marshak. Korolevskii buterbrod*, trans. S. Marshak (Moscow: Detskaia literatura, 1965), pp. 2–7.

Milne, A. A., 'Korol' i brodiaga', trans. Nonna Slepakova, *Kostior*, December 1968, pp. 44–5.

Milne, A. A., *Ia byl odnazhdy v dome*, trans. Nonna Slepakova (Leningrad: Detskaia literatura, 1987).

Travers, P. L., *Mary Poppins Opens the Door* (London: HarperCollins, 2018).

Travers, P. L., *Mary Poppins Comes Back* (London: HarperCollins, 2018).

Travers, P. L., *Mary Poppins* (London: HarperCollins, 2008).

Russian translations

Travers, P. L., *Meri Poppins*, trans. Igor Rodin (Moscow: EKSMO-Press, 2002).

Travers, P. L., 'Meri Poppins', in *Vsie o Meri Poppins: skazochnye povesti*, trans. Boris Zakhoder (Moscow: ROSMEN, 2012), pp. 5–82.

Travers, P. L., 'Meri Poppins vozvraschaetsia', in *Vsie o Meri Poppins: skazochnye povesti*, trans. Boris Zakhoder (Moscow: ROSMEN, 2012), pp. 83–188.

Travers, P. L., *Meri Poppins s Vishnievoi ulitsy*, trans. M. Litvinova (Moscow: ROSMEN, 2012).

Bibliographical sources used for choosing Russian translations of British children's literature for the analysis in Chapter 3

The General Author/Title Catalogue of Books in Russian (1725–1998) of the National Library of Russia (the database of electronic card images), http://www.nlr.ru/e-case3/sc2.php/web_gak (accessed 18 July 2019).

The General Electronic Catalogue of the National Library of Russia, http://primo.nlr.ru/primo_library/libweb/action/search.do (accessed 18 July 2019).

The Universal Digital Catalogue of the Russian State Library, https://www.rsl.ru/en/catalogues/ (accessed 18 July 2019).

The Online Public Access Catalogue of the Library for foreign literature (founder M. I. Rudomino), https://opac.libfl.ru/bjvvv/?type=adv#searchresult (accessed 18 July 2019).

The National Electronic Children's Library of The Russian State Children's Library, http://arch.rgdb.ru/xmlui/ (accessed 18 July 2019).

Brandis, Evgenii, *Ot Ezopa do Dzhanni Rodari: Zarubezhnaia literatura v detskom i iunosheskom chtenii* (Moscow: Detskaia literatura, 1980).

Knigi dlia detei: proizvedeniia zarubezhnykh pisatelei v perevodakh na russkii iazyk. 1918-1978. Bibliograficheskii ukazatel', ed. I. P. Kukhterina (Moscow: VGBIL, 1979).

Startsev, I. I., *Detskaia literatura. Bibliografiia. 1918-1931* (Moscow: Molodaia gvardiia, 1933).

Startsev, I. I., *Detskaia literatura. Bibliografiia* (Moscow: Dom detskoi knigi Detgiza): 1932-9 [1941]; 1940-5 [1948]; 1946-8 [1950]; 1949-50 [1952]; 1951-2 [1954]; 1953-4 [1958]; 1955-7 [1959]; 1958-60 [1961]; 1961-3 [1966]; 1964-6 [1970].

Shiperovich, B. Ia., *Detskaia literatura. Bibliografiia* (Moscow: Detskaia literatura): 1967-9 [1973]; 1970-1 [1981].

Zav'ialova, V. P., T. B. Kaminskaia, and V. I. Latysheva, eds, *Detskaia literatura. Bibliograficheskii ukazatel'* (Moscow: Detskaia literatura): 1972-3 [1984]; 1974-5 [1985]; 1976-8 [1987]; 1979-81 [88]; 1982-4 [1989].

Ezhegodnik Knigi SSSR, 1986-1991 (Moscow: Vsesoiuznaia knizhnaia palata, 1989-94).

Ezhegodnik Knigi Rossiiskoi Federatsii, 1992-1993 (Moscow: Knizhnaia palata, 1995-6).

Ezhegodnik Knigi Rossiiskoi Federatsii, 1994-1995 (Moscow: Rossiiskaia knizhnaia palata, 1997-8).

Ezhegodnik Knigi Rossiiskoi Federatsii, 1996-2001 (Moscow: Book Chamber International, 1999-2002).

Elekytonnyi bibliograficheskii ukazatel' *Knigi Rossii*, 2003-2017, http://gbu.bookchamber.ru/index.html (accessed 16 May 2019).

Archival sources

Bloomington, Indiana, Indiana University, The Lilly Library, Lilly Library Manuscript Collections, Travers, P. L. MSS.

Moscow, Rossiiskii gosudarstvennyi arkhiv literatury i iskusstva (RGALI),
    f. 656: Glavnoe upravlenie po kontroliu za repertuarom pri Komitete po delam iskusstv pri SNK SSSR (Glavrepertkom) (Moscow, 1923-52), '"Triz Dzhoffri.

Drakon, kotoryi ne pokhozh na drugikh". P'esa dlia detei mladshego vozrasta (22 July 1939–31 July 1939)', f. 656, op.3, d. 2650.

Moscow, RGALI, f. 1899: Surkov Aleksei Aleksandrovich (1899–1983) – poet, 'Materialy obschestva "SSSR–Velikobritaniia": ustav obschestva, spisok chlenov obschestva i sostava pravleniia i dr. (1958–1982 gg.)', f. 1899, op. 1, d. 633.

Moscow, RGALI, f. 2939: Tsentral'nyi detskii teatr (TsTD) (Moscow, 1921 – po nastoiaschee vremia), 'Zaiavka B. V. Zakhodera na instsenirovku p'esy D. Barri "Piter Pen", 1959 g.', f. 2939, op. 2, d. 449.

Moscow, RGALI, f. 2939: Tsentral'nyi detskii teatr (TsTD) (Moscow, 1921 – po nastoiaschee vremia), '"Piter Pen" – p'esa v 5 deistviiakh L. Barri. Perevod s angliiskogo B. V. Zakhodera. Pervyi variant', f. 2939, op. 2, d. 446.

Moscow, RGALI, f. 631: Soiuz pisatelei SSSR (SP SSSR) (Moskva, 1934–91), 'Stenogramma ob"edinennogo zasedaniia sektsii kritiki, literaturovedeniia i khudozhestvennogo perevoda Moskovskogo otdeleniia SP RSFSR i Inostrannoi komissii, posviashchennogo sovremennoi angliiskoi literature v russkikh perevodakh i kritike, 1961 g.', f. 631, op. 26, d. 956.

Moscow, RGALI, f. 2949: Moskovskii dramaticheskii teatr im. M. N. Ermolovoi, '"Meri Poppins". Komediia v 2-kh deistviiakh B. Zakhodera i V. Klimovskogo', f. 2949, op. 1, d. 1414.

Moscow, RGALI, f. 2949: Moskovskii dramaticheskii teatr im. M. N. Ermolovoi, 'Stenogramma obsuzhdeniia v Upravlenii teatrov Minesterstva kul'tury RSFSR spektaklia "Meri Poppins"', f. 2949, op. 1, d. 383.

Moscow, RGALI, f. 2949: Moskovskii dramaticheskii teatr im. M. N. Ermolovoi, 'Zametka o spektakle "Meri Poppins". Gazetnaia vyrezka', f. 2949, op. 1, d. 1418.

Secondary sources

Adamov, Daniil, and Viktoriia Sal'nikova, 'Perevodchik Viktor Golyshev – o Brodskom, tsenzure i idealizatsii 60-kh', *Setevoe izdanie m24.ru*, 24 May 2015, http://www.m24.ru/articles/71723 (accessed 18 July 2019).

Aksyonov, Vasily, *Moi dedushka – pamiatnik* (Kemerovo: Sovremennaia otechestvennaia kniga, 1991).

Almond, David, *Menia zovut Mina*, trans. O. Varshaver (Moscow: Azbuka, 2014).

Almond, David, *Skellig*, trans. O. Varshaver (Moscow: Inostranka, 2004).

Almond, David, *Mal'chik, kotoryi plaval s piran'iami*, trans. O. Varshaver (Moscow: Samokat, 2015).

Angliiskie ballady i pesni, trans. S. Marshak (Moscow: Sovetskii pisatel', 1941).

Angliiskie narodnye pesenki, trans. S. Marshak (Moscow: Detgiz, 1944).

Arzamastseva, I. N., and S. A. Nikolaeva, *Detskaia literatura*, 6th edn (Moscow: Academiia, 2009).

Asarkan, A., 'Mir Vinni-Pukha', *Novyi mir*, 8 (1961), 269–71.

Atarova, Kseniia, *Angliia, moia Angliia* (Moscow: Raduga, 2008).

Azov, Andrei, *Poverzhennye bukvalisty: Iz istorii khudozhestvennogo perevoda v SSSR v 1920–1960-e gody* (Moscow: Vysshaia shkola ekonomiki, 2013).

Baer, Brian James, and Natalia Olshanskaya, eds, *Russian Writers on Translation: An Anthology* (Manchester: St. Jerome, 2013).

Bakhtin, M., 'Formy vremeni i khronotopa v romane: Ocherki po istoricheskoi poetike', in *Voprosy literatury i estetiki: Issledovaniia raznykh let*, ed. M. Bakhtin (Moscow: Khudozhestvennaia literatura, 1975), pp. 234–408.

Balina, Marina, 'Creativity through Restraint: The Beginnings of Soviet Children's literature', in *Russian Children's Literature and Culture*, ed. Marina Balina and Larissa Rudova (New York: Routledge, 2008), pp. 3–17.

Balina, Marina, 'Fairy Tales of Socialist Realism: Introduction', in *Politicizing Magic: An Anthology of Russian and Soviet Fairy Tales*, ed. Marina Balina and others (Evanston, IL: Northwestern University Press, 2005), pp. 105–21.

Balina, Marina, and Larissa Rudova, 'Introduction', *The Slavic and East European Journal, Special Forum Issue: Russian Children's Literature: Changing Paradigms*, 49:2 (2005), 186–98.

Baranova, Marina, 'Kazhdaiia novaia kniga delaiet menia drugim' [Interview with Gennady Kalinovsky]', *Detskaia literatura*, 7 (1990), 65–8.

Barker, Ernest, 'An Attempt at Perspective', in *The Character of England*, ed. Ernest Barker (Oxford: Clarendon Press, 1947), pp. 550–75.

Barnes, Julian, *England, England* (London: Vintage Books, 2012).

'Barri Dzh.', in *Literaturnaia entsiklopediia. V 11 tomakh, 1929–1939*, ed. P. I. Lebedev-Polianskii et al., 11 vols (Moscow: Kommunisticheskaia akademiia, 1930), i (1930), 720–1, http://feb-web.ru/feb/litenc/encyclop/le1/le1-7205.htm (accessed 18 July 2019).

Barrie, J. M., 'Dzheims Barri. Piter Pen. P'esa v 5 deistviiakh. Akt 2', *Detskaia literatura*, 12 (1966), 37–8.

Barrie, J. M., *Piter Pen i Vendi*, trans. Nina Demurova (Moscow: Slovo, 1992).

Barrie, J. M., 'Piter Pen i Vendi', in *Pochti kak v zhizni*, ed. Iulii Kagarlitskii, trans. Nina Demurova (Moscow: Pravda, 1987), pp. 443–579.

Barrie, J. M., *Prikliucheniia Pitera Pana*, trans. L. A. Bubnova (Moscow: Detskaia kniga, 1918).

Barthes, Roland, *Image, Music, Text*, trans. Stephen Heath (London: Fontana, 1977).

Batyushkov, K. N., 'Ten' druga', in *K. N. Batiushkov. Polnoe sobranie stikhotvorenii* (Moscow: Sovetskii pisatel', 1964), pp. 170–1.

Berberich, Christine, *The Image of the English Gentleman in Twentieth-Century Literature: Englishness and Nostalgia* (Aldershot: Ashgate, 2007).

Bergsten, Staffan, *Mary Poppins and Myth* (Stockholm: Almqvist and Wiksell International, 1978).

Blium, Arlen V., *Sovetskaia tsenzura v epokhu total'nogo terrora: 1929–1953* (Saint Petersburg: Gumanitarnoe agentstvo 'Akademicheskii proekt', 2000).

Blium, Arlen V., 'Stat'ia dlia entsiklopedii "Tsenzura"', http://www.encyclopedia.ru/news/enc/detail/46922/ (accessed 18 July 2019).

Blium, Arlen V., *Tsenzura v Sovetskom Soiuze. 1917–1991. Dokumenty* (Moscow: ROSSPEN, 2004).

Blium, Arlen V., *Za kulisami 'Ministerstva pravdy': Tainaia istoriia sovetskoi tsenzury. 1917–1929* (St. Petersburg: Akademicheskii proekt, 1994).

Bochkareva, I., 'P. Trevers. Meri Poppins', *Detskaia literatura*, 3 (1969), 62–3.

Borisenko, Alexandra, '"The Good Are Always the Merry": British Children's Literature in Soviet Russia', in *Translation in Russian Contexts: Culture, Politics, Identity*, ed. Brian James Baer and Susanna Witt (New York: Routledge, 2018), pp. 205–19.

Borisenko, Alexandra, 'Istoriia skazki', in *Trevers Pamela Lindon. Vse o Meri Poppins* (Moscow: ROSMEN, 2012), pp. 628–36.

Borisenko, Alexandra, 'Pesni nevinnosti i pesni opyta: O novykh perevodakh "Vinni-Pukha"', *Inostrannaia literatura*, 4 (2002), https://magazines.gorky.media/inostran/2002/4/pesni-nevinnosti-i-pesni-opyta.html (accessed 18 July 2019).

Bramwell, Peter, *Pagan Themes in Modern Children's Fiction: Green Man, Shamanism, Earth Mysteries* (Basingstoke: Palgrave Macmillan, 2009).

Brandis, Evgenii, *Ot Ezopa do Dzhanni Rodari: Zarubezhnaia literatura v detskom i iunosheskom chtenii* (Moscow: Detskaia literatura, 1980).

Breeva, Tat'iana N., and Liliia F. Khabibulina, *Natsional'nyi mif v russkoi i angliiskoi literature* (Kazan': RITs 'Shkola', 2009).

Brodsky, Joseph, 'In Memory of Stephen Spender', in *On Grief and Reason: Essays* (London: Penguin Books, 2011), pp. part X, Kindle edition.

Bukhina, Olga, 'From Narnia to Russia: A History of Translation', *Proceedings of the 33rd IBBY International Congress 'Crossing Boundaries: Translations and Migrations'*, 23–26 August 2012 (2012), http://www.congress2012.ibby.org.uk/transcripts.php (accessed 16 May 2019).

Bunin, I. A., 'Muravskii shliakh', in *Sobranie sochinenii v 9 tomakh*, 9 vols (Moscow: Izdatel'stvo 'Khudozhestvennaia literatura', 1965–7), v: *Povesti i rasskazy 1917–1930* (1966), p. 427.

Bunin, I. A., *Sobranie sochinenii v 9 tomakh*, 9 vols (Moscow: Izdatel'stvo 'Khudozhestvennaia literatura', 1965–7), vi: *Zhizn' Arsen'eva. Iunost'* (1966).

Bunin, I. A., *Stikhotvoreniia* (Leningrad: Sovetskii pisatel', 1961).

Burness, Edwina, and Jerry Griswold, 'The Art of Fiction No. 63, The Interview with P. L. Travers', *The Paris Review*, 86 (1982), http://www.theparisreview.org/interviews/3099/the-art-of-fiction-no-63-p-l-travers (accessed 18 July 2019).

Burnett, Leon, and Emily Lygo, eds, *The Art of Accommodation: Literary Translation in Russia* (Bern: Peter Lang, 2013).

Carpenter, Humphrey, *Secret Gardens: A Study of the Golden Age of Children's Literature* (London: Allen & Unwin, 1985).

Carpenter, Humphrey, and Mari Prichard, *The Oxford Companion to Children's Literature* (Oxford: Oxford University Press, 2005).

Carpenter, Humphrey, Mari Prichard and Daniel Hahn, *The Oxford Companion to Children's Literature*, 2nd edn (Oxford: Oxford University Press, 2015).
Carroll, Jane Suzanne, *Landscape in Children's Literature* (New York: Routledge, 2011).
Chamberlain, John 'Books of the Times', *New York Times (1923-Current file)* (8 August 1935), 15.
Chambers, Iain, *Border Dialogues: Journeys in Postmodernity* (London: Routledge, 1990).
Chekhov, A. P., 'Step': Istoriia odnoi poezdki', in *Izbrannye proizvedeniia v 3 tomakh*, 3 vols (Moscow: Khudozhestvennaia literatura, 1970), i, 422–515.
Cherniavskaia, I., 'O nekotorykh tendentsiiakh v sovremennoi zarubezhnoi literature', *Detskaia literatura*, 3 (1970), 26–9.
Child Sargent, Helen, and George Lyman Kittredge, eds, *English and Scottish Popular Ballads* (London: George G. Harrap, 1904).
Chudinova, Elena, 'Vozvraschenie Sedrika Errola. O tvorchestve Frensis Bernet', *Detskaia literatura*, 5 (1993), 31–6.
Chukovskaya, Lydia, *Procherk. Stikhotvoreniia. Sofia Petrovna. Spusk pod vodu* (Moscow: Art-Fleks, 2001).
Chukovskaya, Lydia, *V laboratorii redaktora* (Arkhangel'sk: OAO 'IPP "Pravda Severa", 2005), http://www.chukfamily.ru/Lidia/Publ/Laboratoria/glava7.htm (accessed 18 July 2019).
Chukovsky, Korney, 'Istoriia moego Aibolita', *Literaturnaia Rossiia*, 30 January (1970), pp. 16–17.
Chukovsky, Korney, 'Kak ia poliubil anglo-americanskuiu literaturu', in Kornei Chukovsky, *Sobranie sochinenii v 15 tomakh*, 15 vols (Moscow: Agentstvo FTM Ltd, 2012), iii: *Visokoe iskusstvo. Iz anglo-amerikanskikh tetradei*, Ebook, pp. 485–8.
Chukovsky, Korney, 'Gorky', in Kornei Chukovsky, *Sobranie sochinenii v 15 tomakh*, 15 vols (Moscow: Agentstvo FTM, 2012), v: *Sovremenniki. Portrety i etiudy*, Ebook, pp. 38–76.
Chukovsky, Korney, *Sobranie sochinenii v 15 tomakh*, 15 vols (Moscow: Agentstvo FTM Ltd, 2012), xiii: *Dnevnik (1936–1969)*, Ebook.
Chukovsky, Korney, 'Tri pis'ma Chukovskogo', *Detskaia literatura*, 4 (1972), 44–5.
Chukovsky, Korney, *Vysokoe iskusstvo. Printsipy khudozhestvennogo perevoda* (St. Petersburg: Azbuka-Klassika, 2011).
Chukovsky, Korney, *Zagovorili molchavshie: Anglichane i voina* (Petrograd: Izd. tov-va A. F. Marks, 1916).
Chukovsky, Nikolai K., *O tom, chto videl: Vospominaniia, pis'ma* (Moscow: Molodaia gvardiia, 2005).
Clark, Katerina, and Evgeny Dobrenko, *Soviet Culture and Power: A History in Documents, 1917–1953* (New Haven: Yale University Press, 2007).
Clifford, Sue, and Angela King, *England in Particular: A Celebration of the Commonplace, the Local, the Vernacular and the Distinctive* (London: Hodder & Stoughton, 2006).

Cogan Thacker, Deborah, and Jean Webb, eds, *Introducing Children's Literature: From Romanticism to Postmodernism* (London: Routledge, 2002).

Colls, Robert, *Identity of England* (Oxford: Oxford University Press, 2002).

Cook, Chris, ed., *Routledge Guide to British Political Archives: Sources since 1945*, (London: Routledge, 2006).

Craik, Georgiana M., *Istorii kuziny Triks. Sbornik dlia detei*, trans. A. Berseneva-Shankevich (Moscow: Izd-vo Sretenskogo monastyria, 2013).

Davidson, Apollon B., *Na putiakh k vzaimoponimaniiu*, 19 March 2014, https://histrf.ru/biblioteka/b/na-putiakh-k-vzaimoponimaniiu (accessed 16 May 2019).

Davidson, Apollon B., 'Obraz Britanii v Rossii XIX i XX stoletii', *Novaia i noveishaia istoriia*, 5 (2005), http://vivovoco.astronet.ru/VV/PAPERS/HISTORY/ALBION.HTM#15 (accessed 16 May 2019).

de la Mare, Walter, *Sygraem v priatki*, trans. Viktor Lunin (Moscow: Detskaia literatura, 1978).

Demurova, Nina, 'Golos i skripka (k perevodu ekstsentricheskikh skazok L'iuisa Kerrolla)', *Masterstvo perevoda*, 7 (1970), 150–85.

Demurova, Nina, 'Malen'kie oborvyshi v bol'shoi literature', *Detskaia literatura*, 7 (1979), 21–33.

Demurova, Nina, 'Peter Pan in Russia: Or Peter Pan, Korney Chukovsky and the Soviet Censor', in *The Neverland: Two Flights Over the Territory*, ed. Nina Demurova and Chris Routh ([n.p.]: Children's Books History Society, Occasional Paper II, 1995), pp. 19–28.

Dobrenko, Evgeny, *The Making of the State Reader: Social and Aesthetic Contexts of the Reception of Soviet Literature*, trans. Jesse M. Savage (Stanford, CA: Stanford University Press, 1997).

Dobrenko, Evgeny, 'The School Tale in Children's Literature of Socialist Realism', in *Russian Children's Literature and Culture*, ed. Marina Balina and others (New York: Routledge, 2008), pp. 43–66.

Dovlatov, Sergei, 'Perevodnye kartinki', in *Sergei Dovlatov. Sobraniie sochinenii v 4-kh tomakh*, 4 vols (Saint Petersburg: Azbuka-klassika, 2005), iv, 328–48, http://www.sergeidovlatov.com/books/perev_kart.html (accessed 18 July 2019).

Düring, Muchael, 'Canon Formation in the Soviet Union: The Case of Swift as an Author of a Children's Classic', in *Canon Constitution and Canon Change in Children's Literature*, ed. Bettina Kümmerling-Meibauer and Anja Müller (New York: Routledge, 2017), pp. 72–84.

Easthope, Anthony, *Englishness and National Culture* (London: Routledge, 1999).

Ehrenburg, Ilya G., 'Angliia', in *Sobranie sochinenii v 9 tomakh*, 9 vols (Moscow: Khudizhestvennaia literatura, 1962–7), vii: *Khronika nashikh dnei. Viza vremeni. Ispaniia. Grazhdanskaia voina v Avstrii. Stat'i* (1966), pp. 444–78.

Ermolaev, Herman, *Censorship in Soviet Literature, 1917–1991* (Lanham, MD: Rowman and Littlefield, 1997).

Erofeev, Nikolay A., *Tumannyi Al'bion: Angliia i anglichane glazami russkikh, 1825–1853 gg.* (Moscow: Nauka, 1982).

Esenin, Sergei, *Stikhotvoreniia. Poemy. Povesti. Rasskazy* (Moscow: EKSMO, 2008).
Etkind, Efim, *Poeziia i perevod* (Moscow: Sovetskii pisatel', 1963).
Even-Zohar, Itamar, 'Polysystem Studies', *Poetics Today*, 11 (1990), 7–193.
Fateev, A. V., *Stalinizm i Detskaia Literatura v Politike Nomenklatury SSSR, 1930-e – 1950-e gg.* (Moscow: Maks Press, 2007), http://psyfactor.org/lib/ detlit5.htm (accessed 18 July 2019).
Fitzpatrick, Sheila, *The Cultural Front: Power and Culture in Revolutionary Russia* (Ithaca: Cornell University Press, 1992).
Fitzpatrick, Sheila, 'Australian Visitors to the Soviet Union: The View from the Soviet Side', in *Political Tourists: Travellers from Australia to the Soviet Union in the 1920s-1940s*, ed. C. Rasmussen and S. Fitzpatrick (Carlton, Vic.: Melbourne University Press, 2008), pp. 1–39.
Flieger, Verlyn, and Douglas A. Anderson, eds, *Tolkien on Fairy-Stories: Expanded Edition with Commentary and Notes* (London: HarperCollins, 2014).
FOM, 'Opinion Poll 'Interes k Velikobritanii. Chto rossiiane znaiut o Velikobritanii? I khotiat li pobivat' v etoi strane?' [Interest in Great Britain. What do Russian people know about Britain? Would they like to visit Britain?]' (24 March 2014), http://fom.ru/Mir/11416 (accessed 19 July 2019).
Ford, Ford Madox, *England and the English: A Trilogy* (Manchester: Carcanet, 2003).
Friedberg, Maurice, *Literary Translation in Russia: A Cultural History* (University Park, PA: Pennsylvania State University Press, 1997).
Friedberg, Maurice, 'Soviet Censorship: A View from the Outside', in *The Red Pencil: Artists, Scholars, and Censors in the USSR*, ed. Maurice Friedberg and Marianna Tax Choldin (Boston: Unwin Hyman, 1989), pp. 15–28.
Gasparov, Mikhail L., 'Briusov i bukvalism', in *Masterstvo perevoda*, 8 (Moscow: Sovetskii pisatel', 1971), pp. 88–128.
Gavin, Adrienne E., 'Grahame, Kenneth', in *The Oxford Encyclopedia of Children's Literature*, ed. Jack Zipes, Oxford University Press, Oxford Reference Online, 2006, DOI: 0.1093/acref/9780195146561.001.0001 (accessed 19 July 2019).
Gervais, David, *Literary Englands: Versions of 'Englishness' in Modern Writing* (Cambridge: Cambridge University Press, 1993).
Gilenson, B. A., and N. Ia. D'iakonova, 'Barri', in *Kratkaia literaturnaia entsiklopediia*, ed. A. A. Surkov, 9 vols (Moscow: Sovetskaia entsiklopediia, 1962–78), i (1962), 459, http://feb-web.ru/feb/kle/kle-abc/ke1/ke1-4591.htm (accessed 18 July 2019).
Giles, Judy, and Tim Middleton, eds, *Writing Englishness 1900–1950: An Introductory Sourcebook on National Identity* (New York: Routledge, 1995).
Golov, V., 'Rastit' patriota – internatsionalista', *Detskaia literatura*, 1 (1985), 2–6.
Goodwin, Elena, *'Dobraia Staraia Angliia' in Russian Perception: Literary Representations of Englishness in Translated Children's Literature in Soviet and Post-Soviet Russia* (PhD thesis, University of Exeter, 2017).
Gopman, V., 'Red'iard Kipling. Mech Vilanda. Skazki staroi Anglii', *Detskaia literatura*, 1 (1986), 73–4.
Goudge, Elizabeth, *Taina lunnoi doliny*, trans. O. Bukhina (Moscow: Zakharov, 2009).

Graham, Kathryn V., 'Grahame, Kenneth', in *The Oxford Encyclopedia of British Literature*, ed. Scott Kastan (Oxford: Oxford University Press, 2006). Oxford Reference Online, DOI: 10.1093/acref/9780195169218.001.0001 (accessed 19 July 2019).

Grahame, Kenneth, *The Wind in the Willows*, ed. Gillian Avery (New York: Penguin Classics, 2005).

Grahame, Kenneth, *The Wind in the Willows: An Annotated edition*, ed. Seth Lerer (Cambridge, MA: Belknap Press of Harvard University Press, 2009).

Green, Peter, *Kenneth Grahame 1959–1932: A Study of His Life, Work and Times* (London: John Murray, 1959).

Grigoriev, V. V., ed, *Knizhnyi rynok Rossii: Sostoianie, tendentsii i perspektivy razvitiia. Otraslevoi doklad. 2018* (Moscow: Federal'noe agentstvo po pechati i massovym kommunikatsiiam, 2018).

Grilli, Giorgia, *Myth, Symbol, and Meaning in Mary Poppins: The Governess as Provocateur*, trans. Jennifer Varney (New York: Routledge, 2007).

Gromyko, Al. A., *Obrazy Rossii v Velikobritanii: real'nost' i predrassudki* (Moscow: Institut Evropy RAN: Russkii suvenir, 2008).

Gubarev, Vitalii, *Korolevstvo krivykh zerkal (povest'-skazka)* (Moscow: Molodaia gvardiia, 1951).

Gubarev, Vitalii, *Korolevstvo krivykh zerkal* (Moscow: Makhaon, 2015).

Gumilev, N., ed., *Ballady o Robin Gude* (Peterburg: Vsemirnaia literatura pri Narodnom komissariate po prosveshcheniiu, 1919).

Habermann, Ina, *Myth, Memory and the Middlebrow: Priestley, du Maurier and the Symbolic Form of Englishness* (Basingstoke: Palgrave Macmillan, 2010).

Hall, Stuart, 'The Question of Cultural Identity', in *Modernity: An Introduction to Modern Societies*, ed. Stuart Hall and others (Malden, MA: Blackwell, 1996), pp. 595–634.

Hall, Stuart, 'Whose Heritage? Un-settling "the Heritage", Re-imagining the Post-nation', *Third Text*, 13:49 (1999), 3–13, DOI: 10.1080/09528829908576818 (accessed 18 July 2019).

Hellman, Ben, *Children's Books in Soviet Russia: From October Revolution 1917 to Perestroika 1986*, 1991, http://www.helsinki.fi/~bhellman/summary.html (accessed 16 May 2019).

Hellman, Ben, *Fairy Tales and True Stories: The History of Russian Literature for Children and Young People (1574–2010)* (Leiden: Brill, 2013).

Hellman, Ben, 'Samuil Marshak: Yesterday and Today', in *Russian Children's Literature and Culture*, ed. Marina Balina and others (New York: Routledge, 2008), pp. 217–39.

Hellman, Geoffrey T., 'The Talk of the Town: Mary Poppins', *The New Yorker*, 38(35) (20 October 1962), 44, http://www.newyorker.com/archive/1962/10/20/1962_10_20_044_TNY_CARDS_000274309?printable=true&currentPage=all (accessed 18 July 2019).

Hodgson, Katharine, 'The Poetry of Rudyard Kipling in Soviet Russia', *Modern Language Review*, 93 (1998), 1058–71

Hollindale, Peter, 'Introduction', in *Peter Pan in Kensington Gardens and Peter and Wendy* (Oxford: Oxford University Press, 2008), pp. vii–xxviii.

Hooker, Mark T., *Tolkien through Russian Eyes* (Zurich: Walking Tree, 2003).

Howkins, Alun, 'The Discovery of Rural England', in *Englishness: Politics and Culture 1880–1920*, ed. Robert Colls and Philip Dodd (London: Croom Helm, 1986), pp. 62–88.

Hunt, Peter, 'Explanatory Notes', in *The Wind in the Willows* (Oxford: Oxford University Press, 2010), pp. 147–70.

Hunt, Peter, 'Introduction', in *Kenneth Grahame. The Wind in the Willows* (Oxford: Oxford University Press, 2010), pp. vii–xxxii.

Hunt, Peter, *The Wind in the Willows: A Fragmented Arcadia* (New York: Twayne, 1994).

Iakovenko, I., 'Krizis adekvatnosti: Razdum'ia kul'turologa', *Vestnik Evropy*, 33 (2012), https://magazines.gorky.media/vestnik/2012/33/krizis-adekvatnosti.html (accessed 18 July 2019).

Iasnov, Mikhail, 'Ot Robina-Bobina do malysha Russelia', *Druzhba narodov*, 12 (2004), 190–200.

Inggs, Judith, 'From Harry to Garri: Strategies for the Transfer of Culture and Ideology in Russian Translations of Two English Fantasy Stories', *Meta*, 48 (2003), 285–97.

Inggs, Judith, 'Censorship and Translated Children's Literature in the Soviet Union: The Example of the Wizards Oz and Goodwin', *Target*, 23 (2011), 77–91.

Inggs, Judith, 'Translation and Transformation: English-Language Children's Literature in (Soviet) Russian Guise', *International Research in Children's Literature*, 8 (2015), 1–16.

Ivanovskii, Ignatii, *Ballady o Robin Gude* (Leningrad: Izdatel'stvo detskoi literatury, 1959).

Ivanovskii, Ignatii, *Ballady o Robin Gude* (Leningrad: Izdatel'stvo detskoi literatury, 1963).

Ivanovskii, Ignatii, 'Fragmenty', *Zarubezhnye zapiski*, 4 (2005), https://magazines.gorky.media/zz/2005/4/fragmenty-2.html (accessed 18 July 2019).

Kalashnikova, Elena, *Interview with Irina Gurova 'Svoi metod ia nikomu ne rekomenduiu, no sudiat-to po resul'tatu . . .'*, Russkii Zhurnal / Krug chteniia, 4 December 2002, http://old.russ.ru/krug/20021128_kalash.html (accessed 18 July 2019).

Kalashnikova, Elena, *Interview with Mikhail Iasnov 'Perevod – iskusstvo poter'*, Russkii Zhurnal / Krug chteniia, 11 January 2002, http://old.russ.ru/krug/20020111_kalash-pr.html (accessed 18 July 2019).

Kalashnikova, Elena, *Interview with Nina Demurova: 'Vse proizvedeniia ia perevodila s udovol'stviem'*, Russkii Zhurnal / Krug chteniia, 15 March 2002, http://old.russ.ru/krug/20020315_kalash.html (accessed 18 July 2019).

Kalashnikova, Elena, *Po-russki s liubov'iu: besedy s perevodchikami* (Moscow: Novoe Literaturnoe Obozrenie, 2008).

Kalinovsky, Gennady, 'Kak sozdaietsia knizhnaia illiustratsiia', in *Panorama iskusstv*, issue 8, ed. Iu. M. Riadchenko (Moscow: Sovetskii khudozhnik, 1985), pp. 15–20.

Kal'm, D., 'Protiv khaltury v detskoi literature!' [Against cheating in children's literature!], *Literaturnaia gazeta*, 35 (1929), 2.

Kanevsky, S., 'Novye prikliucheniia Vinni-Pukha', *Literaturnaia gazeta*, 14 (4 March 1968), 12.

Karasik, Vladimir, and Elena Iarmakhova, eds, *Lingvokul'turnyi Tipazh 'Angliiskii Chudak'* (Moscow: Gnozis, 2006).

Kareev, N. I., 'How Far Russia Knows England', in *The Soul of Russia*, ed. Winifred Stephens, trans. Adeline L. Kaye (London: Macmillan, 1916), pp. 96–101.

Kaznina, Olga A., 'Angliia glazami russkikh', in *'Ia bereg pokidal tumannyi Al'biona . . .': russkie pisateli ob Anglii, 1646–1945*, ed. Olga A. Kaznina and A. N. Nikoliukin (Moscow: ROSSPEN, 2001), pp. 3–24.

Kaznina, Olga A., and A. N. Nikoliukin, eds, *'Ia bereg pokidal tumannyi Al'biona . . .': russkie pisateli ob Anglii, 1646–1945* (Moscow: ROSSPEN, 2001).

Kelly, Catriona, *Children's World: Growing Up in Russia, 1890–1991* (New Haven, CT: Yale University Press, 2007).

Kelly, Catriona, '"Malen'kie grazhdane bol'shoi strany": internatsionalism, deti i sovetskaia propaganda', *Novoe Literaturnoe Obozrenie*, 60 (2003), 218–51.

Khotimsky, Maria, 'World Literature, Soviet Style: A Forgotten Episode in the History of the Idea', *Ab Imperio*, 3 (2013), 119–54.

Kienia, Nataliia, Interview with Viktor Golyshev. *'Esli perevodish' popsu, nechego tseremonit'sia': Viktor Golyshev o prilizannykh tekstakhm 'Garri Pottere' i novoiaze*, Theory&Practice, 25 February 2015, http://theoryandpractice.ru/posts/10266-golyshev (accessed 18 July 2019).

Kliuchevskii, V. O., *Sochineniia: Kurs russkoi istorii* (Moscow: Politicheskaia literatura, 1956).

Knuth, Rebecca, *Children's Literature and British Identity: Imagining a People and a Nation* (Lanham, MD: Scarecrow Press, 2012).

Komissarov, Vilen N., 'Russian Tradition', in *Routledge Encyclopedia of Translation Studies* ed. Mona Baker (London: Routledge, 2001), pp. 694–705.

Koval', Iu., 'S. Marshak. Iz A. A. Mil'na. Korolevskii buterbrod. Ris. E. Meshkova. M., izd. "Detskaia literatura", 1965', *Detskaia literatura*, 3 (1966), 51–3.

KPSS v rezoliutsiiakh i resheniiakh s'ezdov, konferentsii i plenumov, Part I (Moscow: Gosudarstvennoe izdatel'stvo politicheskoi literatury, 1953).

Krupskaia, N. K., 'O Detskoi biblioteke i detskoi knige', in *Pedagogicheskie sochineniia v 10-ti tomakh. Tom 8*, eds. N. K. Goncharov, I. A. Kairov, and I. V. Chuvashev, 10 vols (Moscow: Izdatel'stvo Akademii pedagogicheskikh nauk, 1957–63), viii (1960), pp. 171–9.

Kudriavtseva, T. A., *Prevratnosti odnoi sud'by. Zapiski literatora I perevodchika* (Moscow: R. Valent, 2008).

Kukhterina, I. P., ed., *Izdaniia VGBIL: Vyborochnyi bibliograficheckii ukazatel' 1941–1981* (Moscow: VGBIL, 1982).

Kukhterina, I. P., ed., *Izdaniia VGBIL: Vyborochnyi bibliograficheckii ukazatel' 1975–1986* (Moscow: VGBIL, 1987).

Kumar, Krishan, '"Englishness'" and English National Identity', in *British Cultural Studies: Geography, Nationality, and Identity*, ed. Kevin Robins and David Morley (New York: Oxford University Press, 2001), pp. 41–55.

Kumar, Krishan, *The Making of English National Identity* (New York: Cambridge University Press, 2003).

Kurbatova, I., 'Mir geroev Vinni-Pukha', *Detskaia literatura*, 1 (1973), 29–32.

Kurneshov, Evgenii, *Irina Petrovna Tokmakova predstavliaet knigu 'Piter Pen' Dzh. Barri izdatel'stva 'Moskovskie uchebniki'*, online video recording, YouTube, 31 May 2012, https://www.youtube.com/watch?v=PeA5IpUEzGg (accessed 16 May 2019).

Kutzer, M. Daphne, *Empire's Children: Empire and Imperialism in Classic British Children's Books* (New York: Garland, 2000).

Kuznetsov, Arkadii Iu., 'Britanskii sled v Rossii. Vstrechaia god Velikobritanii', *Biblioteka v shkole*, 2 (317) (2014), 57–61.

Labirint.ru, 'Vneklassnoe chtenie. Otchet dlia pedagogov i roditelei po resul'tatam vserossiiskogo onlain-oprosa' (May 2013), https://en.calameo.com/read/00046390357ebf9393e1f (accessed 18 July 2019).

Latham, Phoebe, 'Liubimye detskie knigi', *Angliia*, 2 (1969), 22–9.

Lefevere, André, 'Mother Courage's Cucumbers: Text, System and Refraction in a Theory of Literature', in *The Translation Studies Reader*, ed. Lawrence Venuti, 1st edn (London: Routledge, 2000), pp. 233–49.

Leighton, Lauren G., 'Translation as a Derived Art', *Proceedings of the American Philosophical Society*, 134 (1990), 445–54.

Leighton, Lauren G., *Two Worlds, One Art: Literary Translation in Russia and America* (DeKalb, IL: Northern Illinois University Press, 1991).

Lentz, Ulrike, 'The Representation of Western European Governesses and Tutors on the Russian Country Estate in Historical Documents and Literary Texts' (Doctoral thesis, University of Surrey, 2008).

Lerer, Seth, 'Introduction', in *Kenneth Grahame. The Wind in the Willows, an Annotated Edition*, ed. Seth Lerer (Cambridge, MA: Belknap Press of Harvard University Press, 2009), pp. 1–43.

Lerer, Seth, ed., *Kenneth Grahame. The Wind in the Willows, an Annotated Edition* (Cambridge, MA: Belknap Press of Harvard University Press, 2009).

Lewis, C. S., *Lev, Koldun'ia i platianoi shkaf*, trans. G. Ostrovskaia (Leningrad: Detskaia literatura, 1978).

Lingerman, Richard R., 'Visit with Mary Poppins and P. L. Travers', *New York Times (1923-Current file)* (25 December 1966), p. A12.

Liubarskaia, A. I., 'Za tiuremnoi stenoi', *Neva*, 5 (1998), 148–72.

Lundin, Anne H., *Constructing the Canon of Children's Literature: Beyond Library Walls and Ivory Towers* (New York: Routledge, 2004).

Lunin, Viktor, 'Vospominaniia: Zakhoder i dr.', *Vyshgorod: literaturno-khudozhestvennyi obschestvenno-politicheskii zhurnal*, 1–2 (2007), 142–59.

Lygo, Emily, *Leningrad Poetry 1953–1975: The Thaw Generation* (Bern: Peter Lang, 2010).

Lyubimov, Mikhail, *Gulianiia s Cheshirskim kotom: memuar-esse ob angliiskoi dushe* (Saint Petersburg: Amfora, 2015), ebook.

Mallett, Phillip, 'Rudyard Kipling and the Invention of Englishness', in *Beyond Pug's Tour: National and Ethnic Stereotyping in Theory and Literary Practice*, ed. C. C. Barfoot (Amsterdam: Rodopi, 1997), pp. 255–66.

Manlove, Colin, *The Fantasy Literature of England* (Basingstoke: Macmillan Press, 1999).

Manlove, Colin, *From Alice to Harry Potter: Children's Fantasy in England* (Christchurch, NZ: Cybereditions, 2003).

Marsh, Richard R., 'The Farmer in Modern English Fiction', *Agricultural History*, 23 (1949), 146–59.

Marsh, Rosalind, *Literature, History and Identity in Post-Soviet Russia, 1991–2006* (Oxford: Peter Lang, 2007).

Marshak, Samuil, *Deti nashego dvora* (Moscow: AST/Astrel', 2008).

Marshak, Samuil, 'Dom, uvenchannyi globusom. Dve besedy S. Ia. Marshaka s L. K. Chukovskoi', *Novyi mir*, 9 (1968), 158–81.

Marshak, Samuil, 'Ia pobyval v triekh stranakh', in *Zhizn' i tvorchestvo Samuila Iakovlevicha Marshaka. Marshak i detskaia literatura*, ed. B. Galanov, I. Marshak and M. Petrovskii (Moscow: Detskaia literatura, 1975), pp. 233–5.

Marshak, Samuil, 'Iskusstvo poeticheskogo portreta', in *Masterstvo perevoda, 1* (Moscow: Sovetskii pisatel', 1959), pp. 245–50.

Marshak, Samuil, *Izbrannye perevody: Angliiskie ballady i pesni* (Moscow: Gosudarstvennoe izdatel'stvo khudozhestvennoi literatury, 1946).

Marshak, Samuil, *Korolevskii buterbrod* (Moscow: Detskaia literatura, 1965).

Marshak, Samuil, *Korol' i pastukh. Angliiskaia narodnaia ballada* (Leningrad: Raduga, 1926).

Marshak, Samuil, *Korol' i pastukh* (Moscow: Detizdat, 1940).

Marshak, Samuil, 'O sebe', in *Marshak S. Ia., Sobranie sochinenii v 8 tomakh*, ed. V. M. Zhirmunskii, 8 vols (Moscow: Khudozhestvennaia literatura, 1968–72), i: *Proizvedeniia dlia detei*, ed. V. I. Leibson (1968), pp. 5–15.

Marshak, Samuil, 'Pocherk veka, pocherk pokoleniia', in *Marshak S. Ia., Sobranie sochinenii v 8 tomakh*, ed. V. M. Zhirmunskii, 8 vols (Moscow: Khudozhestvennaia literatura, 1968–72), vi: *Stat'i. Vystupleniia. Zametki. Vospominaniia. Proza raznykh let*, ed. S. S. Chulkova and E. B. Skorospelova (1971), pp. 351–54.

Marshak, Samuil, *Prikliucheniia stola ii stula. Nebylitsa po Edvardu Liru* (Leningrad: Brokgaus and Efron, 1924).

Marshak, Samuil, *Sobranie sochinenii v 8 tomakh*, ed. V. M. Zhirmunskii, 8 vols (Moscow: Khudozhestvennaia literatura, 1968–72), vi (1971): *Stat'i. Vystupleniia. Zametki. Vospominaniia. Proza raznykh let*, ed. S. S. Chulkova and E. B. Skorospelova.

Marshak, Samuil, *Marshak S. Ia., Sobranie sochinenii v 8 tomakh*, ed. V. M. Zhirmunskii, 8 vols (Moscow: Khudozhestvennaia literatura, 1968–72), vii: *Vospitaniie slovom (Stat'I, zametki, vospominaniia)*, ed. E. B. Skorospelova (1971).

Marshak, Samuil, *Sobranie sochinenii v 8 tomakh*, ed. V. M. Zhirmunskii, 8 vols (Moscow: Khudozhestvennaia literatura, 1968–72), viii: *Izbrannye pis'ma*, ed. S. S. Chulkova (1972).

Marshak, Samuil, *Stikhotvoreniia i poemy* (Leningrad: Sovetskii pisatel', 1973).

Marshak, Samuil, *Vospitanie slovom: stat'i, zametki, vospominaniia* (Moscow: Sovetskii pisatel', 1961).

Maslinskaya, Svetlana, 'Nasledstvo i nasledstvennost': evoliutsiia kritiki russkoi detskoi literatury 1910–1920-x godov', *Revue des études slaves*, 88: 1–2 (2017), 237–55.

Mason, Ian, 'Discourse, Ideology and Translation', in *Translation Studies: Critical Concepts in Linguistics*, ed. Mona Baker (London: Routledge, 2009), iii, pp. 141–56.

Matless, David, *Landscape and Englishness* (London: Reaktion Books, 1998).

McGillis, Roderick, *The Nimble Reader: Literary Theory and Children's Literature* (New York: Twayne, 1996).

Meek, Margaret, 'The Englishness of English Children's Books', in *Children's Literature and National Identity*, ed. Margaret Meek (Stoke-on-Trent: Trentham Books, 2001), pp. 89–100.

Meek, Margaret, 'Preface', in *Children's Literature and National Identity*, ed. Margaret Meek (Stoke-on-Trent: Trentham Books, 2001), pp. vii–xvii.

Mel'nikov, M. N., *Russkii detskii fol'klor* (Moscow: Prosvescheniie, 1987).

Mendelson, Michael, 'The Wind in the Willows and the Plotting of Contrast', *Children's Literature*, 16 (1988), 127–44.

Mendlesohn, Farah, *Rhetorics of Fantasy* (Middletown, CT: Wesleyan University Press, 2008).

Mickelson, Jane L., 'P.L. Travers: 1906–1996', *The Horn Book Magazine*, 72 (1996), 640–4.

Mikhalkov, Sergey, 'Dve udachi', *Literaturnaia gazeta*, 61 (23 May 1961), 3.

Mikhal'skaia, Nina P., *Rossiia i Angliia: problemy imagologii* (Samara: OOO 'Porto-print', 2012).

Milne, A. A., *Dela korolevskie*, trans. Nina Voronel' (Moscow: Art-Bisnes-Tsentr, 1992).

Milne, A. A., *Kristofer Robin i vse-vse-vse. A teper' nam shest'*, trans. G. Kruzhkov, M. Boroditskaia, S. Marshak, N. Voronel' and N. Slepakova (Moscow: AST, 2014).

Milne, A. A., *Kristofer Robin i vse-vse-vse. Kogda my byli esche malen'kie*, trans. M. Boroditskaia, G. Kruzhkov, S. Marshak, N. Voronel' and N. Slepakova (Moscow: AST, 2014).

Milne, A. A., *Vinni-Pukh i vse vse vse*, retold by B. Zakhoder (Moscow: Izdatel'stvo 'Malysh', 1970).

Milne, A. A., *Winnie-the-Pooh* (London: Egmont, 2004).

Mineralova, I. G., ed., *Zarubezhnye detskie pisateli v Rossii: biobibliograficheskii slovar'* (Moscow: Flinta, Nauka, 2005).

Morison, John, 'Anglo-Soviet Cultural Contacts since 1975', in *Soviet-British Relations since the 1970s*, ed. Alex Pravda and others (Cambridge: Cambridge University Press, 1990), pp. 168–92.

Morozov, M., ed., *Ballady i pesni angliiskogo naroda*, trans. S. Marshak, and others (Moscow: Detgiz, 1942).

Motyashov, Igor, 'The Social and Aesthetic Criteria Applied in Choosing Children's Books for Translation', in *Children's Books in Translation: The Situation and the Problems*, ed. Göte Klingberg, Mary Ørvig and Stuart Amor (Stockholm: Almqvist and Wiksell International, 1978), pp. 97–103.

Motyleva, T., 'Kipling', in *Istoriia angliiskoi literaturi. Tom 3*, ed. I. I. Anisimov (Moscow: Izdatel'stvo AN SSSR, 1958), pp. 256–79.

Nabokov, Vladimir, *Mary*, trans. Michael Glenny (Greenwich, CT: Fawcett, 1970).

Narinskaia, Anna, 'Interview with Viktor Golyshev: "Ne nado k perevodu otnosit'sia kak k sviatyne"', *Kommersant Weekend*, 48 (12 December 2008), 93, http://www.kommersant.ru/doc/1091063 (accessed 18 July 2019).

Naumova, I. O., *Frazeologicheskie kal'ki angliiskogo proiskhozhdeniia v sovremennom russkom iazyke (na materiale publitsistiki): Monografiia* (Kharkov: KhNAGKh, 2012).

Nikolajeva, Maria, *Children's Literature Comes of Age: Toward a New Aesthetic* (New York: Garland, 1996).

Nikolajeva, Maria, 'The Development of Children's Fantasy', in *The Cambridge Companion to Fantasy Literature*, ed. Edward James and Farah Mendlesohn (Cambridge: Cambridge University Press, 2012), pp. 50–61.

Nikolajeva, Maria, 'Russian Children's Literature before and after Perestroika', *Children's Literature Association Quarterly*, 20 (1995), 105–11.

Nikolajeva, Maria, 'U istokov angliiskoi detskoi literatury XX veka', *Detskaia literatura*, 7 (1979), 33–7.

Nikolajeva, Maria, 'Translation and Crosscultural Reception', in *Handbook of Research on Children's and Young Adult Literature*, ed. Shelby A. Wolf and others (New York: Routledge, 2011), pp. 404–16.

Nodelman, Perry, 'Grand Canon Suite, Including "A Tentative List of Books Everyone Interested in Children's Literature Should Know"', *Children's Literature Association Quarterly*, 5:2 (1980), 1–8.

Novitskaia, M. Iu., and I. Raikova, *Detskii fol'klor* (Moscow: Russkaia kniga, 2002).

Novye detskie knigi, vol. IV (Moscow: izdatel'stvo 'Rabotnik prosvescheniia', 1926).
O partiinoi i sovetskoi pechati. Sbornik dokumentov (Moscow: Pravda, 1954).
O'Sullivan, Emer, 'Children's Literature and Translation Studies', in *The Routledge Handbook of Translation Studies*, ed. Francesca Bartrina and Carmen Millán (London: Routledge, 2013), pp. 451–63.
O'Sullivan, Emer, *Comparative Children's Literature*, trans. Anthea Bell (London, New York: Routledge, 2005).
Oittinen, Riitta, *Translating for Children* (New York: Garland, 2000).
Ozerov, Mikhail, *Angliia bez tumanov* (Moscow: Detskaia literatura, 1977).
Ozhegov, S. I., *Slovar' russkogo iazyka*, ed. N. Iu. Shvedova (Moscow: Russkii iazyk, 1991).
Parekh, Bhikhu, ed., *The Future of Multi-Ethnic Britain: Report of the Commission on the Future of Multi-Ethnic Britain* (London: Profile Books, 2000).
Parker, Patricia 'What Comes after Mother Goose?', *Elementary English*, 46 (1969), 505–10.
Parrinder, Patrick, *Nation and Novel: The English Novel from Its Origins to the Present Day* (Oxford: Oxford University Press, 2006).
Pavlovskaia, Anna, *Angliia i anglichane* (Moscow: Izdatel'stvo Moskovskii universitet, Triada, 2004).
Pavlovskaia, Anna, *5 O'Clock i drugie traditsii Anglii* (Moscow: Algoritm, 2014).
Pavlovskaia, Anna, 'Osobennosti natsional'nogo kharaktera, ili za chto anglichane liubiat ocheredi', *Vokrug sveta*, 6 (2003), http://www.vokrugsveta.ru/vs/article/512/ (accessed 19 July 2019).
Pearce, Philippa, *Tom i polnochnyi sad*, trans. O. Bukhina (Moscow: Samokat, 2011).
Pervyi Vsesoiuznyi S'ezd Sovetskikh pisatelei, 1934: Stenograficheskii otchet, (Moscow: Gosudarstvennoe izdatel'stvo khudozhestvennoi literatury, 1934; repr. Moscow: Sovetskii pisatel, 1990).
Philip, Neil, 'The Wind in the Willows: The Vitality of a Classic', in *Children and Their Books: A Celebration of the Work of Iona and Peter Opie*, ed. Gillian Avery and Julia Briggs (Oxford: Clarendon Press, 1989), pp. 299–316.
Pinney, Thomas, ed., *The Letters of Rudyard Kipling*, 3 vols (Basingstoke: Palgrave Macmillan, 2004), iii.
Platt, Kevin M. F., 'Doktor Dulitl i doctor Aibolit na prieme v otdelenii travmy', trans. A. Plisetskaia, in *Veselyie chelovechki: kul'turnye geroi sovetskogo detstva*, ed. Il'ia Kukulin, Mark Lipovetskii and Mariia Maiofis (Moscow: Novoe literaturenoe obozrenie, 2008), pp. 80–98.
Podzemskii, A. Ia., ed., *Direktivy VKP(b) po voprosam prosveshcheniia* (Moscow: OGIZ, 1931), pp. 69–74.
Posner, Vladimir, *Angliia v obschem i v chastnosti*, 2015, http://pozneronline.ru/category/filmy-v-poznera/angliya-v-obshhem-i-v-chastnosti/ (accessed 19 July 2019).

Preobrazhenskaia, A. V., 'Kommentarii', in *The Wind in the Willows* (Moscow: Progress, 1981), pp. 315–59.

Prishvin, M. M., *Sobranie sochinenii v shesti tomakh*, 6 vols (Moscow: Gosudarstvennoe izdatel'stvo khudozhestvennoi literatury, 1956–7), i: *Kashcheeva tsep'* (1956).

Proekt dokladnoi zapiski agitpropa TSK Stalinu I.V. po voprosu o ezhenedel'nike 'Britanskii soiuznik', 13 October 1946, Mezhdunarodnyi fond 'Demokratiia' (Fond Aleksandra N. Iakovleva), http://www.alexanderyakovlev.org/fond/issues-doc/69315 (accessed 18 July 2019).

Rakhimov, Azamat, 'Interview with Alexander Livergant: "Perevodchik – professiia smirennaia"', *Nasha gazeta. Shveitsarskie novosti na russkom* (17 December 2014), http://nashagazeta.ch/news/peoples/18739 (accessed 18 July 2019).

Rakhmanova, Natal'ia, 'Vospominaniia', www.kulichki.com/tolkien/arhiv/ugolok/rakhmanova_int.shtml (accessed 18 July 2019).

Reznik, Shaul', 'Galina Zakhoder: "Boris ne pozvolial sebia toptat'"', interview with Galina Zakhoder', *Lekhaim*, 288 (1 March 2016), https://lechaim.ru/events/galina-zahoder-boris-ne-pozvolyal-sebya-toptat/ (accessed 18 July 2019).

Roberts, John C. Q., *Speak Clearly into the Chandelier: Cultural Politics between Britain and Russia 1973–2000* (Richmond: Curzon Press, 2000).

Rosen, Jane, 'Baba Yaga in Brixton', *SCRSS Digest*, Summer (2014), 13–15.

Rubina, Dina, *Dzhentl'meny i sobaki* (Moscow: Eksmo, 2012).

Rudd, David, ed., *The Routledge Companion to Children's Literature* (London: Routledge, 2010).

Rudova, Larissa, 'From Character-Building to Criminal Pursuits', in *Russian Children's Literature and Culture*, ed. Marina Balina and others (New York: Routledge, 2008), pp. 19–40.

Ryzhak, Nadezhda, 'Censorship in the USSR and the Russian State Library', in *IFLA/FAIFE Satellite Meeting 11–12 August 2005/Documenting Censorship – Libraries Linking Past and Present, and Preparing for the Future* (The Nobel Institute in Oslo, Norway: 11 August 2005), http://www.bibalex.org/wsisalex/ faife.htm (accessed 18 July 2019).

Shavit, Zohar, 'Translation of Children's Literature', in *The Translation of Children's Literature: A Reader*, ed. Gillian Lathey (Clevedon: Multulingual Matters, 2006), pp. 25–40.

Sherry, Samantha, 'Censorship in Translation in the Soviet Union: The Manipulative Rewriting of Howard Fast's Novel', *The Passion of Sacco and Vanzetti*', *Slavonica*, 16 (2010), 1–14.

Shestakov, Viacheslav P., *Angliiskaia literatura i angliiskii natsional'nyi kharakter* (Saint Petersburg: Nestor-Istoriia, 2010).

Simonova, Olga, 'Detskaia kniga v fokuse vliianiia (konets 1940-kh – nachalo 1950-kh gg.' [Children's Book as a Subject of Influence Struggle (late 1940s – early 1950s)], in *Detskie chteniia*, 10:2 (2016), 170–89.

Simpson, Jacqueline, and Steve Roud, 'Merrie England', in *A Dictionary of English Folklore* (Oxford: Oxford University Press, 2003).

Singh, Rashna B., *Goodly Is Our Heritage: Children's Literature, Empire, and the Certitude of Character* (Lanham, MD: Screcrow Press, 2004).

Sivokon', S., S. Sivokon', 'Dzh. M. Barrie. Piter Pen i Vendi. Povest'-skazka. Perevod s angliiskogo N. Demurovoi. Stikhi v perevode D. Orlovskoi. "Detskaia literatura". M. 1968. 160 str.', *Novyi mir*, 10 (1969), 282–3.

Sivokon', S., S. Sivokon', 'P. L. Trevers. Meri Poppins. Sokraschennyi perevod s angliiskogo B. Zakhodera. "Detskaia literatura". M. 1968. 240 str.', *Novyi mir*, 5 (1969), 284–5.

Slobozhan, Aleksei, '"Puck" Stories in Russian', *Kipling Journal*, 63 (March 1989), 35–6.

Slobozhan, Aleksei, '"Skazki Staroi Anglii" Red'iarda Kiplinga', in *Red'iard Kipling. Mech Vilanda: Skazki Staroi Anglii* (Leningrad: Detskaia literatura, 1984), pp. 5–12.

Slobozhan, Inna, *A v serdyse moiem – Leningrad ...* (Saint Petersburg: Izdatel'stvo 'Severnaia zvezda', 2013).

Smirnov, Aleksandr A., and M. P. Alekseev, 'Perevod', in *Literaturnaia entsiklopediia*, ed. A. V. Lunacharsky and others, 11 vols (Moscow: Kommunisticheskaia akademiia; Moscow: Sovetskaia entsiklopediia; Moscow: Khudozhestvennaia literatura, 1929–39), viii (1934), 512–32.

Spiering, Menno, *Englishness: Foreigners and Images of National Identity in Postwar Literature* (Amsterdam: Rodopi, 1992).

Teplitskaia, A. V., et al., 'Tysiacha luchshikh proizvedenii mirovoi khudozhestvennoi literatury v russkikh perevodakh, rekomendovannykh dlia komplektovaniia shkol'noi biblioteki', NIO bibliografii RGB, (2004), https://olden.rsl.ru/ru/s3/s331/s122/d311/ (accessed 18 July 2019).

Tokmakova, Irina, 'Zheleznyi chelovek i velosipedist-prizrak: Kratkie zametki po povodu sovremennoi detskoi literatury v Anglii', *Detskaia literatura*, 7 (1979), 40–4.

Tolkien, J. R. R., *Khobbit, ili Tuda i obratno. Skazochnaia povest'*, trans. N. Rakhmanova (Leningrad: Detskaia literatura, 1976).

Tolkien, J. R. R., *Khraniteli: Letopis' pervaia iz epopei 'Vlastelin Kolets'*, trans. A. Murav'ev and V. Kistiakovskii (Moscow: Detskaia literatura, 1982).

Tolstoy, A. N., 'Anglichane, kogda oni liubezny', in *'Ia bereg pokidal tumannyi Al'biona ...': russkie pisateli ob Anglii, 1646–1945*, ed. Olga A. Kaznina and A. N. Nikoliukin (Moscow: ROSSPEN, 2001), pp. 362–9.

Tolz, Vera, *Russia* (London: Arnold, 2001).

Toury, Gideon, *Descriptive Translation Studies – and beyond*, rev. edn (Amsterdam: John Benjamins, 2012).

Travers, P. L., *Moscow Excursion* (New York: Reynal and Hitchcock, 1935).

Travers, P. L., *Moskovskaia ekskursiia*, trans. Ol'ga Maeots (Saint Petersburg: Limbus Press, 2016).

Travers, P. L., 'Only Connect', *The Quarterly Journal of the Library of Congress*, 24 (1967), 232–48.

Trease, Geoffrey, *The Dragon Who Was Different: And Other Plays for Children* (London: Muller, 1938).
Tregubov, Aleksander, 'Vnuk Marshaka o svoiem legendarnom dede: "V 1937 ego spasli deti"', mk.ru, 4 November 2018, https://www.mk.ru/culture/2018/11/04/vnuk-marshaka-o-svoyom-legendarnom-dede-v-1937-ego-spasli-deti.html (accessed 18 July 2019).
Tsvetaeva, M. I., 'Ia bereg pokidal tumannyi Al'biona . . .', in *Marina Tsvetaeva. Stikhotvoreniia. Poemy* (Moscow: RIPOL klassik, 2007), pp. 158–9.
Tsypin, G. E., 'Doklad direktora Detizdata tov. G. E. Tsypina', *Detskaia literatura*, 1 (1936), 15–17.
Turgenev, I. S., 'Forest and Steppe', in *A Sportsman's Notebook*, trans. Charles and Natasha Hepburn (London: The Book Society, 1959), pp. 391–8.
Turgenev, I. S., *A Sportsman's Notebook*, trans. Charles and Natasha Hepburn (London: The Book Society, 1959).
Turgenev, I. S., 'Rasskaz otza Alekseia', in *Sochineniia. Tom 11. Povesti i rasskazy 1871–1877* (Moscow–Leningrad: Nauka, 1966), pp. 291–304.
Vail', Petr, and Aleksandr Genis, *60-e. Mir sovetskogo cheloveka*, 2nd edn (Moscow: Novoe literaturnue obozrenie, 1998).
Vaninskaya, Anna, 'Korney Chukovsky in Britain', *Translation and Literature*, 20 (2011), 373–92.
Vaninskaya, Anna, 'Under Russian Eyes: Foreign Correspondents in Edwardian Britain', *The Times Literary Supplement* (26 November 2014), 17–19.
Varshaver, Ol'ga, 'Razmyshleniia o nekotorykh kul'turologicheskikh aspektakh perevoda detskoi literatury', in *Konstruiruia detskoe. Filologiia. Istoriia. Antropologiia. Kollektivnaia monografiia. Trudy seminara 'Kul'tura detstva: normy, tsennosti, praktiki'. Vypusk 9*, ed. M. R. Balina and others (Moscow: Azimut, Nestor-Istoriia, 2011), pp. 266–82.
Vasil'ev, O. S., *Sovetskie Pisateli ob Anglii* (Leningrad: Lenizdat, 1984).
Vdovenko, I. V., 'Perevod kak "appropriatsiia" teksta. "Aibolit" i "Barmalei"', in I. V. Vdovenko, *Strategii kul'turnogo perevoda* (St. Petersburg: RIII, 2007), http://www.chukfamily.ru/kornei/bibliografiya/articles-bibliografiya/i-v-vdovenko-strategii-kulturnogo-perevoda (accessed 18 July 2019).
Venuti, Lawrence, *The Scandals of Translation: Towards an Ethics of Difference* (London: Routledge, 1998).
Viazemskii, P. A., *Stikhotvoreniia* (Moscow – Leningrad: Sovetskii pisatel', 1969).
Vinogradov, V. S., *Vvedenie v perevodovedenie (obshchie i leksicheskie voprosy)* (Moscow: Izdatel'stvo instituta obshchego srednego obrazovaniia RAO, 2001).
Visel, Mikhail, 'Perevod kalamburov, alliuzii, perekodirovka kul'turnykh kodov na materiale, nakoplennom v khode raboty nad perevodom trilogii Krisa Ridella "Lunnaia Ledi Got" (AST, redaktsiia Mainstream, 2013–2015)', paper presented at the International conference *Detskaia literatura kak sobytie* [Children's literature as happening], The State Educational Institution of Higher Professional Education

of the City of Moscow – Moscow City Teacher Training University, 11–13 December, 2015.

von Mücke, Dorothea E., *The Seduction of the Occult and the Rise of the Fantastic Tale* (Stanford, CA: Stanford University Press, 2003).

Watkins, Tony, 'Reconstructing the Homeland: Loss and Hope in the English Landscape', in *Aspects and Issues in the History of Children's Literature*, ed. Maria Nikolajeva (Westport, CT: Greenwood Press, 1995), pp. 165–72.

Webb, Jean, 'Walking into the Sky: Englishness, Heroism, and Cultural Identity: A Nineteenth- and Twentieth- Century Perspective', in *Children's Literature and the Fin de Siècle*, ed. Roderick McGillis (Westport, CT: Praeger, 2003), pp. 51–6.

Williamson, Henry, *Vydra po imeni Tarka. Ee radostnaia zhizn' i ee smert' v doline dvukh rek*, trans. G. Ostrovskaia (Moscow: Mir, 1979).

Wilson, Anita, 'A. A. Milne's When We Were Very Young and Now We Are Six: A Small World of Everyday Pleasures', in *Touchstones: Reflections on the Best in Children's Literature. Volume Two: Fairt Tales, Fables, Myths, Legends, and Poetry*, ed. Perry Nodelman (West Lafayette, IN: ChLA, 1987), pp. 173–82.

Wintle, Sarah, 'Introduction', in *Rudyard Kipling. Puck of Pook's Hill* (Harmondsworth: Penguin Books, 1987), pp. 7–34.

Witt, Susanna, 'Arts of Accommodation: The First All-Union Conference of Translators, Moscow, 1936, and the Ideologization of Norms', in *The Art of Accommodation: Literary Translation in Russia*, ed. Leon Burnett and Emily Lygo (Bern: Peter Lang, 2013), pp. 141–84.

Yurchak, Alexei, *Everything Was Forever, Until It Was No More: The Last Soviet Generation* (Princeton, NJ: Princeton University Press, 2006).

Zakhoder, Boris, 'Glava nikakaia, iz kotoroi tem ne menee mozhno koe-chto uznat'', in *Lewis Carroll. Prikliucheniia Alisy v strane chudes*, trans. Boris Zakhoder (Moscow: Studiia 4+4, 2012), pp. 9–14.

Zakhoder, Boris, *'No est' odin poet': neopublikovannoe nasledie v 2-kh tomakh*, 2 vols (Moscow: Gala-Izdatel'stvo, 2008), ii: *Moi tainyi sovetnik*.

Zakhoder, Boris, 'Prikliucheniia Vinni-Pukha (Iz istorii moikh publikatsii)', *Voprosy literatury*, 5 (2002), 197–225.

Zakhoder, Galina, *Zakhoder i vse-vse-vse. Vospominaniia* (Moscow: Zakharov, 2003).

Zhitkov, Boris, *Maria i Meri* (Moscow: Gosudarstvennoe izdatel'stvo, 1929).

Index

accommodation as translation strategy 23, 27, 28, 33, 34, 67
  in Kipling's duology about Puck 95
  in *Mary Poppins* 128, 141, 143–4
  in *Peter Pan* 90
  in *The Wind in the Willows* 151, 168
  in *Winnie-the-Pooh* 66–7
adaptation 34
  Alice's Adventures in Wonderland (Carroll) 67
  Doctor Dolittle (Lofting) 59, 206 n.32
  Gulliver's Travels (Swift) 55
  Heather Ale: A Galloway Legend (Stevenson) 63
  Robinson Crusoe (Defoe) 55
  Scouting for Boys (Baden-Powell) 60–1
adequacy, *see* Soviet Realist translation
adventure stories 48, 52, 53, 55, 59, 61, 63, 69, 70, 73, 74
Albion 3, 4, 15, 176–7
Alice's Adventures in Wonderland (Carroll) 25, 36, 60, 62, 65, 67, 73, 148, 197–8 n.70
allusions in translation
  cultural 67, 95, 108, 141–2, 152, 155, 159, 161
  political 68, 83, 86, 90, 97, 100–2, 104–5, 117, 136–7, 174
Angliia, the magazine 42, 68
Anglo-Soviet cultural relations 39–41, 202 n.46
Arcadia 2, 48, 107–8, 152, 154, 159–62
assimilation 5, 29, 37

ballads about Robin Hood 18, 57, 62–3, 69, 205 n.27
Barrie, J. M. 12, 22, 39, 61, 65, 79–80, see also *Peter Pan*
  Peter Pan (play) 79–81, 63, 90–1
  Peter and Wendy, the book 79–80, 82–3, 90–1
Barthes, Roland 175

Bedford, Francis Donkin 87–9
  Hook 87, 89
  illustration 88
  Peter and Wendy (Barrie) 87–9
Berg, Leila 70–1
Bissett, Donald 70–1
Blyton, Enid 42, 74
Bond, Michael 22, 38, 70
Borisenko, Aleksandra 23, 137, 211 n.19
bourgeois values 51, 54–5, 60
  and censorship 30–2
Britanskii soiuznik, the newspaper 41–2, 63
British children's literature
  canon and classics 48, 184–6
  commercially successful, translated into Russian 75
  corpus of British texts compared to Russian translations 49
  corpus selected for the analysis 21–2, 48, 77
  modern classics, translated into Russian 74
  not translated into Russian 75, 190
  themes 48–9, 71, 75
  translated into Russian 54–71, 72–7, 187–9
Burnett, Frances Hodgson 22, 61, 64, 73–4

Carroll, Lewis 12, 16, 22, 39, see also *Alice's Adventures in Wonderland*
censorship in the Soviet Union 4, 6, 29–32, 37–9, 42, 47, 49, 50, 52, 62, 68, 69, 123, 125, 129, 173–4
  in children's literature 30–1, 137
  Detizdat 118
  the editor 31
  Glavlit 30, 31, 39, 44, 82, 91
  Glavrepertkom 123
  Gosizdat 44
  Goskomizdat 45
  in Kipling 95, 97–8, 100, 102
  Narkompros 44, 45

in *Peter Pan* 79, 81–3, 93
  self-censorship 31–2, 44, 130,
    132, 135–6
  spetskhran 37–8
  system of 30–2
  in Travers 130, 132, 134–6
Chelak, Vadim 148–9, 167
  idealized Englishness 167
  illustration 149
  Mary Poppins as a governess 148–9
  Meri Poppins (Zakhoder) 148
  Veter v ivakh (Tokmakova) 167
Chukovsky, Korney 20, 39, 40, 43, 55,
    56–7, 59, 81
  Doctor Dolittle 59, 206 n.32
  on Englishness 15–16
  promoting English culture in Russia 16,
    43, 64, 195 n.54, 196 n.55
  on translation 1–2, 28, 33–5
  on translation of children's literature
    33–4, 64
creative transformations in translation 22,
  24, 95, 174

Demurova, Nina 39, 56, 152
  Alice's Adventures in Wonderland 36, 67,
    197 n.70
  Peter and Wendy (see *Peter Pan*)
  on translation of children's literature 36
Denisov, Sergei 166–7
  landscape 166–7
  reference to illustration 166
  Veter v ivakh (Tokmakova) 166
Detskaia literatura, the journal 45, 56, 64,
    73, 82, 102, 121
didactic 7, 30, 35, 46, 50, 51, 59, 60, 79, 82,
    127, 137–40, 142–3, 148–9, 175
'dobraia staraia Angliia', *see* 'good old
    England'
Doctor Dolittle (Lofting) 59, 206 n.32
Doyle, Arthur Conan 22, 62
duology about Puck (Kipling)
  allusions in translation, cultural 95, 108
  allusions in translation, political 97,
    100–2, 104–5
  censorship/self-censorship 97, 99–102
  countryfolk 109–10
  cultural associations of
    Englishness 107–9
  dialect 109–10

empire 97–106
English national character 99, 101–3
Englishness 98–9, 101–5, 109–10
Enkvist, Anna 97, 103, 107–8, 110,
    213 n.19
examples of translation 101–2, 107–10
Gurova, Irina 103–4, 107–8, 110,
    213 n.19
the fantastic 97, 99, 109
historical past 97–9, 103–6
history of translation 96–8, 103
idealized Englishness 98–9, 102, 104
idyllic Arcadia 107–8
illustrations 103–6
Kruzhkov, Gennadii 103, 107–8, 110,
    213 n.19
landscape 106–10
manipulated in an ideological context
    97–9, 101–2
mysticism 99
patriotic discourse 98, 99, 104–6
political and ideological associations of
    Englishness 98–102, 103–6
Puck 98, 107–8
religion 97–9, 109
reviews 96, 102
Russian cultural context 97, 104, 108–9
Russified/Russianness 105–6, 108–10
Slobozhan, Aleksei 96–9, 100–3,
    107–8, 110
Durrell, Gerald 70–1

empire 8–9, 11, 15, 18, 23, 37, 48, 60–1,
    71, 73, 79, 83, 90–3, 97–106, 153, 174
English folk ballads and tales 38, 57–8, 60,
    62–3, 69, 206 n.30, 215 n.16
Englishness
  attributes of 7–8
  and Britishness 2
  class system 9, 48, 79, 83–4, 89–90, 93
  concept and categorization 2, 7–14
  countryfolk 11–12, 109–10
  cultural associations of 9, 10–11, 13,
    23–4, 71, 73, 76, 107–9, 151, 155,
    158–9, 162–3, 165, 168, 171
  the discourse of the fantastic 10, 13, 54,
    71, 75, 127, 133–4, 136, 140, 143, 148
  the discourse of silliness 10, 12–13, 48,
    53, 54, 65, 66, 71, 76, 113–14, 119–21,
    123, 124–5, 140–1, 143

divided into three groups 8–9
Easthope, Anthony 8, 12
empire 8–9, 11, 48, 79, 83, 90–3, 97–106
Erofeev, Nikolay 15, 195 n.50
features of English national character 9, 10, 11–13, 22–4, 54, 71, 75, 76, 113–14, 119–21, 123, 124–5, 127, 133–4, 136, 140–1, 143, 148, 151, 165–6, 171
gentleman 11, 151, 153, 165–8
governess 12, 127, 134, 144, 146–9
historical past and traditions 9–10, 48, 97–9, 103–6, 124–5
home 10–11, 48, 76, 152, 162–5
idealized 13–14, 17, 18, 73, 98–9, 102, 104, 152, 155, 158–9, 162–3, 165–8, 171, 174–5, 177
landscape 10, 48, 106–10, 153–62, 166–7, 171
Merry England 2–3, 13–14, 25, 98, 107, 121, 151
mythologized 3–4, 14, 74, 76, 98, 151, 154, 159–62, 171, 174, 176, 178
nostalgia 8, 10, 11, 13, 48, 73, 76, 153, 159, 160, 163
political and ideological associations of 8, 9–10, 22–3, 54, 60, 62, 71, 73, 75, 79, 83, 92, 98–102, 103–6
as represented in Russian translations 4–5, 6, 54, 60, 62, 63, 66, 70, 71, 73, 74, 75–6, 92–3, 95, 103–4, 107, 109, 110, 113, 117, 121, 127, 147–8, 151–2, 154–5, 158, 160–2, 173–4
in Russian children's literature 17–19, 182–3
in Russian literature and culture 3–4, 15–19, 179–82, 195 nn.49, 51, 195–6 n.54, 196 n.58
Russian perception of 3–4, 15–19, 191 n.11, 192 n.13, 195 n.50
in Russian studies 193 n.21, 195 n.50
and Russianness (*see* Russianness)
scholarly views of 192–3 n.21
in Soviet non-fictional publications 16–17, 179–80
stereotypes 2–4, 15, 18, 73, 173–4, 175–7
Even-Zohar, Itamar 47, 49

fairy tales 33, 38, 51–2, 60, 70, 72, 80, 113
the fantastic 10, 13, 54, 71, 80, 82, 99, 127

categories 133–4, 136, 140, 143, 148
fantasy 42, 48–9, 51–3, 55, 59, 64, 68, 70, 72, 74, 104, 123, 204 n.12, 210 n.3
theory 13, 133
Farjeon, Eleanor 38, 70, 74

The Gadfly (Voynich) 56
'good old England' 3, 5, 18–19, 174, 175–7
idealization of the Russian past 73, 74, 76
myth of 3, 19, 151, 175, 177
political connotations 73, 76, 177
Russified in translation (*see* Russified)
Gorky, Maxim 27, 43, 51, 57
Grahame, Kenneth 3, 12, 22, 24, 38, 64, 65, 73, 151–3, see also *The Wind in the Willows*
Gulliver's Travels (Swift) 55, 148, 205 n.21

Haggard, Henry Rider 69
The Hobbit (Tolkien) 12, 22, 42, 65, 68, 73, 208 n.63

ideology 4–6, 20–1, 113, 131, 152, 175
and choice of books for translation 7, 30–1, 43, 46–7, 49, 54, 56–7, 61, 63, 66–71, 75–6
concept 7
didactic role 7, 35, 50–1
and Englishness 7–10, 22–3, 32, 54, 60, 62, 71, 73, 75–6, 173–4, 177
ideological context/connotations 20, 32, 45, 55, 67–70, 76, 177
in Kipling 97–9, 101–2
in *Mary Poppins* 131–2, 135–44, 143–4
in Milne 114–15, 119–25
in *Peter Pan* 79–80, 83, 90
and Soviet Realist translation 23, 28–32, 34, 37, 43
in Soviet/Russian culture 7, 17–18, 40, 50–3
in translated children's literature 7
illustrations 24, 60, 85–9, 103–6, 115–17, 121–2, 124–5, 145–9, 161, 166–7, 222 n.45
illustrators
Bedford, Francis Donkin 87–9 (*see also* Bedford)
Chelak, Vadim 148–9, 167 (*see also* Chelak)

Denisov, Sergei 166–7 (*see also* Denisov)
Kabakov, Ilya 85–9 (*see also* Kabakov)
Kalinovsky, Gennady 145, 147–9 (*see also* Kalinovsky)
Konashevich, Vladimir 115–7 (*see also* Konashevich)
Kustodiev, Boris 115–6 (*see also* Kustodiev)
Liubaev, Sergei 103–5 (*see also* Liubaev)
Meshkov, Evgenii 121 (*see also* Meshkov)
Millar, Harold Robert 104, 106 (*see also* Millar)
Miturich-Khlebnikov, May 82, 85–8 (*see also* Miturich-Khlebnikov)
Reznik, Vladimir 166–7 (*see also* Reznik)
Savkevich, Kira 124 (*see also* Savkevich)
Shafranovskaia, Kseniia 148–50 (*see also* Shafranovskaia)
Shepard, Ernest Howard 121–2, 124–5, 166–7 (*see also* Shepard, E. H.)
Shepard, Mary 145–7 (*see also* Shepard, M.)
Traugots, Alexander and Valery 103–4 (*see also* Traugots)
image of England 2, 11, 15, *see also* Englishness
 as 'good old England' 3, 10, 12, 14, 17–19, 159, 162–4
 idealized by Russian translators 178
 in modern Russian perception 176–8
 mythologized 3–4, 14, 76, 175
 in Russian culture 3–4 (*see also* Englishness)
 in Russian translations (*see* image of England in Russian translations)
image of England in Russian translations 92–3, 95, 136, 173–4, *see also* Englishness
 as an imaginary country 171, 175–6
 idealized 65, 148, 151–2, 154–5, 159–61, 162, 164, 171, 175–6
 ideological context 73, 76, 175–7
 mythologized 175, 177
 as the stereotyped image of 'good old England' 24, 73, 163, 176–7

Kabakov, Ilya 85–9
 illustration 87

Hook 85–7, 89
Piter Pen i Vendi (Demurova) 85–9
Kalinovsky, Gennady 145, 147–9
 didactic principle 148–9
 Mary Poppins as a governess 147–9
 Meri Poppins (Zakhoder, Litvinova) 147–8
 reference to illustrations 147–8
The King's Breakfast (Milne) 113–14, 119–23
 the discourse of silliness 113–14, 119–21, 123
 Englishness 114, 121
 examples of translation 119–20
 history of translation 113–14, 122, 125, 215 n.18, 216 n.23
 ideological connotations 114, 119–21, 123
 ideological context 115, 119–23
 illustrations 121–2
 Korolevskii buterbrod, animated film 123
 Marshak, Samuil 113, 114–19, 122–3
 nonsense 113–14, 117
 reviews 121
 Soviet cultural context 114, 122–3
 stereotypes 115–17, 122–3
King Hilary and the Beggarman (Milne) 113–14, 124–5
 censorship 125
 the discourse of silliness 124–5
 Englishness 124–5
 examples of translation 124–5
 history of translation 113–14, 125
 ideological connotations 124–5
 illustrations 124–5
 Slepakova, Nonna 114, 124–5
 Soviet cultural context 125
 traditions 124–5
King John and the Bishop, the English folk ballad 57–8, 206 n.30
Kipling, Rudyard 12, 15, 16, 33, 39, 44
 censorship 95, 97–9, 100, 102
 The Jungle Book 58–9
 Just So Stories 58
 Land and Sea Tales 61
 Puck of Pook's Hill and *Rewards and Fairies* 65 (*see also* duology about Puck)
 Stalky and Co. 61

Konashevich, Vladimir 115–17
  allusion, political 116–17
  illustration 117
  nonsense 117
  review 117
  Tri zverolova (Marshak) 115–17
Kostior, the magazine 58, 114, 124, 197 n.63
Kustodiev, Boris 115–16
  allusion, political and cultural 115
  illustration 116
  Prikliucheniia stola i stula (Marshak) 115–16

Lear, Edward 12, 39, 60, 65, 66, 115–16
Lefevere, André 5
Lewis, C. S. 22, 38, 42, 69, 73, 208 n.63, see also *The Lion, the Witch and the Wardrobe*
The Lion, the Witch and the Wardrobe (Lewis) 42, 68
Literary translation
  and dialect 109
  as 'high art' 28, 33–5
  and norms 23, 29, 50, 67, 132, 144, 162, 165, 174
  Russian theoretical views before 1917 198 n.1
  Soviet children's literature 33–5
  Soviet Realist translation (*see* Soviet Realist translation)
  theoretical views, Soviet period 1, 27–9, 33–5, 199 n.4
  translators as co-authors of the original 28, 34–6
  views of modern Russian translators, including children's literature 35–7
Liubaev, Sergei 103–5
  empire and historical past 103–4
  illustration 105
  Pak s Volshebnykh Kholmov (Kruzhkov) 103–4

Marshak, Samuil 16, 18, 40, 44, 51, 58, 60, 63, 113–14, 117, 141, 215 n.16
  Englishness in his works 18, 195–6 n.54
  Heather Ale: A Galloway Legend (Stevenson) 63
  ideology/Socialist Realism 43, 114–15, 118–19

The King's Breakfast, 63, (see *The King's Breakfast*)
King John and the Bishop (English folk ballad) 57–8, 206 n.30
  the Leningrad branch of Detizdat 118–19
  on literary translation 28, 34, 45
  promoting English culture in Russia 16, 196 n.55
The Table and the Chair (Lear) 60, 115–16
The Three Jovial Huntsmen (English nursery rhyme) 115–17
  on translation of children's literature 33–4
Mary Poppins, the character 133–4, 136–7, 140, 144–9
  character-building and didactic role 137, 140, 148–9
  discourse of the fantastic 134
  as the fantastic Mother Goddess 133, 136–7, 140
  as a governess 127, 134, 144, 146–9
Mary Poppins (Travers), the books
  censorship 128–30, 132, 134–6
  character-building and didactic function 137–40, 142–3, 148–9
  cultural context 137, 141–3, 145
  the discourse of the fantastic 127, 133–6, 140, 143
  the discourse of silliness 127, 134, 140–1, 143
  examples of translation 135–9, 141–3, 144–5
  features of English national character 127, 133–6, 140–1, 143–4, 148
  governess 127, 134, 144, 146–9
  historical context 145–7
  history of translation 128–30, 216 n.2, 217 nn.15, 16, 17
  ideological context 131–2, 135–40
  illustrations 145–50
  Litvinova, Marina 130, 136, 139, 144–5, 147, 217 n.17
  myth 130–3, 145
  reviews 129, 137, 143, 217 n.14, 219 n.38
  Rodin, Igor' 130, 136–7, 139, 141–3, 144, 145, 217 n.17

Russian cultural context 141–3, 145, 149
Russification 140–4
structure of Zakhoder's translation 131–3
supernatural content/mysticism 131–4, 135, 140, 143, 147–8, 218 nn.19, 26
treated ideologically 131–2, 135–7, 140, 143–4
Zakhoder, Boris 128–45, 147, 149, 217 nn.16, 17, 218 n.34
Mary Poppins (Travers), the play 129, 136–40, 142–3
character-building and didactic function 137–40, 142–3
the discourse of silliness 141
examples of translation 136–9, 141
ideological context 136–8
review 138
Zakhoder, Boris 136–40, 142–3
'Merry England' 2–3, 107, 121, 167, 176, 191 n.6
idealized 13–14, 17–19, 25, 177
mythologized 98, 151, 174, 178
Russified in translation (*see* Russified)
Meshkov, Evgenii 121
Korolevskii buterbrod (Marshak) 121
reference to the illustration 121
silliness 121
Millar, Harold Robert 104, 106
empire and historical past 104
illustration 106
Puck of Pook's Hill (Kipling) 104
Milne, A. A. 39, 65–6, 113–14
The King's Breakfast 62, 63 (see also *The King's Breakfast*)
King Hilary and the Beggarman (see *King Hilary and the Beggarman*)
When We Were Very Young and *Now We Are Six* 65
Winnie-the-Pooh (see *Winnie-the-Pooh*)
Miturich-Khlebnikov, May 82, 85–8
Hook 85–8
illustration 86
Piter Pen (Zakhoder) 85–8
Moonfleet (Falkner) 63
mysticism/mystical 50, 51, 64, 99, 131–2, 136, 140, 160–2, 176

myth 50, 98, 107, 130–3, 145, 161–2, 218 nn.19, 26
mythologization 3–4, 14, 19, 52, 73–4, 76, 98, 151, 154, 159–61, 171, 174–8

nationalism 34, 52, 56, 101
Nesbit, Edith 42, 64, 73
Nikolajeva, Maria 5, 6, 36, 48, 64, 134
nonsense 12–3, 16, 18–9, 34, 51, 54–5, 59, 60, 65–7, 70, 72, 73, 80, 113–14, 117, 134, 137, 141–2, 210 n.3
Norton, Mary 42, 64, 70
nostalgia 8, 10, 11, 13, 48, 73, 74, 76, 153, 159, 160, 163
Novyi mir, the journal 81, 129, 209 n.55, 217 n.14
nursery rhymes 16, 34, 39, 60, 62, 63, 138, 141–3

O'Sullivan, Emer 5, 6, 36
Oittinen, Riitta 35

patriotism 8, 9, 48, 51–61, 62, 69, 71, 73, 99, 115, 118, 153, 173–4
Peter Pan (Barrie) 12, 22, 61, 65
allusions in translation, political 83, 86, 90
censorship/self-censorship 79, 80–3, 90–3
character-building and didactic function 79, 82–3
class division 79, 83–4, 89–90, 93
Demurova, Nina 80–5, 89, 90–2, 210 n.5, 211 n.19
empire 79, 83, 90–3
English national character 79, 84–5, 90–1
Englishness 79, 83, 92–3
examples of translation 83–5, 89–90, 91–2, 211 n.19
the fantastic 80, 82
history of translation 79–82, 92, 210 n.5
Hook 79, 83–4, 85–90
ideological context 79, 80, 83
illustrations 85–9
the Lost Boys 79, 91, 93
patriotism 82, 91
political and ideological associations of Englishness 79, 83, 92
reviews 81

Tokmakova, Irina 81–5, 89–90, 92
  treated ideologically 79, 83, 90
  Zakhoder, Boris 80, 82–5, 88, 90–2, 210 n.5
politics of children's literature 6–7
Potter, Beatrix 22, 65

Ransome, Arthur 42, 38
Reed, Talbot Baines 61–2, 63
reviews, critics and media 44, 45, 55, 64, 66–7, 81, 96, 102, 117, 121, 129, 137, 138, 143, 217 n.14
Reznik, Vladimir, 166–7, see also *The Wind in the Willows*
  landscape 166–7
  reference to illustration 166
  Veter v ivakh (Reznik) 166–7
Robinson Crusoe (Defoe) 55, 205 n.21
Rowling, J. K. 20, 22, 74
Russian children's literature
  campaign against fairy tales and fantasy genre 51–2
  historical and cultural context, post-Soviet period 71–2
  historical and cultural context, Soviet period 50–4
  ideological and didactic function 50–1, 53
  ideological influences 50–4
  Krupskaia, Nadezhda 50
  market forces 72
  state control of 50–4, 71, 137
  themes 51–4, 72
Russian translations of British children's books, as analysed in Chapter 3
  adventures 55, 59, 61, 63, 65, 69, 70, 71, 73, 74, 76
  anti-religious rhetoric 54, 56, 58, 71
  bourgeois values 54–5, 60
  censorship/state control of 55, 61–2, 63, 64, 66, 67–8, 72, 173–4, 175
  character-building and didactic function 82, 137–40, 142–3, 148–9, 175
  class struggle 54, 57–8, 69–70, 71
  commercially successful 73, 75
  creative freedom 59–60
  detective stories 74
  empire 60–1, 71, 73
  Englishness 54, 60, 62, 63, 66, 70, 71, 73–6, 173–6, 178
  family 65, 71, 73, 76
  fantasy 55, 59, 64, 65, 68, 70, 73, 74
  frequently reprinted 55, 56–9, 60, 62, 65, 67, 69, 70, 73, 77
  from 1918 to 1930 54–62
  from 1931 to 1950 62–3
  from 1951 to 1991 63–71
  from 1992 to 2017 72–6
  ideological context 67–70, 76
  the list of 187–90
  modern classics 74
  moralistic purpose 59, 70, 72, 74
  NEP 59–60
  nonsense/silliness 54, 55, 59, 62, 65, 66, 73, 76
  nostalgia 73, 74, 76
  political/national rhetoric 54, 55–8, 60–1, 62, 63, 68, 69–70, 71, 73, 75–6
  religion 73, 74, 174
  reprinted popular classics 55, 58–9, 62, 65, 67, 73, 77
  school tale 55, 59, 60–1, 63, 70, 72, 73
  sentimentality 55, 59, 61, 66, 74, 174
  themes 54–5, 57, 59, 61, 62, 64, 65, 68, 69, 70, 71, 72–4, 75–6, 208 n.73
Russianness 24, 104, 105, 110–11, 142, 171, 174, 177
Russification 33, 36, 37, 59, 67, 108–10, 115, 127–8, 140, 144, 152, 155, 157–8, 162, 164–5, 171, 174, 177
Russified/Russian connotations in translation 5, 24, 95, 151–2, 157–8, 160, 162

Savkevich, Kira 124
  allusion, political 124
  Korol' i brodiaga (Slepakova) 124
  reference to the illustration 124
school tale 48, 52, 53, 55, 59, 60–1, 63, 70, 72, 73
Scouting for Boys (Baden-Powell) 60–1
selection of foreign children's books for translation 37–46, 187–90
  and censorship 42, 47, 49, 50, 52, 62, 67–8, 69
  commercial factors 46, 49, 56, 72–3, 75, 173, 175
  cultural factors 47–8

ideological constraints 47–8, 75–6
main actors 43–5
post-Soviet period 49, 72–7
process 43–6
role of Soviet translators 37–43
Soviet period 49, 54–71
theory 47
Shafranovskaia, Kseniia 148–50
  illustration 150
  Mary Poppins as a governess 148–9
  Meri Poppins (Zakhoder) 148
Shavit, Zohar 5, 6
Shepard, Ernest Howard 121–2, 124–5, 166–7
  idealized Englishness 166
  illustrations 122, 125, 167
  The King's Breakfast (Milne) 121–2
  King Hilary and the Beggarman (Milne) 124–5
  silliness 121
  The Wind in the Willows (Grahame) 166
Shepard, Mary 145–7
  illustration 146
  Mary Poppins as a governess 146–7
  Mary Poppins Comes Back (Travers) 146–7
silliness 10, 12–13, 48, 53, 54, 65, 66, 71, 76, 113–14, 119–21, 123, 124–5, 140–1, 143
Socialist Realism 27, 43, 53, 137, 175, 198 n.3
Soviet
  censorship policy in children's literature 30–1
  censorship system 30–2
  criteria for selecting foreign children's books for translation 29
  cultural policy 50–1
  ideology 17, 29–30, 45, 49, 51, 56, 113, 114, 119, 131, 152, 174, 175
  school of translation 27–9
  stereotypes of the West 113–14, 173–4, 175
  writers about England 17
Soviet Realist translation
  adequacy 20, 27, 28
  in the field of children's literature 29, 33–6, 137
  principles of 27–9
  and translatability 29

translators as co-authors 28, 34–6, 81–2, 133
Soviet publishing houses
  Brokgaus and Efron 60, 115
  Detgiz 44–5, 55, 62, 65, 80–1, 203 nn.57, 58, 207 n.53
  Detizdat 58, 62, 118, 203 n.57, 214–15 n.9
  Detskaia kniga 61
  Detskaia literatura 45, 52, 63, 64, 67, 81, 121, 130, 131, 147, 166, 197 n.63
  Detskii mir 65, 207 n.53, 210 n.5
  L. D. Frenkel' 60
  Gosizdat 28, 44, 59, 60, 61, 115, 117
  Iskusstvo 82, 86
  Knebel' 61
  Kniga 61
  the Leningrad branch of Detizdat 118, 215 n.9
  Leningrad educational publishing house 39, 152
  Lenizdat 31
  Malysh 45, 54, 69, 207 n.53
  Mir 45
  Molodaia gvardiia 44, 45, 59, 215 n.9
  Novella 61
  Pravda 92
  Progress 32, 38, 45, 152
  Raduga 45, 58, 59, 60
  Russkoe knizhnoe izdatel'stvo 61
  Sovetskii pisatel' 28
  Svetliachok 59
  Sytin 55, 59
  V. A. Berezovsky 60
  Vremia 61
  Vsemirnaia literatura 27, 57, 59, 60, 198 n.2
  Zemlia i fabrika 44, 59, 61
Stevenson, Robert Louis 22, 39, 55, 62, 63, 108

The Table and the Chair (Lear) 60, 115–16, *see also* Kustodiev
Tarka the Otter (Williamson) 42, 65
The Three Jovial Huntsmen (English nursery rhyme) 115–17, *see also* Konashevich
The Three Little Pigs (Mikhalkov) 60, 206 n.34
Tokmakova, Irina 17, 39, 174

Peter and Wendy (see *Peter Pan*)
  on translation of children's literature 35–6, 64
The Wind in the Willows (see *The Wind in the Willows*)
Tolkien, J. R. R. 12, 22, 38, 68–9, 73, 74, 166, 208 n.63, see also *The Hobbit*
Tom's Midnight Garden (Pearce) 64, 75, 209 n.81
Toury, Gideon 5, 155, 192 n.14
Townsend, Sue 70, 208 n.68
translation of children's literature
  balance between domestication and foreignization 6, 36
  theory 6
  views of modern Russian translators 35–6
  views of Soviet translators 33–5
translation studies
  domestication 23, 28, 33, 34–5, 36–7, 67, 85, 164, 192 n.18
  domestication and foreignization 6, 36, 192 n.18
  principle of the creative translator 35
  theory 5, 47, 109
Translators
  Chukovsky, Korney (*see* Chukovsky)
  Demurova, Nina (*see* Demurova)
  Enkvist, Anna (*see* duology about Puck)
  Gurova, Irina (*see* duology about Puck)
  Iakhnin, Leonid (see *The Wind in the Willows*)
  Iasnov, Mikhail, and Aleksandr Kolotov (see *The Wind in the Willows*)
  Kruzhkov, Gennadii (*see* duology about Puck)
  Litvinova, Marina (see *Mary Poppins*)
  Tokmakova, Irina (*see* Tokmakova)
  Lunin, Viktor (see *The Wind in the Willows*)
  Marshak, Samuil (*see* Marshak)
  Reznik, Vladimir (see *The Wind in the Willows*)
  Rodin, Igor' (see *Mary Poppins*)
  Slepakova, Nonna (see *King Hilary and the Beggarman*)
  Slobozhan, Aleksei (*see* duology about Puck)
  Zakhoder, Boris (*see* Zakhoder)
Traugots, Alexander and Valery 103–4
  empire and historical past 103
  Mech Vilanda (Slobozhan) 103–4
  reference to the illustration 104
Travers, P. L. 22, 24, 65, 128–31, 134, 146–7, 218 n.26
  allusion, mysticism 131–2
  censorship 128–30, 132, 134–6
  fairy tales 132–3, 141–3
  Mary Poppins, the character (*see* Mary Poppins, the character) 133–4, 136–7, 140, 144–9
  Mary Poppins (see *Mary Poppins*) 127, 130–1, 135, 139, 144–5
  Mary Poppins Comes Back (see *Mary Poppins*) 127, 130–2, 146
  Mary Poppins Opens the Door (see *Mary Poppins*) 127, 130–1, 136, 140–1
  Mary Poppins (Travers), the play (see *Mary Poppins*, the play) 129, 136–40, 142–3
  Moscow Excursion 129, 216 n.7
  nursery rhymes 141–3
Trease, Geoffrey 69–70, 123
The True History of a Little Ragamuffin (Greenwood) 22, 56–7, 205 n.25

Uttley, Alison 64, 70

Venuti, Lawrence 5

The Wind in the Willows (Grahame) 12, 65, 73
  allusions, cultural 152, 155, 159, 161
  censorship 152–3, 162, 165
  cultural associations of Englishness 151, 155, 158–9, 162–3, 165, 168, 171
  Englishness, idealized 152, 155, 158–9, 162–3, 165–8, 171
  examples of translation 154, 159–61, 163, 165–6, 168–9
  features of English national character 151, 165–6, 171
  food 168–70
  gentleman 151, 153, 165–8
  the green space 156–8
  historical context 152–5, 158, 163, 165, 168, 170
  history of translation 152–3
  home 152, 162–5
  idyllic Arcadia 151–2, 153–4, 159–62

illustrations 166–7, 222 n.45
Iakhnin, Leonid 153–6, 159–61,
 163–6, 169–70
Iasnov, Mikhail, and Aleksandr Kolotov
 153–4, 156, 159–61, 163–6, 169–70
landscape 153–62, 171
Lunin, Viktor 153–6, 158–61,
 163–6, 169–70
mythologization 151–2, 154, 162,
 166–8, 171
nostalgia 153, 159, 160, 163
Pan 160–2
religion 161–2, 164–5
Reznik, Viktor 153–4, 156, 159–61,
 163–6, 169–70
the road 154–6, 158
Russian cultural context 156–7,
 161–2, 164

Russification 151–2, 157–8, 160, 162,
 164–5, 171
Tokmakova, Irina 153–6, 158–61,
 163–6, 169–70
Winnie-the-Pooh (Milne) 25, 39, 42, 65–7,
 197 n.70, 207 nn.52, 53

Yurchak, Alexei 175

Zakhoder, Boris 39–40, 174, 218 n.34
 Alice's Adventures in Wonderland 67
 Mary Poppins (see *Mary Poppins*, the
  play, and *Mary Poppins*, the books)
 Peter Pan (see *Peter Pan*)
 on translation of children's
  literature 33–4
 Winnie-the-Pooh 39, 65–7,
  207 nn.52, 53

www.ingramcontent.com/pod-product-compliance
Lightning Source LLC
Chambersburg PA
CBHW050324020526
44117CB00031B/1725